# Attempts

# Attempts

## In the Philosophy of Action and the Criminal Law

Gideon Yaffe

OXFORD

UNIVERSITY PRESS

# OXFORD
UNIVERSITY PRESS

Great Clarendon Street, Oxford ox2 6DP

Oxford University Press is a department of the University of Oxford.
It furthers the University's objective of excellence in research, scholarship,
and education by publishing worldwide in

Oxford   New York

Auckland   Cape Town   Dar es Salaam   Hong Kong   Karachi
Kuala Lumpur   Madrid   Melbourne   Mexico City   Nairobi
New Delhi   Shanghai   Taipei   Toronto

With offices in

Argentina   Austria   Brazil   Chile   Czech Republic   France   Greece
Guatemala   Hungary   Italy   Japan   Poland   Portugal   Singapore
South Korea   Switzerland   Thailand   Turkey   Ukraine   Vietnam

Oxford is a registered trade mark of Oxford University Press
in the UK and in certain other countries

Published in the United States
by Oxford University Press Inc., New York

© Gideon Yaffe 2010

The moral rights of the authors have been asserted
Database right Oxford University Press (maker)

First published 2010

British Library Cataloguing in Publication Data
Data available

Library of Congress Cataloging in Publication Data
Data available

Typeset by SPI Publisher Services, Pondicherry, India
Printed in Great Britain on acid-free paper by
MPG Books Group, Bodmin and King's Lynn

ISBN 978-0-19-959066-7

1 3 5 7 9 10 8 6 4 2

For Michael Bratman, teacher and friend.

# Acknowledgments

People often say that the best way to learn about a topic is to teach it. When it comes to the topic of attempted crimes, this has certainly been my experience. Still, I started thinking in a serious way about the issues discussed in this book while taking the first-year criminal law course as a student in 2004. These early thoughts developed into a pair of papers. But my thinking was substantially refined and deepened by co-teaching a seminar on moral luck and attempt in 2005 and, especially, by teaching the first-year criminal law course myself in 2007. Teaching the law governing attempts to those hoping to one day defend and prosecute helped me to recognize the array of different ways in which philosophy, particularly philosophy of action, can help the law. I owe a great debt to my home institution, the University of Southern California, for making it possible for me, while working as a professor there, to study law, and, more importantly, for making space for a non-lawyer in the law school, where I have been trusted, inexplicably, to teach law to law students.

Thanks are owed to several institutions at which material that has found its way into this book was presented. This includes law schools and philosophy departments at the California State University at Northridge, Florida State University, Stanford, the University of California at Berkeley, UCLA, the University of Manitoba, the University of Michigan, the University of St Andrews, the University of San Francisco, and USC. Audiences at all these places were very helpful, as were the participants in the Analytic Philosophy and Law Conference held at UCLA in 2006.

Material from three different published papers made its way into the book, although with significant changes in each case. Those papers are Yaffe (2004), Yaffe (2006) and Yaffe (2008a). While I stand by much of what I said in those papers, I have also changed my mind in significant respects, as reflected especially in chapters 2 and 8.

Michael Bratman, Steve Finlay, Jacob Ross, Mark Schroeder, Walter Sinnott-Armstrong, Gary Watson, and George Wilson all very generously agreed to read virtually the entire manuscript and to discuss it with me over a two-day period. This intensive meeting was invaluable and resulted in important improvements throughout the manuscript. I owe them all a large debt which I hope to repay through careful reading of their next book manuscripts. Three anonymous referees also read the entire book. I am very grateful to them, too, for their helpful and constructive comments. Doug Husak, who has many more ideas about attempts than he admits to, was the only other person to read the entire manuscript. His wonderful and encouraging comments helped me to make the book much better.

Many other people have given me comments on drafts of chapters, or helped me in conversation, or answered emails, often at great length. Although I am surely forgetting people who should not be forgotten, I am grateful to all of the following people for their help with this project: Larry Alexander, Jody Armour, Hrafn Assgeirson, Mitch Berman, Randy Clarke, Meir Dan-Cohen, Jules Coleman, Kory De Clark, David Dolinko, David Enoch, Kim Ferzan, Claire Finkelstein, John Fischer, Harry Frankfurt, Barbara Herman, Pamela Hieronymi, David Hills, Paul Hoffman, Agnieszka Jaworska, Rob Kar, Greg Keating, Christopher Kutz, Barbara Levenbook, Tom Lyon, Michael McKenna, Andrei Marmor, Alfred Mele, Michael Moore, Stephen Morse, Sarah Paul, Lewis Powell, Joseph Raz, Connie Rosati, Scott Soames, Scott Shapiro, Seana Shiffrin, Dan Simon, Dan Speak, Nomi Stolzenberg, Ken Taylor, Manuel Vargas, Kadri Vihvelin, Jonathan Weil, and Ekow Yankah. In addition, Vera Golosker provided valuable research assistance.

The American Council of Learned Societies provided generous support for this project. I received the Fredrick Burkhardt Fellowship for Recently Tenured Scholars. Following a leave from teaching provided by USC in 2008, the Burkhardt Fellowship paid for an invaluable year of residence at the Huntington Library in 2008–09, where very large portions of this book were written. At one point, I had thought this book would have a substantial historical component. Roy Ritchie and the staff of the Huntington are owed thanks for allowing me to occupy valuable office real estate, and wander the gardens at ease, even when the historical side of the project all but vanished. The cactuses in the desert conservatory, on display but rarely, provided me with a wonderful example of striving, in their cases with success, in the face of great difficulty.

Thanks are owed to one person who I have only met once, and too briefly. R. A. Duff's book, *Criminal Atttempts* (Oxford, 1996) was constantly to hand in writing this book. While Duff and I disagree on many things, his identification of the problems in need of solution, and the marvelous way in which he combines philosophy with legal cases, opinions, statutes, and commentaries, was an inspiration to me. It was only after much hard thinking about Duff's book, and about the topics of this one considered independently, that I came to the conclusion that there was something left to say worthy of a book of its own.

Finally, thanks are owed to my family for their love, support, and example. My wife, Sue Chan, reminds me daily why it is worth trying to do anything. And I thank our daughter Oona Yaffe. There's nothing quite like sitting on the floor and playing games with a four-year-old to remind one of the size of the world outside.

# Contents

## Part 4.  Sentencing Attempts

# Introduction

Criminal attempts—failed efforts to complete crimes—are sometimes, despite the fact of their failure, spectacles. Think of John Hinkley's failed effort to kill President Ronald Reagan, or the September 11th terrorists' failed effort to fly United Flight 93 into the White House. Attempts are also very commonly prosecuted and just as commonly punished, even when they are far from spectacular. Prisons are packed with people who never managed to finish the crimes that they were trying to commit. As spectacular as they sometimes are, and as commonly as they are prosecuted and punished, however, there is an undeniable sense in which the punishment of criminal attempts is secondary to the punishment of completed crimes. Attempts are worth punishing only because completions are. We do not devise our criminal law, in the first instance, to fight those who attempt crimes, but instead to fight those who complete them. But, still, the adjudication of criminal attempts makes up a large and important part of the criminal law.

It was not always so. Legal historians usually identify the case of *Rex v. Scofield* (Cald. 397 (1784)) as the first common-law case in which true attempt liability was imposed.[1] Lord Mansfield found the defendant guilty of an attempted arson when he tried and failed to burn down a house. The startling fact about this otherwise banal attempt case is that it did not take place until 1784. So, if the historical claim that this is the first attempt case is true, there were a few hundred years of common law decisions in criminal cases before anyone was taken to be guilty for an attempt. And yet today nothing could seem more natural than to hold people to account in the criminal law, not just for what they succeeded in doing, but also for what they tried to do.

Prior to 1784, the powerful intuition that there can be crime, too, in failures to commit crime was accommodated through the imposition of criminal liability for what the attempter *did* accomplish. The person who stabbed another, intending but failing to kill, was to be held liable not for attempted murder, but for a grievous battery. If the knife were to miss the victim entirely, but cause him

---

[1]  See, e.g. Sayre (1928).

to be aware of impending injury, then criminal liability would be imposed for assault. Of course, it seems much worse to stab someone intending to kill him than to stab him intending merely to hurt him. But this thought too can be accommodated without attempt liability per se. We can define the crime of assault with intent to kill, and give greater penalties for it than for simple assault. Similarly, we can hold a person who broke into another's home in order to steal his things, but was caught before he could take anything, to be guilty of the crime of burglary, a more severe crime than that committed by the person who breaks into another's home but without any intention to commit a felony there. By having crimes of these sorts we do indeed manage to criminalize many attempts to commit other crimes.

But not all. The conduct of the person who swings the blade at another's back but misses entirely, and without even the victim becoming aware that he was attacked, fits at best awkwardly into the category of assault when defined, as assault often is, as "causing another to *apprehend* immediate physical injury". Only under a highly attenuated notion of "apprehend" does a victim apprehend an injury he does not suffer and while entirely unaware that he is even under attack. But, surely, there's a crime there that should not be ignored. The more general point is that backdoor efforts to criminalize attempts by criminalizing completions of the invasion of another's legally protected interests—such as assaults and burglaries—that happen to be, also, attempts, inevitably fail to criminalize some behaviors that are, really, just as worthy of criminalization but can be thought of as completions only by diluting the very notion of completion beyond recognition.

More importantly, efforts to pin crimes on those who attempt crimes, or to enhance their penalties in comparison to others who cause no more harm than they do, but without using the word "attempt", is simply dishonest. It is the *attempt* that we take to be criminal. Why not tell the moral truth in the construction of criminal law? In taking Scofield to be guilty of attempted arson, Mansfield was using the law's voice to tell the truth about what the law was striving to take to be criminal already. The case, then, marked important moral progress on the part of the law. It moved the law towards doing explicitly what it had been aiming to do already.

However, at the point that the step of criminalizing attempts was taken, they needed to be adjudicated. Hard questions therefore needed to be answered: Are all attempts criminal, or only some of them? Are attempts that the defendant could not possibly have completed, crimes? Are some impossible attempts crimes, and, if so, which? Must a person intend to commit the crime in order to be guilty of an attempt? Must he intend *everything* that is involved in the completed crime, or only some of it? If only some of it, which part? Must he intend the presence of the elements of an affirmative defense in order to be shielded from liability for attempt through appeal to that defense? Can a person attempt a crime merely by asking another person to commit it, or does he need to take some other steps to commit it himself? Can people attempt crimes that are typically not completed with intent, such as crimes of negligence or recklessness? Must a person act on his intention in order to be guilty of an attempt? If so, what must he do? How much must a person do to further his criminal intention if he is to be guilty of an attempt? What should we do with the person who abandons his attempt before completion? Should he be convicted as if he had not abandoned his plan? Or acquitted as though he'd never started it? Or something else entirely? How should we sentence attempts relative to the completed crimes of which they are attempts? Should they be given lower sentences, or the same sentences, or what?

This book attempts to answer all of these questions. It offers an account of what attempt law *should* be. In some places, this account serves as a justification of what attempt law *is* already. In others, it serves as a critique of what attempt law is currently and a description of how it should be altered. The book is a work of philosophy. It is not intended as a contribution in criminology, political science, public policy studies, or psychology. These are all fields in which progress can be made on the questions that must be answered in adjudicating attempts. But this book makes progress on the answers to these questions through employing the tools of investigation that are distinctive of analytic philosophy. The guiding idea of the book is that many of the hard questions about attempts to which the law needs answers can be answered by philosophical reflection on the nature of trying to act, and the various kinds of acts and psychological states to which it is inextricably linked, such as that of intending.

While a proper appreciation of what it is to try to act can help us to answer a variety of questions about attempts to which the law needs answers, it cannot do all of the work on its own. Rather, some questions about attempted crimes are to be answered by appreciating what could count as adequate evidence of trying to act, given what trying is. Still other questions about attempts require reflection on what kinds of punishments it is fair to inflict on someone who has attempted a crime, given the sentences that are given for completion of that crime. In the first instance, that is, the nature of trying sets bounds on what behaviors do and do not count as instances of it. But the nature of trying also sets constraints on the evidence for attempt. Trying, it turns out, is a kind of action of which it is rather more difficult to have evidence than other forms of action, a fact that ought to be reflected in some of our legal doctrines concerned with attempted crime. And, further, the nature of trying, and the grounds on which it is criminalized, set constraints on the ways in which it is fair, and unfair, to punish those who attempt crimes in contrast to those who complete them. Most obviously, it is because of what it is to try to act, and why it is justified to criminalize trying to act, that it is never fair to give a *greater* punishment to an attempt than to a corresponding completed crime. Results of this sort concerned with sentencing, too, have implications for the law governing attempts.

So, the answers given here to the questions that must be answered in adjudicating attempts are derived from the following intuitively plausible principles:

- A defendant D committed an attempt of crime C *if and only if* D tried to C.

- A defendant D is rightly held guilty for commission of an attempt of crime C *only if* There is adequate evidence that D tried to C.

- A defendant D is rightly given sentence S for commission of an attempt of crime C *only if* S is a fair sentence for an attempt of C given the sentence issued for completion of C.

The first of these principles concerns attempt commission, the second concerns guilt for commission of an attempt, the third concerns sentencing once guilt for commission has been established. Each of the answers offered here to the questions of legal importance about attempts ultimately derives from one of these three principles. The second, third, and fourth parts of the book correspond to these three principles: part 2 is concerned with the first principle's implications, part 3 with the second's, and part 4 with the third's. Part 1 of the book offers an account of the rationale for criminalizing attempts in the first place and an account of the nature of attempt. Both accounts are essential to the discussion of the principles' implications in the succeeding parts of the book.

The distinction between the first and the second principle rests in part on the distinction between commission of a crime and guilt for it, a distinction to which we return in multiple places in this book. It is possible to commit a crime without being guilty of one. If there is insufficient evidence that D committed a robbery, but D did in fact commit it, then D committed a robbery but is not guilty of any robbery. To "escape on a technicality", also, is to commit a crime without being guilty of one. It is less often noted that it is possible to be guilty of a crime without committing one. If D pays someone to burn down a house, and that person does burn it down, then D is guilty of arson. But D has not committed arson, if commission of arson requires that one burn something, since D has burned nothing at all, but has merely paid someone else to burn something. For some, this will seem an odd usage of the term "guilt", and perhaps, also an odd usage of the term "commission". The terms will serve the purposes they are meant to serve here even if, in the end, they are terms of art that fail to map perfectly on to the terms that are used in ordinary language. For our purposes, to be guilty of a crime is for it to be the case that you are, by the standards of the legal system in which you are charged, rightly held to be criminally liable for the crime. This isn't to say that if you are guilty, in the sense of interest here, you are rightly held to be criminally liable, full stop. Imagine, for instance, a legal system with ridiculously low standards for the exclusion of evidence: much is excluded that should not be. There could be evidence that a defendant committed a robbery that ought not to be excluded, but is excluded given the low bar for exclusion in the system in question. Such a person is rightly held to be criminally liable for robbery, since it would be right for the evidence of his commission of the crime to be admitted, but he is not rightly held criminally liable *by the standards of the legal system in question*, since by those standards the evidence in question is excluded. He is, therefore, not guilty, in the sense in which the term "guilty" is to be used here.

The first of our principles asserts that commission of an attempt is just the familiar act of trying directed toward something that is, already, a crime. The second of our principles notes that guilt for commission requires adequate evidence of commission; this is true not just of attempts, but of any crimes whatsoever. This is only a necessary condition since guilt requires more than this—it requires, also, for instance, absence of immunity, among other things. But it is this necessary condition for guilt that will concern us in this book. The third principle asserts that the fair sentence for commission of an attempt of a crime is constrained by the sentence imposed for the completed crime. As we will see, there are a variety of ways in which the fair sentence for an attempt depends on the sentence for the completed crime.

Some aspects of what attempt law should be, those discussed in part 2 of the book, derive from the first of these three principles. That is, what should and should not count as a criminal attempt is in large part determined by what should and should not count as *trying* to commit a crime. So one of the book's major tasks is the identification of necessary and sufficient conditions for trying to act, in the sense of "trying" that is of relevance to the criminal law. This account is then used in order to explain how the law ought to answer a variety of questions courts have faced in adjudicating attempts. In each case, the question answered has been up until now left unanswered by the courts, or given a wrong answer, or given a correct answer, but on the basis of no reasons or of mistaken reasons.

Other aspects of what attempt law should be, those discussed in part 3 of the book, derive from the second of these principles. As we will see, tryings are a distinctive kind of action and differ in important ways from other sorts of action. One can ordinarily deduce what action an agent completed from a description of his bodily movements and their effects, and a description of the mental states that led to those bodily movements. Not so in attempt. Duplicates in mental state, bodily movement, and effects of bodily movement can nonetheless differ in what they are attempting. The reason is that to try, a particular counterfactual must be true of the agent—it must be true that, roughly, if the agent had ability and opportunity and did not change his mind, he would complete the crime. D1 and D2 both intend to rob the bank, both intend to cook ribs for dinner, and both drive towards the corner where the bank and the grocery store sit opposite. But D1 is motivated by his intention to rob the bank, while D2 is motivated by his intention to cook ribs for dinner: they are thus trying to do different things. The counterfactual in question, when interpreted properly, helps us to distinguish between these two agents.

Give D1 ability and opportunity and he will rob the bank; give D2 ability and opportunity and he will cook ribs for dinner. Duplicates of the relevant sort, of which this is just one example, can differ in what they are trying to do, thanks to differing motivational roles played by their similar mental states. As a result, there is an important difference in what can serve as adequate evidence of trying to act, in contrast to completed action. To have adequate evidence of trying to act, we must have adequate evidence for the truth of the counterfactual. The law ought to reflect this by requiring proof of trying to act that is importantly different from the kind of proof of completed action that the law requires.

And, finally, some aspects of what attempt law should be, those discussed in part 4 of the book, derive from the third principle, concerned with fair sentences. Thanks to the relationship between completed crimes and attempts of them, factors that provide reason to reduce the sentence for a completed crime also provide reason to reduce the sentence for an attempt; fairness requires that mitigators of the sentence for completion mitigate attempt sentences, too. This fact helps us to appreciate how we ought to treat certain factors, found in some attempts, that would mitigate sentence for completion, even if we never actually find them in completed crimes. However, we also find that our principle regarding fairness in sentencing of attempts does not constrain sentence as strongly as one might have thought. It turns out that it can be perfectly fair to give a lower sentence to an attempted crime than to the corresponding completed crime.

Part 1, which discusses what attempts are and why it is justified to criminalize them, comprises chapters 1 through 3. Chapter 1 is the only chapter of the book that does not engage with a problem that judges, and other legal practitioners, need to solve. Rather, chapter 1 is engaged with the question of what, if anything, justifies the default rule according to which it is a crime to attempt to engage in any form of action that is itself a crime. Judges and other legal practitioners do not need to answer this question since they merely silently accept that there is some rationale for this practice when they charge, convict, and punish people for attempted crimes merely on the basis of the fact that that which they attempted was criminal. Still, answering this basic justificatory question provides grounds for much of what follows in the book, in which questions that judges do need to answer are answered.

Chapter 1 reaches both a negative result and a positive result. The negative result is that attempts are not justifiably criminalized as crimes of risk-creation. It is not criminal to attempt a crime because, in so doing, one risks completion of it. This is often true, of course, but it is not on those grounds that attempts are justifiably criminalized. The positive result is that attempts are justifiably criminalized thanks to two facts. First, setting aside irrelevant exceptions, those who attempt crimes and those who complete crimes exhibit the same faults in the way in which they recognize and respond to reasons. This explains why attempters are deserving of censure when completers are. Second, both those who attempt crimes and those who complete them are guided in their conduct by the commitments that are part and parcel of the way in which they recognize and respond to reasons. It is argued in chapter 1 that from this second commonality it follows that attempts that would be justifiably sanctioned were they to succeed are frequently themselves justifiably sanctioned even though they failed. Chapter 1 argues that these similarities between attempters and completers provide sufficient grounds to criminalize the attempt of any kind of conduct that is itself justifiably criminalized.

The argument of chapter 1 provides support for what is sometimes called "subjectivism about attempts": the view that attempts are properly criminalized, not in virtue of the way in which they themselves invade the legally protected interests of others, nor in virtue of their "objective" harmfulness or wrongfulness, but instead in virtue of something about the way in which they are motivated and guided, something about them that is special to, or "subjective" about the agent who engages in them. However, as emerges in later chapters, it is consistent with the subjectivism advocated in this book to hold, as I do, that not all attempts that are worthy of criminalization are rightly punished, even in the absence of justification or excuse.

Chapter 2 addresses the question of whether or not an agent must intend to complete the crime in order to attempt it. While there are some rare cases in which defendants have been found guilty of an attempted crime in the absence of a showing that they intended to complete the crime, by far the dominant legal practice makes an intention to commit the crime an element of the attempted crime. Chapter 2 vindicates this dominant approach by arguing that a person has not tried to do something unless he intends to do it. Therefore, it is not possible to commit an attempted crime without intending to complete the crime. Interestingly, philosophers of action have been close to unanimous in their view that it is possible to try to do something without intending to do it. They have reached this conclusion largely on the basis of examples in which, for instance, a person tries to do something that he believes he cannot do, and does not want to do, in order to demonstrate to someone else that he cannot do it. So chapter 2 argues against the standard view among philosophers of action by showing that the putative counterexamples to the claim that trying involves intending are not, in fact, counterexamples at all. Support for the standard legal practice, then, is provided through refutation of the standard view among philosophers of action.

While chapter 2 is engaged with a problem of legal relevance, it also establishes a philosophically interesting claim, namely that one of the necessary conditions of trying to do something is intending to do it. Thus, chapter 2 takes a first step towards a full account of trying to act, an account, that is, of the necessary and sufficient conditions under which a person has tried to act. Building on the result of chapter 2, a full account of trying to act is provided in chapter 3. The account offered there is labeled the "Guiding Commitment View". According to the Guiding Commitment View, a person has tried to act just in case he has an intention that commits him to each of the components of success and his behavior is guided by each of those commitments. While various plausibility arguments are offered for the Guiding Commitment View, ultimately the argument for it is in the form of an inference to the best explanation provided in later chapters: the Guiding Commitment View provides us with useful and explanatory answers to a wide variety of questions that need to be answered about attempted crimes.

The Guiding Commitment View invokes the notion of "a component" of successful action in its definition of attempt. The components of crimes, in contrast to informally defined types of action, are what interest us here. So, an advocate of the Guiding Commitment View bears a burden to explain what the components of crimes are. With the aim of meeting this burden, chapter 3 provides an account of the elements of crimes, arguing that the traditional divide between act, result, and circumstantial elements of crimes is to be understood by appeal to variation in prosecutorial burdens. There are conditions that must be shown by the prosecution when an element is an act element that need not be shown if the element is a result or circumstantial element. And, similarly, there are conditions that must be shown by the prosecution when an element is a result element that need not be shown if the element is a circumstantial element. Circumstantial elements thus pose the weakest burdens on the prosecution, result elements are next, and act elements involve the most stringent burdens. This account reverses what might have been the expected order of explanation according to which the prosecutorial burdens are different because the elements are of different sorts. By contrast, according to the view presented in chapter 3, the elements belong to different sorts, thanks to the fact that there are different prosecutorial burdens associated with them. Thus, under the Guiding Commitment View, a person has attempted a crime just in case he has an intention that commits him to *each of the conditions that the prosecution bears a burden to show* in the completed crime and is guided by each of these commitments. This position plays a substantial role in what follows, especially in part 2 of the book.

Having determined that in order to show that a defendant committed an attempted crime, the prosecution must show the defendant to have been committed to each of the components of completion of the crime by his intention, there remains a question about precisely what intention a defendant needs to be shown to have had. A full answer to this question is provided by the specification of a procedure for determining, with respect to each component of the completed crime, precisely what intention an attempter must have in order to be properly committed to that component. In part 2, which includes chapters 4 through 7, an account of such a procedure is offered, and its implications for several questions of legal importance are drawn. The view of the intention in attempt offered there, which fits snugly with the Guiding Commitment View of trying, is labeled "The Elemental Conception of the Intention in Attempt". The discussion in part 2 is divided by the different sorts of conditions that are involved in completed crimes, for the Elemental Conception has different implications with regard to the intention needed with respect to different sorts of conditions.

Chapter 4 first considers the way in which an attempter's intention commits him, or need not commit him, to the legal properties of the completed crime, for example the property of being legally prohibited, or the property of being unjustified legally. There it is argued that an attempter need not be committed to the *legal properties* of the completed crime in order to attempt it. A person can attempt a murder, for instance, without intending to break the law, as when he attempts a mercy killing in the false belief that mercy killings are legal. It is shown that this common-sense position follows from the Guiding Commitment View. Similarly, it is shown that under the Guiding Commitment View, an attempter need not ordinarily be committed by his intention to the mental elements involved in completion of the crime. It is enough, instead, that he be committed to that which the mental elements involved in completion concern. So, for instance, if completed arson requires the belief that the fire one starts will burn something, the attempter need only be committed by his intention *to burning something*, and need not also be committed to *believing* that he will. By having an intention to burn something, the attempter thereby has sufficient commitment to the mental state involved in completion, even though that mental state is not something that he is committed to by his intention *in the way* that he is committed to burning something.

The chapter also considers the intention needed with respect to the acts and results involved in the completed crime, arguing that an intention *to* act is essential to attempt, but only an intention *that* the results involved in completion come to pass. The distinction between intending *to* and intending *that* developed in chapter 4 is applied in other ways later in the book. But in this section it is used, also, to explain the central place in attempt law to be given to the distinction between intending a result and foreseeing it as a consequence of what one intends. It is uncommon to find jurisdictions in which a person can be convicted of an attempt when merely foreseeing a result, but not intending it. The common approach is the right approach if the arguments of this section succeed.

Notably absent from chapter 4 is any discussion of the commitment that an attempter need have to the circumstantial elements of a crime. Imagine a defendant who tries to buy a television off the back of a truck not knowing whether it is stolen when it is in fact stolen. Is such a person sufficiently committed to the television's being stolen to have attempted receipt of stolen property? Chapter 5 answers this question arguing, through appeal to the Guiding Commitment View and the accompanying Elemental Conception of the intention in attempt, that there is a class of special cases in which what a person's intention commits him to is determined *by what is the case*. Hence the defendant in this example is committed to the television's being stolen by his intention to receive it *if the television is actually stolen, but he is not so committed by his intention if it is not*. It is also argued that the actual status of the television is typically irrelevant if the defendant believes it to be stolen. In that case he has the intention needed for an attempt to receive stolen property even if the television is not stolen. The implications of these surprising results for a wide range of cases are discussed.

Chapter 5 also engages for the first time in the book with the question of whether or not it is possible to attempt the impossible, an issue to which we return later. The reason that this issue comes up here is that historically, and misleadingly, courts and commentators have labeled cases of absent circumstantial elements—for example, cases of receipt of property that was not stolen tried as attempts to receive stolen property—to be cases of "impossible" attempts. This is misleading, since to say that a circumstantial element is absent and to say that it could not be present are importantly different things; property that is not stolen ordinarily *could* have been. Still, it is argued in chapter 5 that "impossible" attempts of this sort are not disqualified from being attempted crimes, and so are not disqualified from deserving punishment as such, except in those rare and interesting cases in which the absence of the circumstantial element establishes that the defendant actually lacks the intention needed for attempt since he lacks an intention that commits him to the relevant circumstantial element of the crime. So, while the "impossibility" in such cases—the absence of the relevant circumstantial element—does not all by itself shield the defendant from criminal liability, it does undermine the claim that the defendant actually attempted the crime at all in a rare subset of such cases. The reason is that in that rare subset of cases in which the circumstantial element is absent, its absence undermines the claim that the defendant had the intention needed for an attempt.

While the topic of chapter 6 is importantly different from the topics of chapters 4 and 5, it bears a close relation to them. Chapter 6 addresses the question of whether it is possible to attempt crimes of recklessness and negligence, crimes that necessarily cannot be completed with intent. Is there some kind of tension between the claim, argued for in chapter 2, that intention is necessarily involved in attempt, and the claim that it is possible to attempt a crime that necessarily does not involve intent? Courts and commentators have without exception held that there is. There can be no attempts of crimes that cannot be completed with intent, in their view. This chapter shows that this view is mistaken. There can be, indeed there *are* such cases, and the chapter provides some examples.

The chapter proceeds by identifying two different arguments that have been offered for the claim that attempts of crimes of recklessness and negligence are impossible, and shows that both arguments fail. The chapter then identifies a category of attempts in which such a crime is being attempted. In all members of the relevant class of cases, the defendant takes steps to manage his future mental states, and, in particular, to arrange it so that he will later act without, at the time of action, acting on his intention. Such a person might, for instance, while acting on an intention to kill someone else, try to get that person to bait him so that he will lose his temper and kill him. If he anticipates that he himself is someone with a nasty temper, likely to over-react and use deadly force in expressing his anger, without knowing that he's doing so, then precisely what he is doing in trying to get the victim to bait him is attempting to kill recklessly. Chapter 6 argues that such plans are doomed to failure. Someone who tries to manipulate his future self in such a way, and succeeds, acts intentionally, contrary to his goals. But, the fact that the plan is doomed to failure does not mean that the defendant in such a case is not attempting to engage in it: he is. And, in fact, when we know what to look for we find such cases in courtrooms. People who intend to commit crimes by using such self-management techniques are committing attempts to commit crimes of recklessness and negligence, and ought to be treated as such.

In addition to solving the problem of attempts to commit crimes of recklessness and negligence, chapter 6 makes further progress on the question, discussed in chapter 4, of whether the attempter must have an intention that commits him to the mental states involved in completion. In chapter 4 it was shown that he need not, since the intention itself can serve as sufficient commitment to those mental states when it involves commitment to that which they concern. However, the argument of chapter 6 shows that there is one important exception to that claim: those cases in which the agent plans for himself to be in certain mental states later. If those later mental states are required for completion, and the crime cannot be completed with intent, then those mental states themselves must be things that the attempter intends to have. We do not usually need to commit ourselves to be in later mental states in order to attempt, but the exceptions are those special cases in which such later mental states are crucial to our succeeding in our (hopeless) plans to act unintentionally.

Chapter 7 is the final chapter of part 2, and is therefore the final chapter in which progress is made merely by appeal to what it is to commit an attempt. The chapter tackles the problem of drawing the line between solicitations and attempts. When a defendant asks an undercover police officer to kill another for money, has the defendant attempted murder, or merely solicited murder? The question is of legal importance for several reasons, not least of which is that the penalties for solicitation are typically far lower than those for attempt. There are two extreme possibilities: solicitations are never attempts, or solicitations are always attempts. But the truth lies in between: some solicitations are attempts, and some are not. The hard question is how to draw the line.

Chapter 7 solves the problem, arguing that whether or not a solicitor has the intention needed for attempt depends on the formal structure of the completed crime. Roughly, "result" crimes—such as arson in which a lead element is the result element of something burning—are attempted when solicited, while "act" crimes—such as rape, in which a lead element is the act of sex with another person—are not. Put more carefully, a solicitor typically has the intention needed for attempt when the lead element of the crime is a result, but typically lacks it when the lead element is an act. Of course, there is more to attempt than the intention—under the Guiding Commitment View, there must also be guidance by each of the commitments the intention constitutes. But, still, a difference in the intention needed for attempt when the crime is a result crime rather than an act crime provides us with principled grounds on which to draw the line between those solicitations that are attempts and those that are not. This view is refined, developed, and defended in chapter 7.

Part 3 of the book, which consists of chapters 8, 9, and 10, is concerned with legal doctrines about attempts that are best understood through consideration of the special sort of evidence of attempt that is required, given what attempts are. Where the intention involved in attempt plays a central role in the preceding chapters, the chapters included in part 3 focus on the other important aspect of attempt under the Guiding Commitment View, namely what it is to be guided by the commitments that one has in virtue of one's intention. In part 3 it is suggested that the distinctive feature of the guidance by one's commitments involved in attempt is the support that it gives to, roughly, the following counterfactual: "If the agent had ability and opportunity to do as he intended and did not change his mind, he would have completed the crime." The role that a person's intention-based commitments play in guiding his behavior is of the sort involved in attempt just in case this counterfactual is true of him. It follows that if we are to have adequate evidence that a person attempted a crime, we need to have evidence that this counterfactual is true. The implications of this are explored in part 3.

One of the reasons that it took so long to impose criminal liability for attempts as such was that it was assumed that to criminalize attempts was to criminalize mere thoughts, and that was held, and with good reason, to be an abhorrent practice. However, from its inception, criminal liability for an attempt was never imposed without a showing to the effect that the defendant performed some act in furtherance of his criminal intention. Attempts have never been crimes of pure thought, but have always involved action. It seems to most people that this is an essential feature of attempt law; it would be completely unjustified to punish someone for an attempt without such a finding. Chapter 8 explains why this is. The explanation is not that there is no trying without action in furtherance of one's intention. Since basic acts—acts that are performed without performing any act on the way to their performance—can be attempted, it must be possible to try to act without doing, strictly speaking, anything. Nor is the explanation that without action nobody is endangered by the attempt. This is not true, and would not provide an adequate explanation, it is argued, even if it were. Rather, the explanation is that in the absence of action in furtherance of one's intention, there is insufficient evidence that the defendant would have completed the crime given ability, opportunity, and no change of mind. In other words, without action in furtherance of one's intention, there could be guidance by one's intention, but there cannot be adequate *evidence* of such guidance. A person who confesses to intending to complete a crime, for instance, has not provided adequate evidence to believe that he would have gone through with it given ability, opportunity, and no change of mind. I might confess my intention to, for instance, climb Mount Denali some day, without providing you with any evidence to believe that I will go through with it when given the chance. By contrast, if I take steps towards doing as I intend, which I do not merely by confessing my intention, then I do provide you with such evidence. Chapter 8 makes a detailed argument for this claim.

The basic idea of the argument is that rational agents who have done *anything* to further their intentions will do *everything* they need to do, given ability and opportunity, and in the absence of change of mind. Hence, we can conclude from the fact that a defendant has done something to further his intention, that he would fulfill it given the chance, assuming that he is rational. It seems very unlikely that anything other than action in furtherance of intention could serve to support an inference of the sort that is needed. Action in furtherance of intention, then, ought to be required for criminal liability for attempt, since without it there is insufficient evidence that the defendant was guided by the commitments constituted by his intention, and so insufficient evidence that he committed an attempt.

The idea that the act element of attempt serves an evidential function, and the identification of precisely what it is evidence *of*—namely, the counterfactual claim that the defendant would have completed the crime given ability, opportunity, and no change of mind—is used, in chapters 9 and 10, to resolve two long-standing legal problems. Chapter 9 is concerned with the issue of so-called "inherent impossibility". We do not typically take people to be guilty of attempted crimes when it was not just impossible, but *wildly* impossible for them to have completed the crime in the way they planned. The person who tries to kill another by sticking pins in a voodoo doll is not guilty of attempted murder. The problem is that while attempts by voodoo rarely attract the attention of police and prosecutors, it is very common to find people charged with attempting crimes who have adopted monumentally stupid plans for completing them. How do we draw the line between the stupid attempt that had no chance of succeeding and the inherently impossible attempt?

The first thing to recognize is that the distinction is not to be drawn by appeal to what it is to commit an attempt: the person who tries to kill with voodoo *tries* to kill; such a person has committed an attempt. If he is not to be held guilty of one, it must be for reasons that undermine guilt without undermining commission. Chapter 9 argues that the line is evidential: we lack sufficient evidence that the person trying to kill by voodoo is trying to kill. As indicated in chapter 8, to have the evidence we need, we need to be confident that the defendant would have completed the crime given ability, opportunity, and no change of mind. But to be confident of this, we need to be confident that the defendant *would take advantage of his ability and opportunity if he had it*. But to be confident of that, we need to be confident that the defendant understands his own abilities well enough to be in a position to recognize what he can and cannot do. The term "practical competence" is given in chapter 9 to the person who is competent in this regard. The problem with someone who tries to kill by voodoo is that he seems to be seriously handicapped in this respect. He is not someone whom we could necessarily expect to drink when led to water, as it were, despite his intention to drink. For all we know, when given ability and opportunity to kill with a gun, he might still persist with the voodoo. By contrast, somebody who has a stupid plan might still be somebody who we are confident would take advantage of ability and opportunity, were he to have it.

Just as the solution to the problem of inherent impossibility emerges from reflection on what, exactly, we need evidence *of* in order to know that a person is attempting a crime, the solution to one of the oldest and most discussed problems about attempts can be solved by such reflection: namely, the problem of specifying precisely what a person must have done in order to be guilty of an attempted crime. This issue is tackled in chapter 10. What emerges there is that there are two ways in which an act performed in furtherance of a criminal intention can provide us with adequate evidence that the defendant is trying to commit the intended crime. First, *any* such act serves when performed by a person who is rational and practically competent. So, for such agents, the so-called "first act" test suffices for guilt for attempt: a rational and practically competent agent who does anything motivated by his intention to commit a crime has provided us with adequate evidence that he is trying to commit it. However, many defendants are either irrational or practically incompetent, or both. Can such defendants provide us with adequate evidence that they are trying to commit crimes? They can, it is argued, when they perform so-called "last acts", acts that will lead without further conduct on the defendant's part to completion, if not interrupted. Even the person who cannot be trusted to take the best road to completion, even the practically incompetent person, can be held guilty for an attempted murder when he points a gun at someone else and pulls the trigger. But if he is stopped when there is more for him to do than this, then he is properly taken to be guilty of attempt only if we can be confident that he would do it, and such confidence requires us to be confident that he is both practically competent and rational. The test offered in chapter 10 for the act element of attempt, then, is a hybrid of the two extreme positions that are to be

found in the literature on this topic—the first act test and the last act test—
neither of which is adequate on its own, as has been widely recognized by both
legal practitioners and commentators. Still, while divided the two tests fall,
when properly united they stand.

Part 4, which consists of chapters 11 and 12, turns to issues of sentencing.
The idea that drives the discussion in this part of the book is, simply, that just as
the criminalization of an attempt is parasitic on the criminalization of the
associated completed crime—it is never justifiable to criminalize an attempt
to act in a way that is not, itself, justifiably criminalized—the sentencing of an
attempt is parasitic on the sentencing of the completed crime of which it is an
attempt. It emerges in these two chapters that this idea has some unexpected
consequences.

Chapter 11 considers the question of what to do with the defendant who
attempts a crime—he has the needed intention, is guided by the commitments
it constitutes, and provides us with adequate evidence of this through action
in furtherance of his intention that meets the test proposed in chapter 10—
but abandons it before completion. There are, at the moment, jurisdictions
that take abandonment in such conditions to be irrelevant; jurisdictions that
take abandonment to mitigate sentence, but not to speak to the question of
guilt; and jurisdictions that follow the *Model Penal Code* in granting a complete
affirmative defense to an attempt charge to those who abandon. Chapter 11
argues against the two extreme positions and offers an argument in support of
mitigating the sentences of those who abandon before completion, after having
attempted a crime and done enough to provide adequate evidence that they
have. The argument proceeds in two stages. The first half of the argument
proceeds, roughly, as follows: note, initially, that one way in which a factor
can mitigate punishment is by cancelling a reason that is usually present in
favor of issuing a particular sentence rather than a lower one. Generally, a judge
who issues a particular sentence to a defendant for a completed crime—say,
a year in prison—can offer the following reason for his decision not to issue a
lower sentence: had the defendant anticipated a lower sentence at the time
of the crime, he would not have recognized sufficient reason to refrain from
completing the crime. This explanation is not always available and is not
always sufficient even when available. Sometimes a lower penalty would
have, by the defendant's lights, given sufficient reason to refrain, and, still,
the penalty given is justified for other reasons. And sometimes a lower sanction
would not have sufficed to give the defendant sufficient reason to refrain, but,
still, a lower sentence would have been appropriate. Nonetheless, this is one
reason that can be given for the decision to issue a particular sentence rather
than a lower one. However, when the defendant has abandoned the crime
before completion, and has done so from an appreciation of sufficient reasons
to abandon it, then this reason for issuing a particular punishment rather than a
lower one is undercut. But something that undercuts a reason of this sort is a

mitigating factor; it provides a reason to give a lower sanction, or even no sanction, even if that reason is outweighed by other competing reasons that support sanctioning at a particular level. Thus, abandonment mitigates. This argument, however, does not support mitigation on the basis of remorse, where that is understood as the recognition of sufficient reason not to complete the crime *after* the crime has been completed. It is crucial to the argument that the reason that is cancelled by abandonment concerns the conception that the defendant had of his reasons *prior* to completing the crime.

The argument just rehearsed, namely the first stage of the argument for abandonment-based mitigation, does not show, all by itself, that abandonment mitigates *attempt*; it shows only that abandonment mitigates *completion*. Consider someone who *completes* a crime despite having abandoned it before completion; he sets a causal sequence in motion and then tries unsuccessfully to stop it. Still, when the causal chain reaches its end—when the building explodes, for instance, despite his efforts to stamp out the fuse that he lit—he has completed the crime. The argument just offered gives us good reason to take abandonment to mitigate sentence in such a case. But the case of an abandoned attempt is importantly different from this kind of case. The person who attempts the crime and then abandons is being held criminally liable for something, namely the attempt, that was completed before he abandoned, while the person who abandons and then completes the crime nonetheless, is being held criminally liable for something that was not completed until after he came to appreciate sufficient reason not to do it. Thus, the abandoned attempt looks more like a case of remorse following completion than it looks like a case of completion that was previously abandoned. We therefore need a further argument to bridge the gap between the claim our argument establishes, namely that abandonment mitigates completion, and the claim we seek to support, namely that abandonment mitigates attempt. The gap is filled in chapter 11 by noting that, with exceptions that can be set aside, the reasons to punish attempts are all of them reasons to punish completions. A judge deciding how to punish an attempt ought to ask himself, first, how he would have punished the crime had it been completed. If some of the reasons that he might have had for such a punishment are undercut by factors in the defendant's case, then those factors mitigate. It follows that abandonment mitigates sentence for attempt by undercutting a reason to give a particular punishment, rather than a lower punishment, to the crime that the defendant was trying to commit before he abandoned. So, the linkage between attempts and completions places constraints on the sentencing of attempts that direct us about what to do with those who abandon: mitigate, but do not grant an affirmative defense.

Chapter 12 turns to a more fundamental issue in the sentencing of attempts: the question of whether it is unfair to sentence attempts, particularly "last act" attempts, less severely than corresponding completed crimes. There are arguments against differential punishment that do not appeal to its unfairness.

Some think, for instance, that people need more control over outcomes than those who complete crimes typically have, in order to justify punishing them as severely as we do. Such people are not troubled by the *unfairness* of punishment discrepancies between completions and attempts. They are concerned, rather, with the mismatch between punishment and the control given defendants had over what they did, rather than the unfairness of giving different punishments to relevantly similar defendants. While we might call that issue one of fairness, it is not one of *comparative* fairness: it does not concern a kind of unfairness present only because of the way in which we treat people in different, but similar groups. In any event, chapter 12 does not weigh in on the question of whether those who complete crimes had enough control over what they caused to warrant the punishments we give them. The chapter addresses only the question of whether it is unfair to give attempters and completers different sanctions.

The chapter argues that it is not unfair. The argument proceeds in two stages. First, the following appealing thought is developed into the best argument it can be: the thought that the reason it is unfair is that the last act attempter and the completer *did the same thing*, even though they caused different results. It is argued that, even in its most polished form, this argument fails. It either employs premises that presuppose its conclusion, or else it employs false premises. The fundamental problem is that it is either false, or true in a trivial and unhelpful sense, that the last act attempter and the completer do the same thing. Hence, a difference in punishment of last act attempters and completers can be predicated on a difference in conduct, and there's nothing unfair about that. Second, it is argued that, by contrast, a similar kind of argument succeeds in showing that it is unfair to give a lesser punishment to the non-last act attempter than it is to the last act attempter. Those two types of agents *have* done the same thing in a non-trivial and important sense: they have both tried to commit the crime. Given that virtually everyone recognizes no unfairness in giving a lower punishment to the non-last act attempter and the completer, it follows (given some further, but plausible, assumptions) that there is no unfairness in giving a lower punishment to the last act attempter and the completer. In fact, it might be unfair to give them *the same* punishment, since to do so would be to give the last act attempter an unfair punishment relative to the non-last act attempter who is given less. The result is that the widespread practice of giving lower punishment to attempts than to completions is not unfair; it may have other problems, but it doesn't have that one.

Overall, then, the book provides a unified set of answers to a diverse and complicated set of legal questions about attempted crimes, questions that courts must answer in adjudicating particular cases, and which we would like them to answer on principled grounds. What unifies the variety of answers given in this book is the picture of trying to act offered and defended here. It is a picture that bears fruit, but which, I hope, has intuitive appeal, as well. Criminal attempts involve, like attempts to do things that are not crimes, an intention that commits the agent to success and guides him towards completion. From this basic idea, and its implications for the evidence needed of attempt, and the sentences that are properly imposed for it, a wide array of difficult problems can be solved, problems that judges confront when those charged with attempted crimes walk into their courtrooms.

Part 1

# What Are Attempts and Why Do We Criminalize Them?

# 1

# Rationalizing the Criminalization of Attempt

## 1. Introduction

When the legislature defines a crime—when it specifies a punishment for a person shown beyond a reasonable doubt to have acted in a certain way in certain circumstances and with certain results—it succeeds in defining a second crime as well, namely the crime of attempting to commit the crime defined. The legislature could choose specifically not to proscribe the attempt to commit a crime defined, but in the absence of an explicit statement to that effect, by defining the crime the legislature grants the state the power to punish also for the attempt. We seem to accept, that is, the following principle: "*If a particular form of conduct is legitimately criminalized, then the attempt to engage in that form of conduct is also legitimately criminalized.*" Call this "The Transfer Principle", since, under it, the legitimacy of criminalization transfers from completion to attempt. In accepting the Transfer Principle, the criminal law reflects our acceptance of a deeply entrenched principle of moral thought: if you shouldn't do something, then you shouldn't try to do it either. Moral prohibition, like justifiable criminalization, seems to transfer from completion to attempt.

Generally, it is through appeal to the Transfer Principle that attempts become crimes. The legislature might have a long debate about whether to pass a law making a certain kind of behavior a crime. But it does not then have a separate debate about whether to criminalize attempts to engage in that kind of behavior. Rather, when the law is passed, the attempt, too, has *ipso facto* become a crime. The Transfer Principle, then, is of great practical importance: it serves as a silent premise in the legislature's reasoning about what to criminalize. As such, it is in need of justification. Why do we think that justifiable criminalization transfers automatically from completed crimes to our efforts to engage in them? The principle is in particularly pressing need of justification, given that the first thing (although not necessarily the only thing) that one would cite in defense of criminalizing many completions—think of murder, rape, or robbery—is the harm that such acts cause. But attempts often cause no harm at all. What, then, justifies the Transfer Principle?[1]

Under consequentialist justifications of criminalization, the Transfer Principle is at best a reliable rule of thumb, and not an unqualified truth. The consequentialist thinks that the act of criminalizing a completed crime, like any other action, is justified because doing so results in better consequences, all told, than the alternative. But even when we assume this is true of the criminalization of the completed crime, it does not follow that it is true of the criminalization of the attempt. In criminalizing attempts, we take on the costs of policing, prosecuting, and punishing a large class of acts. These costs are not insignificant. And they are not offset to the same degree as the costs of punishing completions by the harm that is averted by preventing attempts since, after all, many attempts cause no harm at all. Of course, we also might punish them less harshly than completions, as many jurisdictions do, thus lowering at least one of the costs associated with their punishment, namely the pain and deprivation inflicted on the offender. And in threatening punishment we also manage to prevent some completed crimes as well as some attempts, thus offsetting the costs further. Do the consequentialist calculations come out in favor of criminalizing attempts? Not simply in virtue of the fact that they happen to come out in favor of criminalizing the corresponding completion. The fact that they come out in favor of criminalizing completions is *evidence* that they will also come out in favor of criminalizing attempts, but it is no more than evidence. Under consequentialist approaches to criminalization, the question of whether to criminalize an attempt is a new question from the one we asked in deciding whether to criminalize the completed crime. Among other things, this

---

[1] In Husak (2008), Douglas Husak decries the lack of attention given by philosophers of law and criminal law theorists to the following question: What are the necessary and sufficient conditions that legislation specifying punishment for a type of conduct must meet if it is to be justifiable? Husak's complaint is well-founded. An answer to this question is of the first importance—both to the creation of a complete theory of criminal law, and to the task of retarding what is, by all measures, a scandalous growth of the criminal law in the United States—and its importance far outstrips the attention that has been given to it. Husak identifies several necessary conditions that must be met if legislation criminalizing a particular type of conduct is to be justified, and notes whole categories of American criminal legislation that fail to meet one or more of these conditions. As Husak recognizes, however, necessary conditions for the legitimacy of criminal legislation are much easier to come by than are sufficient conditions. How harmful, or in what way, must harmful conduct be harmful, before it is legitimately criminalized? How wrong or offensive, or in what way, must wrongful or offensive conduct be before it is legitimately criminalized? Still, in the case of attempts, we appear to have a sufficient, albeit recursively defined, condition for the legitimacy of criminalization, namely the Transfer Principle. A full theory of justified criminalization—a full set of necessary and sufficient conditions—must respect that principle: it must turn out that the principle is true under the theory. And so further reflection on the principle can probably aid in the construction of a defensible theory of criminalization. However, reflection on the principle and its rationale can also tell us a great deal about the nature of attempted crimes.

implies that under the consequentialist approach we shouldn't expect the same answer across all crimes. Perhaps it is true that if the consequences of criminalizing murder are good enough to justify that practice then so are the consequences of criminalizing attempted murder. The same might be true for rape and for robbery. But from these facts we shouldn't conclude that this is also true of fraud, or larceny, much less of truancy, or bigamy, or unlicensed possession of a dangerous animal, or any of the other wide variety of crimes that we find in any mature criminal code, the attempts of all of which are automatically criminalized under the Transfer Principle. The consequentialist calculation would need to be made in each instance. So it seems that under the consequentialist approach, the Transfer Principle, in its unqualified form, is not justified, although it might be justified when limited or qualified in certain ways. However, what we seek here is a true justification of the principle; it is that principle, and not a qualified one, that we find in our criminal law, and in the silent, background reasoning of our legislature. And it is that principle, and not a qualified one, that is reflective of a deeply entrenched element of our common-sense moral thought. Can it itself be justified? If so, the justification of it must be nonconsequentialist.

Justifications of the Transfer Principle have implications for the adequacy of accounts of the elements of an attempted crime. To see the point, consider the following nonconsequentialist justification of the Transfer Principle:

Attempts and completed crimes both involve action furthering an objectionable intention to a substantial degree. These two features of completions—objectionable intention and action that takes one a substantial distance towards fulfilling it—are what justifies criminalizing completions. So, when the completion is justifiably criminalized, so is the attempt.

There is a question as to whether this is an adequate justification of the Transfer Principle. Among other things, since often whether a person acts on his intention at all, much less how far he manages to go in doing what he intends, is a matter of luck, this approach involves a commitment to the existence of so-called "moral luck", something of which many people deny the possibility. But put that issue aside for now (it is discussed in connection to the act element of attempt in chapter 8, and in connection to sentencing in chapter 12). Someone who endorses this line of thought is under pressure to hold that an attempted crime must involve conduct that furthers an intention in something like the way and to the degree in which completions involve such acts. Less action than what is required to complete the crime might still suffice for attempt, on this view, but probably not much less. So, one who endorses this line of thought might on those grounds rule out some candidate accounts of the act element of attempts. On some such accounts, behavior will count as an attempted crime even though it does not deserve to be criminalized under the

Transfer Principle, according to this rationale of the principle. Alternatively, consider the following justification of the principle:

Attempts and completed crimes both involve an objectionable intention. This feature of completions alone is what justifies criminalizing completions. So, when the completion is justifiably criminalized, so is the attempt.

As it stands, this line of thought is at odds with our practice of requiring an intention for an attempt even when intention is not required for the completed crime (this issue is discussed in chapter 2). But putting that aside, we can see that someone who accepts this line of thought is under pressure to see much less action than would be needed to complete the crime, maybe even no action at all, as sufficient for a criminal attempt when coupled with the appropriate objectionable intention. There will be comparable implications of our rationalization of the Transfer Principle for our understanding of the *mens rea* elements of attempt (although the two justifications just described won't differ in this regard). In general, the point at this stage is merely that what we think must be shown to convict for an attempt is not independent of what we think justifies criminalizing attempts in the first place. The results of this chapter, then, serve as premises in the chapters to come.

Section 2 considers the prospects for justifying the Transfer Principle on the grounds that when a type of act is morally wrong, then so is the attempt of it. Section 3 considers the prospects for justifying the principle by conceiving of attempts as risking completions. Both views are rejected. Section 4 offers an alternative rationale that identifies the deep features shared by attempts and completions that warrant the criminalization of an attempt, when criminalization of completion is warranted; namely, that both reflect corruption in the modes of recognition and response to legal reasons employed by the actor, and further that these modes of recognition and response to reasons play a role in guiding the actor's conduct. As we'll see, this amounts to a defense of a view distinct from, although allied to, the position just described, according to which both attempts and completions are justifiably criminalized, when they are, on the grounds that they involve the same objectionable intention and conduct in furtherance of it. Under the assumption that the *mens rea* elements of the completed crime are indicators of the modes of recognition and response to legal reasons of defendants who complete crimes, the corresponding intention of the person who attempts a crime is an indicator of the same or worse modes. What matters is not commonality in the mental states between completion and attempt, but commonality in what those mental states express, namely modes of recognition and response to reasons. But this is not the only thing that matters. Completion involves completed action, while attempt (usually) does not, but, for reasons to be explained, it is not the fact that completion involves completed action, but rather a concomitant of this fact that contributes to the justifiability of criminalizing completion. The concomitant fact is that completion involves a kind of guidance of behavior in accordance with one's modes of recognition and response to reasons that we also find in attempt. These two commonalities between completion and attempt, then, serve to justify the Transfer Principle.

## 2. The Wrong of Trying to do What's Wrong

One might think that the Transfer Principle is justified because its moral analogue—the moral principle that if acting in a particular way is wrong, then so is trying to act that way—is true. Such an approach requires supplementation with some set of claims to the effect that the moral and the legal bear a close relation. If one held, for instance, that the moral wrongness of a type of act is both necessary and sufficient reason to criminalize it, this claim would link with the moral analogue of the Transfer Principle to yield an argument, a justification, for the Transfer Principle. It seems likely that weaker claims concerning the relation between the moral and the legal would also serve. In particular, this line of thought only requires the view that the moral wrongness of completed crime *when found in conjunction with other features of the completed crime that are also found in the attempt* is necessary and sufficient to justify criminalizing completion. One might hold, for instance, that moral wrongness is necessary and sufficient to justify the criminalization of conduct *that invades or threatens to invade an interest of the sort that the state has a duty to protect*. In what follows I will grant, for the sake of argument, that the moral wrongness of a type of behavior is the leading feature to be found in a complex condition met by both completion and attempt, and the meeting of which is both necessary and sufficient to justify criminalizing completion. However, as I will suggest in what follows, even granting such claims, the Transfer Principle cannot be justified simply by appeal to the truth of its moral analogue. The true moral principle in the neighborhood of the Transfer Principle does not provide adequate support for the Transfer Principle.

As a first step in this argument, note the distinction between "last act" attempts, also known as "complete" attempts, and the rest. A last act attempt involves performance by the defendant of all the conduct that the defendant believes he personally needs to perform in order to complete the crime. When a defendant engages in a non-last act attempt, by contrast, his course of conduct ends before he's done all that he thinks he needs to do. If a defendant fires a gun at the head of another with the intention of killing him, his attempt is (ordinarily) a last act attempt: he doesn't ordinarily think that more action is required of him in order to fulfill his intention to kill. If, by contrast, he administers several doses of a poison and thinks more doses will be needed to cause death, his attempt is non-last act. The distinction between these two kinds of attempts seems significant, since an agent who engages in a non-last act attempt can be acting while coherently conceiving of the possibility that he won't go through with his plans. The normative relevance to attempts of (a) the belief that one could still change one's mind, (b) the actual possibility of doing so, and(c) actual change of mind itself, will be discussed in chapters 10 and 11. If any of these three things are significant, then there is a normatively signifi-cant difference between last act and non-last act attempts.

However, for those who hold that non-last act attempts are at least sometimes criminal—as is the case in every jurisdiction in the United States, and in both Britain and Canada—a successful rationalization of the Transfer Principle will be such as to justify the criminalization of *both* last act and non-last act attempts, when the completed crime is justifiably criminalized. The rationali-zation of the principle will not, that is, imply only that last act attempts are to be criminalized. Justifiable criminalization extends to trying to act criminally, and is insensitive to the difference between last act and non-last act attempts. It is possible that non-last act attempts are not to be punished as harshly as last act attempts. But the question of criminalization and the question of the degree of punishment are distinguishable and must be distinguished. Even if last act and non-last act attempts are to be split when it comes to degree of punishment, they are to be lumped together when it comes to criminalization. Both derive their criminality from the criminality of the completed crime.

R. A. Duff's brilliant book on attempted crimes includes a less satisfying account of the grounds for their criminalization than one might hope to have. Part of the problem with Duff's discussion of that issue is that he is committed to thinking that we can justify criminalization of attempts through arguments that justify only the criminalization of *last act* attempts. Consider the following passage:

[W]e must surely agree that if it is wrong to cause a harm intentionally or recklessly, it is also (and not much less) wrong to attempt to cause such harm, or to take unreasonable risk of causing such harm. A law that condemned and punished actually harm-causing conduct as wrong, but was utterly silent on attempts to cause such harms, and on reckless risk-taking with respect to such harms, would speak with a strange moral voice.[2]

The problem with Duff's argument is that wrongness varies in kind and magni-tude, and there is little reason to think that non-last act attempts are wrong in quite the same way, or to the same degree, as completed crimes. Last act attempts, by contrast, are quite plausibly thought to be just as wrong as com-pleted crimes. So, Duff's argument seems to support the Transfer Principle when it is confined to last act attempts: they seem to be justifiably criminalized because they are just as wrong as the relevant completed crimes (on the assumption that the moral and the legal are related in such a way that the wrongness of the completed crime is both necessary and sufficient to justify its criminalization when found alongside other features shared by the completed crime and the last act attempt). But we can't reach any conclusion from this

---

[2] Duff (1996), 134.

argument as it stands about non-last act attempts. Some acts, while wrong, are not wrong enough, or wrong in the right way, to justify criminalizing them, as anyone who has told a small lie, or broken even a big promise, knows. But if non-last act attempts are not wrong in quite the same way or to the same degree as the completed crimes they are attempts of, then perhaps they are wrong in a way or to a degree which fails to justify criminalizing them even when the completed crime is justifiably criminalized on the basis of its wrongness. Of course, that doesn't seem likely. But that's not the point. The point is that we cannot justify the Transfer Principle simply by noting that when completion is wrong, so is attempt; for that argument to work without supplementation, attempt and completion must be equally and equivalently wrong, and at least non-last act attempts rarely are.

The true moral principle that is analogous to the Transfer Principle is something like this: "If a type of behavior is wrong in some way and to some degree, then trying to engage in that behavior is also wrong in some related way or in some related degree." But since this true principle is compatible with significant variation between the kind and degree of wrongness in completion and attempt, it cannot serve to support the Transfer Principle without supplementation.

## 3. Criminalization as Risk-Suppression

The idea that the justified criminality of a completed crime transfers to the attempt because the attempt *risks* the completed crime is deeply ingrained in the law. We find the idea in Oliver Wendell Holmes's discussion of attempt in *The Common Law*,[3] but we also find it in a different form in the *Model Penal Code*, which has a radically different conception of both the nature of attempt and the value of criminal punishment generally from that which we find in Holmes. The idea can take one of two very different forms. In the first, a particular defendant's attempt is to be criminalized because it risked the completion of the crime *on that very occasion*. In the second, a particular defendant's attempt is to be criminalized because it is evidence of his dangerousness, and so is evidence that there will be a completed crime on some later occasion, or that there was one which went undetected on some earlier occasion. Holmes takes the first approach, the *Model Penal Code* the second.

Ordinarily, when we say that a particular event risks some result we mean at least that the conditional probability of the result, given the event, is significantly higher than the prior probability of the result.[4] On the first approach,

---

[3] Holmes (1881), 68–9.

[4] This is almost certainly not all we mean. We mean, in addition, that the result is something that typically follows events of that sort, and we probably mean more, even, than these two things.

attempts are to be criminalized because the conditional probability of completion of the crime *begun in the attempt*, given the attempt itself, is significantly higher than that completed crime's prior probability. On this view, to say that attempts risk completion is like saying that the conditional probability that the runner will complete the race, given that he has made it to the halfway point, is higher than the prior probability of his completing the race: we bet less on his completion before we learn that he's made it halfway. Similarly, on this first approach, the occurrence of some of the events that would make up a completed crime—namely the attempt—increase the probability that there will be that very completed crime: we bet less on the defendant's completing the crime on this very occasion before we learn that he attempted it. On the second approach, attempts are to be criminalized because the conditional probability of a token of that type of crime being performed by the defendant, given the attempt, is significantly higher than the prior probability that the defendant would perform such a crime. To continue the runner analogy, on this second approach, the fact that the runner has made it halfway increases the probability that he will complete, or has completed, *a* race—either the one that he is halfway through, or some other race on some other future or past occasion. The first approach involves conceiving of attempts as analogous to crimes of immediate risk creation, such as drunk driving. By driving drunk, the driver significantly increases the probability that he will injure others or damage their property on this occasion and through the activity of driving drunk in which he is engaged. The second approach involves conceiving of attempts as evidence of dangerousness of disposition that might in future, or might have in the past, resulted in crimes. On the second approach, attempts are criminalized, not because they themselves create risks of completed crime, but rather because thanks to them we come to recognize a risk that the offender has completed, or will complete a crime.

A problem with the first approach is that the occurrence of many a legitimately criminalized attempt fails to raise the probability that the attempt will blossom into a completed crime. Under the first approach, there appears to be no good reason to criminalize such attempts. In fact, this line of thought can drive an argument to the effect that impossible attempts are not to be criminalized. The thought is that if the crime could not possibly have been completed, then the attempt did not raise the probability of completion. The prior probability of completion was zero, and so is the conditional probability of completion, given the attempt. But if it did not raise the probability of completion then, on this view, the attempt should not be criminalized. The right response to this bit of *modus ponens*, however, is *modus tolens*: since the fact of impossibility is (almost) never legitimately a defense, attempts are not rightly criminalized in virtue of the fact that they impose risks of blossoming into completion, but for some other reason. In short, the fact that impossible attempts are justifiably criminalized under the Transfer Principle indicates that the first approach's rationale for the Transfer Principle is flawed. (More on impossible attempts in chapters 5 and 9.)

The point about impossible attempts is actually a symptom of a deeper problem with the first approach, namely that if the relevant question from the point of view of criminalization is the increased probability of completion, then the fact that the defendant *tried* to act criminally is of no direct relevance, but only of indirect relevance, to the justification of the Transfer Principle. Someone who tries very hard, but is incompetent, or just very unlucky, might increase the probability of completion by very little through his efforts. In fact, he might even have such a 'brown thumb' that we think him more likely to succeed if he doesn't try at all. While it is obvious that the fact of incompetence per se should not undermine the justifiability of criminalization, the problem here does not rest on that claim. The problem is that the Transfer Principle is not justified by a view according to which attempts only sometimes bear the right relation to completions to justify criminalizing them. There is great variety among attempts in how much, if at all, they increase the probability of completion, and the degree to which they do has little to do with any of their other normatively relevant properties. Some non-last act attempts, for instance, have a higher probability of blossoming into completed crimes than do some last act attempts. The person who fires a bullet at the chest of someone wearing a bulletproof vest has hardly increased the chance of completing a murder through his act, although he has performed the "last act". By contrast, a person who aims and has yet to fire at the person who is wearing no protective gear, may have increased the probability of a completed murder by a great deal, even though he hasn't performed the last act. The degree to which an attempt increases the probability of completion just does not align with the normatively relevant features of attempts. But the thought that drives the Transfer Principle is that attempts *themselves*, because they are tryings to act, bear the right relation to the completed crimes to warrant criminalization, quite independently of the further accidental property that some of them possess of significantly raising the probability of completion.

Consider, now, the approach that we find in the *Model Penal Code*, according to which attempts are to be criminalized because where there is an attempt there is an increased probability that an instance of the crime will be, or has been performed by the actor on this or some other occasion. In the commentary, the *Model Penal Code* says that attempt law "should focus on the dangerousness of the actor, as a person manifesting a firm disposition to commit a crime."[5] The view avoids one of the objections that arises with respect to the position that attends to the risk that the attempt itself will be completed. Even if there is no chance at all that the attempt will be completed—and so no increase

---

[5] *Model Penal Code*, Commentary to §5.01, 298.

in the probability of completion in light of the attempt—it is still probably true that someone who attempts a crime is more likely to complete that crime on some occasion than someone who does not. What we attempt, that is, is evidence of character, and character is evidence of criminal behavior.

To some, the *Model Penal Code's* approach seems to involve punishing people not for what they have been proven beyond a reasonable doubt to have done, but for what we think they will do, or what we think they might have done, but have not been proven beyond a reasonable doubt to have done. The approach, that is, seems to involve a violation of the presumption of innocence. It is possible that this criticism succeeds. But if it does, it serves as the basis for a critique of a broad class of crimes, and not just of criminal attempts. Consider what are sometimes called "ancillary" crimes: conduct that is criminalized, not because it is worth criminalizing considered in itself, but because it is frequently found alongside conduct that is justifiably criminalized in itself. A typical example of an ancillary crime is the crime of "structuring" a transaction, as when a large amount of cash is deposited in a bank in several small increments so as to avoid triggering reporting requirements.[6] An eccentric, or someone with a strong sense of privacy, might do this without it being true that there is some other conduct in the vicinity that is deserving of criminal sanction. But we criminalize this behavior because, typically, those who do this kind of thing are taking steps to conceal something that we have independent reasons for wanting to criminalize. Those who are opposed to ancillary crimes will be opposed, for the same reasons, to the *Model Penal Code's* rationale for the Transfer Principle. After all, if the *Model Penal Code* is right, then it seems that attempts are closely analogous to ancillary crimes. They are punished not because they are worth punishing considered in themselves, but because they are often found before or after completed crimes that are worth punishing in themselves.[7]

However, there is room to reject the *Model Penal Code's* rationale for the Transfer Principle, even by those who accept the legitimacy of at least some ancillary crimes. Under that rationale, the legitimacy of criminalization transfers from completion to attempt without appeal to any kind of deep, and morally relevant linkage between attempt and completion of the sort that fuels the recognition of the truth of the Transfer Principle. To see the point,

---

[6] The Federal crime is defined at 31 U.S.C.A. § 5324.

[7] Another problem with the *Model Penal Code's* approach: say a defendant attempts petty larceny. This fact raises the probability that he committed petty larceny in the past or would do so in the future. But it also raises the probability that he committed grand larceny in the past, or would do so in the future. Petty larceny, after all, is a "gateway" crime to grand larceny. Why punish this defendant for attempted *petty* larceny, but not attempted *grand* larceny? If the attempt in which he actually engaged deserves criminalization because it shows the defendant to be dangerous in a particular way, why not punish him for *all* the different ways in which it shows him to be dangerous?

consider again the moral analogue of the Transfer Principle: "If a type of action is morally wrong, then so is the attempt of it." As the remarks in section 2 reflect, we cannot justify the Transfer Principle simply by citing this moral version of it: the problem is that there are differences between the wrongness of the completed crime and that of the attempt. But, at the same time, it seems clear that a justification of the Transfer Principle must serve to see it as reflective of a thought of the same sort that underlies the moral analogue of the principle. Moral wrongness transfers from completion to attempt, but it is clear that it does not do so *because* those who attempt are likely to complete the wrong act on some other occasion. There is, instead, some kind of deep moral commonality between completion and attempt which is registered in the thought that when the one is wrong, so is the other. The *Model Penal Code's* rationale for the Transfer Principle serves to justify it only at the cost of cleaving it away from the logic of the moral principle that is its close cousin. As we will see, it is possible to justify the Transfer Principle while respecting its grounding in our moral thought. What we need is a rationale for the principle that explains, as Duff says, why to deny it would be to "speak with a strange moral voice".[8]

## 4. Justifying the Principle: Censure, Sanction, and Our Modes of Response to Reasons

The justification of criminal punishment and the justification of criminalization must be linked.[9] It is not justifiable for the state to punish conduct that is not criminal, and it not justifiable for the state to criminalize a type of conduct, no tokens of which can be justifiably punished. However, it does not follow from this that the criminal punishment of an act is justified if, and only if, the act is of a type that is justifiably criminalized. And, in fact, a variety of legal doctrines make sense only if it is possible for a person's conduct to be criminal, and legitimately considered so, even though punishment of it is not justifiable. This thought is required, for instance, to make sense of various immunities. Under the US Constitution, members of Congress are immune from libel charges for things they say on the floor of the House or the Senate.[10] But this does not mean that a libelous remark made on the floor is not a crime: it is—it is simply not a crime for which a member of Congress can be justifiably punished. To take another example, consider the fact that with few exceptions, when a principal in a crime has an excuse, his accomplice can still be convicted for the crime. It is a crime to help an insane person rob a bank, even though the insane person has an excuse for his conduct, and so is not justifiably punished for it.

---

[8] Duff (1996), 134.
[9] For discussion, see Husak (2008), especially chapter 1.
[10] U.S. Const. art. I, §6, cl. 1.

Typically, this doctrine is explained by saying that the conduct of the excused principal is still criminal, and so the accomplice is still implicated in a crime. The thought is that the excuse of insanity does not nullify the criminality of the principal's conduct but, instead, nullifies the appropriateness of punishment of that conduct, even in the face of its criminality. To hold that this aspect of the criminal law is justified is to hold that conduct can be justifiably criminalized without being justifiably punished.

To see why justifiable criminalization does not entail justifiable punishment, it helps to be reminded that criminal punishment involves two distinct things: censure and sanction. To punish for conduct is to express the judgment that the conduct is an appropriate object of disapproval and condemnation: this is censure. But it is, of course, also to inflict the agent with pain or deprivation or both: this is sanction. While I don't have an argument for the claim, it seems to me that the following is true:

(*) Criminalization of a type of conduct is legitimate if (1) Censure by the state of every unexcused and unjustified token of that type of conduct is deserved, and (2) Some of the unexcused and unjustified tokens of that type of conduct are legitimately sanctioned by the state in some way or other.[11]

This view explains how it is possible for conduct to be legitimately considered criminal without being legitimately punished. This can happen in at least two ways. First, consider an unexcused and unjustified token act that is of a type that is justifiably criminalized under (*). Such an act is deservedly censured by the state. But it does not follow that it is legitimately sanctioned, since it might be among the tokens of the type that are not. Such is the case with the congressman's libel. Second, consider an excused or justified act that is of a type that is justifiably criminalized under (*). Such conduct might not be deservedly censured—justified conduct never is, and excused conduct rarely is—and it is certainly not legitimately sanctioned; but this is consistent with its being criminal since it remains of a type that is justifiably criminalized under (*). Such is the case with the insane person's robbery; we are not barred from conceiving of such conduct as a crime by (*).[12]

---

[11] This principle should be understood to be saying that the desert of censure of all the tokens, and the legitimacy of sanction of some, derives from the fact that the tokens are tokens of the type. Otherwise, it might turn out to be justified to criminalize public lies of all sorts merely because all are deserving of censure and it is legitimate to sanction lying under oath. This result is blocked, however, when the principle is understood as described in this footnote, since it is not legitimate to sanction lying under oath thanks to the fact that it is an instance of lying, but thanks to the fact that it is an instance of lying *under oath*. (Thanks to Jacob Ross for pressing me in a way that forced this refinement and to Gary Watson for suggesting it.)

[12] Many hold that justified conduct is not criminal. (*) might appear to run contrary to this view. And it is inconsistent with it *if* justified conduct is of the same type as unjustified conduct that is legitimately criminalized under (*). However, this last claim can be denied. To do so, criminal proscriptions must be taken to have tacit "unless"-clauses that are met when the elements of a justification are in place. The law does not proscribe killing people, on this

As we will see, if a type of action is deservedly censured by the state when unexcused and unjustified, then unexcused and unjustified attempts of it are also deservedly censured by the state. And if some such completions are appropriately sanctioned, then it is also appropriate to sanction some such attempts (last act attempts to engage in legitimately sanctionable conduct in the absence of immunity, for instance, are legitimately sanctionable, and more). From these two facts, together with (*), we are able to conclude that the Transfer Principle is true. There are two relevant shared properties between completions and attempts. There is the property of completions and attempts that underlies desert of censure of completions, and so helps to account for the fact that their criminalization is justifiable. And there is the property of justifiably sanctioned completions that it shares with some attempts. What are these properties? I will suggest that the first is the agent's improper mode of recognition and response to legal reasons. The one who completes the crime and the one who attempts it may differ in what sanctions they deserve, but since they recognize and respond to legal reasons in the same way, the first is deserving of censure by the state only if the second is too. The second property—the property in virtue of which sanction of completions is deserved and which we find also in some attempts—is the property of being guided in one's conduct by one's mode of recognition and response to reasons in a way that brings one close to completion. This position will be explained in what follows.

## 4.1 *The Commonality Between Legitimately Sanctioned Completions and Some Attempts*

First consider sanction and the question of whether it follows from the fact that some tokens of a type of completed behavior are deservedly sanctioned that some tokens of attempts to engage in it are deservedly sanctioned. A fully adequate explanation for why this is so would draw on a genuine theory of the penal sanction—an account of the necessary and sufficient conditions that a bit of behavior must meet if it is to be legitimately sanctioned. I do not have such a theory to offer. However, an argument can be made for the claim even in the absence of such a theory. Here's the argument.

Two assumptions are made in this stage of the argument. First, assume that if a particular kind of conduct is deservedly censured when unexcused and unjustified, then so are unexcused and unjustified attempts to engage in it. This assumption is harmless, since an independent argument for it will be produced in section 4.2. Second, in line with current legal practice, assume that the mere

---

view, but instead proscribes killing *unless required for purposes of self-defense*, for instance. If this is right, then there is no conduct of type C that is justified, which is why justified conduct is not criminal. All justified conduct is necessarily not of the type that the law proscribes. For discussion of the issue see, for instance, Finkelstein (2000).

fact that unexcused and unjustified conduct is deservedly censured by the state does not entail that it is legitimately sanctioned. For the legitimacy of sanction, we need at least absence of immunity, for instance.

The argument is a *reductio ad absurdum*. From the following assumption, we will derive an absurdity: imagine that although some completions of a kind of conduct are legitimately sanctioned, no attempts of that kind of behavior are. To make as plausible a case for the opposition as possible, imagine that the completed behavior is truancy, and we are further assuming that although some truant behavior is legitimately sanctioned, it is not legitimate to sanction anyone who merely attempts to be truant. It follows that each of the relevant completions must possess some feature which is necessary for the legitimacy of sanction, and which is not possessed by any attempts. There may be no single feature shared by all legitimately sanctioned completions, but, still, all attempts must differ in some crucial way from each legitimately sanctioned completion. For each completion that is legitimately sanctioned, that is, we can point to some feature of it that justifies sanctioning it, and which is not possessed by any attempt.

First, note that none of these features, whatever they are, can be possessed in virtue of the mental state involved in completion. The reason is that attempts always involve intention (an argument legitimizing this legal practice is offered in chapter 2), and there are very good reasons to think that a person who is sanctionable and who falls short of intention—he is merely reckless, for instance—is *less* deserving of sanction than someone who does the same objectionable thing with intent. So although attempters might differ in their mental states from those who complete the relevant type of crime and are deserving of sanction, it cannot be on those grounds that the attempters are not legitimately sanctioned. So, the features that we are imagining possessed by the legitimately sanctioned tokens of conduct must be features of the acts, results, or circumstances involved.

The next step is motivated by the observation that there are virtually limitless ways to fall short of achieving the acts, results, and circumstances involved in any crime. We can imagine features of the acts, results, and circumstances that entail that they are fully achieved, of course (such as the trivial feature of being the conjunction of the acts, results, and circumstances needed for completion). But with the exception of features that fall into this category, the following is true: if F is a feature possessed by any state of affairs in which the acts, results, and circumstances of the completed crime are realized, it is possible for a state of affairs to possess F even though it is also the case that the acts, results, and circumstances of the completed crime are not realized in that state of affairs. To put the point another way, we can divide features of states of affairs into two sorts: there are those that are "completion-entailing"—if a state of affairs possesses a feature in this category, then the acts, results, and circumstances of the completed crime are realized in that state of affairs—and those that are "completion-insufficient"—they are not completion-entailing.

Now, the following is a fact about attempt: for any completion-insufficient feature, it is possible to try to commit the crime, to fail, and for the state of affairs realized by one's efforts to *possess* the completion-insufficient feature. For instance, merely being absent from school is not enough for truancy: you also need to lack permission. So, absence from school is a completion-insufficient feature. And it is possible for a person to try to be truant and to fail, despite succeeding in being absent from school; imagine, for instance, that unbeknownst to the student, the principal grants him permission to be absent in order to allow the police to follow him to his drug-supplier.[13] The lack of permission is also completion-insufficient, since a student has failed to be truant if he fails to leave school grounds even while lacking permission to do so. There is a failed attempt possessing this feature when the student leaves class without permission to leave school, but is nabbed before leaving school grounds. What follows is that, if the crucial features of the justifiably sanctioned completions are completion-insufficient, then some attempts possess those same features and so are justifiably sanctioned also. We are then halfway towards showing that if some completions are justifiably sanctioned, then so are some attempts.

What if, instead, the crucial features of the justifiably sanctioned completions are completion-entailing? In that case, no failed attempts possess those crucial features, since, by definition, any attempt that did would be a completion, and so would not be a *failed* attempt at all. Someone who holds that the crucial feature of truancy, thanks to which some of its tokens are justifiably sanctioned, is *the conjunction* of absence from school and lack of permission would see the crucial feature as completion-entailing. If all of the crucial features, then, of the justifiably sanctioned completions are completion-entailing, then no attempts of that type of crime are justifiably sanctioned. However, this cannot be the case. To see why it can't, notice that every crime, without exception, involves the causation of a particular event. Sometimes this is folded into the definition of the act element of an attempt, as when a statute bans "killing" in certain circumstances. Sometimes, instead, the causation element is explicitly identified as such, as when a statute bans "causing death" in certain circumstances. (The importance of the distinction between these two ways of writing a statute is discussed in chapter 7.) What this implies is that it is possible to get arbitrarily close to completion of a crime without actually getting there. If a statute bans the causation of death, a person can fall short of completion by causing a person to be in a state only just this side of death; if a statute bans being absent from school, a person can fall short of absence by being arbitrarily close to the school boundary, or by being only "technically" present, as when the statute overlooks the fact that school buses—even when parked at the mall—are,

---

[13] For a case with a similar structure, see *United States v. Berrigan* (482 F.2d 171 (3d Cir. 1973)). Cases of this sort are discussed in chapter 5.

technically speaking, school grounds. Many of the cases in which a person causes something that is close to, but not quite, what needs to be caused for completion of the crime, are complete attempts, "last act" attempts. How could it be that the appropriateness of sanction should be so black-and-white as to be present when a line is crossed, but absent when it is all but crossed by someone who intends to cross it? This seems particularly implausible when we are reminded that sanctions can be arbitrarily small: for every sanction there is a lesser sanction possible. Someone who insists that the crucial features of the justifiably sanctioned completions of a particular sort of crime—the features in virtue of which they are justifiably sanctioned—are all completion-entailing, insists that although sanction admits of degree, and although attempts can differ from completions by a very small amount, they differ entirely from completions in the justifiability of sanction. This is possible—there is no contradiction in such a position—but it seems very unlikely to be true.

It is worth summarizing the argument just offered for the claim that when some completions are justifiably sanctioned, so are some attempts. We start by assuming this is false. This implies that justifiably sanctioned completions are different from attempts in crucial respects. We then note that there is a distinction between two kinds of features of completions: some are completion-entailing, and some are not. Since all of those of the second sort are possessed by some attempts, the completion-insufficient features are not those that distinguish the justifiably sanctioned completions from the attempts. But it seems virtually certain, given the role of causation of events in the definitions of crimes, that the crucial features of justifiably sanctioned completions, the features in virtue of which they are justifiably sanctioned, are not completion-entailing. But since every feature of a completion is either completion-insufficient or completion-entailing, our assumption entails a contradiction. And therefore we are able to conclude that if some completions are justifiably sanctioned, then so are some attempts.

It is important to note an implication of this argument that will turn out to be of importance later. Sometimes the way in which a crime involves causation of an event is that an element of the crime is a basic action which would not be performed were the defendant not the cause of some event. A basic action is an action the performance of which does not require performance of any prior *act* that causes or contributes to its performance. While every example of a basic act is controversially classified as such, simple bodily movements appear to be good examples. To raise one's arm certain things need to take place—nerve impulses and muscle contractions, for instance—but these events needn't be *actions*. When one raises one's arm, one may not *do* anything else first that contributes to one's arm rising. Crimes of trespass, and loitering, are good candidates for crimes that require causation only because they require basic action. Such crimes require that one's body be in a certain place. More needs to be true for trespass than this: among other things, perhaps, the place one's body is must be another's property, and one must lack permission to be there. But in so far as trespass involves causation, it merely involves causation by the defendant of his body's position. A person can get arbitrarily close to, while falling short of causing an event such that, were he to cause it in the normal way, it would be a basic act. To fall just short of causing one's arm to move, or causing one's body to be on another's property are examples. In such cases, one necessarily falls short of any form of action other than trying itself (on the assumption that trying is action); if there were action in such a case, then the act one falls short of completing would not be basic at all. Now the argument above, if it succeeds, shows that a person who gets arbitrarily close to causing that which needs to be caused in a legitimately sanctionable completion is also legitimately sanctionable. This is true even when the causation requirement of completion derives only from the fact that completion involves a basic act. Thus the argument implies that the feature of a completion, in virtue of which it is legitimately sanctioned, may not be that it involves any kind of completed conduct. Something falling short of conduct, which is shared with the attempt and that gets close to completion, suffices.[14] In chapter 3 a precise specification of what this is, is provided. For now it is enough to say that in both legitimately sanctionable completion and attempt we have guidance by the agent's way of recognizing and responding to reasons, despite the fact that such guidance might fall short of any form of action on the agent's part (other than, perhaps, the act of attempting itself). As we will see, this is part of the reason that the argument offered here for the Transfer Principle cannot be employed in support of principles that justify the criminalization of other forms of conduct that do not rise to the level of attempt.

## 4.2 The Commonality Between Completions Deserving of Censure and Attempts

Move now to the other half of the argument for the Transfer Principle and consider censure, and the reasons for thinking that if completion is justifiably censured, then so is attempt. Under what conditions does a person's conduct

---

[14] This implies that behavior can be justifiably sanctioned even if the defendant does not engage in any voluntary bodily movement. This might appear to be a violation of the voluntary act requirement. However, as we will see in chapter 8, there is good reason not to sanction any attempts of justifiably criminalized basic actions which, necessarily, involve no action on the part of the defendant: in such cases we lack sufficient evidence that the defendant is attempting, and so are unwarranted in sanctioning. So, the conclusion reached here can be put more precisely: we are justified in sanctioning attempts of justifiably sanctioned basic acts *if we have adequate evidence that they are attempts*. However, we never do have such evidence. Still, the conditional conclusion reached here is sufficient for the purposes of justifying the Transfer Principle. The reason is that even crimes like trespass that *can* be completed through basic action can also be attempted in a way that involves performance of some act. A person can attempt trespass by climbing a fence, for instance, despite the fact that it is also possible to complete a trespass without doing something else first.

warrant censure? It is an old idea, that has been developed in a wide variety of different ways, to answer by citing certain facts about the person's deliberations, or about his underlying modes of recognition and response to reasons, expressed by his deliberations and resulting conduct. The idea is that the root of the censurability, or blameworthiness of conduct are facts about the modes of recognition of reasons employed by the person in reaching a conception of the reasons on the basis of which he acts, and the modes of response to reasons that he employs in acting on that conception. There are many kinds of flawed modes of these sorts that people employ in reaching such a conception, or in guiding conduct in accordance with it. Some people fail to grant any weight to considerations that do, in fact, give reasons for and against action, as when a person simply doesn't consider in his deliberations the fact that a form of action might cause pain. Some people grant too much or too little weight, or weight of the wrong sort, to considerations that they take to be reason-giving, as when a person weighs the destruction of the whole world less heavily than a scratch to his little finger, or weighs his own financial losses more heavily than the life of another person. Others fail to consider actions that have a chance of turning out, on reflection, to be favored by the balance of reasons. Yet others consider too much, wasting deliberative effort in considering conduct that won't, in the end, be undertaken. This list is not exhaustive: there are many ways to err. But all of the errors here are errors *because* there are better ways than those the agent employs for guiding the creation of his conception of what is favored by the balance of reasons, and for translating that conception into action. Although I can't claim to have defended it, and it would, doubtless, require many caveats to defend, I will move forward on the assumption that the following claim is true:

(**) Unexcused and unjustified conduct deserves censure *if and only if* it is a product of a faulty mode of recognition or response to reasons for action.

There are many different kinds of reasons for action, and so there are many different kinds of justifiable censure. Since what concerns us is the kind of censure that figures in a sufficient condition for justified criminalization, we will be concerned with legal reasons, and not with all of them, but only with those legal reasons that are provided by statutes and other legal provisions specifying that certain sorts of conduct are to be criminally punished. Call these the "criminal legal reasons". For our purposes, then, unexcused and unjustified conduct deserves censure by the state *if and only if* it is a product of a faulty mode of recognition or response to criminal legal reasons for action.

To show, then, that unexcused and unjustified attempts to engage in a certain kind of behavior deserve censure by the state if unexcused and unjustifed completions of that type of conduct do, it is sufficient to show that attempters recognize and respond to reasons in the same ways as those who complete crimes. Is this the case? One central reason for thinking so is that the practical question of whether to try to do something seems, usually, to collapse into the question of whether to do it. Often, that is, deliberation that issues in an effort to do something just is deliberation about whether or not to do it. It is because we reach the conclusion that completion is supported by reasons that we attempt. And, perhaps equivalently, when we cite the reasons that support an attempt to do something—that account for the fact that attempting makes sense—we cite reasons for completion. When we ask why the chicken *tried* to cross the road, we are satisfied by an explanation indicating that there was reason to get to the other side.

Although this is usually so, it is not always the case. The reason is that it is not the case that either all, or only, the reasons for trying are reasons for completion, and so it is perfectly possible to find that the question of whether to act and the question of whether to try are, and need to be, considered separately by the deliberator. Note first that not all reasons for and against trying are reasons for and against succeeding. Jennifer Hornsby, who has thought in a more penetrating way than most about trying, shows this convincingly:

Someone who applies for a job although her chances of getting it are negligible and although she is not at all sure that she wants it, may need practice at job interviews, and it may be that she would gain practice only by doing her best to get this one, which would require her to try to get it. Someone who knows that she wouldn't succeed in saving the person, but who is anxious to be seen to have tried to, might be motivated in an attempt at rescue by a desire that she should at least have tried.[15]

Hornsby's examples illustrate that it is common enough for trying to have consequences that are not consequences of success (except in so far as success involves trying). Trying to get a job can cause you to get better at job interviews; trying to save someone can cause you to be perceived as a good person. And when those consequences matter, they can supply reasons for or against trying that do not provide corresponding rational support to succeeding.[16] This possibility, however, does not create a problem for the claim that those who attempt, recognize, and respond to reasons in a way that makes them deserving of censure when completion is so deserving. The reason is that in such cases, the reasons for and against *attempt* are among the reasons the *completer* recognizes and responds to. The person who needs practice with interviews and who manages to get the job offer, perhaps contrary to his expectations, recognizes and responds to the reason for trying to get it—namely, that by doing so he would get better at job interviews—in just the way that the attempter who failed did. Conversely, he recognized and responded to reasons for completion that the attempter, too, recognized and responded to in the same way. The fact that there are reasons for attempt that are not reasons for completion, that

[15] Hornsby (1995), 526.

[16] The same point is illustrated, not with respect to trying, but with respect to intention, by Gregory Kavka's well-known "toxin puzzle". See Kavka (1983).

is, does not show that there is a difference between the completer and the attempter's modes of recognition and response to reasons.

However, it is not just that there can be reasons for trying that are not reasons for succeeding. In addition, succeeding can, in principle, have consequences that supply reason for or against succeeding, but won't come to pass, or won't supply reason for or against success, if the agent tries to succeed. To use a stark example, if an eccentric millionaire promises me $1,000,000 to do something so long as I don't try to do it—it's got to be done effortlessly—then I have a reason to do it and a powerful reason not to try. More commonly, there are types of action in which the consequences of trying will interfere naturally with the possibility of success, and without the fanciful machinations of eccentrics. The golfer who tries to sink the putt will find himself, as a result of his trying, thinking hard about sinking the putt; this will in turn cause the motion of the club to be less smooth, too calculated, and so he'll miss the putt. Aware of this, he undertakes strategies to sink the putt without trying; he empties his mind and "lets his body take over" before hitting the ball, for instance. Each reason he has to sink the putt provides him with a reason *not* to try to sink it, since trying, in such a case, is counterproductive. (Cases in which trying to act requires efforts to manage the mental states that will cause and accompany action are discussed in chapter 6.)

Now imagine a kind of conduct C that is legitimately criminalized and that has the feature that sinking the putt was just imagined to have: were a person to try to C, he would fail to C. As hard as it might be to find examples of such conduct, defense of the Transfer Principle ought not to insist that there isn't any such conduct that is legitimately criminalized. (Under the view offered in chapter 6, crimes of negligence and recklessness that cannot be completed with intent are examples of such crimes.) But in fact, the possibility of such a crime creates merely the *appearance* of a problem. To see this, consider that there are two significantly different kinds of people who we might describe as "trying to C". There are those who try to C *because* they want to C, or take themselves to have reason to C. They are adopting means to C—namely trying to C—that are guaranteed to fail. And there are those who try to C in order *to avoid* C-ing. Recognizing that they will not C if they try to, they come to take trying to C as a means to refraining from C-ing and thus as a means to *obeying* the law against C-ing. People in the first group exhibit the same or worse modes of recognition and response to reasons as those who complete C. Like those who C, they exhibit a failure to restrain themselves in the face of reasons against C, the reasons in virtue of which C was properly criminalized in the first place. Thus, the fact that there are reasons not to C that are not reasons against attempting to C, in this case, is compatible with the claim that the argument needs, namely the claim that the attempters are deserving of censure if the completers are. *This* kind of attempter recognizes or responds to reasons in a way which is just as bad or worse than the completer, and so is deserving of just as much, or more censure by the state. Assuming that negligent homicide, for instance, is a crime that a person will necessarily fail to complete by trying, the person who tries to commit a negligent homicide because he hopes to succeed in committing one, takes another's death as a positive reason in favor of conduct that he hopes to lead to it, while the person who completes the crime of negligent homicide merely fails to recognize a powerful reason not to act as he does, a reason that he should recognize, namely that his conduct will cause another's death. Thus, the person who attempts in this case is actually *more* deserving of censure than the person who completes the crime. (Some see attempted crimes of negligence or recklessness as contradictions in terms. For a reply to them, see chapter 6.)

The second class of attempters of crimes that will fail if attempted—those who try to C in order to refrain from C-ing—are somewhat more problematic. They seem to be recognizing and responding to reasons in just the way we would like them to: they recognize all the reasons against C-ing that there actually are, grant those reasons appropriate weight, and respond to those reasons by taking steps to see to it that they do not run afoul of the law's ban on C-ing. In what sense are they deserving of censure at all? The solution is to admit that they are not deserving of censure, but to deny that they are actually attempting to C in the sense of relevance to the criminal law. The reason that they are not attempting to C in that sense is that they intend to *refrain* from C and are acting on that intention. It is argued in chapter 2 that attempts always require an intention to succeed. Assuming that the argument of that chapter works, it follows that a person necessarily cannot try to C while acting from an intention not to C, which is just what must be imagined in the seemingly problematic cases.[17] If we want to call such conduct "trying to C", it is in some sense of the term "try" different from that of relevance to the criminal law.

The argument of this section has proceeded as follows: criminalization of a type of conduct is justified, on the view assumed here, if all unexcused and unjustified tokens of the type are deserving of censure, and some are justifiably sanctioned. It was first argued in section 4.1 that if some tokens of a type of completed conduct are justifiably sanctioned, then so are some tokens of the attempt of it. The alternative requires the implausible claim that the features of justifiably sanctioned completions which account for the fact that they are justifiably sanctioned are possessed only by completions. We then turned to censure and the question of whether the fact that a type of conduct is deserving

---

[17] It is possible, in theory, for a person who aims to refrain from C to take steps to place his later self into the position of trying to C while acting on an intention to C. Perhaps he takes steps to make himself into the kind of person who will actually aim at C and he does so precisely because he knows that's a good way to see to it that he does not C, knowing as he does that trying to C is a sure way to fail to C. But such a person arranges for his future self to recognize and respond to reasons in a way which is as bad or worse than those who complete C. He thus arranges for his future self to be deserving of censure for his attempt to C. Thus even this kind of case is not problematic for the claim that the argument needs.

of censure implies that attempts to engage in it are. A form of conduct is deserving of censure by the state if it springs from a faulty mode of recognition or response to criminal legal reasons. If we find that two sets of agents employ the same modes of recognition and response to reasons, or that the second's are worse than the first's, then it follows that if the first's conduct is deserving of censure, then so is the second's. This is true of those who complete crimes and those who attempt them. And so the Transfer Principle follows from a plausible, albeit undefended position concerning a sufficient condition of justified criminalization and a necessary and sufficient condition of deserved censure.

### 4.3 Some Implications of the Justification of the Transfer Principle

The justification for the Transfer Principle offered here bears an interesting relation to the rationale rejected in section 2. The justification discussed in that section merely points to the moral analogue of the Transfer Principle. As was suggested in section 2, the true moral principle analogous to the Transfer Principle is not sufficient to support the Transfer Principle, even when we grant a variety of contestable claims about the degree to which moral facts dictate facts about legality. However, it was also suggested that what is right about the view discussed in section 2 is that there must be some close link between the Transfer Principle and its moral analogue. The view defended in this section avoids the problem encountered by the position criticized in section 2 and, at the same time, benefits from its insight. It avoids the problem because the argument for the Transfer Principle does not depend on a commonality between completion and attempt—like moral wrongness—that can be found even in the presence of differences that might make the difference in the justifiability of criminalization. But the justification offered here benefits from the insight of the view rejected in section 2, since the moral analogue of the Transfer Principle is almost surely true for something like the reasons that are offered here in favor of the claim that censure of attempt is deserved if censure of completion is. The fundamental reason, that is, that it is wrong to try to do things that are wrong is that both those who succeed in doing wrong and those who try have faulty modes of recognizing and responding to reasons, the very faulty modes that ground desert of censure in the first place. Of course, there are important differences between the legal and the moral case. Most notably, the moral analogue of the Transfer Principle makes a claim about wrongdoing, and thus a claim about desert of censure, not a claim about liability to sanction or even blame. Hence the moral analogue of the Transfer Principle does not require any argument analogous to the argument of section 4.1 for the claim that if some completions are justifiably sanctioned then some attempts are. Thus under the moral analogue of the Transfer Principle, moral wrongness of completion transfers even to those who recognize and respond to reasons in just the way that those who complete objectionable conduct do, but are not guided in any way by their distinctive modes of recognition and response to reasons. Not so for the Transfer Principle. The argument of section 4.1 is essential to the argument for the Transfer Principle, but it is far from clear that any analogous argument is needed in support of its moral analogue. Be that as it may, the deep connection between the Transfer Principle and its moral analogue is that both are justified in part through appeal to the deep commonality in the modes of recognition and response to reasons of those who act and those who try.

Recall the justification for the Transfer Principle discussed in passing at the opening of this chapter, the justification according to which what makes criminalization of completion appropriate is the objectionable intention that guides the relevant behavior, which is the same intention that we find in attempt. As noted, one problem for this justification is that attempt and completion actually often have different *mens rea* elements. When completion requires recklessness or knowledge, for instance, attempt requires intent. (This is discussed at greater length in chapter 2.) The Transfer Principle, then, cannot be exploiting a precise similarity in the mental states of the completion and the attempt. Now, although it is common enough for criminal law theorists to use the term "culpability" synonomously with "mental state", as though there was no more to the question of the sense in which one's behavior redounds to one's credit or discredit than what mental states animated that behavior, this is something of a mistake. Mental states matter to culpability, not intrinsically, but because of what they reflect about the way the agent recognizes and responds to reasons. A rational person who intends to act in a particular way, for instance, does not consider actions that he believes to be incompatible with doing as he intends. Therefore, his intention tells us something important about the way he handles reasons: he does not consider reasons for actions that conflict with what he intends. Similarly, a person who knows that some result will follow from his behavior, but does not intend that result, is happy to entertain actions that allow him to do as he intends without the expected results coming to pass. This tells us something different about the way in which he recognizes and responds to reasons. And so on. Mental state matters. But it matters because of what it tells us about the deeper facts constitutive of culpability, facts about the agent's ways of navigating the terrain of reasons. The proposed rationale for the Transfer Principle, then, takes what's right about the rationale appealing to an intention shared between completion and attempt, while avoiding that approach's errors.

Further, the argument for the Transfer Principle does not support a principle according to which a mere intention to engage in some kind of behavior is properly criminalized when the intended behavior is. The second half of the argument for the Transfer Principle probably[18] applies to such a principle—the

---

[18] I say "probably" because there's a question as to whether commitments about what reasons one will respond to in one's conduct are constituted solely by one's intention. Perhaps one has those commitments thanks, also, to what one is moved by.

person with an intention probably recognizes and responds to reasons in the same mode as the person who commits the crime—but the first half does not. The form of argument employed above in support of the contention that at least some attempts are justifiably sanctioned when some completions are does not go through when applied to mere intention. No intention, by itself, is "arbitrarily close" to completion to give us confidence that it is justifiably sanctioned. Thus, the argument for the Transfer Principle offered here justifies only principles under which the conduct falling short of completion involves some kind of guidance by the modes of recognition and response to reasons held in common with the person who completes the crime.

However, the argument for the Transfer Principle supports criminalizing more than would be criminalized under the following principle: "*If a type of conduct is justifiably criminalized, then so is the conjunction of an intention to engage in that conduct and action in furtherance of that intention.*" The consequent of this conditional identifies a proper subset of the attempts. Thus, under this principle, many attempts are not criminalized. In particular, this principle does not allow the criminalization of any failed attempt to engage in a basic act that is an element of a crime; by definition, an agent cannot engage in *action* on his way to performance of a basic act. Hence, although the argument for the Transfer Principle could be used to support this alternative principle, it can be used to support a broader principle of criminalization, namely the Transfer Principle itself.

Given the point about the importance of mental state, we might wonder if the argument for the Transfer Principle offered here shows that we are justified in criminalizing harmless, reckless, or negligent behavior, not rising to the level of attempt, which would have involved a completed crime had it been harmful. We might wonder, that is, if we can justify the following principle on the same grounds as the Transfer Principle: "*If a particular form of harmful conduct is justifiably criminalized, then so is equally censurable conduct that fails to cause harm.*" This seems, at first glance, as plausible as the Transfer Principle, given the justification for the Transfer Principle offered here. After all, there are surely some reckless drivers who get close enough to injuring others to warrant sanctioning them, given that sanction would have been appropriate had others been injured. And, after all, isn't the reckless driver who damages someone's property, recognizing, weighing, and responding to reasons in the same way as the person who drives recklessly but, fortuitously, causes no damage? Put these two points together and it appears that we have just as strong an argument for the imposition of criminal liability for non-harmful versions of any justifiably criminalized harmful behavior as we have for attempts.

In fact, I believe this is true with this caveat: it is very possible that no tokens of reckless or negligent acts that have a low probability of harm, and do not cause harm, are justifiably sanctioned; if this is right, then such acts are not justifiably criminalized. Thus, probability of harm might matter to the justifiability of criminalizing reckless or negligent harmless acts in a way that such probabilities do not matter to attempts; some complete attempts are justifiably sanctioned even if there was a very low probability of success. But, even putting aside this caveat, it is important to see that the fact that the form of argument used to support the Transfer Principle would support other principles of criminalization does not supply an objection to anything to be said here. That there are good reasons to criminalize certain forms of reckless and negligent endangerment does not show that there are not also good reasons to criminalize attempts. Nor does it show that attempts are justifiably criminalized thanks to the fact that they are forms of endangerment. An attempt is justifiably criminalized, when completion is, thanks to the fact that it is a trying, and tryings possess a variety of features that are sufficient to warrant criminalizing them when completion is justifiably criminalized. In particular, they involve the same or worse modes of recognizing and responding to reasons, and they involve guidance by that way of recognizing and responding to reasons of a sort that sometimes takes the attempter as close to completion as is needed to justify sanction. It is probably also true that particular acts of reckless or negligent endangerment, such as those that impose a high risk of harm, possess some of the very same features, and so are justifiably criminalized thanks to that fact. But it does not follow that attempts are criminalized because they are endangering, or that endangerments are criminalized because they are attempts. In fact, neither of these things is true, and yet both types of conduct are justifiably criminalized for reasons that parallel one another. Only tryings are criminalized under the Transfer Principle, even if the argument for the Transfer Principle can be amended so as to justify other principles of criminalization that support the criminalization of forms of conduct that are not tryings.

## 5. Conclusion

When attempts are justifiably criminalized, they are so in virtue of the fact that the Transfer Principle applies. When trying to act is rightly taken to be a crime, it is thanks to the fact that acting is rightly taken to be one. In rejecting the rationalization of the Transfer Principle discussed in section 3, according to which attempts are to be criminalized because they risk completions, we are committed to thinking that the legislative act of appealing to the Transfer Principle to criminalize an attempt is a very different sort of act from the legislative act of criminalizing an act of risk-creation. There may be good reasons to criminalize risk-creating behaviors, but they cannot be criminalized through the Transfer Principle. The feature of our moral thought that makes its way into our criminal law in the Transfer Principle is the idea that trying is a type of behavior of peculiar normative importance. So we should expect that the right theory of attempted crimes will bear a very close relation to the philosophical theory of trying. Given that we employ the Transfer Principle in the criminalization of attempt, we need to understand what it is to try to act, and what the relation is between trying to act and completed action. However, as will become important in chapter 3, in which an account of the kind of trying of relevance to the criminal law is identified, there are multiple and distinct "ordinary" senses in which people try to act. What we need to understand is the nature of just one of the ordinary kinds of trying to act, namely, the kind that is criminalized under the Transfer Principle. The better we understand that, the closer we will be to resolving difficult questions about the nature of attempted crimes.

# 2

# The Need for an Intention

## 1. Introduction

In the middle of a June night in Fort Wayne, Indiana, Curtis Jones, a member of a gang, went to the home of a rival gang member where a party was taking place. Jones fired four bullets into a crowd of people inside the home. Three of the bullets struck Troy Williams, who bled to death. The remaining bullet struck Latrail Gamble, who was injured, but not killed. Jones was charged with the murder of Williams and the attempted murder of Gamble. In Indiana, as elsewhere, an intention to kill is not required for murder. A person who causes another's death is guilty of murder in that jurisdiction if he knew his action was likely to kill another person, even if he did not intend to do so. The jury found that Jones did indeed know that it was likely that firing bullets into the crowd would kill someone, and so convicted Jones of Williams's murder. However, in Indiana, attempted murder, by contrast, does require an intention to kill. The jury acquitted Jones of the attempted murder of Gamble. After all, they presumably reasoned, although Jones knew that it was likely that he would kill someone, he didn't intend to; he intended, instead, to fire his gun, to frighten those associated with the rival gang, and probably even to injure them, but killing, the jury thought, was not his intention, even if he thought it might happen. Or, to put it another way, the jury seems to have thought that Jones could have done all that he intended even if nobody died. But if Jones didn't intend to kill, then, under Indiana law, he didn't attempt to. The Supreme Court of Indiana affirmed this pair of verdicts.[1]

As it is in Indiana, so it is almost everywhere: intention to complete a crime is required for the attempt of it, even when the crime in question can be completed without such intent. However, despite the fact that this is the dominant position, dissent can be found. In Colorado, for instance, "A person commits criminal attempt if, acting with the kind of culpability otherwise required for commission of an offense, he engages in conduct constituting a substantial step

---

[1] *Jones v. State* (689 N.E.2d 722 (Ind. 1997)).

toward the commission of the offense."[2] In applying this statute in Colorado, a guilty verdict was upheld in *People v. Thomas* (729 P.2d 972 (Colo. 1986)), in which the defendant was convicted of attempted manslaughter after firing warning shots, intended to frighten and not to kill, at a man he believed to be a fleeing rapist. Since Thomas's mental state would have sufficed for *mens rea* for manslaughter had the victim been killed, it suffices for attempted manslaughter in the actual situation in which the shots missed.[3] So, to return to the Indiana case, had Jones done what he did in Colorado, instead of Indiana, he would have been guilty of the attempted murder of Gamble: he knew he was likely to kill someone in firing the shot that hit Gamble, and only that "kind of culpability" is required for attempt in Colorado.

There are a variety of possible ways of characterizing the fundamental source of disagreement between these two approaches to the *mens rea* of attempt. Perhaps, for instance, while in Indiana it is tryings, true attempts, that are criminalized, Colorado uses the word "attempt" to refer to risk-creating behaviors that are not tryings at all. So construed, very different kinds of behaviors are criminalized under the rubric of "attempts" in the two jurisdictions. However, assuming that both Indiana and Colorado criminalize attempts under the Transfer Principle, discussed in chapter 1—the principle that attempts are justifiably criminalized if completions are—then the fundamental disagreement regards what mental states are involved in trying to act. When the disagreement is construed in this way, Indiana legislators can be understood as committed to the claim that to try to act one must intend to act, while Colorado legislators can be understood to be committed to denying this. So understood, it follows that which statutory scheme is just turns on the question of whether or not one can try to act only if one intends to.

From this point of view, Colorado can be seen to be siding with Oliver Wendell Holmes. Holmes, who thought of attempts as justifiably criminalized merely because they risk completed crimes—an approach that, as we saw in chapter 1, cannot serve to justify the Transfer Principle—thought that the demand that attempt requires intent, even when the completed crime does not, is without justification. He writes:

It may be true in the region of attempts, as elsewhere, the law began with cases of actual intent, as those cases are the most obvious ones. But it cannot stop with them, unless it

---

[2] Colo. Rev. Stat. §18-2-101(1).

[3] Colorado follows the *Model Penal Code* in its definition of the act element of attempt under which such an act must be "strongly corroborative of the actor's criminal purpose". See *Model Penal Code* §5.01(2), Colo. Rev. Stat. §18-2-101(1). In some jurisdictions that also follow the *Model Penal Code* in this, such as Utah (see *State v. Norman* (580 P.2d 237 (Utah 1978)), this definition of a substantial step has been taken to entail that attempt requires intent. The requirement of intent, then, has been thought to enter indirectly into the definition of attempt. However, Colorado does not follow Utah, or other *Model Penal Code* states, in this interpretation.

attaches more importance to the etymological meaning of the word attempt than to the general principles of punishment. Accordingly, there is at least color of authority for the proposition that an act is punishable as an attempt, if, supposing it to have produced its natural and probable effect, it would have amounted to a substantive crime.[4]

Holmes assumes that the idea that attempt requires intent is merely a contingent fact about language—a fact, that is, about how we use the words "attempt" and "try". Why should our laws be constrained by such contingencies? Shouldn't they, instead, be constrained by correct principles of criminalization and punishment? However, the rationale for at least one of those principles— namely the Transfer Principle—depends on tethering what we criminalize *as* attempt to what attempts really are.

My aim here is to argue, not that it is a linguistic fact that "attempts" implies "intends", but that it is a fact, instead, about *the nature* of attempts that they involve intention. The argument to be offered is intended to establish not, merely, that trying to act requires *some* kind of intention. It is not intended to show merely, for instance, that one cannot try to kill without, say, intending to pull a trigger (or swing a knife, or drop poison in a coffee cup, etc.). Rather, the claim is that one cannot try to kill unless one's intention commits one to killing, as when one intends *to kill*. Trying to commit a crime requires an intention that commits one to *completing the crime*, not merely an intention that commits one to something distinct from, even if in the neighborhood of, the completed crime.[5] As we'll see, the claim to be established here is of particular interest because it has been almost universally denied by philosophers of action: they hold that it is possible to try to act without intending to act that way. In establishing that philosophers of action have been mistaken on this point, we reach the following result: if attempts are to be criminalized through appeal to the Transfer Principle, then intent must be an element of every crime of attempt, even when the crime can be completed without intent. The conclusion also marks a first step towards an account of the necessary and sufficient conditions that are met when a person is trying to do something in the sense of relevance to the criminal law; such conditions will be supplied in chapter 3.

Section 2 of this chapter describes and criticizes an argument of Michael Bratman's that implies, if it's successful, that one can try to act without intending to act. The argument depends on the theory of intention developed by Bratman in his book *Intention, Plans and Practical Reason*, as well as in a number of important papers on the topic.[6] Bratman calls the theory "the planning theory of intention".

---

[4] Holmes (1881), 66.

[5] There are hard questions about what conditions the content of a person's intention must meet for it to commit one to *completing the crime*. It is obvious, for instance, that the person need not conceive of what he intends to be a crime: one can have the intention needed for an attempt while having false beliefs about what conduct is criminal. This is just one issue, but it serves to illustrate a large family of problems that will not be addressed in this chapter, but in chapter 4.

[6] Some of these are collected in Bratman (1999a).

Section 2 begins by examining the planning theory of intention, which informs many of the chapters to follow, especially those in part 2 of this book. This discussion is followed by an argument for the claim that the planning theory does not in fact imply, as Bratman claims it does, that it is possible for an agent to try without intending. Section 3 goes one step further by employing the planning theory as a premise in an argument intended to show that, in fact, one can try only if one intends. If this argument succeeds, then not only does the planning theory fail to imply what Bratman takes it to imply, it implies the exact opposite. Indiana's law, requiring intention for attempt, is correct because of the very nature of trying and the nature of intention. Given what trying and intending are, one can criminalize attempts through appeal to the Transfer Principle only if intention is an element of attempt.[7]

---

[7] It is important to head off a misunderstanding. One might reason like so: if the jury is right that Jones did not intend to kill anyone (although he knew he was likely to), then he did not kill intentionally. But if he did not kill intentionally, then he is not responsible *for killing* (although he is responsible for those things that he did do intentionally, such as injuring and frightening people). So, the mistake in both Indiana and Colorado law that gives rise to the puzzling legal state of affairs described is not a mistake in those states' laws proscribing attempts, but in their murder laws. Their murder laws proscribe unintentional killings, and that's unjust. Colorado, in order to maintain a coherent legal code, then doubles the mistake by proscribing "attempts" that do not involve intention, and so don't promise, even if completed, to end in intentional, and thus responsible, action.

This bit of reasoning is flawed, for it rests on a pair of claims, both of which are initially appealing, but at least one of which is likely to be false: (1) An agent can act intentionally only if he intends to so act. (This is what has been dubbed by Michael Bratman "the simple view". Cf. Bratman (1987), 111–138.) And, (2) An agent is responsible for his action only if the act was intentional. (1) admits of counterexamples in which agents intend something distinct from, but "close" to, what they end up doing and so do the act intentionally. For instance, say that Jones had intended to kill someone, but had no idea who would be at the party. Did he intentionally kill Williams? It seems so, even though he did not intend to kill *Williams*, whom he may not have even known to exist, much less expected to be at the party that night. Further, arguably, although not intending to kill anyone, in knowing that he might, and being willing to live with or even welcome that result, Jones thereby killed intentionally. It's possible, that is, that together with his intention to injure and frighten, his foreknowledge was sufficient to make his act of killing intentional, despite never having been intended.

How many counterexamples (2) admits of will depend on what one's view of (1) is. If, for instance, you deny that Jones killed Williams intentionally, in the actual case in which he had no intention at all to kill, you might take his act of killing as an example of one for which an agent is responsible despite its being unintentional. Be that as it may, however, we ought to accept that, for instance, people are responsible for results springing from negligence, despite the fact that negligence often involves an absence of any mental representation, and necessarily absence of any foreknowledge, of the results that figure in the description of the agent's act. It would be an absurdity to suggest that the man who kills a pedestrian after failing to refill his brake fluid necessarily killed the pedestrian intentionally; precisely what makes the case the peculiar tragedy it is for not just the pedestrian, but also the driver, is that the killing is *unintentional*, and yet one for which the driver very well may never, and ought never, forgive himself.

In any event, in what follows, I will be assuming that both (1) and (2) are false and thus that both Indiana and Colorado have defensible murder laws, although only one of them has a defensible view about attempted crimes.

## 2. Against an Argument for the Possibility of Trying without Intending

### 2.1 *Bratman's Planning Theory of Intention*

Bratman's planning theory of intention, which with the qualifications developed here, I endorse, will be used in a variety of different ways in this book. The theory was developed in response to problems discovered with the views of the nature of intention prominent in the 1970s, particularly Donald Davidson's. In his seminal paper "Actions, Reasons and Causes",[8] Davidson built a theory of the nature of intention from consideration of the role that intentions play in the explanation of action. Generally, we explain an agent's action by citing two mental states that led to performance of the act: a belief and a desire. In particular, Davidson noted, we cite a desire to perform an act of a certain type, and a belief that the particular token act performed belonged to that type. In Davidson's famous example, we explain the fact that a person flipped the switch by citing his desire to turn on the light—a desire to perform some act of the type "turning on the light"—and his belief that the particular bodily movement that he made was, indeed, an act of turning on the light, or a token of that type.

Although Davidson himself never quite came out and said it, he is often taken to have expressed the view in "Actions, Reasons and Causes" that intentions *just are* the belief-desire pairs that we cite in explanation of action. On this view, the mental state of intention is built out of two "simpler" parts: the relevant belief and the relevant desire. This "belief-desire model" of intention can be varied in many different ways. We might agree that intentions are belief-desire pairs while disagreeing with Davidson about the particular belief-desire pair that they are. Perhaps, for instance, an intention should be understood to consist of a desire to reach a particular end (rather than a desire to perform an act type), and a belief that the act one performs will bring one closer to reaching it (rather than a belief that a token act is of the type). Or perhaps some third belief-desire pair is more accurately equated with intention. Still, the advocate of any particular version of the belief-desire model of intention accepts that intentions are reducible; under such views, an intention just is a complex of beliefs and desires.

Davidson himself repudiated the belief-desire model in a later paper entitled "Intending".[9] "Intending" is a difficult paper, admitting of multiple possible interpretations. However, it seems clear that Davidson there rejects the belief-desire model primarily on the grounds that it is possible to intend to do something while engaging in no act at all that is explained by that intention.

---

[8] Davidson (1980c).     [9] Davidson (1980a).

Hence it is often true that an agent has an intention, and false that there is any belief-desire pair that explains any of his behavior and is, at once, properly identified with the intention he has. A person who intends to build a squirrel house, to use Davidson's example, may be in a mental state that as yet plays no role whatsoever in explaining anything that he has done to date. He therefore has no belief that any particular token act of his is an instance of building a squirrel house and so, under Davidson's version of the belief-desire model, he does not have the intention to build a squirrel house. Since it seems possible to have an intention and yet to have done nothing at all in furtherance of it, it follows that there is something wrong with Davidson's version of the belief-desire model. But rather than responding to this worry by rejecting the reduction of intention to some other set of mental states, in "Intending" Davidson replaces the belief-desire model with a different reduction. He holds there that an intention is to be equated with "an all-out evaluative judgment" in favor of the intended act. What precisely an intention is being equated with in this view—a complex of beliefs? of desires? of some mix between them? of something else entirely?—need not concern us. What is important for our purposes is merely that Davidson has attempted an alternative reduction, of some sort, of intention to some other mental state or set of mental states.

In his now classic paper, "Davidson's Theory of Intention",[10] Bratman offered what many now see as a refutation of theories that equate intention with complexes of beliefs and desires. Although Bratman's argument is subtle, the fundamental idea involves noting that intentions appear to be subject to norms of rationality that complexes of beliefs and desires are not. There is no irrationality, for instance, in desiring to do two things that cannot both be done; there is no irrationality in wanting to go to Paris for your vacation and also wanting to go to the Bahamas. With important qualifications that need not concern us, it follows that it is possible to have a belief-desire complex that adds up, under a belief-desire theory of intention, to an intention to go to Paris, and another that adds up to an intention to go to the Bahamas, without being guilty of any kind of irrationality. But since it is clearly irrational to *intend*, rather than merely to desire, to do each of two things while believing that one cannot do both, there is something wrong with such a belief-desire theory. The norms of rationality that apply to agents, thanks to the fact that they have certain beliefs and certain desires, are simply different from those that apply to agents, thanks to the fact that they have certain intentions. We thus need a theory of intention that respects the contours of the rational pressures that agents with intention labor under. Theories that reduce intention to complexes of beliefs and desires, as both Davidson's theories do, fail in this respect.

[10] Bratman (1999c).

Bratman's criticism of belief-desire theories of intention naturally sets the stage for a new research program aimed at developing an alternative theory of intention. His positive view starts with the important insight that what makes the mental state of intention distinct from other practical mental states—mental states, that is, that play a role in deliberation and in the motivation and guidance of action—are the norms of rationality that govern it. The new research question, then, is this: "What norms of rationality govern intention?" To put Bratman's insight another way, we might say that intentions are in an important way belief-like (although Bratman does not think they are to be equated with beliefs). Beliefs, too, are governed by norms of rationality that do not govern other mental states like, for instance, hopes. Someone might hope that something occurs, and hope that it doesn't without being guilty of irrationality: it makes perfect sense to see a possible future state of affairs as both attractive and unattractive, depending on how you look at it. But someone who believes that something will occur, and that it won't, is irrational: that's just not a set of mental states that it could make sense to have. What is distinctive about both intention and belief is that the having of such a mental state qualifies an agent to be assessed by certain norms of rationality appropriate to the mental state in question.

Bratman calls the theory that emerges from pursuing the question of what norms of rationality govern intention "the planning theory of intention". He gives his view this name because the norms of rationality that govern those with intentions are grounded in the aims of planning agency. Planning serves certain roles in helping us to reach our ends. In particular, it serves a *coordinating* role, helping us both to mesh what we do with what others do so as to reach joint goals, and to mesh what we do now with what we do later, and did before, so as to reach individual goals that require time-slices of the agent to work together. Thus, stated in its most general form, the planning theory of intention comprises the following pair of claims:

(A) An agent who has an intention is subject to assessment by certain distinctive norms of rationality.

(B) The norms of rationality governing those with intentions meet the following condition: by conforming to these norms the agent's intentions support the forms of inter- and intrapersonal coordination that are available to planning agents.

Notice that, as stated, the planning theory of intention could be filled out in a variety of different ways, depending on the precise specification of the norms governing those with intentions. In fact, Bratman's argument for the claim that one can try without intending relies on his view of the particular norms of rationality governing intention, namely what he has called norms of "strong consistency", "means-end coherence", and "agglomerativity".

The strong consistency requirement is this: an agent cannot rationally intend to do A if he believes that he will not do A. This is not to be confused with the view that if you intend to do A, then rationality requires you to believe that you will. Bratman's condition is weaker than this, for under it you could intend to do A, fail to believe that you will, and also fail to believe that you won't, without falling into irrationality.

The strong consistency requirement has attracted more attention in the literature than the other two requirements and is, therefore, fairly well-understood.[11] The requirement of means-end coherence has been much less carefully examined. It imposes at least two distinct limitations on intention. First, it requires that an agent cannot choose just anything as his means to the achievement of a particular end and maintain rationality; rather, the means must fit the end appropriately or must, at least, do so relative to the agent's beliefs. The requirement of means-end coherence, that is, places an agent under rational pressure to select an action as a means to his end only if he believes it to be a possible means to that end. Further, an agent's intentions are means-end coherent only if he intends all those acts that are believed by him to be necessary means to other acts he intends. This isn't to say that rationality requires that, for every action an agent intends, he also intends a means to that action: our plans are often left open without being worthy of rational criticism. However, if the agent believes an act to be *required* if he is to do as he intends, then rationality requires him to intend that act.

Bratman is not as explicit as one might like as to what pressure is imposed by the agglomerativity condition. He says, "Given the role of intentions in coordination, there is rational pressure for the agent to put his various intentions together into a larger intention."[12] For reasons that need not concern us here, this condition ought to be understood like so:[13]

---

[11] Cff. Grice (1971); Harman (1976); Davidson (1980a), 83–102; Bratman (1987), esp. 37–41; Velleman (1989), esp. 113–21; Mele (1992), esp. 146–49.

One of the central questions under discussion in this literature is this: "Is the strong consistency requirement violable?" That is, is it possible to intend to act while believing you will not, as Bratman assumes? There are difficult questions here linked, at bottom, to difficult questions about the distinction between logical and metaphysical possibility. On the one hand, it seems that, since there is no logical contradiction in the idea of any particular combination of mental states present in a particular mind no matter what their content—just as there's no logical contradiction in the idea of a library containing books that contradict each other—there is no impossibility in it. However, if there could be metaphysical impossibility without logical, then this inference does not follow; perhaps *the nature* of certain mental states is such as to exclude others from the mind. Even if there is such a thing as metaphysical impossibility, however, it doesn't follow that it is metaphysically impossible to intend while believing in failure. In any event, I will be assuming that Bratman is right: the pressure not to believe you will fail that is imposed by an intention is normative rather than metaphysical. The same goes, I assume, for the other rationality requirements on intention.

[12] Bratman (1987), 194.

[13] For an argument in favor of this construal of the condition, see Yaffe (2006).

*Agglomerativity*: It is irrational to intend A and intend B if the intention to do both A and B would itself be irrational according to some other principle of rational intention.

This principle does not require that the agent actually formulate an intention to both A and B if she intends each individually; it doesn't require that the agent put all of her perfectly compatible intentions into larger conjunctive intentions. A person who intends to go to San Francisco today and to Paris a year from now needn't, to maintain rationality, formulate a single intention to go to San Francisco today and Paris a year from now. Rationality requires only that such an intention would not be irrational on the grounds, for instance, that the agent believes he cannot go to both places (and thus is in violation of the strong consistency requirement), or on the grounds that going to both places would undermine his ability to take some means to one of his ends (and thus be in violation of the requirement of means-end coherence). Agglomerativity, then, requires that agents avoid having sets of intentions that cannot be combined into conjunctive intentions while maintaining rationality on independent grounds, and so it places agents under pressure to combine their individual intentions, and thus make conflicts evident to themselves, when there is doubt as to the rationality of the conjunctive intentions in question.

Claims (A) and (B) then, together with the three rationality conditions on intention, constitute Bratman's planning theory of intention.

## 2.2 Does the Planning Theory Imply that One Can Try Without Intending?

Under the planning theory of intention, what makes a practical mental state an intention is that, by virtue of having it, the agent is subject to assessment by the norms of strong consistency, means-end coherence, and agglomerativity. This view lies at the center of Bratman's argument for the claim that an agent can try to do something without intending to do it. The argument starts with reflection on examples with the following structure: consider a person who wants either to A or to B, but not to do both. In order to do this, he decides that he'll try to do each, knowing that his chances of doing both are very low, but that his chances of doing one or the other are much higher if he tries to do each than if he invests his energies in one course of conduct at the expense of the other. There are many examples of this sort. Every year high school seniors take steps towards attending Yale and take steps towards attending Harvard—they apply to both, pay exorbitant application fees to each, travel for interviews, exort relatives to contact old friends in the admissions offices, etc.—knowing full well that they cannot attend both, and that, even if they could, to do so would be a sure way to fail to realize the benefits of attending either. Bratman's example is simpler: imagine that there are two video games in which the player is to maneuver missiles towards a target. Further, imagine that the two games are wired in such a way that if one hits the target of game 1, then both games shut down. This is similarly true with game 2. Further, were one to get very close to hitting the two targets simultaneously, both games would shut down before either target was hit. An agent who knows all this sits down to play both games simultaneously on the reasoning that if he divides his energies between both games he is more likely to hit one target or the other.

If this agent is rational, then, given Bratman's rationality conditions on intention, the agent is trying to do each of two things, but does not intend to do either. To see this, start by asking if Bratman's game-player intends to hit target 1. If the answer is "yes", then by symmetry he must also intend to hit target 2. However, if he intends to hit target 1 and he intends to hit target 2, and yet he believes that he will not hit both targets, he must have irrational intentions, for (by agglomerativity) an intention to hit both targets would have to be rational for him to maintain rationality; but it is not, for (by strong consistency) he cannot believe that he will not hit both targets given this pair of intentions. However, it is simply manifest that he is trying to hit target 1 and that he is trying to hit target 2. Hence one can try without intending.

Bratman's example is mirrored by a recent case. Consider *People v. Smith* (124 P.3d 730 (Cal. 2005)). As a mother drove slowly away from the defendant with her infant in a car seat immediately behind her, the defendant fired one shot toward the car, missing both mother and baby. Evidence indicated that both the mother and the baby were in the line of fire at the moment that the gun was fired, although the bullet would have struck the baby first and would not have passed on to the mother, had the car not moved at just the right moment. The defendant was charged with both the attempted murder of the mother and the attempted murder of the baby. Smith's conviction for both attempts was upheld. Assuming, as seems plausible, that Smith believed that he could not kill both mother and child with a single bullet, he seems to have adopted a strategy analogous to Bratman's game-player: he recognized that he had time to fire only one shot, so he fired the gun in an effort to kill the mother, and he fired it in an effort to kill the baby—he was trying to do each of these things—but he expected that he would kill at most one. If Bratman's argument succeeds, then Smith neither intended to kill the mother nor intended to kill the baby. And given the legal rule that intention is required for attempt, Smith should not have been convicted of either crime, or, correlatively, the legal rule should be revised.

Bratman's argument is not easy to reject. Notice that neither of two natural ways to reject the argument—by rejecting the strong consistency requirement, or by rejecting the agglomerativity condition—are, in the end, attractive. To see why, recall that the whole point of the rationality conditions on intention is their connection to the forms of coordination that are available to a planning agent. An agent who intends to do things that she flatly believes she will fail to do frequently faces a variety of insurmountable obstacles to the maintenance of both inter- and intrapersonal coordination. In general, the problem is that we can count on people to do as they intend; but we cannot count on people to do as they believe they will not do. For instance, imagine that I intend to pick up my daughter at daycare at four o'clock today, but believe that I will not; perhaps I expect myself to be hopelessly absorbed in my own work come this afternoon.[14] When my wife calls to ask if she should plan to pick up our daughter, what should I tell her? On the one hand, she can count on me to do it (I intend to) and, on the other, she can count on me not to (I believe I won't). The outcome that we both want—our daughter gets picked up and only one of us makes the trip to the daycare center—would be made more likely if I were to live up to the standards of a rational agent, but given my belief and intention, this outcome is no more likely than either of the suboptimal outcomes (we both go to the daycare center, or neither of us does). What follows is that my intention is less than fully rational, and it is so precisely because I believe I will not do as I intend. We can just as easily generate cases in which violation of the strong consistency requirement undermines *intra*personal coordination: imagine, for instance, that I am wondering what to do with myself at five o'clock today. Can I count on having already picked up my daughter? Yes and no, depending on whether I consult my present intentions or my present beliefs.

Obeying the agglomerativity condition seems no less essential to the achievement of the forms of inter- and intrapersonal coordination that are the hallmark of planning agency, and for the same reasons. The fact that an agent intends to A gives us reason to count on him to do so; similarly, when he intends to B. But if he believes that he won't do both, then that gives us reason to think that he will fail to do at least one or the other, and he might do neither. What, in such a case, can we count on him to do? There's no saying, and so the forms of coordination that require that we can count on agents to act in certain ways will be undermined when agents violate the agglomerativity condition. This is similarly the case if the conjoined intention—the intention to A and B— violates the requirement of means-end coherence by, say, requiring a means that the agent specifically intends not to do. In such a case, the intention not to undertake the necessary means allows the agent and others to count on him not to do it, while the pair of intentions, the intention to A and the intention to B, allows the agent and others to count on him to do so. Again, without being able to count on the agent either to act or not to, coordination is undermined.

We can think up examples in which an agent does better by violating, rather than obeying, the requirements of strong consistency, agglomerativity, or even means-end coherence. A case in point is Gregory Kavka's "toxin puzzle", in which an eccentric billionaire offers to give you a large sum of money today now to *intend* to drink a sickness-inducing toxin tomorrow that you know you will have no reason to drink when the time comes. Assuming that you believe

---

[14] Of course, this is just the sort of thing that those who take the strong consistency requirement to be inviolable would deny to be possible.

yourself, in general, to do only what you prospectively see yourself as having reason to do, you have good reason to believe that you won't drink the toxin; you'll already have the money, so drinking will promise sickness and no reward. Still, you do better—you get the money—if you nonetheless intend to.

Notice that the kinds of cases in which inter- or intrapersonal coordination are undermined when agents violate the strong consistency requirement appear much more common than cases in which violation of that requirement actually furthers such coordination. It is an empirical matter whether this appearance is accurate. But imagine that it were not. Imagine a world in which people are constantly being rewarded when they intend to do things they believe they will not do. Imagine a world, even, in which the very forms of inter- and intrapersonal coordination that planning helps us to achieve are achieved by those agents who violate the requirement of strong consistency and, for whatever reasons, are not achieved by those who obey it. Imagine further that the violators of the strong consistency requirement are not merely lucky to achieve coordination any more than the man who intends to drink the toxin while believing he will not is merely lucky to get the money; rather, the violators of the strong consistency requirement manage to put themselves into just the mental states that they need to be in, that it *makes sense* to be in in this world, if coordination is to be achieved. Who are the rational ones in this world: those who follow the demand of strong consistency, or those who violate it?

Which answer to this question one is drawn to is a function of one's conception of instrumental rationality. According to one conception of the instrumental rationality of a person's collection of mental states—what I will call the "causal conception"—the rational person is the one whose mental states conform to the model that there is good reason to believe will in fact serve his ends, given the causal structure of the world in which he lives. Under this conception, the violators of the strong consistency requirement are the rational agents, for there is good reason to believe that in the world in which they live it is through such violation that inter- and intrapersonal coordination is to be achieved. According, however, to another conception of rationality—what I will call the "attitudinal conception"—the rational person is the one whose mental states conform to a model dictated by the characteristic function or purpose of those mental states. To justify a claim to the effect that a particular set of mental states is not attitudinally rational we point to the purpose that such mental states are to serve, and the way in which a set of mental states of the sort in question tend to frustrate that purpose. To clarify with an example: it appears, just by reflecting on the notion of coordination, that coordination requires people to be able to count on themselves and others to act in certain ways; further, it appears, just by reflecting on the notion of "counting-on", that we cannot count on agents to act in certain ways if some of their authoritative mental states, such as their intentions, represent them as acting that way, and others, such as their beliefs, as not acting that way. On the attitudinal conception of rationality, that is, the mental states in question impose constraints on an agent quite independently of any facts about what will and will not earn the agent goods in the particular circumstances in which he finds himself; the constraints are imposed simply by virtue of the nature of the attitudes in question. Those attitudes, by their nature, serve a particular purpose (such as inter- and intrapersonal coordination), and this purpose dictates the conditions under which such attitudes are rational or irrational; it dictates, that is, the norms of rationality governing agents who have the attitudes in question. Under the attitudinal conception, it is the agents who obey the strong consistency requirement, in our hypothetical world, who are the rational ones, even though, as it happens in that world, they do not achieve any of the forms of coordination with themselves and others that intentions are to make possible.[15] An agent who obeys the strong consistency requirement in this hypothetical world is like a person who takes steps to heal his ailing appendix, rather than have it removed, even when healing it is more painful and promises no special benefit. It's true that, given the way of the world, a healthy appendix will never serve its natural function. Still, from the point of view of that function, the thing to do is to heal the organ rather than remove it. Similarly, from the point of view of the function of intention, the thing to do is to obey the strong consistency requirement, even if, given the way of our hypothetical world, this is to follow a less than optimal course.[16,17]

---

[15] Newcombe's paradox places in tension not the causal and the attitudinal conceptions of instrumental rationality, but, instead, two different forms of the causal conception. One-boxers take the past financial success of one-boxers to show that there is good reason to think that in the circumstances they are more likely to reach their ends by taking one box. Two-boxers, by contrast, think that given that the decisions they make cannot cause events that preceded those decisions, they do best by taking both boxes. The disagreement, then, is about what one has reason to think will lead to the best outcome, given the odd circumstances of the example, and not a disagreement of the sort that can be found between those accepting the attitudinal and those accepting the causal conception of rationality.

[16] In the first instance, the properties of being causally or attitudinally rational or irrational are possessed not by mental states, or by actions, but by the agents who have those mental states or perform those actions. They are possessed by agents thanks to their attitudes and actions, but not, except in a derivative sense, by the attitudes and actions of those agents. Further, the properties bear no logical relations to one another. All the various possible combinations of causal and attitudinal rationality and irrationality are possible. Our intuitions about rationality, however, are not often so fine-grained as to support, by themselves, claims about the particular form of rationality or irrationality enjoyed by a particular agent.

[17] As a further illustration of the attitudinal conception of rationality, notice that that conception can be used to explain the peculiarity of Moore's paradox, which begins by noting that there is something peculiar about asserting "p, but I don't believe it". (The paradox is noted in Moore (1942), 543.) The man who asserts "p, but I don't believe it" might be accurately reporting his own beliefs: he might believe both p and that he does not believe that p. Nobody denies, that is, that this is possible. Nor is there any logical contradiction in the contents of the two reported beliefs: one, the belief that p, concerns an extra-mental fact; the other, the belief that he does not believe that p, concerns a fact about his mind. So what's peculiar about the man's statement? The answer might be that the following is a norm of attitudinal rationality governing belief: an agent's belief that p is rational only if he does not also believe that he does not believe that p. Whether or not this really is a norm of the

Return to Bratman's argument, seemingly showing that one can try to act without intending to do so. The argument depends crucially on the claim that the game-player, and others like him, would have irrational intentions were he to intend to hit target 1 and intend to hit target 2, given that he believes that he will not hit both. But would his intentions be causally or attitudinally irrational? They would not be causally irrational: the game-player has good reason to believe that the having of both intentions is a good way, in the circumstances, to reach his goal of hitting exactly one target. The same point goes for any similar example: by intending to go to Harvard and intending to go to Yale, the high school senior increases his chances of going to one or the other; by intending to kill the infant, and intending to kill the mother, Smith increases his chances of killing one or the other. However, the game-player, the high school senior, and Smith all have attitudinally irrational intentions, and for just the reasons that Bratman suggests, reasons that have been rehearsed above: the point of intentions is to provide for inter- and intrapersonal coordination, and the norms of strong consistency and agglomerativity are linked to such coordination through the notion of counting on someone to act, an essential element in coordination that is undermined when agents violate strong consistency and agglomerativity. So once we see that there are two different sorts of rationality informing our intuitions about which hypothetical agents are rational and which not, the assertion that the agent in the example is rational is seen to be equivocal: he is causally rational and attitudinally irrational. So, although he is manifestly trying to hit target 1 and trying to hit target 2, it does not follow that one can try without intending; the game-player very well might have the two intentions in question.

To see the point in sum, it might be helpful to state the heart of Bratman's argument in syllogistic form as set out below, where it is assumed that the game-player is trying to hit target 1 and trying to hit target 2, and believes that he will not hit both:

1. The game-player is rational.
2. If he intends to hit target 1 and intends to hit target 2, then he is irrational.
∴ He does not intend to hit target 1 and intend to hit target 2.

---

attitudinal rationality of belief will depend on what beliefs are for, and whether or not there is a link to be found between obeying this norm and the function or aim of belief. Perhaps, for instance, the point of belief is to help us to reach knowledge and thus to motivate us to search for justifications for the things that we do believe. But such a search for justification requires self-conscious awareness of what one's beliefs are, and it is precisely this which is undermined by the presence of beliefs that one lacks the beliefs one actually has. Be that as it may, the point worth emphasizing is only that the notion of attitudinal rationality might be precisely what guides our intuition in reaction to Moore's paradox, an intuition that something has gone wrong in the statement, even if it is far from clear, at first glance, precisely what.

What I have suggested is that this is "a syllogism with two middle terms", and so its conclusion doesn't follow from its premises. The term "rational" in premise 1 refers to causal rationality, while the term "irrational" in premise 2 refers to attitudinal rationality.

Bratman can resist this argument by insisting that the game-player is attitudinally rational or, in other words, by insisting that "rational" in premise 1 refers to attitudinal rationality. However, it would be a mistake to support this assertion merely by appeal to intuition. Our intuitions about rationality are not terribly fine-grained and are influenced by various irrelevant factors, such as the way in which an example is described. Say, for instance, that one tells the story of two game-players who happen to be named Hesperus and Phospherus. Hesperus is trying to hit target 1, Phospherus target 2. Each knows that both targets can't be hit, and each is extremely confident in both his own abilities and his superiority to the other. Further, they are working together, aiming to make it the case that between them one target is hit, by having each of them do their utmost to hit their respective targets. They assume, and let's assume they are right, that the chances of them hitting the two targets simultaneously are inordinately slim, and that the chances of one or the other hitting a target would reduce drastically were each to do anything less than his utmost to hit his assigned target. I think it would seem to most people that each is rational and that each intends to hit his respective target. Why does anything change when it turns out that Hesperus and Phospherus are one and the same person?

Further, and more importantly, it is possible to support the claim that the game-player in Bratman's example is attitudinally irrational with reasons, and not just with intuitions. Where we have the violation of a principle of rationality there is a call for explanation, a need to say how what is before us makes sense. Imagine that you are given only the following pieces of information: the game-player is trying to hit target 1 and trying to hit target 2; he wants to hit at least one target; he believes that he cannot hit both. Now if the player's behavior is to make sense, we need an answer to the following question: "Why is he trying to hit each target, rather than just trying to hit one or the other?" The answer, of course, is that he thinks it more likely that he'll hit one if he tries to hit each, than if he tries to hit only one. But the answer isn't the point; the point is that the question *needs answering* if we are to find the game-player's conduct intelligible. Further, and importantly, we wouldn't need an answer to that question if the game-player did not believe that he could not hit both targets. What this shows is that given that the agent in the example is trying to hit each target, he is under rational pressure not to believe that he can't hit both and, importantly, that pressure goes away only by imagining alterations in his mental states, such as absence of the relevant belief. The presence of this pressure needs explanation, and it is provided by the presence in the game-player of the intentions to hit the targets, for where there is intention there are the pressures under which the game-player labors.

Notice that we can't explain the pressure to explain himself by appeal to different intentions from the intentions to hit each target. If, for instance, the game-player merely intended *to try* to hit target 1 and intended *to try* to hit target 2, there would be no pressure to explain, for he believes that *he can* do both of those things, just as he believes that he can take all the steps short of succeeding in his efforts to hit both targets. The same would go for any other retreat in the content of the intentions associated with his tryings. So long as he's trying to hit each target while believing that he can't hit both, he owes us an explanation; that debt can't be explained by appeal to any intentions other than the intentions to hit each target. (There remains the possibility, to be headed off in the next section of this chapter, that the need for explanation is to be explained by the tryings themselves, independently of any associated intentions. But for now, let that pass.)

Bratman is right that we assent to the claim that the agent in the example is rational, but he is wrong about why we assent. We assent, not because the game-player is under no pressure to explain why trying to hit each target makes sense in the face of the belief that he can't hit both, but because we see that, although he has crafted his set of mental states in a way that violates norms of attitudinal rationality, he has done so because doing so is the best way to reach his goals in the circumstances. In other words, our assent to the game-player's rationality derives from our allowing causal rationality to trump attitudinal, in this case, in our all-out assessment of the agent's rationality. Whether it would do so across the board is unclear, but it doesn't matter for our purposes. What matters is that the pressure to explain himself under which the game-player labors indicates that, whatever we think of his rationality all told, he is not attitudinally rational.

It's important to see that there is a deflationary move that could be made here, and which would be attractive to someone skeptical of the very idea of attitudinal rationality. We might say that the only kind of rationality is causal rationality. This is not to say that there isn't *appeal* to principles like strong consistency and agglomerativity. However, we might understand such principles, not as exceptionless norms of attitudinal rationality, as I, following Bratman, have suggested, but, instead, as rules of thumb specifying how, generally, one's mental states ought to be ordered if they are to help one to coordinate one's behavior inter- and intrapersonally.[18] Under this deflationary line of thought, what we learn from the game-player example is merely that the norms of strong consistency and agglomerativity admit of exceptions: there are rare cases when it makes sense to violate them. Where I have painted the pressure to explain himself under which the game-player labors as speaking to the violation, on his part, of the norms of attitudinal rationality governing

---

[18] This is, essentially, the position expressed in Kolodny (2005).

intention, the advocate of this deflationary line of thought would suggest that this pressure arises merely from the fact that the game-player is not obeying a rule that, in most circumstances, it makes sense to follow; he explains himself to us simply by showing that his circumstances are not of the usual sort, and so are not covered by the rules in question.

The advocate of this deflationary line of thought might support his position by directly attacking the very coherence of the notion of attitudinal rationality. In fact, the notion seems to have a very soft spot: what gives a particular mental state its "aim" or "function"? If the answer were to appeal to, say, the fact that, characteristically, mental states of the relevant sort cause certain attractive results—intentions, typically, cause coordination, for instance—then it might seem that there is no more to attitudinal rationality than causal: the conditions under which a mental state can be reasonably expected to bring about a certain result are determinative of the norms of rationality that the mental state is to meet. But if the actual causal role of the mental state is not what determines its aim or function, then what does? What makes it the case that one mental state is to play a role in producing inter- and intrapersonal coordination and another is not?

Someone who conceives of the principles of strong consistency and agglomerativity as mere rules of thumb, and who supports the position with this sort of attack on the very notion of attitudinal rationality, is in partial agreement with me, for such a person accepts that Bratman's argument fails to show that it is possible to try to act without intending to. However, such a person goes on to insist on something that I deny, namely that Bratman's game-player is rational in every meaningful sense. Under this view, the game-player *seems* irrational at first glance, in the same way that someone who harms another *seems* to be doing something that falls short of maximizing utility. In this last case, we can dispel that impression by indicating how causing harm will result in more utility, given the agent's very special circumstances; analogously, we can indicate how the game-player is actually more likely, rather than less, to achieve intrapersonal coordination by violating the principle of agglomerativity, given his very special circumstances.

The notion of attitudinal rationality, as a kind of rationality distinct from causal, will, in the next section of this chapter, serve as a premise in a positive argument for the claim that one tries to act only if one intends to. So, the deflationary position just sketched is not available to me, despite the fact that both its advocate and I deny that Bratman's argument shows that claim to be false. What I can hope to do here, however, is merely to acknowledge a debt that, unfortunately, I will not pay fully in this book: a full defense of the argument to be offered below would require defense of the notion of attitudinal rationality. However, one thing can be said here in defense of that notion: an analogy to biological functions at least gives one pause in acquiescing to the deflationary claim that principles like agglomerativity and strong consistency are nothing more than rules of thumb. Eyes have the function of helping us to detect the properties of objects that are at some distance from our bodies, and not in immediate contact with them. A large part of the reason for believing this is that, in fact, our eyes *cause* us to detect remote properties. There is a meaningful sense in which one hasn't done what's healthy for one's self when one gouges one's eyes out, even if, for some strange reason, this results in an improvement in one's ability to detect the remote properties of objects. We might say that the function of one's eyes places one under pressure not to gouge them out, even when gouging them out will help one to realize the very goods that eyes have the function of providing. In similar fashion, the thought goes, the function of one's intentions places one under pressure not to violate strong consistency or agglomerativity, even when doing so will help one to realize the very goods that intentions have the function of providing. In short, the notion of attitudinal rationality, as something distinct from causal, is no less appealing than a natural and appealing conception of health as linked to the biological function of one's organs.

In summary, then, we can ask two different questions about the rationality of an agent's mental states: (1) Do his mental states conform to patterns that fit with their aims or functions? (That is, is he attitudinally rational?) and (2) Do his mental states conform to patterns that there is good reason to believe will further his ends, under the circumstances? (That is, is he causally rational?) There is little reason to think that reflection on the second of these questions can tell us very much about intention or trying. After all, there is so much variation in the circumstances that agents face that there is little reason to expect there to be anything in common among the sets of mental states possessed by the causally rational or the causally irrational. By contrast, we can ask ourselves whether or not an agent's mental states make him assessable by the norms of attitudinal irrationality appropriate to intention, and thus determine if he has an intention, rather than some other mental state. Thus, we have a tool for assessing whether or not an agent has an intention that is far better than the usual appeal to linguistic or conceptual intuition. Instead of asking, of a particular agent, "Would we *say* that he intends to A?" we can ask "Would we take him to be irrational were he to fail to meet the demands of strong consistency, means-end coherence, and agglomerativity?" What we've learned from discussion of Bratman's views is that it is important that this question is confined to consideration of attitudinal rationality, to the exclusion of causal; if we allow consideration of both we end up concluding that the game-player and others like him lack intention, a conclusion which is unwarranted for the reasons already given.

## 3. The Functional Role of Trying

Arguing against an argument against a claim is not the same, of course, as arguing for the claim. So far it's been argued only that the planning theory of intention ought not to be construed in such a way that it implies the falsity of the claim that an agent tries to act only if he intends to. This section goes farther by arguing that, in fact, when construed as described in section 2, the planning theory actually implies *the truth* of that claim. That is, when we take seriously the idea that to have an intention is to be subject to the norms of strong consistency, means-end coherence, and agglomerativity, understood as above and understood only as norms of attitudinal rationality, it follows that one tries only if one intends.

At the end of the last section it was suggested that one of the virtues of the planning theory of intention is that it supplies a tool for systematically determining if an agent or hypothetical agent has an intention that does not require appeal to the vagaries of linguistic or conceptual intuition. We need only determine if the agent is subject to the distinctive norms of attitudinal rationality that govern intention, namely strong consistency, means-end coherence, and agglomerativity. However, we now need to look more closely at this claim. In particular, we need criteria for determining whether or not an agent really is to be assessed by the norms of attitudinal rationality governing intention. Such criteria, however, are not as difficult to produce as one might think. Notice that whenever a person seems to violate a norm of rationality, of whatever sort, he owes an explanation that shows how, at least by his own lights and perhaps by ours as well, his seemingly incongruous mental states or behavior actually make sense. When an agent seems to violate a norm of attitudinal rationality he can meet this explanatory demand, and thus show that, in fact, he is not in violation of the norm, in one of two ways. He can show that either (a) he actually lacks the relevant attitude on the basis of which the norm applies to him, or (and more importantly for our purposes) (b) the violation of the norm of attitudinal rationality actually, in the circumstances, is a means to some end that he possesses, and he is, therefore, causally rational.

For instance, if a person announces that he intends to win the lottery we first want to know if he believes it to be fixed, or if he has peculiar beliefs about probability that don't imply, as ours do, that he won't. When we find out that, in fact, he, like us, believes that he will not, then we expect some further explanation, for the agent appears to be in violation of the norm of strong consistency. He can, at this point, suggest that he doesn't *really* intend to *win*, but merely to buy a ticket and keep a positive attitude, say. This is to adopt the first approach in explanation of his apparent violation of the norm: it amounts to saying that the norm doesn't actually apply to him at all, that he is not to be assessed by it, since a presupposition of its application in this case is the intention to win, an intention that he says he lacks. Alternatively, the agent can give us an explanation of how having the intention to win, in the face of the belief that he will not, is causally rational. He might say, for instance, that he's influenced by social-psychological research that shows that those who intend to win, whether or not maintaining attitudinal rationality, are much more likely to win. He might say that he really doesn't know why this is—he can't think of any explanation himself—but he badly wants to win, and so sees the having of the intention to win, in the circumstances, as worth the pain of attitudinal irrationality. This is to explain his behavior by appeal to its causal rationality, its likelihood to serve his ends, given the circumstances, even in the face of its attitudinal irrationality.

The question, then, of whether or not an agent who is trying to A also intends to A has reduced to this: "Does the agent owe an explanation if his mental states fail to conform to the norms of attitudinal rationality governing intention?" Would he owe an explanation if, say, he is trying to A while believing he will fail, that either indicates that he is not, despite appearances, trying to A at all, or that trying to A, in the circumstances, and in violation of the norm of strong consistency, is a good way to reach his ends? He would. To see the argument for this claim, consider, first, why we might think that an agent who is trying to act while believing he will fail owes us an explanation of the relevant sort. The argument will extend to the other two norms of attitudinal rationality governing intention.

There is a wide variety of circumstances in which agents try to do things that they believe they will not do and whom we would not pronounce irrational. In a recent paper, Carl Ginet has identified three kinds of case.[19] First, an agent might believe he can't do something, but also believe that he's far from infallible in the assessment of his own abilities. He might then try to do the thing he thinks he can't in order to find out if he's right. He might do this because he has strong reason to succeed in acting, but he also might do it because he has reasons for *wanting to know* his own abilities, even though he has no reason to succeed in acting. Second, an agent might believe he can't do something but be challenged by someone else who claims he can. To prove this other person wrong, he might try to do that thing. Such an agent might lack a reason to succeed in acting and might also lack a reason to know his own abilities; he might only, that is, be trying to act in order to prove another wrong. It is worth looking at the example that Ginet uses to illustrate the third sort of case. He writes,

Suppose Sam knows that [a] log is far too heavy for him to move by pushing on it. But Sam is a soldier under the command of Rudy, and Rudy has ordered Sam to try to move the log by pushing on it. Sam would very much prefer that Rudy not find out that he (Sam) cannot move the log by pushing on it, but the penalty for refusing to obey the command would, in Sam's view, be a worse consequence than Rudy's knowing that Sam cannot move the log by pushing on it. So Sam pushes on the log as hard as he can in order to

---

[19] Ginet (2004). Ginet takes all three cases to illustrate that an agent can try to do something without intending to do it. However, Ginet is simply assuming that an agent does not intend to do what he believes he will not do, and so concludes that the people in all of his examples lack the intention to act. Thus, the argument to follow, if it succeeds, refutes this aspect of Ginet's position.

comply with Rudy's command to try to move it by pushing on it, but very much regretting... that by so doing he will reveal to Rudy that he cannot move it by pushing on it.[20]

By making it part of the example that Sam does not want Rudy to know that he can't move the log, Ginet distinguishes this case from the second sort of case in which the agent hopes to show another person that he can't do the thing he is trying to do; Sam's reason for trying, in Ginet's example, is his desire to comply with the command. Notice that Ginet has provided a blueprint here for generating an arbitrarily large number of categories of agents who try to act while believing they can't. Abstractly, Ginet's example is constructed as follows. Assume that D believes that he cannot A and that he has no reason to successfully A. Assume also that agents sometimes have reasons of types R1, R2...Rn for trying to A that are not also reasons for successfully A-ing (i.e. sometimes they want to see if they can A, despite their belief that they can't; sometimes they want to prove to someone else that they can't; etc.). Now imagine that, for some reason, D is positively averse to trying to A for reasons of any of these n types (in Ginet's example, instead of wanting another to know that he can't A, he wants that other person *not* to know that). But he has a stronger reason for trying to A nonetheless (in Ginet's example, he wants to avoid whatever penalty would befall him were he to fail to obey the command). Using this blueprint, we can generate an arbitrary number of distinct types of example in which an agent has reason to try to A but, by the nature of the construction, lacks any of the previously identified possible reasons for doing so. The point can be put another way: since anything can cause anything else, we can construct examples in which trying to act can cause anything one likes. In order to generate an example of an agent who tries to A while believing he can't and maintains rationality, we merely set things up so that his trying to act will cause something that he wants more than he wants to avoid any of the other things that trying to act will cause.

The point is that in all of Ginet's examples and in all of the possible examples that one might construct by following in Ginet's footsteps, we pronounce in favor of the agent's rationality in trying to act in the face of belief in failure, only because we see how, in light of his ends, it makes sense for him to do so. These are pronouncements of causal rationality, not of attitudinal. They amount to the giving of the second sort of explanation identified above for deviance from the norm of strong consistency; instead of denying that the agents in question are really trying to act, we show how, in light of their circumstances, trying to act in the face of belief in failure is a good way to reach their ends. What follows is that we are yet to find an example of an agent who tries to act while believing he can't and maintains *attitudinal* rationality.

---

[20] Ginet (2004), 95–6.

To say this much isn't to say that such agents are attitudinally irrational, but only that our reasons for thinking them rational derive from our recognition of their causal rationality. We need more in order to support the point sought here, namely that those who try to act while believing they will fail are attitudinally irrational. But to support this point we need an argument for thinking that there's a link between compliance with the norm of strong consistency and the point or purpose of trying. Bratman identified a link between that norm and the purpose of intending (namely, inter- and intrapersonal coordination) through the connection between coordination and the need to count on those with whom action is being coordinated. Is there a similar link in the case of trying? Yes. To see this, start by noting that the function of intention and the function of trying must be quite closely intertwined, for the function of trying to act is, in part, to support the function of intending to act. It is by trying that we translate our intentions into behavior. But it is *behavior* that must be coordinated if we are to reach our individual and joint ends; plans can mesh as much as we like, but until we act on them we don't get where we want to go. Plans by themselves don't give us coordination, although they are essential to it: we also need to *act* on our plans, and it is by trying to act that we do so. Just as intending is a universal means to coordinating our behavior, trying to act is a universal means to acting, and thus to coordinating our behavior (among other things). If we can't count on ourselves or others to try to act, then we can't count on them to act, and if we can't count on them to act, we can't coordinate our behaviors with them in ways that are essential for reaching our ends.[21]

This isn't yet an argument; it just amounts to the observation that the roles of intending and trying are not so easily disambiguated. However, we are now in a position to produce the needed argument: trying to act serves all the ends that action serves. In fact, its function is to enable agents to achieve whatever ends are achieved through action. Now, if trying to act is to serve this purpose, then we must be able to count on ourselves to act when we try; that, after all, is why we try. But if the norms governing those who intend apply to them because we need to count on them to act, the very same norms apply to those who try. So, if you try, you are assessible by the very norms that apply to you when you intend. Since assessibility by such norms is what makes an agent's mental state one of intending, it follows that if you try to act, you also intend to.[22]

---

[21] Bratman is well known for having shown that intention has "two faces": one having to do with intentional action, the other having to do with the mental states involved in planning. Bratman takes trying, like aiming, to contribute to intentional action. However, what is being suggested here is that trying, like intending, has a second face, as well, for in addition to playing a role in generating intentional action, it is essential to the kind of coordination that is the hallmark of planning agency.

[22] Are there asymmetries between the rational pressures governing those who try and those who intend? Under the argument here, every norm of rationality that applies to someone who intends also applies to someone who tries, although the reverse need not be true for the argument to go through. We would thus expect a causally rational agent to find it no easier

The argument just offered can be put more carefully:

(1) If an agent has a mental state the content of which is to-A, and the function of that mental state requires that the agent can be counted on to A, then she is on those grounds assessible by the norms of strong consistency, means-end coherence and agglomerativity. [(p&q) → r]

(2) If an agent has a mental state the content of which is to-A, and she is on those grounds assessible by the norms of strong consistency, means-end coherence and agglomerativity, then she has an intention to A. [(p&r) → s]

(3) ∴ If an agent has a mental state the content of which is to-A, and the function of that mental state requires that the agent can be counted on to A, then she has an intention to A. [(p&q) → s]

(4) If an agent is trying to A, then she has a mental state the content of which is to-A, and the function of that mental state is to make it the case that she A's. [t → (p&u)]

(5) If the function of a mental state is to make it the case that an agent A's, then the function of that mental state requires that the agent can be counted on to A. [u → q]

(6) (from 4 & 5) If an agent is trying to A, then she has a mental state the content of which is to-A and the function of that mental state requires that the agent can be counted on to A. [t → (p&q)]

(7) ∴ If an agent is trying to A, then she has an intention to A. [t → s]

The stretch of argument of premises (1)–(3) employs the driving ideas behind the planning theory of intention. The stretch of argument from premise (4) to the conclusion extends those ideas to determine what mental states the trying agent must have.

It is worth making a few comments about this argument, by way of clarification. First, notice that the argument does not imply, nor do I believe it's the case, that one cannot act without trying to act. Just as one can achieve coordination without intention, one can act without trying to. Nonetheless, the point of trying is to act, just as the point of intending is coordination.

Second, as Ginet's examples, and the other examples that we can generate following his lead, show, it is perfectly possible for an agent to serve some other end, besides acting, by trying, an end that is achieved *just by* trying, independently of action. This, however, is no objection to the argument just offered, for

to try to do something that he believes he will not do, than to intend to do it. In fact, this is, I believe, what we find. Both those who try to do what they believe they cannot, and those who intend to do so must "compartmentalize" their minds; they must somehow "set aside" their belief that failure is inevitable in order to try or intend. This is a difficult task, but it is no more difficult in the case of intending than it is in the case of trying, which is just what the view defended here implies.

in this respect trying is just like intending: as the toxin puzzle shows, intending can serve some other purpose besides inter- and intrapersonal coordination. Just as this fact is compatible with the fact that the point of intending is to achieve coordination, the fact that Ginet's examples illustrate is compatible with trying's function being to bring about action.

Third, to say that we must "count on" people to act as they intend or as they are trying to act, is not to say that action is, or need be, *guaranteed* if trying and intending are to serve their respective purposes. We might count on ourselves to act as we try in just the way that we count on ourselves and others to do as we intend; it's always possible that people won't do what we are counting on them to do, but there is nonetheless a presumption of action where there is trying or intending. There's another way to put the point: unless it's hopeless, it always makes sense to advise those who hope to coordinate their behavior to make plans. This is true even though we all recognize that sometimes the best-laid plans don't get us coordination, and even though we all recognize that sometimes people achieve coordination fortuitously and without planning. Similarly, unless it's hopeless, it always makes sense to advise someone who hopes to act, to try. This is true even though we all recognize that sometimes we fail despite our best efforts, and sometimes we succeed effortlessly. The reason that these are both good pieces of advice, despite the fact that they don't identify certain routes to success, is that what is being advised is to use the tool that you can count on to work: planning is the tool for coordinating, and trying is the tool for acting; we can count on those tools to work, even though they don't always.

This point should go some way to answering concerns that might be raised about premise (5), the claim that the function of trying to act requires counting on the trying agent to act. It might be objected that the sense in which the aim of coordination requires that we can count on agents to do as they intend is quite different from the sense in which the aim of acting requires that we can count on agents to do as they are trying to do. Our chances of coordination are low when we can't count on agents to do as they intend. But there is no comparable problem when it comes to acting; it's not as though an agent's chances of acting are lower if the agent can't be counted on to do as he tries. Counting-on serves a clear instrumental role in generating coordination, but no comparable instrumental role in generating action. While this is correct, it doesn't serve to undermine the argument, for there is another sense in which counting on agents to do as they act is necessary for accomplishing the characteristic aim of trying: it's what provides reason to try. Counting-on is necessary to make trying worthwhile (when trying isn't serving some purpose distinct from its characteristic purpose); similarly, counting-on is necessary to make intending worthwhile (when intending isn't serving some purpose distinct from its characteristic purpose). So, while counting-on is necessary to the purpose of intending for different reasons from those for which it is necessary to the purpose of trying, it is nonetheless necessary for both, and that's all that the argument requires.

In any event, we have now reached the result at which this chapter aimed: in trying to act, and thereby employing a mental tool the function of which can be realized only if we can count on the agent to act, the agent becomes subject to the very norms of attitudinal rationality that govern those with intentions. Since, as the planning theory of intention has shown us, to have an intention is to have a practical mental state that makes one appropriately assessible by such norms, it follows that if one tries to act, one intends to act.

## 4. Conclusion

The argument of this chapter has taken us one step towards an account of the nature of trying, since it has served as a defense of one of trying's necessary conditions, namely an intention that commits one to completion. Necessary and sufficient conditions for trying will be offered in chapter 3. In addition, the result reached here provides an answer to the following question: "Which of two statutory schemes proscribing attempted crimes is defensible, the dominant one (like Indiana's) that makes intent an element of attempt even when the completed crime does not require intent, or, instead, one (like Colorado's) that requires for attempt only the mental states required for the completed crime?" The answer is the first, for without intent nothing that a person does could be a case of trying to act, regardless of the question of what mental states one must have in order to successfully act. Since laws against attempts are justifiable because of the Transfer Principle, any just law proscribing attempt will have intent to act as an element. To criminalize attempts through even a silent appeal to the Transfer Principle is to commit oneself to a construction of the elements of attempted crimes that respects the nature of trying to act. And so an account of the *mens rea* element of attempt must also respect it in this.

# 3

# The Nature of Trying

## 1. Introduction

This chapter offers a general account of the nature of trying which I call "The Guiding Commitment View". By combining the Guiding Commitment View with an account of the elements of crimes, also offered in this chapter, we are able to provide an account of what it is to try to commit *a crime*, in contrast to other things that people attempt. This account is then used in different ways in the next seven chapters, which comprise parts 2 and 3 of the book. The position plays a role, but a lesser role, also in part 4's discussions of the sentencing of attempts. In chapter 4, the Guiding Commitment View is used to explain what mental states are involved in the attempt of a crime. In chapters 5, 6, and 7, three long-standing problems about attempted crimes are solved through appeal to the account of the mental states involved in attempt implied by the Guiding Commitment View. In chapter 8, the Guiding Commitment View is used in a different way to justify the practice of never convicting for attempt in the absence of action performed as a means to fulfilling a criminal intention. It is argued in chapter 8 that that practice is justified on the grounds that such action constitutes indispensable evidence that the defendant is trying to act as trying is construed under the Guiding Commitment View. The Guiding Commitment View's implications about evidence of trying are then used in chapters 9 and 10 to solve two more difficult problems encountered by courts adjudicating attempted crimes.

Ultimately, a theory like the Guiding Commitment View ought to be judged less by the soil in which it is planted than by the fruit that it bears. So, although this chapter will offer some arguments for the position, the more important case for it is made in the succeeding chapters. In those chapters it is shown that the Guiding Commitment View provides us with principled grounds on which to make decisions about defendants that have with rare exceptions been made, until now, either on faulty principles or on no principles at all. The fact that the view allows for a principled resolution of various legal problems itself counts in favor of the view. But, of course, a view that gives the wrong advice is no more likely to be true than one that gives no advice at all. However, it is also argued in the succeeding chapters that the advice the Guiding Commitment View implies is at least *not the wrong advice*; what the view tells us to do might not be right, but there's no reason to think it's wrong. And sometimes the view's implications are clearly the right ones: sometimes it tells us to do what we ought to do. Putting all these results together, we reach the conclusion that the Guiding Commitment View is to be preferred to alternative theories of what it is to try to commit a crime.

The discussion to follow is driven by the following intuitive idea: *to try to do something is to be committed to each of the components of success and to be moved by those commitments*. Without commitment, there is no investment of one's agency in success, and so there is no trying. But without being moved by one's commitment, there is no striving towards success, and so no trying. The Guiding Commitment View is a formalization of this intuitive idea.

The Guiding Commitment View builds on the result of chapter 2. There we learned that, despite appealing arguments to the contrary, trying necessarily involves intending. As we saw there, and as we will see in greater detail here, to have an intention is to be thereby committed to that which one intends: intentions constitute commitments. So, the lesson from chapter 2 that will be incorporated here is that the commitments that are involved in trying are intention-based. A person is committed to success in the way involved in trying just in case he has a certain intention. As we will see in chapter 4, the Guiding Commitment View can be used to determine precisely what intention is required to attempt a crime, given a description of the elements of the completed crime.

Since this entire chapter is devoted to explaining and defending the Guiding Commitment View, it helps in what follows to have a statement of the view to refer to even though it invokes several notions to be explained below. Here, D is an agent (a defendant, for instance) who has an intention, the content of which is X. C is a type of action (a crime, for instance) and E1, E2 . . . En are all those things that are true when a person C's (as we will see, when C is a crime, these conditions are a function of the elements of C).

*The Guiding Commitment View*: D attempts C *if and only if* ∀Ei, the following criteria are met:

*Commitment Criterion*: ((Ei is included in X) OR (If D's intention plays its proper causal role, then Ei)), &

*Guidance Criterion*: D is guided by his commitment to Ei.

In what follows, this position will be elucidated and defended. Section 2 explains what the E's are; it explains what, exactly, a person who is trying must be committed *to*. Most importantly for our purposes, it explains this for the case when C is a crime, through an account of the elements of crimes. Section 3 explains the Commitment Criterion through a discussion of the nature of intention, a discussion that builds on some of the ideas introduced in chapter 2. This section explains, that is, what the commitment involved in trying really amounts to. Section 4 explains the Guidance Criterion. It is suggested there that there is guidance by one's intention-based commitment when the intention causes something on the way towards performance of an act that one believes to be a means to doing as one intends, or is what, itself, is intended. However, it is suggested that a good test for determining if this condition is met is to see if the following counterfactual is true: had the agent had ability and opportunity to commit the crime, and did not change his mind, he would have committed it. Section 5 offers two reasons for thinking that the Guiding Commitment View captures the sense of trying that is of relevance to the criminal law of attempt. First, it is suggested that in contrast with competing theories, the Guiding Commitment View licenses us to describe what a person is trying to do in a way that aligns with the descriptions that we need to give in the context of the criminal law. Second, the Guiding Commitment View counts as attempts of crimes all and only those behaviors that are criminalized under the Transfer Principle, introduced in chapter 1. Given that attempts are criminalized under the Transfer Principle, this is just what we would hope for from a theory of the nature of attempt.

## 2. The Elements of a Crime

The account of trying to act offered here depends on a particular way of construing success. Outside of the legal context, the account is very straightforward: to succeed to C is for your action to fall under the concept of C. Hence the concept of the action in question dictates what success entails. Typically, maybe even always, our ordinary action concepts allow for multiple forms of instantiation. The concept of "building a bird house" applies to the act of building it from a kit, to building it from basic materials of a wide variety of different sorts, to building any number of very different bird houses for any number of different kinds of birds, or for no birds at all. In the ordinary case, the set of conditions that one needs to be committed to in order to be trying to C are any set of conditions satisfaction of which would involve an act that falls under the concept of C.

When we move to the legal context, however, things get more complicated. The reason is that the conditions that are involved in completion are dictated by the elements of crimes, and at best indirectly by our ordinary action concepts. As a brief look at murder law confirms, what counts as murder in the ordinary sense does not correspond perfectly to what counts as murder in the legal sense. The same is true of rape, robbery, burglary, destruction of property, criminal trespass, kidnapping, etc. In fact, there may be no crime that corresponds perfectly with the ordinary concept that its name expresses.

To understand what is involved in succeeding in completing a crime, we need to know more, that is, about the elements of crimes.

Uncontroversially, the elements of a completed crime are all and only those conditions that must be shown beyond a reasonable doubt to hold if the prima facie case against the defendant is to be established. The elements of crimes are typically divided into four categories: acts, results, circumstances, and mental states. Some have held that nothing of legal importance ought to turn on this division of the elements.[1] They hold this view because they think that it is too often a vexed question whether a particular element is correctly characterized as act, result, or circumstance. For instance, they think that there is no way to decide whether it is correct to characterize murder as including the act element *killing* and the circumstance that *the victim is a human being*, or, instead as including an act element of *killing a human being*. If anything of legal importance turned on the question of which characterization is correct then there would be a serious problem, they think. As we will see in chapter 4, 5, and 7, the Guiding Commitment View implies that, in several different ways, whether a person's behavior is an attempt turns on how the elements of the completed crime are to be classified. Therefore, it is important to defend the claim that the lines between these four categories are sharp; there is, it will be argued, a right and a wrong way to classify the elements. And, as we will see, a correct classification of the elements dictates what conditions are involved in the successful completion of a crime.

Typically, both skeptics about the distinctions between different elements of crimes and those who try to vindicate those distinctions assume that, if the distinctions are meaningful, then which category a particular element falls into is determined prior to the determination of what the prosecution is required to show beyond a reasonable doubt in order to establish the prima facie case. However, what will be suggested here is that the question of how to classify a particular element *just is* the question of what the prosecution bears a burden to show beyond a reasonable doubt. An element counts as, for instance, an act element rather than a result element precisely because the prosecution is required to show something beyond a reasonable doubt in order to meet its burden that it would not be required to show were the element in question a result element. Thus, the view offered here reverses the ordinary order of explanation: instead of determining what the prosecution must show by determining how the element in question is to be classified, it is suggested here that how the element is to be classified is determined by what the prosecution must show with respect to it. This position will become clearer, and the details of it will be specified, in what remains of this section.

The line between the mental state elements and the rest of the elements of a crime is not questioned: the mental state elements are just that, mental states,

---

[1] Cff. Duff (1991), Williams (1991).

while the rest of the elements are not. So what is required is to defend the claim that there is, in any given instance, a correct way to classify any particular non-mental element of a crime as act, result, or circumstance. For our purposes, the circumstantial elements will be defined, unhelpfully, as follows:

An event[2] is a circumstantial element of a crime *if and only if* The prosecution meets its burden with respect to that element just in case (1) The prosecution shows that the event occurred, and (2) The element is neither a mental state of the defendant nor an act or result element of the crime.

Of course, this is unhelpful, since this definition requires definitions of the act and result elements of crimes. How are acts and result to be defined?

The thought that it is arbitrary to classify a particular element as act, result, or circumstance derives from the mistaken assumption that the classification is to be determined by the nature of the event or state in question. In fact, it is determined by the nature of the burdens that the prosecution bears with respect to that element. To say that an element of a crime is an act element or a result element is to imply that the prosecution has a variety of burdens that it lacks when the element is circumstantial. Further, the burdens are different when the element is a result than when it is an act. To see this, consider the following definition of a result element:

An event is a result element of a completed crime *if and only if* The prosecution meets its burden with respect to that element just in case (1) The prosecution shows that the event occurred, & (2) The prosecution shows that the event was caused by the defendant.

The causal fact—not the fact that, for instance, Victim died, but the fact that Defendant caused Victim's death—is something that the prosecution bears a burden to establish, if the event in question is a result element of the completed crime. For every result element of a crime, the prosecution is required to show, and only required to show, that a certain event occurred, and, further, that the defendant caused that event. The existence of this second burden is what distinguishes result elements from circumstantial elements. So, in jurisdictions in which murder is defined, in part, as "causing another's death", death is a result element of murder since the prosecution is required to show both that a death occurred and that the defendant caused it.

By contrast, the fact that the owner did not grant permission to the defendant to occupy his house is a circumstantial element of criminal trespass, since the prosecution bears no burden to prove that the defendant caused the owner not to grant permission. Notice that the phrase "caused the owner not to grant permission" is ambiguous. On one reading, this is true of someone who acts in

---

[2] Throughout I use the term "event". Some of the elements of crimes are better described as conditions or states. However, to use a disjunctive term like "event, state or condition" is awkward. Instead, the term "event" should be understood broadly to incorporate states and conditions.

an offensive way towards the owner and his offensive conduct causes the owner to demand that he leave.[3] That is one way to cause the owner not to grant permission to be on his land. On another reading, however, this is true of someone who differentially selects land to occupy that he lacks permission to occupy. That is, if such a person is choosing between entering two plots of land, one of which he has permission to enter and one of which he does not, he chooses the latter in part because of the fact that he lacks permission to enter that land. Such a person does not cause any given person not to grant permission; rather, he causes it to be the case that the property he occupies is one that he lacks permission to occupy. To say that a condition, like the absence of the owner's permission, is a circumstantial element of a crime is to say that the prosecution bears *neither* burden with respect to it. The prosecution need not show that the defendant caused the condition, and it need not show that the defendant performed the act that he performed, as opposed to an alternative similar act (such as entering a different piece of land), in part because of the fact that the condition held. A person can have committed the crime, that is, even if it is pure accident that the condition holds, or even if the condition was caused in either or both senses by other people. (The import of this construal of circumstantial elements of crimes will become important in chapter 5.)

To identify something, like a killing, as an act element of a crime is to imply that the prosecution has a rather complicated burden distinct from that involved in either results or circumstances. To understand the nature of this burden we must digress at some length into discussion of the nature of action.

Start by noting that acts are rarely referred to with descriptions that pick out their intrinsic properties. Instead, they are referred to by reference to what they cause.[4] To say that someone "killed" another is to say that he performed an act that caused a death; to say that someone "raised his arm" is to say that he performed an act that caused his arm to rise. In these cases, and in almost all cases, we say what a person did by saying what the act caused.[5] So, to say

---

[3] This is true, in any event, if it is possible for one person to cause another's voluntary act, in this case the act of withdrawing permission. No point of substance, however, depends on this possibility. After all, many circumstantial elements are the sorts of things that no defendant has ever caused. Defendants don't cause it to be night or day, but the fact that it was night at the time of the crime is an element of burglary in many jurisdictions.

[4] So-called "basic acts" are sometimes cited as the exception to this rule. So, to say that "He moved his finger" is not to say that he did something that caused his finger to move. The thought is that there is nothing more causally "basic" than the moving of the finger. (The *locus classicus* of this thought is Danto (1965).) While there probably are basic acts, when they are elements of crimes (as in the examples mentioned in chapter 1), they affect the elements of attempts in just the way that non-basic acts do.

[5] There is at least one very important exception to this rule: trying. To say that a person tried to A is not to say that he did something that caused a trying to A. There may be other exceptions also. Mental acts, in particular, may be exceptions. To say that someone "thought about Agatha Christie" might not be to say that he did something that caused a thought about Agatha Christie. Descriptions of mental acts, that is, might not always be rightly said to work by picking out a result that is caused by the act referred to. See McCann (1974).

"D A'd" is to imply that D caused an A. However, to say "D caused an A" is not to imply that D A'd; sometimes this is true, sometimes it is not. A person calls to his dog from across the street; the dog runs to his owner and is hit by a car. The owner caused the dog to be crushed, but it is not the case that the owner crushed the dog. This commonplace example alone shows that there is a gap between result elements of crimes and act elements. The distinction is not "just drafting" as many legal practitioners assume. After all, an imaginary statute that proscribes "crushing dogs" does not proscribe prima facie the behavior of the person who calls his dog from across the street and thereby causes it to be crushed. Such a person might have done something wrong; he may even have done something which warrants his being held *guilty* under the imagined statute. But he has not *committed* the crime that the statute defines for he has not crushed a dog. This point will become clearer as we move forward.

Joel Feinberg uses the term "the accordion effect" to pick out those cases in which we can move from "D caused an A" to "D A'd".[6] When D fires a bullet and a death results, we can (ordinarily) say *both* that D caused someone's death and that D killed someone; here we have the accordion effect. It is absent in our example of calling the dog and thereby causing it to be crushed. There are also cases in which the move from "D caused an A" to "D A'd" would be licensed *were there an appropriate verb of action in our language*, but there happens not to be such a verb. It is a quirk of our language that even when "You caused me to be happy" is true "You happied me" is not; after all, it is often, although not always, the case that both "You caused me to be frightened" and "You frightened me" are true.

So we have three kinds of cases in which it is true that "D caused an A": there are those in which it is also true that "D A'd" (above, the case of killing by causing a death with a shot); those in which it would be true that "D A'd" were there an appropriate verb associated with events like A (above, the happiness case); and those in which it is not true that "D A'd" even if there is an appropriate verb (above, the dog case). Feinberg seems to use the term "the accordion effect" to apply only to cases of the first sort, although there are hints that he would take there to be an accordion effect also in cases of the second sort.[7] However, it is clear that he thinks that, where there is an accordion effect, there is a deeper involvement of the agency of the actor in the event caused than when there is not. The thought is that the agency of the person who crushes a dog is more involved in the dog's being crushed than is the agency of the person who causes the dog to be crushed but does not crush it. If this is right, then there is a comparable degree of agency involvement in those cases of the second

---

[6] Feinberg (1970a), 134.
[7] See Feinberg (1970b), 184.

sort in which there is no appropriate verb, but it would apply were there one. Agency involvement, after all, is not language-relative. It would be strange, that is, if one's agency is more involved in what one causes under Chinese than under English, if it so happens that there is an appropriate verb in Chinese, but not in English.

So as to avoid confusion of terms, let's use the term "the agency-involvement factor" to refer to those conditions, whatever they are, that set the first two kinds of case apart from the third. The presence of the agency-involvement factor is what licenses the move from "D caused an A" to "D A'd", or would license it were there an appropriate verb in our language. Although we have little trouble sorting those cases in which the agency-involvement factor is present from those in which it is absent, it is far from clear what, exactly, the agency-involvement factor is. However, for our purposes what will matter is only that there is such a factor, and that we are capable of recognizing it when it is there.

Feinberg seems to think that when the agency-involvement factor is present, there is action, and when it is absent there is mere causation of an event, falling short of action; he seems to think that when the agency-involvement factor is absent, as in the dog case, then there is *no* involvement in the relevant event of the agency of the actor. In fact, Donald Davidson was deeply influenced by this claim in his account of action, despite not endorsing it entirely.[8] But we needn't follow Feinberg this far. Perhaps the dog's being crushed is relevant to a proper characterization of what the owner *did* in our example above; perhaps it figures somehow into a full account of his actions. We can admit this while also asserting that his agency was not so intimately involved in that event as to license the claim that he crushed the dog. It matters little for our purposes here where in the spectrum of agency involvement we place the dividing line between action and mere happening. Perhaps there is no single dividing line. What matters is only that there is a difference in the intimacy of our agency involvement in those cases in which we can move (or could if there was an appropriate verb) from "D caused an A" to "D A'd" in comparison to those in which we can't.

It is important to see that the presence or absence of the agency-involvement factor does not turn merely on the mental state of the agent; hence, to say that a particular event is an act element of a crime is not to imply that the prosecution is under any particular burdens with respect to the mental state elements of the crime. In particular, the agency-involvement factor can be present even when the agent is far from intending the event that figures into the act's description. The drunk driver who causes the death of a pedestrian typically also kills someone; the agency-involvement factor is present in such a case even though

---

[8] For discussion, see Bratman (2006).

the death was not intended, not foreseen, and perhaps not even consciously risked. In fact, that the presence or absence of the agency-involvement factor is not immediately established by noting the mental state involved in a person's behavior is an essential presupposition of the criminal law's view to the effect that the act element of a crime can be accompanied by any of a variety of different mental states. If, by contrast, whereever there is action there is intention, then it would not be possible for the act element of a crime to be realized recklessly or negligently. Conversely, a result can be intended, and caused by the intention, with the agency-involvement factor absent, as is indicated by Donald Davidson's famous example of deviant causation: the mountain climber intends to drop his fellow climber and reflection on his intention to do so makes him so nervous that his hand shakes and his fellow climber falls.[9]

This is not to say that mental state is irrelevant to the determination of the presence or absence of the agency-involvement factor. When one intends something, the agency-involvement factor will be present with respect to far more of the actually occurring consequences of what one intends than when one is merely reckless or negligent with respect to that same thing. Compare, on the one hand, a person who intends to burn his house and causes his neighbor's to burn to, on the other hand, one who merely negligently burns his own house but also causes his neighbor's house to burn. It is more appealing to think that the first person *burns* his neighbor's house than that the second does; both claims might turn out to be false, on reflection, but the first is, still, more likely to be true than the second. Mental state seems to matter to such questions. Let me be clear: I am not offering a theory of the nature of the agency-involvement factor; I am merely trying to make clear what I mean by it. For our purposes what matters is only that when the agency-involvement factor is present, then what one causes can be appealed to to characterize what one does (or could be if our language provided a relevant verb), and when it is absent this is not the case.

We are now in position to say what distinguishes act elements of crimes from results and circumstances.

An event is an act element of a crime *if and only if* The prosecution meets its burden with respect to that element just in case (1) The prosecution shows that the defendant engaged in a voluntary[10] bodily movement, & (2) The prosecution shows that the bodily movement caused some specified event, & (3) The prosecution shows that the agency-involvement factor was present.

---

[9] See Davidson (1980b). Davidson describes the example as one in which the person has a relevant belief-desire pair, and not one in which the agent has a relevant intention. Under a view of intention that Davidson advocates, but repudiates following the publication of this essay, the belief-desire pair is the only thing in the head that we could be referring to with the term "intention". For brief discussion, see chapter 2.

[10] The notion of "the voluntary" here is a topic of its own. For discussion see, e.g., Moore (1993), chapters 2–6, and Husak (2007).

Here the "specified event" mentioned in condition (2) is the type of event that the statute defining the crime mentions in order to refer to the act in question. So, for instance, if the statute says that "killing" is an element of the crime, then a death is the event in question. So, consider three different characterizations of some of the elements of murder:

(A)  Act: Killing; Circumstance: The victim is a human being
(B)  Result: Death; Circumstance: The victim is a human being
(C)  Act: Killing a human being

The question of whether (A) or (B) is correct will depend on whether the prosecution bears a burden to show that the agency-involvement factor was present in the causation of the death. This will in turn depend, in part, on the question of whether the statute defining the crime bans killing or, instead, bans causing death. The precise wording of the statute will become important to that determination, although probably not decisive, since standard principles of interpretation would not prevent a court from interpreting a statute that says "killing" to mean "causing death" or vice versa. The question of whether (C) is correct will, again, turn on what burdens the prosecution bears. However, it seems unlikely that the prosecution should be required to prove that the defendant caused his victim to be a human being, in either of the senses mentioned above, much less that the agency-involvement factor was present in that causal event. A defendant is probably rightly held guilty for murder even if, for all that the prosecution can show, he would have killed his victim even if his victim had been a deer rather than a person. Thus it seems that either (A) or (B) will be superior to (C) in the following sense: neither (A) nor (B) requires the prosecution to show something that appears to be normatively irrelevant, namely that the defendant caused his victim to be a human being.

The classification of an element of a crime as act, result, or circumstance is, then, a question about prosecutorial burdens. Answering that question requires interpreting statutes, and so interpreting legislative intent, in so far as that matters to statutory interpretation. This task, in turn, often involves making normative inferences of the form, "The prosecution *ought* (or ought not) to have the burden to prove X, therefore such-and-such an element of this crime is an act element (or result, or circumstance)." Interpretive questions of this kind, not to mention the entwined normative questions, are almost never easy to answer. I will not be making any proposal here about how they are to be answered, either in general or in any particular case. Instead, I will be assuming that in each case they can be answered, and so we can, in turn, classify the elements of crimes as acts, results, and circumstances. Still, one observation is worth making. To define a particular event, such as damage to a piece of property, as an act element of a crime—and so someone who causes damage but did not *damage* anything is not guilty—is to say that part of what makes the proscribed behavior wrongful is that it involves a misuse of one's agency. By contrast, to define such an event as a result element of a crime—and so some-one who causes damage but did not *damage* anything would be guilty—is to say that part of what makes the proscribed behavior wrongful is that it involves carelessness. And to define an event, such as the absence of permission, as a circumstantial element of a crime is to say that part of what makes the pro-scribed behavior wrongful is that it was not properly restrained; the agent, for instance, did not take the absence of permission to be a sufficient reason not to act in a way which, in the end, damaged something. Defects in agency, defects in carefulness, and defects in restraint are different from one another. The question, then, about whether to define the relevant events as acts, results, or circumstances depends on what combination of these defects we are trying to minimize and punish.

To determine, then, what is involved in successful completion of a particular crime, we first identify the elements of the crime and classify each as act, result, or circumstance. For each act element (for example, killing), we find that there are three conditions involved in success: that the relevant event occurred (for example, a death), that the event was caused by the defendant, and that the agency-involvement factor was present. For each result element we have the first and second of these conditions, but not the third; and for each circumstan-tial element we have the first condition only. The conjunction of all of these conditions might be called "C's components": they are the full set of conditions involved in the successful completion of C. Analysis of our ordinary concepts of action rarely allows for a comparable degree of precision, since their application is not guided in the same way by prosecutorial burdens. This implies that often the question of whether a person is trying to act in some ordinary sense is often less easily answered than the question of whether he is trying to commit a crime. It is sometimes less easily answered, since it is sometimes less clear what success involves in the ordinary case than in the legal.

## 3. Intention-based Commitments: Content and Role

Attempts include intentions because intentions constitute commitments of just the sort that are involved in trying; this is the upshot of the positive argument for the claim that trying involves intention offered in chapter 2. But what is one committed to in virtue of having an intention? As we will see, there are two importantly different kinds of commitments of a person who has an intention: those deriving from the content of the intention, and those deriving from the proper motivational role of the intention. The commitment here is not a distinct attitude from the intention. Rather, to be committed to X is to be subject to a variety of norms of rationality—it is, for instance, to be criticizably irrational for possession of a belief that not-X, and to be criticizably irrational for failing to form an intention for, and thus a commitment to the occurrence of, those conditions that one believes to be necessary for the occurrence of X. A person who is subject to such norms owes an explanation for violation. He might provide such an explanation by citing the goods that he achieves by, for instance, intending something that he believes he will fail to accomplish, but, nonetheless, he is committed to that which he intends in virtue of the fact that he is subject to such norms, and owes such explanations. The distinction between commitments deriving from an intention's content and those deriving from its proper causal role requires substantial elaboration.

## 3.1 Content-based Commitments

Although it has its limits, there is an analogy between intentions and pictures. A picture has a variety of qualities—it hangs in a certain museum, it was created on a certain day, it consists of paint on canvas inside a frame—but among its most important qualities are its representational qualities: it represents, for instance, a man and a woman sitting at a bar with a glass of absinthe. The discussion here is guided by a realist view of intention under which intentions are as real as pictures. They are states of the mind, almost certainly with neural correlates, with a variety of properties, including, but not exhausted by, their representational qualities. Intentions, that is, have features in virtue of which they represent certain events or states of affairs. If we were to try to build a creature that has not had an intention, we would need to dedicate a part of the creature to, among other things, represent events and states of affairs. That which an intention represents is what will be termed the intention's "content".

It is well known by philosophers of language that, when expressed in ordinary language, there is often ambiguity as to what, exactly, a statement about a person's intention is saying about that intention's content.

(1) He intends to enter the house on the corner.

is ambiguous between the following two sentences:

(1a) He intends to enter the house, and intends that the house that he enters is on the corner.

(1b) He intends to enter the house, and the house he intends to enter is on the corner.

The person described in (1a) intends to enter a house, but the world would not come to match his intention if it turned out that the house he enters is not (perhaps as he thought) on the corner. (Perhaps if he does not enter the house *on the corner* he fails to signal his confederates as he plans to.) By contrast, the man described in (1b) will succeed in doing what he intends even if the house that he enters is not on the corner. He is aiming to enter a house which is, in fact, on the corner, but that fact is not part of what he aims to realize in having the intention that he has. To avoid ambiguity of this kind, it is helpful when writing of intention to place the content of an intention in square brackets so that (1a) and (1b) can be represented, respectively, like so:[11]

(1a′) He intends [to enter the house on the corner].
(1b′) He intends [to enter the house] on the corner.

Notice that the content of an intention can be expressed using "to". This is not true of the contents of many other attitudes, such as belief, much less of many content-bearing entities, such as pictures. Nobody believes [to p]; instead they believe [that p]. However, intentions, like beliefs, can take "that"-clauses. A person can intend [to kill] or he can intend [that a person is killed]. When a person's intention is best expressed using the word "to" this implies that the content of the intention will not match the world unless it comes to pass that *the person himself* performs the action described in the intention. I might intend [that you act], but if that is the case then the content of my intention cannot be expressed using "to".[12] If I intend [to cause you to act], my intention will not match the world unless you act, but it will also fail to match the world if you act on your own without being caused to do so by me. So, even in this case, my intention will not match the world unless the act described—namely the act of *causing you to act*—is performed by me. The content of an intention [that Y] matches the world when Y is true. In this way (although not in other ways) it is the same as a belief [that Y] or a hope [that Y]. So, an intention [to X] could be understood as a particular species of intention [that Y]: they are intentions [that I X].[13]

Thanks to its content, an intention [to X] constitutes a commitment to the occurrence of X and to the presence of the agency-involvement factor in X's occurrence. (As we will see, thanks to its proper causal role, such an intention also constitutes a commitment to causing X.) By contrast, thanks to its content, an intention [that X] constitutes only a commitment to the occurrence of X, and not a commitment to the presence of the agency-involvement factor in X's occurrence. Someone who intends [to give a toast at dinner] is committed both to a toast being given, and to its being given in such a way as to make it true that *he* gives a toast. By contrast, someone who intends [that a toast is given at dinner] is committed to a toast being given, but need not be committed to giving a toast himself. The person with the *to* intention might be under rational pressure to, for instance, request that the master of ceremonies call on him when the moment comes. By contrast, the person with the *that* intention might

---

[11] This notation is used, also, by R. A. Duff. See Duff (1996), 6.

[12] There are those who think that an intention that someone else act is an impossibility; we can only intend our own actions, they say. See, for instance, Baier (1997), Stoutland (1997); Velleman (1997). For a response, see Bratman (1999b).

[13] For a general defense of the very idea of *that* intention, see Vermazen (1993).

be under rational pressure to, for instance, encourage someone else to make a toast, or, if nobody is willing, to do it himself. So intentions *that* often place agents under rational pressure to form intentions *to*, but they do not, in and of themselves, and thanks to their content, constitute commitment to *doing* anything. (As we will see, thanks to their proper causal role, they sometimes constitute a commitment to causing the world to be as they represent.)

In what follows I will say that "X is in an intention's content" or that "X is intended", just in case the relevant intention is either an intention [to X] or an intention [that X]. It is common for a condition to be in an intention's content because the content of the intention is a complex condition that includes it and more. The death of someone or something is in the content of an intention [to kill]; that another person fails to give consent is in the content of an intention [to have non-consensual sex]; that the building that one burns is a residence is in the content of an intention [that a residence burns]. To say that the condition is in the intention's content, then, is not to imply anything about *how* exactly it is in that content, but only that it is included in the often complex condition that is intended *to* or intended *that*. To say that X is in an intention's content is to imply that the agent has one of two importantly different commitments: a commitment to an action or a commitment to the world's being a certain way.

## 3.2 Role-based Commitments

The content of an intention is distinct from the intention's function, what we might refer to equivalently as its proper causal role. Analogously, the picture might play the role of filling empty wall space, not to mention the role of occupying the attention of the museum's visitors. The picture's role is quite different from its representational content. Its *proper* causal role differs also from the roles that it might in fact play, as when, for instance, it plays the role of a doorstop. An intention's primary, but not sole, function is to make it the case that its content matches the world. This distinguishes intentions from beliefs, hopes, or even desires. While these other states may, on occasion, cause it to be the case that the world matches their content—such is the case, for instance, in certain forms of self-fulfilling wishful thinking—it is not their *function* to do so; they are not failing to function well when they fail to cause the world to be as they describe. So, an intention [that Y] has the function of making it the case that the world is Y; an intention [to X] has the function of making it the case that the agent who has that intention performs an action, namely X-ing.

The distinction between content and causal role is nicely illustrated by well-known cases of "deviant causation". A man intends [to run over Victim] and so backs out of his driveway in order to find Victim and run him over. But unbeknownst to the man, Victim is passing by and is run over by the man as he backs out of the driveway.[14] Did the world come to match the content of the man's intention? Yes: he ran over Victim. But we recognize that something implicated in saying that the man intends [to run over Victim] has not come to pass: it is not the case that the intention to run over Victim functioned properly in bringing it about that its content matched the world. The intention caused the result that it represented, but it is not thanks to the fact that the intention functioned properly that it is true that the man ran over Victim.[15]

There is a difference between the content of an intention [to X] and the content of an intention [that Y]. But is there also a difference in the proper causal role of these intentions? No. Whatever an intention's content, it plays its proper causal role only if it causes the world to match its content: that's the main thing an intention is *supposed to do*. There is more to proper causal role than this, as the deviant causation cases show: they are cases in which there is causation by the intention of the conditions, thanks to which its content matches the world, but the intention fails to play its proper causal role. What constraints must a causal chain that begins with the intention and ends with the world matching its content meet if it is to be an instance in which the intention plays it proper causal role? This is a very difficult question for which I do not have a complete answer, and I do not have an answer that "solves" cases of deviant causation.[16] Still, more can be said about the proper causal role of an intention, and more is required for what follows.

A properly functioning intention causes it to be the case that the world comes to be as it represents *by* playing a role in coordinating the agent's behavior over time and in coordinating the agent's behavior with the behavior of others. As we saw in chapter 2, following Michael Bratman, this implies that intentions, unlike other attitudes such as desires and hopes, are governed by a particular set of norms of rationality. An intention is not rational, for instance, if the agent believes that he will not do as he intends. An agent with an intention who violates this norm has trouble coordinating with his future self and with others and so, in turn, has

---

[14] The earliest appearance of this example of which I know is in Chisholm (1964), 617.

[15] Some take a different moral from such cases. They take such cases to show that an intention [to X] is actually an intention [to X intentionally]. (e.g. Wilson (1989), 270). Thus, they conclude that in this example the world has not actually come to match the content of the man's intention: he ran over Victim, but not intentionally, as he intended. As I see it, this line of thought involves two claims, one of which I accept and the other of which I reject (as indicated in the main text below). The first claim is that to perform an act intentionally is for that act to bear a certain special relation to an appropriate intention; I accept this. The second is that the relation that an act must bear to an intention for the act to be intentional must be included in the content of the intention if the act is to be intentional; this I deny. In the main text I put this point by saying that the proper causal role of an intention need not be included in the intention's content. See chapter 6 for related discussion.

[16] In the typical case, when an intention [to X] properly causes it to be the case that the agent X's, it is also true that the agent *X's intentionally*. Similarly, in the typical case, when an intention [that Y] properly causes it to be the case that there is a Y, it is also true that the agent *causes Y intentionally*, although it may be true neither that the agent Y'd intentionally nor even that he Y'd. Doubtless, however, there are untypical cases too.

trouble making the world match his intention. So part of what an intention does when it functions properly is to influence what other mental states an agent has. A properly functioning intention, for instance, excludes a belief to the effect that the world will never come to match the intention's content. But this is not all that a properly functioning intention does. It also imposes structure on the deliberations of the agent who has it.

We can see that intentions impose structure on further deliberations by considering commonplace examples: a rational person who intends this morning to buy milk this afternoon doesn't deliberate this morning about how to go about getting milk this evening; it would be irrational to do so. Nor does he deliberate about whether to do things this morning that would (relative to his beliefs) preclude the possibility of his getting milk this afternoon. He deliberates about what to do tonight under the assumption that he will have already gotten milk this afternoon, and he deliberates about what to do this morning under the assumption that he will be getting milk this afternoon.

Our purposes here will not require greater precision about the way in which intentions structure deliberation than the identification of two different ways in which they do so. First, a person with an intention is under pressure not to consider, when deliberating, courses of conduct incompatible (relative to his beliefs) with the conduct he intends. And, secondly, such a person is under pressure to reach certain conclusions about what to do when he deliberates. Following Bratman, we can capture the first sort of pressure by saying that intentions "filter options" for consideration in deliberation: if you intend [to X], then you must not consider courses of conduct that are incompatible with your performing X. This does not imply that you consider only courses of conduct in which you do X; some courses of conduct are neutral with respect to the question of whether or not you X. To violate this demand is to waste deliberative effort. One of the benefits that we gain from the formation of intention is the simplification of our further deliberations: if you intend to do something then there are fewer courses of conduct to consider in future deliberations, for you need not (in fact, ought not) consider courses of conduct incompatible with what you already intend. A standard example of the second sort of pressure, pressure regarding what conclusions to reach in deliberation, derives from the need for means-end coherence in one's intentions: if you intend [to X], then you must decide to take the means to X-ing, and you must decide to perform acts that are required, in addition to X, in order to reach the end that X serves.

An intention places these kinds of pressures on the agent who has it; an agent with an intention falls short of rationality if he fails to comply with these pressures.[17] But such an agent's intention thereby fails to play its proper causal role. So, for our purposes, the following is true:

---

[17] The form of rationality at issue here is what is referred to in chapter 2 as "attitudinal rationality".

An intention plays its proper causal role *only if* (1) It non-deviantly causes it to be the case that the world matches the content of the intention, (2) It causes the agent to revise his mental states so as to comply with the rationality conditions on intention, and (3) It structures deliberation by (a) causing the agent to refrain from considering acts incompatible with what he intends and (b) causing him to decide to perform acts believed by him to be necessary to the world's coming to be as he intends.

This is expressed as a necessary condition on proper causal role because, as we will see in chapter 5, there are a class of intentions that place agents under rational pressures not yet described here. Such intentions play their proper causal role only if they cause agents to comply with these special pressures. In fact, there may be more pressures yet, even beyond those identified here and those discussed in chapter 5. But it is only those necessary conditions on proper causal role identified here that need concern us.

Earlier in this section it was said that there are two kinds of commitments of a person with an intention: there is that which he is committed to in virtue of the intention's content, and there is that which he is committed to in virtue of the intention's proper causal role. We can now see better what this actually means. A person who intends [to X] is not just committed to X's occurrence and to the presence of the agency-involvement factor in X's occurrence: these are the things that he is committed to thanks to the content of his intention. But he is also committed to all of the various things that would be true were his intention to play its proper causal role. After all, the commitments in question amount to subjection to norms of rationality, and a person who has an intention would be irrational were his intention to fail to cause any of the various things that are involved in its proper causal role. Therefore, a person with an intention is committed to each of the three things that are described above as necessary conditions of the intention's playing its proper causal role. He is committed, that is, to his intention's non-deviantly causing the world to be a certain way. He is also committed to revising his mental states when necessary to comply with norms of rationality governing intention. And he is committed to deliberating in a certain way in order to comply with other such norms.

Consider those things that are true when an agent's intention plays its proper causal role. I have said that these are things that the agent is committed to occurring. But is it wrong to say that they are things *that the agent intends?*[18] After all, all the same norms of rationality that apply to an agent in virtue of those things that are in the content of his intention apply to him with respect to those things that are true when his intention plays its proper causal role; this is the force of saying that *he is committed* to both. Add to this the further view, taken for granted in chapter 2, that applicability of such norms in virtue of the possession of an attitude is sufficient for that attitude to be an intention, and it

---

[18] Thanks to Randy Clarke and Alfred Mele, among others at Florida State University, for a very helpful discussion of this question.

appears that the commitment to what is true when an intention plays its proper causal role simply amounts to an intention in favor of those things. In fact, I believe this is correct: those conditions that are true when an intention plays its proper causal role are also intended. However, to indiscriminately refer to both the conditions that are in the content of an intention with content X, and those that are true when the intention plays its proper causal role *as intended* is to risk implying that it matters to what follows which of the following views is correct: when a person intends [X] there is (a) one intention with the content X that constitutes a commitment to, among other things, all those things that are true when it plays its causal role, or (b) two intentions, one with the content X and another intention [that the intention play its proper causal role], or (c) one intention [X & that this intention plays its proper causal role].[19] In what follows, I will speak as though (a) is true, but, in fact, for our purposes it matters not at all which of these three things is the best way of characterizing the situation. What matters is only what a person with an intention [to X] is committed to, and not where to draw the line, if anywhere, between the contents of our intentions and the contents of our commitments. Everything to follow that is said in a way that is consistent with (a) could be said in a way that is, instead, consistent with either (b) or with (c).

## 3.3 *The Commitment Criterion*

The Commitment Criterion is intended to capture the idea that to be trying to do something, a person must have an intention-based commitment to each of the components of success. For the Commitment Criterion to capture this idea, the conditional in the second disjunct— "If D's intention plays its proper causal role, then Ei"—must be understood to be asserting a logical implication. It is to be interpreted, that is, as true just in case in every possible world in which the intention plays its proper causal role, Ei is also present. Hence a person who intends [to seriously injure Victim] is not attempting murder under the Guiding Commitment View, for Victim's death is not in the content of D's intention, and there are possible worlds in which the defendant's intention plays its proper causal role in bringing it about that Victim is seriously injured, but Victim does not die. As long as Ei is not included in X, and not logically necessary given that the intention plays its proper causal role, then, under this position, the agent fails to have the intention-based commitment to Ei needed for an attempt.

---

[19] There's a lively debate over issues in this neighborhood. See Bratman (2007a), Bratman (2007b), Bratman (2007c), Davis (1984), Donagan (1987), 88, Harman (1976), Harman, (1986) ch. 8, Harman, (2000), Mele (1992), ch. 11, Mele (1999), Searle (1983), Velleman (1989), Wilson (1989), 270.

The Commitment Criterion in the Guiding Commitment View is the position's heart. To see in what sense this is so, consider the following remark made by H. L. A. Hart:

In…attempts the *actus reus* is not…directly identified but is indirectly identified by reference to the accused's intention. In such cases, the intention plays a double role: it fixes what is to count as an *actus reus* and is also an element of *mens rea* required for liability. If this double role were objectionable there could be no law of attempt at all.[20]

The distinction between *actus reus* and *mens rea* with which Hart is working here is, roughly, the distinction between what is done, on the one hand, and what attitude the agent has towards what is done, on the other. An accurate description of what is done might include reference to the mental states of the agent in doing it—a person does not lie, for instance, unless he intends to deceive. But what is done almost never turns entirely and exclusively on the agent's mental states—whether he lies, for instance, turns in part on whether what he said was actually false, independently of what he happened to think. By contrast, what attitude a person has towards what he has done—what he thinks he's done, what mental states he acted on in doing it—is determined entirely by his mental states. However, what Hart is noticing is that in the case of trying, the agent's mental states play a much more prominent role in characterizing what he is doing than they do in other cases. To be trying is, in large part, to be in a certain mental state. This is not all that is involved; as the Guiding Commitment View makes clear, one must also be moved by the relevant mental states, or, anyway, by the commitments they constitute. But, still, the heart of trying is the mind of the person who is trying. The Commitment Criterion captures the idea that trying to do something involves having an intention-based commitment to each of the components of success. What our discussion of intention has made clear is just what it is to have such commitments: it is to be subject to a variety of norms of rationality that apply in virtue of the fact that the agent has an intention.

## 4. Guidance

### 4.1 *Motivational Influence and the Completion Counterfactual*

The idea that trying involves more than a commitment to success is motivated by the observation that a person can be committed to something—can have, in fact, an intention-based commitment to it—and not be trying to do it at all. I intend to climb Mount Denali some day. But I am not, currently, trying to do so; after all, I am not in any way moved, at the moment, by that commitment.

---

[20] Hart (1981), 163.

Intention, therefore, is not sufficient for trying. Now, the observation that trying must involve more than just intention tempts one to the position that what distinguishes the two is that the person who tries actually *does* something in furtherance of his intention. But this cannot be quite right. The reason is that, as hinted in chapter 1, it is possible to try to engage in a *basic* action—an action that is performed without any other action being performed on the way to its performance. If that is so, then trying need not, itself, involve any action in furtherance of the intention that it involves. Say, for instance, that raising one's arm is a basic action. Someone who believes this will insist that, although one must first flex one's muscles to raise one's arm, flexing one's muscles is not something *done*—it is not, itself, an action, performed on the way to raising one's arm. Similarly, flexing a muscle requires reception of acetylcholine by the nerve that animates the muscle. That itself requires release of acetylocholine by a presynaptic nerve cell. But neither of these things is an action performed by the agent. If the agent is to raise his arm, things need to happen after he forms the intention to raise it and before the arm is raised—reception of acetylcholine, flex of a muscle, etc.—but none of those things are *actions*, if the raising of the arm is basic. But it is surely possible to try, and fail, to raise one's arm. This is what happens, for instance, when the paralyzed patient does his best to comply with the doctor's instruction to raise his arm. And trying seems, like the reception of acetylcholine, to be something that occurs on the way to success. What should we say about this?

Although the conclusion is not strictly forced, it is natural to say that we learn from this that trying need not be, itself, action.[21] It is certainly possible to try by acting—as when one throws one's shoulder against a door in an effort to open it—but it is also possible to try without acting, as one does who tries to raise his arm but the process goes no farther than, say, the release of acetylcholine by the presynaptic nerve without reception by the postsynaptic nerve animating the muscle (perhaps the acetylcholine receptors in the postsynaptic nerve are blocked).[22] If this is right, then we need an account of "guidance" under

---

[21] The conclusion is not forced since there are two other avenues open. One can deny that anything other than trying is basic action; so, the fact that one can try on the way to raising one's arm while falling short merely shows that raising one's arm is not basic. (Such a position commits one to holding that trying cannot be attempted, an unembarassing result.) Or, in theory, one could deny that the fact that trying is action undermines the status of the raising of one's arm as basic. Such a position would require supplementation with an account of basicness that had this implication, since the usual account—that the doing of which does not require the doing of anything else—does not imply it. For related discussion, see McCann (1998).

[22] Davidson held that an act is a bodily movement that is intentional under some description. See Davidson (1980d). If the release of acetylcholine by the presynaptic nerve is intentional under the description "trying to raise his arm", then that bodily motion (if bodily motion it be) is action, albeit not intentional under the description "release of acetylcholine by the presynaptic nerve". But this is very counterintuitive. Better to resist the claim that trying is always itself action.

which the commitments constituted by an intention can guide one, even if one engages in no action at all thanks to their guidance. Our account of guidance, that is, must not preclude this possibility.

However, things are more complicated yet, for our account of guidance must respect the fact that intentions can have effects without it thereby being the case that the agent is trying to do as intended. Intending to confront a friend who has behaved badly, I tap my finger nervously on the table awaiting his arrival. My tapping is guided *in some sense* by my intention—the explanation for my tapping will require mention of my intention—but it is not thanks to the role that it is playing in animating *that* behavior that I am rightly said to be trying to confront my friend, even if, in fact, I am. We can even fall short of guidance in the relevant sense when the effects of our intention are, themselves, intentional actions, which, arguably, my tapping is not. My intention to climb Mount Denali might cause me to tell you that I have this intention. But even though my confession is guided, again, *in some sense* by my intention, it must not be guided by that intention in the sense that is of relevance to trying, since I am not thereby trying to climb Mount Denali.

From all of this, we are able to reach the following conclusion. There is guidance by one's intention of the sort that is involved in trying just in case one's intention causes something. But we have yet to describe the nature of that which one's intention must cause for guidance. The effects needn't be actions. And the kind of effects of my intention resulting in my tapping my fingers or confessing my intention are not of the requisite sort either, even though they are actions. But then what kinds of effects are of the requisite sort?

The answer is this: *there is guidance by a commitment if and only if the intention that constitutes the commitment non-deviantly causes an event as part of motivating an action that the agent believes will fulfill, or believes will serve as a means to fulfilling, the intention.* This condition is met by the person who performs an act as a means to doing as he intends. The act performed as a means is the event caused by his intention, and it is also the action that his intention motivated and which is believed by the agent to be a means to doing as he intends. However, this condition is also met when the event caused and the action motivated are distinct from one another. The person whose presynaptic nerve releases acetycholine, which is not received by the postsynaptic muscle nerve meets the condition: his intention non-deviantly causes the release of acetycholine while motivating an act that the agent believes will fulfill his intention to raise his arm, namely the act of raising his arm. No matter where we stop the sequence of events caused by an intention, provided that that sequence was launched as part of the role that the intention is playing in motivating action believed by the agent to be useful, either directly or as a means, to fulfilling his intention, we meet this necessary and sufficient condition on guidance by the commitments that the intention constitutes.

It is important to head off some possible misunderstandings about this account of guidance. First, consider a seeming counterexample to the view. A person intends to run a race tomorrow morning and believes that he needs a hearty breakfast if he is going to do so. Seeing that he has no eggs, he heads to the store to buy some. He is motivated to go to the store because he intends to run the race. But he is not, when he is going to the store, trying to run the race. Or, imagine that as he makes his first move towards the store the acetylcholine receptors in a crucial nerve become blocked so although he releases acetylcholine, it does not reach the postsynaptic nerve. In this case, he is that much farther from trying to *run the race*—although he is trying to go to the store. Despite appearances, however, this is not a counterexample to the position offered here. The reason is that what motivates his going to the store is not the intention to run the race, but, instead, the intention to go to the store, an intention that he formed as a result of the fact that he intends to run the race. The account of guidance offered here requires us to identify the intention *on which the agent is beginning to act*. The crucial intention, that is, is the one that is in fact causing, in the normal motivational way, the acts or other events that are involved in guidance. It is not always the case that an agent who acts on an intention to perform a means is thereby acting on an intention to reach an end, *even if he formed the intention to perform the means as a result of his intention to reach the end*. This is the case here, for it is the intention favoring the means that is actually moving him.

Notice, and this is also important, it is *possible*, even in a case such as that just described, to be acting on the intention to reach the end when one pursues the means. A person, for instance, whose act of going to the store is intentional under the description "taking a means to running the race" is acting on the intention to run the race; it is that intention that is motivating him, which is why it contributes its content to a description under which his act is intentional. We thus have a difference between two agents both of whom intend to run the race and both of whom have an intention to go to the store, an intention which is formed because the agent believes going to the store is a means to running the race. One of them is moved by the first intention (and perhaps the second, as well); the other is moved only by the second. So under the account of guidance offered here, the first is guided by the commitments constituted by his intention to run the race, the second is not. Thus, under the Guiding Commitment View, the first is trying to run the race when he goes to the store; the second is not.[23]

The underlying picture here is that there is a distinctive kind of causal role that an intention is playing when it motivates. It must cause something, and it

---

[23] While the distinction here is sharp, one might hesitate to place any normative weight on it. We might object to any view according to which the first of these agents is to be held responsible for some crime while the second is not. The difference between them might not seem to be of the sort that supports a difference in punishment or blame. This concern will be addressed in chapter 8.

must cause it in the way that is distinctive of motivation. It is extremely difficult to specify the necessary and sufficient conditions under which an intention is motivating. What, exactly, is distinctive about its causal role in such cases? I will not try to answer this difficult question here. However, something of importance can be said which bears on the answer, and will be of great importance in part 3 of this book. The distinctive feature of motivation by intention is that, if all goes well, it leads to doing as one intends. The person who is moved by his intention to confess to a friend that he has it, is not *motivated* by his intention, because even when all goes well, the causal sequence launched by the intention does not culminate in his doing as he intends; it culminates, instead, in his confessing that he has the intention. Similarly, the person who is motivated by his intention to take the means to his end, such as the intention to go to the store, but is not motivated by his intention to reach the end, such as the intention to run the race, will, when all goes well, go to the store; he will only run the race when all goes well if he is motivated by his intention to run the race. Put more carefully, when an intention that commits an agent to all the components of C motivates a person D at time t1, then there's a later time t2, such that the following is true:

*The Completion Counterfactual*: If (1) from t1 to t2 D has the ability and the opportunity to C and does not fall prey to "execution failure", and (2) D does not (at least until after t2) change his mind, then D would C.

Clause (1) identifies three different things that can defeat one from doing as one intends when motivated by the intention: one can turn out not to have what it takes to do so (inability), one's circumstances can interfere (inopportunity), or one can simply fail to execute. The last of these is the least familiar. J. L. Austin gives a famous example:

Consider the case where I miss a very short putt and kick myself because I could have holed it. It is not that I should have holed it if I had tried: I did try, and missed. It is not that I should have holed it had conditions been different: that might of course be so, but I am talking about conditions as they precisely were, and asserting that I could have holed it.[24]

The golfer in the example is motivated by his intention to sink the putt and has the ability and the opportunity to do so. He does not change his mind and the intention continues to motivate all the way through the completion of the club's motion. But he does not sink the putt. The problem is one of execution failure.

While it is possible, in the end, that the execution failures are really just a combination of cases in which the agent either lacks ability or opportunity (perhaps they are the cases in which he lacks one or the other, but we can't tell what he lacks), nothing to follow will hang on that. We are motivated by an intention, in the sense that matters, when in the absence of those factors that

[24] Austin (1979), 218n.

defeat motivation from leading to fruition, we succeed. Among the factors that can defeat success is change of mind. Change of mind comes in at least two flavors. One can change one's mind by giving up one's intention entirely, or one can change one's mind by deciding to stop being motivated by one's intention now, while still retaining it. The person who, for instance, walks away from a bank robbery when he sees that the cops are watching changes his mind in the second sense, but not necessarily in the first, since he may continue to intend to rob the bank despite deciding not to do it *now*.

I am advocating, then, the following:

The causal influence of an intention on a person's behavior is *motivational* in the sense of relevance to guidance *if and only if* the Completion Counterfactual is true.

So, to show that a person's intention-based commitments are guiding his behavior, we must show *both* that the intention has had effects on him, and that the causal process that includes these effects is such that the Completion Counterfactual is true.

This is not *an account* of motivation since it does not involve any description of the particular way in which the intention is "animating D's behavior" when it motivates him. Rather, it is a test for determining whether or not the particular way in which the intention animates D's behavior counts as motivating D. It does so count if, and only if, the Completion Counterfactual is true. As we will see in part 3, what this implies is that the truth of the Completion Counterfactual is important and indispensable evidence that the agent is being motivated by his intention, and so it is important and indispensable evidence that he is guided by the commitments that his intention constitutes, and that in turn implies that it is important and indispensable evidence that he is trying to act, as trying is understood under the Guiding Commitment View. Motivation by intention is what is crucial to guidance, but what is crucial to *knowing* if a particular person is motivated by his intention is knowing that the Completion Counterfactual is true. Or, to put the point another way, unless we know that the Completion Counterfactual is true we cannot rule out the possibility that the agent's intention is animating behavior in the way that it does when I tap my fingers awaiting my friend's arrival, or confess my intention to climb Mount Denali. To rule out these non-motivational roles, we need to know if the Completion Counterfactual is true.

## 4.2 *How the Completion Counterfactual Is and Is Not to be Interpreted*

The truth value of counterfactual conditionals, like the Completion Counterfactual, often vary with the accompanying choice of possible worlds in which their antecedents are true. In general, to assess a counterfactual conditional, we consider those possible worlds in which the antecedent is true, and see whether, in those worlds, the consequent is also true. If so, then the counterfactual conditional is true. But, as is well known from the literature on conditionals, we frequently do not consider *all* the possible worlds in which the antecedent is true. Consider the counterfactual conditional, "If Nader hadn't run, then Gore would have won in 2000." One possible world in which the antecedent is true is one in which Gore, also, chooses not to run; in that world, Gore does not win. But it doesn't follow from the fact that such a world exists that the conditional is false. Typically, in assessing the counterfactual conditional, we consider only worlds in which Nader does not run, but Gore does. And there are many further limitations, too: we limit ourselves, for instance, to worlds in which the election rules in the United States are as they actually are, to worlds in which Gore's campaign was run roughly as well as it was actually run, and so on. We limit ourselves, in short, to the consideration of possible worlds similar to the actual world and in which the antecedent holds.

But how similar to the actual world, and in what ways, must a possible world in which the antecedent of the Completion Counterfactual is true be, in order to merit consideration? To see why the problem is pressing, imagine someone who is trying to kill another, points a gun at his head and misses. Imagine, further, that this defendant is very squeamish: he would not adopt any means to killing the other that risked getting blood on his clothes. So, there are possible worlds in which the defendant has the ability and opportunity to kill the victim with a knife, does not suffer from "execution failure", and does not change his mind, but does not kill the victim, since to take the means available to him in that possible world he would have to risk getting blood on his clothes. If the existence of such possible worlds showed the Completion Counterfactual to be false, there would be a very serious problem for the view of guidance proposed here. After all, this is plainly a case in which the defendant is guided by his intention-based commitments. The solution to the problem is this: the possible worlds just described are not among those that need to be considered in determining whether the Completion Counterfactual is true.

Why not? The answer is that we must limit the relevant possible worlds at least to those in which the act that will serve for completion of the crime has just the same support by reasons as the act that the defendant actually performed. If the defendant takes himself to have a reason not to perform an act that will risk getting blood on his clothes, and he did not expect that anything he was actually doing involved such a risk, then in considering possible worlds in which he has ability and opportunity to complete the crime, we must limit ourselves to worlds in which he can do so without risking blood on his clothes. The hypothetical acts that would suffice for completion must be matched to the defendant's actual behavior in their rational support. The route to completion available in the relevant possible worlds must be no less rational, relative to the agent's beliefs, than the behavior animated by his intention.

This is not simply an ad hoc limitation designed to avoid counterexamples such as that of the would-be killer who is squeamish about blood. We are trying to determine if the defendant is motivated by his intention to commit the crime. So we need to see whether the causal influence of that intention is of the sort that would lead to commission of the crime in hospitable circumstances. But to discover that it would not lead to commission of the crime in circumstances in which there were reasons not to commit it that are absent in the actual world is not to make any progress on our guiding question. The fact that the agent would not commit the crime in such circumstances is irrelevant to the question of whether he is being motivated by his intention to do so in the actual circumstances, in which such reasons are absent. The goal that we are trying to reach by assessing the Completion Counterfactual—the goal of determining if the criminal intention's influence is motivational—is furthered by limiting our gaze to possible worlds in which the road to completion is no rougher, in his mind, than the road that the defendant is actually traveling. (As we will see, this view of the proper way to limit the class of possible worlds to consider in assessing the Completion Counterfactual will be of some importance to the argument of chapter 9.)

There are a set of cases, in addition, that indicate that further restrictions on the relevant set of possible worlds are warranted when assessing the Completion Counterfactual. Consider someone who has an aversion to getting blood on his clothes so powerful that he will not choose to do as he intends if the required means will result in his getting blood on his clothes; however, unlike the person just discussed, this agent takes his aversion to be completely irrational. He sees himself as having no reason whatsoever to avoid getting blood on his clothes. But, nonetheless, he will not elect any course of conduct, no matter how much reason he takes himself to have to engage in it, if it will lead to his getting blood on his clothes. Thus, there is a possible world in which he has the ability and the opportunity to complete the murder by stabbing and does not complete it, despite the fact that the stabbing is just as supported and opposed by reasons as the shooting that he performed in the actual world. Now in this case, we have an explanation for his failure in the possible world in question that does not impugn the hypothesis that the influence of his intention on his actual conduct is motivational. We recognize, that is, that someone motivated by an intention to kill might nonetheless not be motivated to do something else that would also lead him to kill; in this case, he has an aversion that defeats that intention from continuing to motivate in this alternate circumstance. In general, then, the fact that a defendant does not complete the crime in a possible world in which the antecedent of the Completion Counterfactual is satisfied does not show, all by itself, that the Completion Counterfactual is false. If the failure to complete is explained in a way that does not show the influence of the criminal intention not to be motivational, then the possible world in question is not one of those that needs to be considered in assessing the Completion Counterfactual. The point, in short, is that so long as we recall why we care about the Completion Counterfactual—again, it helps us to see if the intention is motivating when it animates the defendant's behavior—we are not likely to be misled. Some possible worlds in which the antecedent is satisfied and the consequent is not show the Completion Counterfactual to be false and some do not. The relevant question is whether the existence of such possible worlds speaks to the claim that the intention is not motivating in the actual world. Differences between what the agent would need to do to complete the crime in the possible world and what he was doing in the actual, may support excluding that possible world from consideration when assessing the Completion Counterfactual.

For similar reasons, extraneous evidence supportive of the Completion Counterfactual might not serve to support the claim that the intention's influence is motivational. Consider, for instance, a supernaturally fully resolute being: such a person always, without exception, does what he intends. We therefore know that, given that he is fully resolute and intends to C, he will C in all possible worlds in which he is fully resolute and has the ability, opportunity, and does not change his mind. But can we conclude from this that such a being is actually motivated by his intention in the actual world, at the moment that concerns us? No. He might have an intention to do something far in the future that does not require any conduct on his part now. In this case, every possible world which shares with the actual the agent's resoluteness is an irrelevant possible world: his resoluteness defeats any inference that we might make about the nature of his intention's influence on his conduct. Given that he is fully resolute in a particular possible world we cannot conclude from the fact that he completes the intended crime in that world that the intention either is, or is not, influencing his conduct in the distinctively motivational way. The result: possible worlds in which we hold fixed his resoluteness are not among the relevant possible worlds.

In general, in assessing the Completion Counterfactual we consider all and only those possible worlds in which its antecedent is satisfied *and in which there are no contributors to the agent's completion and non-completion that prevent us from making inferences about the nature of the particular way in which the intention is animating the agent's conduct.* If the agent completes the intended crime in all of those possible worlds, then he is guided by the commitments constituted by his intention, and so is trying to commit the crime.

## 5. The Legally Relevant Sense of Trying

### 5.1 *Describing What We Are Trying to Do*

One of the lessons of the fact that we criminalize attempts under the Transfer Principle is that someone who tries to do something has engaged in wrongdoing of the sort that warrants criminalization just in case he has tried *to C*, where C is a crime. That is, what makes an attempt wrongdoing of the sort that is relevant to the criminal law is that it is an attempt *to commit a crime*; other sorts of failed attempts are not instances of wrongdoing warranting criminalization. But what must be true for it to be warranted to enrich our description of what a person is trying to do with reference to all of the various conditions involved in the completed crime? The question concerns the descriptions that we attach to tryings: what can and cannot be appealed to to correctly characterize what a person is trying to do?

The Guiding Commitment View provides an answer. Under it, there are two situations in which we are warranted in enriching our description of what the agent is trying to do with reference to a particular condition: (1) when the person has an intention-based commitment to that condition and is guided by that commitment, or, (2) the condition is realized when all that the agent is committed to comes to pass, but the condition is not itself a component of success. It is probably clear why we can enrich our description with reference to a condition under (1), but it may be less obvious why we can do so under (2). The reason is that when (2) is met, appealing to the condition to describe the act that the agent is trying to perform does not imply that the agent has an intention-based commitment to the condition; rather, citing the condition is just a way of directing attention to the set of components of success that do not include it, but happen to accompany it. To illustrate, consider a would-be mercy-killer who intends [to kill] and believes falsely that mercy killings are not prohibited. The Guiding Commitment View allows us to say that this person is attempting *murder*. Since this person is committed by his intention to killing, and is guided by that commitment, we are warranted in describing what he is trying to do with reference to killing, as we do in this case. But it is also true that were the conditions his intention commits him to to come to pass—were he to kill—he would have performed a prohibited act. Hence, we are warranted in describing what he is trying to do with reference to the fact that the act is prohibited, as we do when we say that he is attempting *murder*. Since the act's being prohibited is a feature of a completed murder, but is not a component of the crime—it need not be shown beyond a reasonable doubt by the prosecution—the defendant need not be committed to it by his intention, as the would-be mercy killer is not, in order to be said to be attempting the crime. However, since it is nonetheless a feature of that which he is committed to realizing, it can be appealed to in describing what he is trying to do.

Notice that the Guiding Commitment View's account of the conditions under which we can enrich our description of what a person is trying to do with reference to a condition is not the only possible account, by any means. In fact, the Guiding Commitment View stands between two extremes. In a very strict sense, what might be called the "narrow" sense, what a person is trying to do is determined entirely by the content of the intention that he has in trying to do it. Someone who intends [to hit that man] is trying to hit that man. In the narrow sense, he is not trying to hit the president, even if the man he is trying to hit is the president. In fact, in the narrow sense, he is not trying to hit the president even if *he knows* that the man he intends to hit is the president. To try to hit the president, in the narrow sense, he would need to intend [to hit the president].[25] The narrow sense of trying differs from the Guiding Commitment View at least in this: under the Guiding Commitment View, and not in the narrow sense, what would be true were the agent's intention to play its proper causal role can be legitimately appealed to to characterize what he is trying to do, even if it is not included in the intention's content.

The Guiding Commitment View and the narrow sense of what a person is trying to do do not exhaust the ordinary ways in which we attach descriptions to what a person is trying to do. In what might be called the "broad" sense, what a person is trying to do is what he would in fact do were the world to come to match his intention as a result of the intention playing its proper causal role. In the broad sense, a person might be trying to hit the secretary of the treasury, even though she intends [to hit the president], if she swings at the secretary of the treasury in the mistaken belief that he is the president. She is trying to hit the secretary of the treasury, in the broad sense of "trying", for were she to hit the man at whom she swings she would hit the secretary of the treasury.

Neither the narrow nor the broad sense is the one which is relevant to the legal context. Consider, again, the would-be mercy killer who believes mercy killing to be legal. He is attempting a prohibited killing, even if he believes that the killing he is attempting is not prohibited. So much for the narrow sense. We are, at least, allowed to enrich our description of what a person is trying to do through appeal to what is, in fact, prohibited and so we can go beyond what appears in the content of her intention. As just indicated, this is implied by the Guiding Commitment View. Like the Guiding Commitment View, the broad sense can accommodate this example: were the mercy killer to do as he intends, he would do something prohibited, and so we are licensed, under the broad sense of trying, to refer to what he is trying to do as *murder*.

The broad sense, however, is no closer than the narrow to the legally relevant sense. A person who intends [to take that car] while falsely and reasonably

---

[25] Some are attracted to the view that the person who intends [to hit that man] and knows that that man is the president is actually *intending* [to hit the president]. To hold such a view is to say that the content of our intentions is determined, in part, by the content of our other attitudes, such as our beliefs (at least when those beliefs amount to knowledge). (Such a thought is probably related to the use of the term "oblique *intention*" to refer to the attitude one has to that which one expects to occur as a result of what one intends, and to the misleading slogan that "a man intends the natural consequences of his acts".) But this understanding of the content of an intention elides mental contents of distinctly different sorts. There is such a thing as intending [to hit that man] while merely foreseeing that one would thereby hit the president, and *not* intending [to hit the president]. For such a person, the successful execution of the intention does not depend on the man being the president. On the narrow view of trying, then, such people are not trying to hit the president.

believing that he has permission to take it, is not attempting to steal a car, even though he would indeed steal it—that is, take it without permission—were he to do as he intends. So much for the broad sense. We cannot in general enrich our description of what a person is trying to do with reference to facts that he is not committed by his intention to obtaining. And, in fact, we are barred from doing so under the Guiding Commitment View. In this case, the lack of permission is one of the components of the completed crime, and so we are licensed by the Guiding Commitment View to appeal to it in describing what the agent is trying to do only if the agent is committed by his intention to that condition and is guided by that commitment. The agent in the example is not, and hence cannot be described as trying *to steal*.

What we have learned then, is that at least to a first approximation, the Guiding Commitment View characterizes what a person is trying to do in a way that harmonizes with the way in which we need to characterize that in criminal law. This is one argument in its favor.

## 5.2 A Further Argument for the Guiding Commitment View

As the existence of both the narrow and the broad senses of trying makes clear, the term "try" is not univocal. We use it in various ways in different circumstances. There is more than one "ordinary" or "common-sense" notion expressed by the term. What is important for our purposes, however, is to identify the notion that is particularly crucial for the assessment of criminal responsibility. In particular, we need an account of what it is to try which labels as "trying to commit C" all and only those tryings that are justifiably criminalized under the Transfer Principle. So, we need to label as "trying to commit C" all and only those tryings that are justifiably criminalized if C is justifiably criminalized. The Guiding Commitment View meets this requirement. To show this, we need to show that the argument for the Transfer Principle offered in chapter 1 goes through when "trying to C" is equated with "counts as trying to C under the Guiding Commitment View". It suffices to show, that is, that if trying is conceived of as suggested in the Guiding Commitment View, then the Transfer Principle is true for the reasons offered in chapter 1.

A crucial premise in the argument for the Transfer Principle offered in chapter 1 is the claim that the person who attempts the crime is recognizing and responding to reasons in the same, or a worse way than the person who completes the crime. In fact, this is true under the Guiding Commitment View. After all, to explain what reason a person would have not to complete a crime, we need to appeal to the complex of conditions involved in the completion of that crime. But if there is a legal reason not to realize that complex of conditions, then there is a legal reason not to have a set of commitments that amount to a commitment to realizing that complex. This is precisely the set of commitments held by the person who is attempting to C, under the Guiding

Commitment View. However, to hold those commitments that one has legal reason not to hold, given that one has legal reason not to C, is not yet to try: one must also be moved by those commitments. This fact plays a crucial role in the justification of the Transfer Principle offered in chapter 1. Under that justification, it is only because trying has, in common with completion, guidance by one's commitments that some tryings are justifiably sanctioned when some completions are. This implies that there are no behaviors that are rightly criminalized under the Transfer Principle as tryings to C, and that also fail to count as such under the Guiding Commitment View. The Guiding Commitment View labels as tryings to C exactly those tryings that are criminalized as such under the Transfer Principle.

There are, then, principled reasons for accepting the Guiding Commitment View of trying to act. If attempts are criminalized through appeal to the Transfer Principle, then what counts as an attempt must be such that it is legitimate to criminalize it under that principle. The fact that the Guiding Commitment View meets this requirement counts in its favor, although nothing said here rules out the possibility that another incompatible view of trying would also meet it.

## 6. Conclusion

While the Guiding Commitment View formalizes an intuitively appealing conception of trying to act, it is also important that it be grounded in a theory of mind and action. Intuitive plausibility is of very little worth in the absence of such supporting architecture. What I hope to have demonstrated in this chapter is that the intuitively plausible picture that underlies the Guiding Commitment View sits easily with a defensible theory of intention aligned with and inspired by Michael Bratman's, and with a defensible theory of motivation. The fact that the Guiding Commitment View is supported by these theories is an argument, of sorts, in its favor that can be added to the arguments advanced in section 5. Still, as indicated in the introduction, a more powerful argument for the Guiding Commitment View derives from its capacity to help us to find principled grounds on which to solve either correctly, or at least not incorrectly, puzzling problems concerned with attempted crimes. Its capacity to do this will be demonstrated over the course of the remainder of this book.

# APPENDIX: A COMPETING CONCEPTION OF TRYING

Thomas Pink has accused many philosophers of failing to recognize the distinction between decision, on the one hand, and what he calls "conation", or trying, on the other.[1] For Pink, decision is a distinctive exercise of agency that produces action through, as he puts it, "motivation-perpetuation".[2] Our decisions, that is, produce action by first producing intentions, or other pro-attitudes, that persist and cause the actions decided upon. By contrast, to try is to exercise one's agency in a different way. It is to generate action without producing any motivational mental state that leads to that action. As Pink puts it,

Deciding to raise my arm causes my arm to rise by ensuring that thereafter I am motivated to raise my arm . . . [T]rying causes my arm to rise simply by way of causing nerve impulses and muscle motions.[3]

Deciding is thus an instance of what Pink calls "second-order agency": it is an exercise of agency leading to action by way of further exercises of agency, namely intentions, that it produces. By contrast, trying is an instance of "first-order agency". When a person tries, he brings about action without necessarily first bringing about any other exercises of his agency. Further, Pink seems to hold that trying need not involve, itself, any mental state. He writes,

[C]onations may not be mental events at all. It is a sensible matter for discussion whether attempts at bodily action occur within the mind, or outside it—and whether their status as mental or non-mental is determinable a priori at all.[4]

In the first instance, Pink is here denying that there is an a priori identity between trying and any particular mental state. However, he aims to deny more than just identity. His claim appears to be that, a priori, there is no reason to think that trying involves any mental state at all; it might not consist, even, in some set of mental states plus more.

The first of Pink's claims—that trying is importantly different from deciding—is compatible with the Guiding Commitment View of trying. The Guiding Commitment View implies that trying causes action by causing nerve impulses and muscle motions, and not necessarily by causing further motivational mental states. The second claim, however,

---

[1] Pink (1996). Pink equates conation with trying on p. 52.
[2] E.g. Pink (1996), 264.
[3] Pink (1996), 264.
[4] Pink (1996), 58.

103

is not. Under the Guiding Commitment View, trying necessarily involves a particular mental state—namely an intention—even though there is more to it than that (it also includes guidance by the commitments the intention constitutes). Thus a full defense of the Guiding Commitment View requires engaging with Pink's claim that trying need not involve any mental states at all.

In one sense the issue has already been addressed in chapter 2. Trying necessarily involves intending, since trying's function entails that the trying agent is governed by those very norms that govern an agent with an intention. However, the argument of chapter 2 assumed that trying involves *some* mental state; the question there was only whether the mental state it involves is an intention to complete the action attempted. Why should we think, a priori, that trying involves any mental state at all? Couldn't it be that to try to A is simply to move towards A-ing?

It is possible that what Pink is calling "conation", and equating with trying, is little different from that by virtue of which a person satisfies the Guidance Criterion in the Guiding Commitment View. It is possible, that is, that a person has a conation, in Pink's sense, just in case he is guided by a particular intention-based commitment. If that's correct, then conation, in Pink's sense, is just one part of trying in the sense identified by the Guiding Commitment View. And since it is perfectly sensible to ask whether guidance by one's intention "occur[s] within the mind, or outside it—and whether [its] status as mental or non-mental is determinable a priori at all"—perhaps there are, or perhaps there are not, mental states causally downstream of intention whenever a person is guided by his intention-based commitments—the same applies to conation. However, one then starts to wonder whether the conflict between Pink's position and the Guiding Commitment View is merely verbal. Pink thinks that a person who tries to A intends to A and moves towards A-ing; only the movement towards A-ing is the trying, but the intention is at least a common concomitant of trying. Under the Guiding Commitment View, also, a person who tries to A intends to A and moves towards A-ing, but both are part of the trying to A. Why does it matter whether we say that there are two things here that are (virtually or necessarily) always found together, or one thing with two parts?

For many purposes, it probably does not matter. But when we are discussing responsibility, whether moral or legal, it does. In general, an account of the nature of a wrongful act that includes all and only those features of the act in virtue of which it is wrongful is to be preferred over an account that needs to cite more, or less, than is included in the account of the act in order to explain its wrongfulness. Theft is wrong, in part, because it involves the taking of someone else's property. We can imagine a definition of theft that left this feature out, while admitting that most, maybe even all, "thefts", as so defined, involve it. Such a definition, however, would leave out of the account of theft a feature that is crucial for explaining why theft is wrongful. Similarly, given that our interest (although not Pink's) is with responsibility, we ought to prefer an account of the nature of trying that includes in the account all and only those features of trying in virtue of which it is wrongful (when it is). We ought not to have to appeal to something that goes along with trying, but is not part of it, in order to explain why wrongful trying is wrongful. And it is clear that the intention involved in trying is essential to the explanation for wrongful trying's wrongfulness.

This is true of most, if not all, wrongful conduct—mental state contributes mightily to wrongfulness. But it is doubly clear in the case of trying as one can see when one reflects on the fact that the description that we give to a trying—we describe it as a "trying *to A*", for instance—is determined, in large part, by the intention on which the agent is acting. It is a commonplace, that is, that whether a person buying a screwdriver is trying to fix his car, or trying to kill his roommate, depends on the intention on which he is acting. More is often involved in fixing the appropriate description of a trying than this, as we have seen already, and will see again in chapter 4. But, still, intention matters crucially. Hence, on Pink's view, a feature of a trying that is essential to explaining its wrongfulness, namely that it is performed with a given intention, is not part of what makes it a trying. Such a view may serve Pink's purposes—interested, as he is, in the metaphysics of mind, in the fundamental categories of the psychological states involved in free action—but it does not serve ours, interested as we are in responsibility.

# Part 2

# The Elemental Conception of the Intention in Attempt and Its Implications

# 4

# The Intention in Attempt

## 1. Introduction

Under the Guiding Commitment View of trying, offered in chapter 3, to try to do something is to have a commitment, deriving from one's intentions, to each of the components of success, and to be moved by those commitments. In the case of trying to commit a crime, the components of success are all those conditions that must be shown beyond a reasonable doubt by the prosecution in order to establish guilt for the completed crime. It follows that to attempt a crime, each such condition must be something to which the defendant is committed by his intention. So, it seems clear what intention someone who attempts a crime has: he has an intention that commits him to each of the conditions that must be shown by the prosecution to establish that a defendant committed the completed crime. True as this is, it is expressed at a level of abstraction that makes it difficult to determine precisely what its implications are to various difficult problems that courts face in trying to determine whether or not a defendant's intention is of the sort that is required for an attempt of a particular crime. We need guidance in determining whether or not a particular intention, had by a particular defendant, is such as to commit him to each of the conditions that are involved in the completed crime. This chapter provides such guidance, and thereby articulates what will be called "The Elemental Conception of the Intention in Attempt", which is the conception of the intention involved in attempt implied by the Guiding Commitment View, the conception under which the intention in attempt is an intention that commits the agent to each of the components of completion.

We will proceed here by looking at each of the various kinds of conditions involved in completion and consider, in each case, what intention a defendant needs to have in order to be properly committed to that condition. As we will see, a defendant charged with attempt needs to have a different intention with respect to different kinds of elements of the completed crime. A particular sort of intention will suffice for commitment, for instance, to one of the result elements of the completed crime, but would not suffice were the element in question classified as an act element. One important set of elements of crimes, however, will not be discussed in this chapter, namely circumstantial elements. Discussion of the intention needed in order to be properly committed to a circumstantial element of a crime will be saved for chapter 5, in which the closely related question of whether the circumstantial elements of the completed crime need to actually be in place for the attempt is also discussed. That is, we will discuss in chapter 5 what kind of commitment a defendant needs to have, for instance, to the absence of consent in rape, alongside the question of whether or not an attempted rape requires that the victim be in fact non-consenting.

One conceptual tool that will be used in more than one place in this chapter, and in chapters to come, is the distinction between commission and guilt, mentioned briefly in the introduction to this book. Although it can seem quite counterintuitive until explained, *commission is not required for guilt.*[1] This is clearest in the case of accomplice liability. If A holds Victim while B rapes her, A and B are both guilty of rape. However, in such a case, only B *committed* rape, since rape requires sex and only B engaged in it. Thanks to facts about one's relation to the commission, such as intentionally lending aid, one can be guilty of a crime that one did not commit.[2] As we will see, several potential objections to the Guiding Commitment View's implications about the intention needed for attempt can be overcome by noting that there are good reasons to take someone who falls short of commission of an attempt by the Guiding Commitment View's standards to be nonetheless guilty of one. This will become clearer in what follows.

Section 2 considers the question of what kind of intention-based commitment the attempter must have towards the legal properties of the completed crime—the property of being legally prohibited, for instance, or the property of lacking an affirmative defense. At various times, courts have become confused about this issue, and have asserted that there is no attempted homicide when a person, for instance, tries to kill someone else from the false and unreasonable belief that he is justified in doing so in order to defend himself. Rather, as we will see, there are good reasons to conceive of such a case as one in which a homicide has been attempted, but the attempt is mitigated by the defendant's false and unreasonable beliefs, just as a completed homicide would be. In general, as we will see, the Guiding Commitment View implies that a

---

[1] Douglas Husak draws a distinction between what a person is guilty of and what a person is punished for. See Husak (1996a). Husak's notion of guilt seems to correspond with my notion of commission, and Husak's notion of what a person is punished for seems to correspond to my notion of guilt. Husak holds that a person, for instance, who unintentionally kills a bystander while trying to kill someone else—a classic transferred intent case—is not guilty of murder but is rightly punished for murder. In the terminology to be used here, such a person has not committed murder, but is guilty of it.

[2] For discussion, see Robinson (1984).

commitment with respect to a legal property of completion is required for attempt only if the possession of the legal property by a person's behavior is necessary for commission of the crime. Most legal properties are necessary for guilt, but not for commission.

Section 3 turns to the question of what commitment an attempter must have towards the act and result elements of the completed crime. In the course of discussion of this issue, it is explained when foresight of a result is sufficient for guilt for an attempt, although it is argued that it is never sufficient for commission of an attempt. Section 4 considers what commitment an attempter must have to the mental state elements of the completed crime. A large class of cases in which this issue arises—cases in which the crime cannot be completed with intent—are discussed, not in this chapter, but in chapter 6. It is argued here that in all other cases, however, an intention-based commitment to each of the act, result, and circumstantial elements of the completed crime necessarily involves sufficient commitment to each of the mental state elements of the completed crime. There is, therefore, no additional intention that is needed with respect to the mental states involved in completion in the class of cases under discussion in this chapter.

This chapter draws throughout on the details of the Guiding Commitment View. For reference, therefore, it is helpful to have the view to hand. Here, as before, D is a defendant, C is a crime, X is the content of D's intention, and E1, E2 . . . En are those conditions that must be shown beyond a reasonable doubt for commission of C:

*The Guiding Commitment View*: D attempts C *if and only if* ∀Ei, the following criteria are met:

*Commitment Criterion*: ((Ei is included in X) OR (If D's intention plays its proper causal role, then Ei)), &

*Guidance Criterion*: D is guided by his commitment to Ei.

Recall, also, that the conditional in the second disjunct of the Commitment Criterion is to be interpreted as a logical truth: it is true just in case in every possible world in which its antecedent is true, its consequent is true also. It is shown here that the Guiding Commitment View, which springs, as we have seen, from a plausible and intuitive picture of trying, implies also a plausible and intuitive picture of the mind of the attempter, and of those whose minds are close enough to that of the person who commits an attempt to warrant being held guilty for one, despite falling short of commission.

## 2. The Legal Properties of Completion

The legal properties involved in completed crimes are a diverse lot. They include, for instance, properties of particular objects, such as the property of being on one's land, that are possessed in part in virtue of what the law says:

whether the tree whose trunk is on my neighbor's land, and most of whose branches overhang mine, is "on my land" will depend on what the law says. They include, also, the property of being legally prohibited. Entering a dwelling at night with the intent to commit a felony therein is legally prohibited. That form of conduct possesses that property. But the legal properties do not end there. Also of importance to our purposes are the legal properties of being unjustified and unmitigated. Someone who enters a dwelling at night with the intent to commit a felony therein *in order to prevent a fire* may have a necessity defense. In such a case, his conduct possesses the property of being legally justified. Similarly, someone who intentionally kills another person *with reasonable provocation and in the heat of passion* has engaged in conduct possessing the legal property of being mitigated. We should not expect the diversity of legal properties of completed crimes to be treated uniformly by an account of the commitment involved in attempt. Perhaps some legal properties of completed crimes are things to which defendants need to be committed, and others are not.

## 2.1 *Legal Prohibition*

For a time, although much less frequently now, courts would distinguish between attempts in which completion was "legally impossible" and those in which it was "factually impossible", and would excuse defendants whose attempts fell into the former category. Courts have moved away from this practice, largely because the fact-law distinction is difficult to make out—is the feature of belonging to someone else, for instance, a legal feature or a factual feature of a particular piece of property?—and also because the fact that it was impossible to succeed has come to be seen as insufficient, in itself, for excuse for an attempt, regardless of whether the impossibility in question is "legal" or "factual". Several confusions, undoubtedly, gave rise to the formulation and employment of the distinction between legal and factual impossibility. However, the notion of the legally impossible was designed to excuse a set of defendants who deserve to be excused, albeit not on any grounds having to do with the impossibility of completion: namely, those who falsely believe that what they are trying to do is legally prohibited. (Such cases are sometimes referred to as cases of "pure legal impossibility".) As R. A. Duff puts it, "[A] repentant adulterer who walked into a British police station to give herself up for this supposed crime would be told to go home."[3] And, we can add, she would be sent home that much more quickly if she had merely tried and failed to commit adultery while falsely believing it to be illegal. Although this is certainly true, why is it true? In fact, the result is implied by the Guiding Commitment View.

---

[3] Duff (1996), 93.

The Commitment Criterion in the Guiding Commitment View implies that a person is attempting a crime, in the sense of relevance to criminal responsibility for attempt, only if *there is a crime*, each of the components of which he is committed to by his intention. The adulterer who falsely believes adultery to be a crime fails to meet this condition for, although she is committed to each of the components of adultery, she is not thereby committed to each of the components of any crime, since adultery is not a crime.

Notice, however, that when we describe as "trying to commit a crime" the act of a person who is, under the Guiding Commitment View, trying to C, where C is a crime, we move from the Guiding Commitment View to the broad view of attempt, introduced in chapter 3, under which we are licensed to enrich our description of what a person is trying to do with reference to properties of the act that he would do were he to succeed. We refer to what he is trying to do as "a crime", even though he may not be committed, much less guided by a commitment, to the criminality of the behavior that he aims for. As I suggested in chapter 3, the broad view of attempt, as well as the narrow (according to which what a person is doing is fixed by the content of his intention), is perfectly legitimate in certain contexts. The Guiding Commitment View is not intended to impugn uses of the terms "try" and "attempt" that are inconsistent with it, but, instead, to identify the crucial sense of those terms for criminal responsibility. So it is harmless enough to say that what a person is trying to do is "to commit a crime", so long as we recognize that this fact alone is of no relevance to criminal responsibility. What matters to criminal responsibility is what the Guiding Commitment View tells us matters: there must be some crime C such that the agent is committed to each of the components of C and guided by those commitments, a fact that we sometimes misleadingly register by saying that the agent is "trying to commit a crime".

To see the point here more clearly, notice that one gets puzzled about the repentant attempted adulterer when one reasons like so:

(a) The repentant attempted adulterer is trying to commit a crime.
(b) If someone is trying to commit a crime, then there is some crime C such that he is trying to C.
(c) If there is some crime C such that a person is trying to C, then that person has committed an attempted crime.
(d) ∴ The repentant attempted adulterer has committed an attempted crime.

(c) is true. In fact, it follows from the fact that attempts are criminalized under the Transfer Principle—the principle, discussed in chapter 1, that says that if it is legitimate to criminalize a particular type of behavior, then it is legitimate to criminalize the attempt of it. After all, if attempts are criminalized for this reason, then one is justified in criminalizing an attempt to C if C is, itself, justifiably criminalized. The problem with this line of reasoning, that is, is not its appeal to (c). The problem is that there is no interpretation of "trying to commit a crime" under which both (a) and (b) are true. (a) is true, in the narrow sense of trying, only if the repentant attempted adulterer intends [to commit a crime]. But one can intend [to commit a crime] without it being true that there is some crime C such that one intends [to C]. This is true for just the same reasons that one can intend [to buy a house] without there being any particular house that one intends to buy. On the other hand, if we interpret "trying to commit a crime" under the broad sense of trying, then (a) asserts that there is something that the agent is trying to do that is, in fact, a crime. This is false, since adultery is not a crime (in Britain, where the repentant adulterer tries to commit adultery). So, even if (b) is true under the broad sense—and it is a bit unclear one way or the other—we still do not have an interpretation of "trying to commit a crime" under which both (a) and (b) are true. And, importantly, the Guiding Commitment View does not supply one either. There is a way of construing the repentant attempted adulterer under which (a) is true under the Guiding Commitment View: imagine that the repentant attempted adulterer is committed to having sex with a married partner, and is committed to the criminality of that act. But if this is true, (b) is false under the Guiding Commitment View: its antecedent is true, but its consequent is false since there is no set of conditions that are both involved in a completed crime and things to which the agent is actually committed. The confusion over cases like that of the repentant attempted adulterer arises, in short, from vacillation among various natural ways of interpreting the phrase "trying to commit a crime".

What has been shown so far is that under the Guiding Commitment View, it is possible to attempt a crime without having any commitment with respect to the criminality of the behavior one is committed to, and, conversely, the mere fact that one is committed to the criminality of the behavior to which one is committed does not, thereby, make it true that one is attempting a crime in the sense of relevance to the criminal law. However, there is a class of crimes that requires commitment to their criminality, if they are to be attempted. These are crimes, like certain forms of tax evasion, the commission of which requires the belief that what one is doing is legally prohibited. To underpay on one's taxes *while believing that one is legally required to pay more* is a much more severe offense than is underpaying in the absence of that belief.[4] Where there is a *mens rea* requirement with respect to a condition, as there is here, the condition itself is one of the components of the completed crime. Hence, when the completed crime is one like tax evasion, attempt of it will require an intention-based commitment to its criminality. Since the criminality of behavior in such cases is much like a circumstantial element of a crime—it is certainly not something that needs to be caused by the defendant for completion of the

---

[4] Cf. U.S.C. §7201.

crime—a full treatment of it will have to wait until chapter 5, in which the commitment involved in attempt to the circumstantial elements of completion is discussed. (The relevant issues are discussed in the appendix to chapter 5 where the famous hypotheticals of Lady Eldon and Mr Fact and Mr Law are discussed.)

## 2.2 Unmitigated or Unjustified

The property of being legally prohibited is not the only property of completed crimes that needs to be considered here. Also of importance are the properties of being legally unjustified and unmitigated. For instance, in the case of *State v. Grant* (418 A 2d 154 (Maine 1980)), the defendant claimed that he had tried to kill a man named Nicholson believing that he had to do so in order to repel Nicholson's attack. However, he admitted that his belief that he needed to use deadly force to repel the attack was unreasonable: a reasonable person would have recognized that less than deadly force would have done the trick. Had Grant succeeded in killing Nicholson, his would have been a case of so-called "imperfect self-defense"—a case, that is, in which all the beliefs required for self-defense are present, but since some of them are unreasonable, justification is lacking. Imperfect self-defense mitigates a successful homicide in some, although not most, jurisdictions. Under *Model Penal Code* §3.09(2), what would otherwise be a purposive homicide is treated as a reckless homicide when performed in imperfect self-defense. Many jurisdictions that mitigate for imperfect self-defense classify such homicides as voluntary manslaughters. It thus seems natural to conceive of Grant as having committed an attempted murder that is deserving of mitigation in the same way that a completed murder would be so deserving were it performed in imperfect self-defense. We might then say that his crime is one of attempted reckless homicide, or attempted voluntary manslaughter (depending on which term is used for completed imperfect self-defensive homicides in the jurisdiction in question).

However, two forces press in opposition to this conclusion. First, it is the consensus view that there are no attempted crimes of recklessness or negligence; after all, many have reasoned, attempt requires intent, and crimes of recklessness and negligence are necessarily committed without intent. Hence, although it might make sense to reduce a completed homicide committed in imperfect self-defense to a reckless homicide, one cannot reduce an attempted homicide committed in imperfect self-defense to an attempted reckless homicide without thereby imposing liability for a non-existent crime.[5] We will see in chapter 6 that the consensus view that attempted crimes of recklessness and negligence are impossible is mistaken. However, even if we grant that

---

[5] The court in *People v. Reagan* (99 Ill.2d 238 (1983)) reasoned in just this way.

position, it is ridiculous to object on this ground to treating attempted homicides performed in imperfect self-defense as attempted reckless homicides. Even if an attempted reckless homicide is impossible, we still know how it would be sentenced were it possible. To say that an attempted homicide performed in imperfect self-defense is to be treated as an attempted reckless homicide is simply to say that it is to be sentenced as that crime would be *were it ever committed*; this is perfectly consistent with the assertion that it is impossible to commit it. The mistake here is, at its heart, the confounding of commission and guilt. To say that an attempted homicide of imperfect self-defense is to be punished as an attempted reckless homicide is not to imply that it involves *the commission* of an attempted reckless homicide. After all, a completed imperfect self-defensive homicide is not actually reckless. It is an intentional homicide that is to be punished *as if* it were reckless. Thus to punish someone like Grant as though his crime were an attempted reckless homicide is to imply only that it involves *guilt for* such an attempt on the theory that it was just as bad as such a crime would be were it ever committed.

However, there is a second more pressing ground of opposition to the claim that an attempted homicide performed in imperfect self-defense is an attempted murder deserving of mitigation. The problem is that it seems to distort things to say that the defendant is trying to commit murder. Rather, what seems appropriate to say is that he is trying *to kill in self-defense*. On the assumption that you are committing a crime when you attempt to C *because C is a crime*, it seems that someone who is trying to kill in self-defense is committing no crime at all.

The Guiding Commitment View implies that imperfect self-defensive attempts to kill are *attempts to commit murder*, in one sense of the term "murder" but not in another. To see this, recall the case of the would-be mercy killer, discussed in chapter 3, who attempts to perform a mercy–killing, believing falsely that mercy-killing is legal. It was suggested in chapter 3 that the Guiding Commitment View allows us to say that this defendant is attempting murder, since the quality of being prohibited is a quality that his act would have were he to realize all that he is committed to by his intention, but it is not a component of success. In this sense of the term "murder", to say that a homicide is a murder is to imply that it is prohibited. In fact, it is also to imply that it is unmitigated. Say that, unbeknownst to the would-be mercy killer, mercy-killings are not murders, but manslaughters. In that case, it would be false, in this sense of the term "murder", to describe what he did as an attempted murder. That would be to imply that the homicide he attempted was unmitigated, which it was not, since it was, in fact, a manslaughter that he attempted. In this sense of the term "murder", the attempted homicide performed in imperfect self-defense is not an attempted murder. After all, the quality of being unmitigated is not a quality that the defendant is committed to by his intention, nor is it a quality possessed by the conduct that would come to pass were the defendant to realize his intention-based commitments. It is in this sense of the term "murder" that it sounds wrong to say that the imperfect self-defensive attempt is an attempted murder; it sounds wrong because it is wrong.

There is, however, another sense of the term "murder". In this sense, an act falls under the term just in case all of the components of murder are realized. In this sense of the term, there is no implication that a murder is either prohibited or unmitigated. It is, instead, merely a homicide performed with certain mental states, such as an intention to kill. Even a fully justified self-defensive intentional homicide is, in this sense, a murder. It is in this sense of the term that the imperfect self-defensive attempt is an attempted murder. So, what the Guiding Commitment View implies is that imperfect self-defensive attempts are attempted murders, in this second sense of the term, deserving of mitigation. They are therefore commissions of attempted murder (in the second sense), but those who commit them ought to be held guilty of attempted reckless homicides or attempted voluntary manslaughters (depending on how the corresponding completed crimes are classified).

## 3. Acts and Results

Using the Guiding Commitment View, and in particular the Commitment Criterion, we can determine the content of the intention needed for attempt by working backwards from a list of all the things that are true when an agent completes the crime, and putting all of those into the content of the intention that are not made true merely by the intention playing its proper causal role. If the completed crime requires the act of killing, then the following three things are true when the crime is completed: (1) another person dies, (2) the death is caused by the defendant, and (3) the agency-involvement factor is present. So, we consider each of these in turn.

Must another's death appear in the content of the intention? Say that it does not. Say, for instance, that the defendant intends [that another is badly injured]. Now since the death is not in the intention's content, the first disjunct in the Commitment Criterion is not met. And since the intention could play its proper causal role in bringing it about that another is badly injured without that person dying, it follows that if something short of the death of another figures in the content of the intention, the intention will not suffice for attempt under the Guiding Commitment View. So, to attempt murder, the death must be intended.

How about the second requirement, namely that the death is caused by the defendant? To attempt a murder, must a defendant not just intend another's death, but also intend [that the death is caused by me]? No. The reason is that if the defendant intends [that another dies] or intends [to kill another] and his intention plays its proper causal role in bringing it about that the world is as intended, then it will be true that the defendant causes another's death.[6] Since the causal fact will be generated by the intention's playing its proper causal role, it need not figure in the content of the intention. By having an intention with the death in its content, the defendant has a role-based commitment to causing the death.

An inference was just made that it is important to highlight. The inference employed the following claim:

(\*) If R is a type of event that is included in the content of an intention and the intention non-deviantly causes the world to match its content, then the intention causes an R.

Add to this that, for instance, the death of another human being is included in the content of an intention [to kill another human being] or an intention [that another human being dies], and we reach the conclusion reached in the previous paragraph: were such an intention to play its proper causal role, then the intention, and hence the agent, would be the cause of the death. Notice, however, that (\*) is not generally true. After all, the condition that the other is a human being, which is included in the content of both the intention [to kill another human being] and the intention [that another human being dies], is not caused by the intention when the intention plays its proper causal role in making the world match its content. In fact, as we will see in chapter 5, this fact will be of some importance to understanding the intention of the attempter with respect to the circumstantial elements of crimes (such as the condition that the other is a human being). Despite this, however, the inference is valid in the present context. The reason is that over a restricted range of cases, (\*) is true, and that is the relevant range for our immediate purposes here. In particular, (\*) is true whenever R is the sort of thing that it makes sense to require the prosecution to show to have been caused by the defendant, such as a death, or damage to property, or any event that figures into the definition of an act element of a crime as something that the prosecution must show to have been caused in order to establish that the defendant committed the crime. It follows that *whenever R is an event that figures into the definition of the act or result element of a crime*, it is further true that an intention that includes R in its content, and which non-deviantly causes the world to match its content, also causes R.

From what has just been said we can reach the following conclusion. *If R is a result element of crime C, then a defendant attempts C only if he intends [that R].* An intention *that* suffices for attempt when the element in question is a result element of the completed crime, since it constitutes a commitment to the two things that the prosecution bears a burden to show, thanks to the result

---

[6] What if the defendant intends [that Victim dies] and, acting on this intention, induces another to cause Victim's death? Even in this case, *were the intention to play its proper causal role* (which it might be thought not to do in the actual circumstances), the defendant would cause the death. See the discussion of the Voluntary Intervention Principle in chapter 7.

element: that the event occurred, and that the event was caused by the defendant. R's occurrence is generated by the intention's content matching the world; the causation of R by the defendant is generated by the intention's playing its proper causal role. Since these are the only two conditions that the prosecution bears a burden to show when a result element is at issue, it follows that an intention *that* will suffice. An intention *to* would do also, but it is not necessary for an attempt since, as we are about to see, such an intention involves commitments over and above the minimum that are imposed by the result element.

If the needed intention is merely an intention [that another die], then the intention could play its proper causal role without also making it the case that the agency-involvement factor is present in the causation of the death. It follows that the agency-involvement factor must be in the *content* of the intention if the element is an act element of the completed crime. Or, put more simply, *if A is an act element of crime C, then a defendant attempts C only if he intends [to A]*. So, the intention [to kill] is what is needed to attempt the crime; an intention *that* will not do. In general, under the Guiding Commitment View, when crime C has act elements A1, A2, ..., Ak and result elements R1, R2, ..., Rj, to attempt C, a defendant must intend [to A1], intend [to A2], ..., intend [to Ak], and must intend [that R1], intend [that R2], ..., intend [that Rj]. Or, put more simply, an attempter must intend *to* do all the acts needed for the completed crime, but must only intend *that* the results come to pass. As we will see in chapter 7, this difference in the *mens rea* of attempts with respect to acts and results is essential to a principled resolution of at least one difficult problem in the law of attempts.

### 3.1 *The Problem of the Foreseen but Unintended Consequence*

The *Model Penal Code* takes the act-result distinction to matter to determining the *mens rea* needed for an attempt in a different way from that just proposed. Under the *Model Penal Code*, act elements of the completed crime must always be intended for an attempt of the crime. Results too need to be intended except in "last act" cases: those in which the defendant believes "that [his act] will cause such result without further conduct on his part".[7] In cases of this sort, it is enough for the *mens rea* of attempt to foresee the result. So, to use one of the *Model Penal Code*'s examples, a person who places an explosive on a timer in a building, foreseeing but not intending the deaths of the inhabitants (perhaps he is aiming only to get the insurance money, and would prefer not to kill anyone) is guilty of attempted murder when the explosive fails to detonate.[8] However, although this is not explicitly noted in the code's commentary, a

---

[7] *Model Penal Code* §5.01(1)(b).
[8] *Model Penal Code*, Commentary to §5.01, 305.

person who does the same thing for the same purpose but is stopped instants before he can press the detonation button—imagine such a defendant to differ from the first only with respect to the time apprehended—has not attempted murder under the *Model Penal Code*, since he did not intend the deaths and believed that he needed to do more (namely push the button) before the deaths would result. Although some disagree,[9] it seems that there is no normatively significant difference between these two defendants, and so something has gone wrong with the *Model Penal Code*'s approach here.[10] I do not mean to be implying that both defendants are guilty of attempted murder, but, instead, that attempt law should not split them, but lump them together.[11]

However, it can seem that the Guiding Commitment View, in implying that an intention with respect to result elements is required for attempt, implies problematically that some defendants are to be split who, intuitively, ought to be lumped together. Say that the defendant is charged with attempted murder and he did not intend [to kill Victim], but intended, instead, [to crush Victim's brain]. Of course, when the jury hears the defendant testify to this, they are not likely to believe him; they are likely to think that he really intended [to kill Victim], despite what he claims. But let's stipulate that if the jury draws such a conclusion, they are mistaken. Our defendant genuinely does not intend [to kill Victim], although he's certain that Victim will die if he succeeds in doing as he does intend. A world in which Victim survives with his brain crushed is logically possible; but let's stipulate that it is nomologically impossible: it is compatible with the axioms of logic, but incompatible with the laws of nature. This defendant is not attempting to kill under the Guiding Commitment View. The death is not in the content of the defendant's intention, and an intention [to crush Victim's brain] could play its proper causal role in making the world match its content without Victim dying. This is the force of saying that the conditional in the Commitment Criterion is to be interpreted as a logical

---

[9] R. A. Duff appears to be among them. See Duff (1996), 358.

[10] The *Model Penal Code* justifies criminal liability for attempts on grounds of dangerousness. The idea, then, is that since the first bomber is more dangerous than the second, it is fair to impose a lower *mens rea* bar for the attempt. However, there is little reason to think that the first bomber is any more dangerous than the second. The first, for instance, is apparently not very good at picking out non-defective explosives while, for all that's been said, the second is very good at that and so is much more likely to actually blow up a building.

[11] The best case for splitting these cases is that in the second there is still a chance for the defendant to alter course as a result of change of mind, while in the first this is not so. Whether the possibility of effective changing of mind is normatively relevant is discussed in chapters 10 and 11. However, even if it is normatively relevant, the best way to capture that in the law is not to require a different mental state with respect to the result of the one defendant than of the other. If the relevant difference is to be registered in the *mens rea* elements of the attempt then it should be registered in the attitude towards change of mind; some defendants really are leaving open the possibility that they will change their mind, others are firmly decided on not changing their minds, even if there is a chance to do so effectively. If the relevant difference is to be registered, instead, in the act elements of the attempt, then, too, there should not be a difference in the mental state with respect to the result that is required for the attempt.

implication: there are possible worlds in which the intention plays its proper causal role and Victim survives, although these are worlds with different laws of nature from the actual. Assuming that we want to hold such a defendant guilty of attempted murder, what should we say about this kind of case?

There are two options. The first, which is not the option I accept, is to hold that examples of this sort show that the Guiding Commitment View is in need of revision. In particular we might expand the Commitment Criterion, so that in addition to being committed to that which is in the content of the intention, and that which would be true were the intention to play its proper causal role, we take defendants to be committed, also, to that which they foresee (or foresee with certainty) will result from those other conditions. Call the resulting position the "Guiding Commitment + Foreknowledge View". So, we are allowed to say under the Guiding Commitment + Foreknowledge View that the person who intends [to crush Victim's brain] attempts to kill Victim, for although Victim's death is not included in the content of the defendant's intention, it is included in the content of the conjunction of the content of the intention and the content of the belief that death is an unavoidable result of a brain being crushed. And if the intention plays its proper causal role, and Victim dies, then our defendant caused Victim's death.

The problem with this approach is that it collapses the distinction between intent and foreknowledge in such a way as to mishandle cases in which that distinction is important. Consider the case of *State v. Caine* (652 So.2d 611 (La. App. 1995)). In a tussle with a convenience store employee who was trying to eject him, Caine pulled a syringe full of clear liquid from his pocket, plunged it into the arm of the employee, and yelled, "I'll give you AIDS!". He appealed his conviction for attempted murder on the grounds that no reasonable juror could infer an intent to kill from his statement. His conviction was upheld. The court conceptualizes the relevant issue here as one of *evidence* of intent. That is, the question is whether a reasonable jury could have taken Caine's statement to express not merely intent [to give the victim AIDS] but intent [to kill]. The court takes the issue as concerning what intentions it is reasonable to infer a person to have given his statements. That is the right way to conceptualize the issue. But it would be improper to conceptualize it that way were the Guiding Commitment + Foreknowledge View correct. After all, under that view, and assuming that Caine did indeed believe, falsely, that anyone infected with HiV will die, there is no evidential question to weigh: the question is settled by the legal test for determining what intention is required for attempt. A reasonable jury could indeed have concluded that Caine intended [to·kill], but a reasonable jury also could have concluded that Caine did not have that intention, but had, only, the intention required for an attempted grievous assault of some sort. Reasonable people could disagree on the issue. But in that case it must be possible for a defendant like Caine to fall short of attempt because he falls short of having an intention that commits him to killing. The Guiding Commitment +

Foreknowledge View removes this possibility by stipulating that, as a matter of law, the distinction between intent and foresight is irrelevant in attempt. That view then forces a jury to turn its attention away from the defendant's intention, in a case like Caine's, and towards the defendant's beliefs. But as the case illustrates, this amounts to misdirection.

We need not give up the Guiding Commitment View in the face of examples like the brain-crushing example. There is an alternative way to respond to cases of foreseen but unintended consequences that is consistent with that view. To see this, we need only be reminded again of the distinction between commission and guilt. Although it is rarely recognized as such, a well-known rule appearing in the *Model Penal Code* implies that there can be guilt without commission, for reasons quite different from those involved in accomplice liability or in any of the other examples discussed so far. Under the *Model Penal Code* §2.02(5), when a particular type of mental state is an element of a crime, a "higher" mental state will serve for guilt. If negligence is required, then recklessness, knowledge, or intent will serve; if recklessness is required, then knowledge or intent will serve, and if knowledge is required, intent will serve. Why should this be? After all, a person who does something negligently or recklessly necessarily does *not* do it intentionally; negligence and recklessness necessarily exclude intent, so why should intent serve to meet requirements of negligence and recklessness? Why hasn't a defendant charged with a crime of negligence, say, exonerated himself when he shows that he actually intended the result he caused, and so was not negligent with respect to it? The answer is that it is generally worse to do something bad recklessly than it is to do it negligently, worse to do it knowingly than recklessly, and worse to do it intentionally than knowingly. Therefore, we shouldn't acquit a defendant of a crime of negligence if he was actually aware of the risk and so was, in fact, not negligent but reckless, or not reckless but purposive.

Under the *Model Penal Code*'s rule, a defendant can be guilty of a crime that he did not commit. Imagine, for instance, that a defendant is charged with negligently damaging public property in contrast to the crime of intentionally damaging public property. A person who commits the crime damages public property while unaware that his conduct was even likely to do so, and in circumstances such that a reasonable person would have recognized that acts like the defendant's would indeed do such damage. Since there is a more severe crime of intentionally damaging public property, a person who actually intended to damage public property—not only was he not unaware of the risk that he would, but instead consciously aimed at doing so—did not commit the crime of negligence. But a jury member who is convinced beyond a reasonable doubt of the defendant's intention [to damage public property] ought to vote to convict, not to acquit, under the *Model Penal Code*'s rule. Such a jury member believes that the defendant did not commit the crime, but is nonetheless guilty of it. Thus two members of the jury could disagree about what crime the defendant committed—one thinks the defendant intentionally damaged property, the other recklessly—and nonetheless agree that the defendant is guilty as charged. This is another kind of case, then, of guilt without commission. Here, as in most cases of guilt without commission, "just as bad or worse" is the driving justificatory principle for punishment of those who do something objectionable that falls short of behavior that meets the definition of the crime charged.

The crushing-the-brain example is one in which there is a plausible case for guilt for an attempted murder, even though there is not commission of attempted murder. There is no commission because commission requires an attempt *to commit murder* and, under the Guiding Commitment View, that is not what the defendant attempted. We cannot enrich our description of what this person attempts by reference to killing—as we would were we to describe him as attempting murder—since his intention does not commit him to the death of the victim. But there is guilt for the same reasons that there is guilt without commission under the *Model Penal Code*'s rule just discussed: the conjunction of the intention of the person who intends [to crush Victim's brain] together with his belief to a certainty that Victim's death will result, is just as bad as the intention [to kill]. The *Model Penal Code*'s rule is guided by the general idea that for guilt what is needed is either the mental state involved in commission, *or a mental state that is just as bad*. The mental state of the defendant in the crushing-the-brain example is different from that involved in attempted murder, but it is just as bad, and that warrants a finding of guilt.

It is rarely recognized that the *Model Penal Code*'s evaluative hierarchy of mental states—intent is worse than knowledge, knowledge worse than recklessness, etc.—only roughly approximates the moral truth. Sometimes knowing what will happen if one acts is just as bad as intending it; usually it is not. (In fact, a case can be made that sometimes doing something negligently is worse than doing it recklessly. At least the reckless person considers the other's interests when he acts; the negligent person is so selfish as to not even notice that his conduct risks violating them.) It is extraordinarily difficult to codify the relevant principle here. It is very hard to specify the precise conditions under which foresight is just as bad as intent. All of the following factors, and perhaps more, probably matter to the calculation: the severity of the foreseen harm, the actual likelihood of its coming to pass, and the degree to which the intended act is itself wrong independently of the foreseen harm. Further, whatever the algorithm for determining when foresight is just as bad as intent, it remains true that, in general, it is not. A true account of the relevant guilt-without-commission principle that guides our intuitions in the crushing-the-brain example would need to accommodate these facts. However, for our purposes here, what matters is only the general point that the Guiding Commitment View does not falter in the face of such examples since our intuitions about them are driven, not by our conception of what it is to attempt a crime, but by our conception of what it is to do something that is not an attempt but is just as bad as one, and bad enough to warrant guilt for attempt.

Those familiar with the philosophical literature concerned with the so-called "Doctrine of Double-Effect"—the view, held by the Catholic Church, among others, that there is a moral difference between intending a bad result and foreseeing that it will come to pass when one does as one intends—will recognize the issue just discussed. In his classic article on the topic, Jonathan Bennett uses examples similar to the crushing-the-brain example to argue that the Doctrine of Double Effect is false.[12] There is no moral difference, thinks Bennett, between intending [to kill Victim] and intending [to crush Victim's brain] while fully recognizing that doing so will kill Victim. But what has just been shown here is that, even if Bennett is correct—even if the Doctrine of Double Effect is false for just the reasons he says—this fact does not undermine the criminal law's distinction between intent and foreknowledge, at least as it appears in attempt law. This distinction is often useful for drawing distinctions in commission, and it is therefore useful for drawing distinctions in guilt when guilt is predicated on commission. But there are cases, also, in which although there is a difference in commission, there is no difference in guilt, precisely because there is no moral difference in those rare cases between intent and foresight. Such is the case in the crushing-the-brain example.

## 4. Mental States

In thinking about what kind of commitment someone guilty of attempt must have with respect to the mental states involved in completion, we need to remind ourselves of what purpose is served in the first place by the mental state elements of completed crimes. It is a very old idea, as old as the distinction between *mens rea* and *actus reus*, that the prosecution bears a burden to show the defendant to have been in various mental states because, in addition to wrongdoing, culpability is required for just punishment. It is wrong to pass confidential government information downloaded from a server to someone unauthorized to receive it and likely to use it to damage the United States.[13] But it is not culpable when done by someone who falsely and reasonably believes, for instance, that the information can do no damage, and that the person to whom he is giving it is authorized to receive it. Even disputes about the line between wrongdoing and culpability evolve in front of mutual acceptance of the obvious idea that mental state matters because what is done is not the sort of thing that deserves to be punished except when accompanied and guided by

---

[12] Bennett (1981). The literature that Bennett's article spawned is quite large. See, for instance, Quinn (1989), Fischer, Ravizza, and Copp (1993), Scanlon (2008).

[13] This is a crime under U.S.C §1030.

some relevant conception in the mind of the defendant of what he is doing. Mental state, the thought is, transforms wrongful behavior into the kind of thing that the criminal law is to respond to.

Given this rationale for *mens rea* requirements, it appears that there is not, generally, a good reason to require that the defendant who attempts be shown to have any particular mental state *with respect to the mental states* needed for completion. The mental states involved in completion are what promote the acts, results, and circumstances involved *in completion* to the level of the punishable. Similarly, the mental states involved in attempt are what promote the acts, results, and circumstances involved *in attempt* to the level of the punishable. Thus, it seems that the mental states involved in attempt need be directed only towards those elements that are relevant to the wrongdoing involved in the attempt. We should no more require the attempter to have thought about the thoughts involved in completion than we should require the defendant who completes the crime to have thought about the mental states involved in completion: it is enough merely *to have* the relevant mental states—to have thought about what you're doing—and not to have thought *about* them. From this point of view, although there is a hard question to ask about what mental state the attempter needs to have with respect to the acts, results, and circumstances involved in completion, to ask any comparable question about his attitude towards the *mental states* involved in completion is to get bogged down in confusion about what the point of mental state requirements is.

Things are in fact more complicated than this, however, because, as noted, the act involved in attempt amounts to legal wrongdoing only if the defendant has a certain mental state with respect to it. Each and every component of success in the crime is something towards which the attempter must be aimed if he is to be rightly said to be attempting *the crime*, and so to be involved in wrongdoing of the sort that criminal attempts involve. Since mental states are components of the completed crime, these too are things that the defendant must be committed to occurring. So, although the attempter needn't think about the mental states involved in completion in order to be *culpable* for attempt, maybe he needs to think about them in order for his act to amount to legal *wrongdoing*.

At this point, we encounter two importantly different kinds of crime. One kind can be quickly dispensed with here, the other will be separately considered in chapter 6. The two kinds of crime are those that cannot be completed with intent, and those that can. The former are referred to in chapter 6 as "intent-excluding crimes". The latter are those crimes in which, for instance, for commission, the defendant must know that he will cause a bad result, but there is no more severe crime reserved for those who intended to bring about that result. Such crimes are implicitly, if not explicitly, disjunctively defined. In order to show that defendant D *committed* such a crime, the prosecution is not required to show that D knew something, period, but is, instead, required to show *either* that D knew something *or* intended it. Both a defendant who intends to bring about a result and has grave doubts that he will succeed, and one who does not intend to bring it about but is certain that he will, *committed* the crime when the result is actually brought about and the crime is of this second sort. By contrast, crimes in the first category are such that while there may be guilt if the defendant had a relevant intention, there is not commission by such a defendant. Negligent homicide is in the first category: a defendant who intends to kill has not committed negligent homicide (although he might be guilty of it). Homicide requiring only knowledge that death will result is ordinarily in the second category: there is no other crime reserved for the person who intends [to kill] or intends [that Victim dies]. A person with such an intention commits such a homicide when he kills. Intent-excluding crimes will be discussed in chapter 6. There the Guiding Commitment View will be used to show what attitude a defendant must have towards the mental states involved in such completed crimes in order to attempt them. But we can consider the second class of crimes—those in which intent does not preclude commission of the completed crime—here.

With respect to this category of crimes, the Guiding Commitment View implies that any defendant charged with attempt, and whose intention serves for *mens rea* with respect to the acts, results, and circumstances of the completed crime, necessarily has the mental state needed with respect to the mental state elements of the completed crime; he is necessarily committed to having the mental states needed for completion in the way that warrants a description of what he is trying to do that incorporates them. The reason is that if the Guidance Criterion is met—if he is actually guided by his intention-based commitment to the relevant acts, results, and circumstances—then he has intent with respect to both those conditions that are in the content of the intention and with respect to those that are realized thanks to the intention's playing its proper causal role. A person who, for instance, kills as a result of his intention [to kill] playing its proper causal role has the mental state needed for the completed crime with respect to the element of killing: he intends it. And similarly, he has the *mens rea* involved in completion with respect to the causation of the death by him.[14] Thus each mental state element of the completed crime is realized thanks to his intention playing its proper causal role. It follows that he need not include the mental states involved in completion in the content of his intention in order to attempt. He is committed to their occurrence since they would be present were the intention to play its proper causal role, even when they are not included in its content.

---

[14] Notice that, for this to be true, it must be possible to have intent with respect to X without X being in the content of one's intention. This seems plainly true in the case in which X is "defendant causes R" and it is true that the defendant causes R when the intention plays its proper causal role.

This solution does not serve for crimes that cannot be committed with intention. After all, if the crime is of that sort, then when the defendant's intention guides his conduct, he necessarily *lacks* the mental states involved in completion, for what he has is intention, and that, by definition, precludes commission of the completed crime. As I say, we will consider the mental state needed for an attempt of such crimes in chapter 6. As we will see there, in those cases, a defendant must intend to have a certain mental state later.

## 5. Conclusion

There are, in essence, two questions that need to be asked about the intention of the defendant charged with an attempted crime: "Does his intention commit him to each of the components of the completed crime?" and "If it does not, is it just as a bad as an intention that does?" If we answer "yes" to the first question, then we have a defendant who satisfies the most important necessary condition for trying: the Commitment Criterion. Such a defendant may very well have committed an attempted crime. The conditions under which the answer is "yes" are specified by the Elemental Conception of the intention in attempt articulated in this chapter, where that view is to be understood as the conjunction of claims about what intention is needed to commit one to each of the different sorts of components of completed crimes discussed in the preceding sections. If we answer "no" to the first question—the defendant lacks an intention that commits him to all of the components of the completed crime—but "yes" to the second, then we have on our hands a defendant who may very well be guilty of an attempted crime, despite the fact that he did not commit one.

Discoveries made while tinkering in the philosopher's laboratory do not always develop into machines capable of threshing wheat in the wild. I imagine that many a reader has had the thought much earlier in this chapter or the last that, while the Guiding Commitment View may express the truth about the kind of trying of relevance to the criminal law, and may imply the truth about the intention involved in attempt, namely the Elemental Conception of that intention, these truths are untranslatable into a simple "test" of the sort that we instruct jurors and trial judges to apply. Perhaps that is true when fact-finders are faced with the question of whether a particular defendant had the intention needed for attempt. They are not likely to have the patience to distinguish, for instance, between intending *that* and intending *to*, much less the perspicuity to determine which intention any particular defendant happened to have. In fact, the behavioral evidence often radically underdetermines the question of the precise content of the defendant's intention, and defendants themselves may know no better than we what they intended. Fact-finders are likely to consult their gut intuitions about the concept of trying, and just decide without much reflection whether the defendant was really trying to commit the crime. Even if this is what they inevitably do, however, it is important that we have a standard by which to assess the accuracy of their judgments, a standard that is rooted, not in intuition, but in principle. Even if we cannot hope to show fact-finders how to apply principle, we need to know what principles we strive for them to apply if we are to know what criticisms of their decisions are apt and inapt. The Guiding Commitment View, and the Elemental Conception it implies, provides such a standard; it tells us when gut intuition has gone astray and so provides us with a tool with which to criticize or affirm decisions made in trials.

# 5

# Circumstances and "Impossibility"

## 1. Introduction

Melvin Dlugash, Joe Bush, and Michael Geller went drinking together one night. Geller repeatedly demanded that Bush give him $100 towards the rent of Geller's apartment, where Bush was staying. Bush repeatedly refused. When Geller pressed the point one last time, Bush, angry with him, shot him three times. Geller lay motionless for several minutes, and showed no signs of life. At that point, Dlugash fired five bullets into Geller's head. It is not clear why Dlugash did this, although one possibility is that he did it to demonstrate to Bush that he was in league with him, and not an innocent witness whom Bush would have a motive to kill. But whatever his motive, did Dlugash murder Geller? If Geller was dead when Dlugash shot him, then Dlugash did not commit murder, but merely mutilated a corpse—a crime, perhaps, but a far lesser crime than murder. And since the prosecution cannot prove beyond a reasonable doubt that Geller was alive, they choose to charge Dlugash with *attempted* murder.[1] One question one needs to answer to resolve the case is whether an attempted murder requires that the victim is alive at the time of the attempt; if so, then the prosecution's inability to establish that fact undermines their case against Dlugash, not just for completed murder, but also for attempted. We also need to know what *attitude* Dlugash needs to have had towards the question of whether his victim was alive or dead in order to be guilty of an attempted murder. If Dlugash was intending to finish Geller off, then he would not have fired had he been certain that Geller was already dead. Is *that* the attitude he needs to have had to have attempted murder? Or is it enough for the attempt that Dlugash believed that Geller was alive? Or is uncertainty about the question, together with a willingness to go ahead whatever the facts, enough for attempted murder? It is quite possible, that is, that Dlugash was at the time no more certain than we can be in retrospect whether Geller was alive. If that's right, did Dlugash attempt murder?

---

[1] *People v. Dlugash* (41 N.Y.2d 725 (1977)).

As it is in *Dlugash*, so it often is: where the question of *mens rea* with respect to circumstances arises in an attempt case, there is often a question also about whether the relevant circumstantial element needs to be in place. This chapter solves both problems. It offers principled grounds for deciding what attitude an attempter must have towards the circumstantial elements of the completed crime, and it provides principled grounds for deciding when the circumstantial elements of the completed crime need to be in place for the attempted.

Cases like *Dlugash* are often misleadingly labeled as involving "impossible attempts". After all, if Dlugash was trying to kill Geller, then he very well may have been attempting the impossible feat of killing a dead man. Another well-known example of such a case, which has occupied the imagination of many a criminal law theorist, is *People v. Jaffe* (185 N.Y. 497, 78 N.E. 169 (1906)), in which the defendant, a suspected "fence", was charged with an attempt to receive stolen property after he purchased some fabric that he believed to be stolen, but which was in fact falsely represented to him as stolen as part of a sting operation. Or, for a more recent example with exactly the same structure, consider *United States v. Crow* (164 F.3d 229 (5th Cir. 1999)). Crow had multiple conversations in an internet chat room with someone going by the name of "StephieFL". During the course of their conversations, StephieFL claimed to be a 13-year-old girl. In fact, the messages were written by an undercover (adult) police officer. Crow tried to convince StephieFL to send him sexually explicit photographs of herself, and was charged with attempting sexual exploitation of a minor. The completed offense requires a showing to the effect that the person exploited is indeed a minor. Did Crow attempt sexual exploitation of a minor, or does the fact that it was an adult he was actually in contact with show that he did not?

The court in *Jaffe* conceptualizes the case as one in which the defendant tried to receive stolen property but could not possibly have succeeded, since the property was not stolen, and then struggles with the question of whether success was impossible in the right sense of "impossible" for acquittal. We might find ourselves down this road, also, in considering *Crow*. The literature that cases like *Jaffe* has spawned is very large, and most of it engages directly with the question that the court in *Jaffe* takes to be crucial: the question of the sense, if any, in which it must be possible to succeed if one is to be guilty of an attempt.[2] As we will see in chapter 9, there is a very thin sense in which attempt requires the possibility of success; so-called "inherent impossiblity", when properly specified, does indeed provide a sound basis for acquittal: consider the person who attempts murder by incantation. But there is no need to tackle

---

[2] There is too much literature on this topic to list it all. Some of the best-known early discussions include Strahorn (1930); Skilton (1937a); Skilton (1937b); Keedy (1954); Smith (1957); Hall (1960), 586–99; Williams (1961), 633–53; Smith (1962); Hart (1981). Helpful recent discussions include Duff (1996), 76–115, 378–85; Hasnas (2002).

the issue of impossibility's relevance to attempt in connection with cases like *Jaffe*. If it was possible, in some given sense, for the fabric that Jaffe bought to have been stolen, then it was possible, in that sense, for Jaffe to have successfully received stolen property. But the *Jaffe* court does not inquire whether it was possible, contrary to fact, for that property to have been stolen; that's not what concerns the court. What concerns the court, whether it knows it or not, is not the *possibility* that the fabric was stolen, but *the simple fact* that it was not. But if that is their concern, then the question of the possibility of success just isn't the crucial question even by their own standards. What courts in cases like *Dlugash* and *Jaffe* need to answer are the two intertwined questions addressed in this chapter: "What mental states must an attempter have towards the circumstantial elements of the completed crime?" and "Under what conditions, if any, must the circumstantial elements of the completed crime be present for the attempt?"

The temptation to conceive of cases like *Jaffe*, *Crow*, or *Dlugash*, as involving impossibility derives from the fact that circumstantial elements of crimes are very rarely things that defendants are committed to causing; they, instead, typically assume them to be in place already in their deliberations about what to do, or simply ignore them. When we imagine someone "doing as he is trying to do" we ordinarily, in our imaginations, add to the world all of those conditions that he is committed *to causing*, leaving the rest of the world as he found it. The picture is that those things that he is not committed to causing are *given*, or immutable to him for practical purposes. Under that picture, such conditions are not things that the defendant aims to change and so they are to be treated *just like* things that cannot be otherwise. Of course, it isn't literally true that such conditions cannot be otherwise: many things that we take for granted are things that we *could* cause to be the case, and that *could* fail to be the case for various reasons. Jaffe took it for granted that the goods he received were stolen; for practical purposes, this was just as much a settled matter for him as that the sun rises or that $2 + 2 = 4$. Given that the goods were not stolen, it can seem that Jaffe's conduct, predicated as it was on the goods being stolen, was, for practical purposes, just like conduct predicated on the impossible claim that it is not the case that $2 + 2 = 4$. Is a person really attempting X if success in that endeavor would require $2 + 2$ to equal something other than 4? Perhaps not. But nothing follows about *Jaffe*. Even if *for practical purposes* Jaffe's conduct is like that of the person who acts on the assumption that $2 + 2 = 5$, it is importantly different from such conduct. That the goods were stolen was settled for Jaffe, but he did not take it to be a necessary truth, nor was it a *necessary* falsehood. In short, there is *similarity*, but not *identity*, between what is considered by an agent to be given for practical purposes, and what could not possibly be otherwise. We are thus mistakenly moved by the force of the analogy between "given for practical purposes" and "impossible to be otherwise" into conceiving of cases where a circumstantial element of completion is absent, and the defendant is not committed to causing it, as cases involving the impossibility of completion.

So in consideration of cases in which a circumstantial element of the completed crime is absent in the attempt—the property isn't really stolen, the defendant actually has permission to take it, the victim isn't really under age, etc.—we should not make the mistake of entering into debate about whether the possibility of success is necessary for either the commission of an attempt, or guilt for one. But that is not the only misleading road that one can find oneself on in consideration of such cases. Consider those cases in which the defendant has an intention-based commitment *to causing* a particular circumstantial element of a crime. Imagine, for instance, the intending rapist who is uninterested in consensual sex: if he sensed that his victim was consenting, he would take steps to make her change her mind before he had sex with her, or he would find a victim who was not consenting. In cases of this sort, it seems intuitively that the circumstantial element of the completed crime need not be in place for the attempted. If this intending rapist is stopped before there is sex, it seems perfectly true that he attempted rape, even if he had not yet achieved the absence of his victim's consent, or had not yet found an unconsenting victim. It is tempting to conclude from this that the circumstantial elements of the completed crime *never* need to be in place for the attempted crime. The relevant issue, we might think, is *always* the defendant's mental state, not the facts. But this would be a rash conclusion to reach. Perhaps the circumstantial elements of the completed crime need to be in place in at least some of those cases in which the defendant falls short of a commitment to causing them to be the case. In fact, as we will see, this is so.

Section 2 criticizes the two best-known efforts to resolve the dual problems of the mental state with respect to circumstances required for an attempt and the circumstances themselves, if any, required: the positions, that is, of John Stannard and R. A. Duff. Section 3 offers an alternative resolution. The issue is in particularly pressing need of resolution under the Guiding Commitment View. For reference in what follows, recall the details of the position. Here, as, before, D is a defendant, C a crime, the E's are those conditions that must be proven beyond a reasonable doubt to prove completion of C, and X is the content of D's intention:

*The Guiding Commitment View*: D attempts C *if and only if* $\forall$ Ei, the following criteria are met:

*Commitment Criterion*: ((Ei is included in X) OR (If D's intention plays its proper causal role, then Ei)), &

*Guidance Criterion*: D is guided by his commitment to Ei.

Under this view of trying, a person is trying to act only if *his intention* commits him to each of the components of success. If everything that our intentions commit us to are things that they also commit us to causing, then it would seem that the Guiding Commitment View implies too lenient a standard for the *mens rea* of attempt with respect to circumstances. Since the prosecution bears no burden to show that the defendant caused the circumstantial elements of the crime to be in place, why should a defendant have to be committed to causing them in order to attempt the crime? The prosecution needn't show, in a statutory rape case, that the defendant would have chosen a different victim had his victim not been underage and thereby caused it to be the case that he had sex with an underage victim. It is enough that she was underage, even if the defendant would have had sex with her even if she had not been. But then it is too lenient to require an intention in attempted statutory rape that commits the defendant to causing the victim to be underage. Such a requirement would require the attempter to be committed to more than is involved in the completed crime. In fact, this would be a just objection to the Guiding Commitment View were it the case that everything that one's intention commits one to is something that one is also thereby committed to causing. As we will see, this is not the case. The solutions to be offered in section 3 exploit a distinction between conditions that are in the content of an intention which the agent is thereby committed to causing, on the one hand, and those that he is not, on the other, despite their presence in the content of his intention. The circumstantial elements of crimes need only be included in the content of the attempter's intention in the latter way.[3] Hence the Guiding Commitment View does not imply too lenient a standard for the *mens rea* of attempt with respect to circumstances.

As we will see, also in section 3, there is a set of cases in which a person's intention commits him to the presence of a circumstantial element only if the circumstantial element is actually in place. Not all cases are like this—sometimes the circumstantial element can be absent and still be something that one's intention commits one to—but, still, some are. Section 3 distinguishes the cases. One result we will find is that an intention that can be imputed to Dlugash, consistent with what we know of him, commits him to Geller's being alive prior to being shot only if Geller was indeed alive at the time that Dlugash shot him. Since this cannot be proven beyond a reasonable doubt, it follows that nor can it be proven beyond a reasonable doubt that Dlugash attempted murder. By contrast, Jaffe's intention [to buy stolen goods] commits him to the goods being stolen even if they were not in fact stolen. Hence Jaffe has attempted to buy stolen goods. Section 3 also traces the implications of the solution offered there for several other kinds of problematic cases.

---

[3] This distinction was mentioned briefly in chapter 4 in connection with the claim that an attempter need not include *the causing* of the results and acts involved in completion in his intention, since he would cause them were his intention to play its proper causal role.

## 2. Stannard and Duff

The two most prominent positions to be found in the literature about the mental states with respect to circumstances involved in attempt, namely John Stannard's and R. A. Duff's, both, in different ways, link the question of what mental states are required with the question of whether the circumstantial elements themselves need to be in place for attempt. Stannard observes that in every attempt there is a "missing element"—there is some condition, that is, that needs to be proven for commission of the complete offense but which is not proven, or is in fact absent, in the attempt. Then, distinguishing between his approach and others, he makes the following suggestion:

A more sensible approach would be to distinguish between the missing element and the other elements, and to say that while the missing element must be intended, the other elements require only the *mens rea* appropriate for the full offense.[4]

In *Dlugash*, there are several "missing elements", all deriving from the absence of proof that Geller was alive when Dlugash shot him. Most obviously the circumstantial element *that Geller was alive* is missing. But, as a result, there is also insufficient proof *that Dlugash caused a death*. And this, in turn, implies that there is insufficient proof that Dlugash's act was one of *killing*. On Stannard's view, since all of these elements are missing, Dlugash would have to be shown to have intended all these things in order to be shown to have committed attempted murder, as he would be if he were shown to have intended [to kill]. If, in fact, Dlugash thought that Geller was dead, then that would be evidence that Dlugash did not intend [to kill]. Although it might be possible in a certain addled and agitated state to intend [to kill] what you believe to be dead, it is not likely to have been Dlugash's state of mind. So it appears that on Stannard's view there is insufficient evidence that Dlugash committed attempted murder.

As we will see, this is the right result to reach in *Dlugash*. But Stannard's view does not succeed across the full range of different kinds of elements of completed crimes. It leads us to criminalize as attempts behaviors that are not tryings, and so are not properly criminalized under the Transfer Principle. To see this, first consider Duff's proposed counterexample to Stannard's position, intended to support precisely this line of objection:

Fearing damage to my expensive drill in a tricky DIY task, I decide to use my neighbor's identical drill without her consent. However, I mistake my drill for hers, use mine, and damage it. Stannard's principle convicts me of attempted criminal damage since I act with intent as to the missing element of the complete offence (that what I damage is another's property), and with the fault required for the complete offence as to its non-missing

---

[4] Stannard (1987), 199.

element (with recklessness as to whether damage is caused). Surely, though, I should not be convicted, since I have not attempted to damage another's property.[5]

The agent here has not attempted to damage another's property, as Duff says, since he does not intend [to damage something], nor does he intend [that something is damaged]. This result aligns with the council of the Guiding Commitment View. In fact, the defendant may very well be trying *not* to damage the drill he's using: he may be committed by his intention to not damaging it and be guided by that commitment. However, there is room for Stannard to object to this example on the grounds that it trades on intuitions to the effect that an attempt is absent when certain circumstantial elements, in this case that the drill is someone else's, are absent. Stannard's view is, in the first instance, a theory about the *mens rea* of attempt, and is compatible with the claim that there is no attempt in a case like this unless the drill is not, in fact, the defendant's. Imagine, that is, that Stannard's view is supplemented with independent reasons, reasons separate from his characterization of the mental state involved in attempt, for thinking that in a case like this, there is no attempt unless the drill is not, in fact, the defendant's. Perhaps, for instance, this would fall out of some particular account of the act element of attempt. So supplemented, Stannard's view would imply that the agent in Duff's example has the *mental state* needed for attempt, but has not attempted because the drill he uses is his. Our intuitions are probably fine-grained enough to say that this agent is not attempting to damage anything, but they may not be sufficiently fine-grained to identify *the reason* why there is not such an attempt. This fact can be exploited by Stannard to respond to the example, since there is no incompatibility with making a claim about what mental state is required for attempt *when an element is missing*, and making a claim to the effect that a certain class of elements (namely the circumstantial) cannot be missing. Still, so conceived, Stannard's view would require an account of the conditions under which the circumstantial elements of the crime need to be in place for the attempted, and that account would have to imply that Duff's case is one in which they are required. But perhaps Stannard could supply such an account.

However, the objection that Duff is after cannot be bypassed in this way in another set of cases. This is illustrated nicely by any crime which requires the causation of two different events, the first of which is intended by the defendant and the second of which is not, but only the second of which comes to pass. Consider, for instance, *United States vs. Neiswender* (590 F.2d 1269 (4th Cir. 1979)). Neiswender approached the attorney for the defense in a high-profile trial and offered to "fix" the jury for a fee. There was evidence to suggest that Neiswender was bluffing. His plan appeared to be to take the fee and disappear

---

[5] Duff (1996), 15. Duff gives a slightly different example to the same effect in Duff (1991), 112.

without taking any steps at all to influence the jury. Importantly, he seems to have been aware that there was a good chance that his proposal would cause justice to be obstructed, not by causing the jury to be fixed, but by causing the attorney to put up less than his strongest possible case. In fact, Neiswender tried to minimize this risk by informing the attorney that it was very important that he present the strongest possible case in order not to let on that the jury was fixed. Neiswender was charged with attempting to obstruct justice by deception. To prove the complete offense, although not the attempt with which Neiswender was charged, the prosecution would need to show, among other things, both that another person was deceived *and* that justice was obstructed. Now let's imagine that Neiswender did not cause anyone to be deceived—the attorney could tell he was bluffing—but did cause justice to be obstructed—the attorney was rattled enough by the incident that he provided a less than adequate defense of his client. Under Stannard's analysis, Neiswender has the *mens rea* of attempted obstruction of justice. After all, he intends the missing element (that another is deceived), and he has the *mens rea* of the completed crime, recklessness, with respect to the non-missing element (that justice is obstructed). But under such facts Neiswender is clearly not trying to obstruct justice. He's trying to *avoid* obstructing justice while still getting the money; that's why he insists that the attorney should put up the very best defense he can.

Since nobody can plausibly insist that elements of the completed crime *that the attempter must be committed to causing* must be *in place* for an attempt—they are precisely what is typically absent in an attempt—this example cannot be accommodated by Stannard in the way it was suggested that he might accommodate Duff's proposed counterexample to his view. Stannard cannot reply, that is, that in a case like this there is no attempt to obstruct justice by deception if there is not deception; after all, Neiswender was committed *to causing* someone to be deceived. However, what this example illustrates is only that Stannard's proposal is inadequate as a *full* account of the *mens rea* of attempt. It is consistent with this example that Stannard's view succeeds as an account of the *mens rea* of attempt when it comes to circumstantial elements of the completed crime. However, the view is only defensible against Duff's example, which involves *mens rea* with respect to a circumstantial element, when coupled with the further claim that such elements must be in place for attempt in such cases. So, for our purposes in this section, Stannard's view has been reduced to the position that, for attempt, the circumstances of the completed crime must be in place, and the defendant must have the mental states with respect to them required for completion. Nothing said so far suggests that this is not right, but, even if it is right, to follow the route to that conclusion that Stannard's view requires is to follow a more convoluted path than is necessary or, in the end, defensible.

Stannard offers us a principle for sorting those elements that must be intended for attempt from those with respect to which the *mens rea* of the completed crime suffices: the missing elements fall into the first category, the non-missing into the second. Thus, on Stannard's view, the question of what mental state with respect to circumstances is required for attempt is not distinct from the question of what circumstantial elements of the completed crime need to be present for the attempt. Duff's own positive position links these questions also, although in a different way. Duff holds a position more closely allied to the Guiding Commitment View, although, as we will see, importantly different from it in several respects. Duff puts his position this way:

> Would the agent necessarily commit the relevant complete offence if she succeeded in doing what she is trying to do? ... If the answer is "Yes", she is guilty of attempting to commit that offence.[6]

As stated here, Duff's test requires a prior identification of what the agent is *trying* to do. However, he seems to have in mind the narrow view of trying, under which what a person is trying to do aligns perfectly with the content of his intention. So understood, "doing what [one] is trying to do" can be understood in our terms as the conjunction of two things: the world matching the intention's content, and the world's coming to be that way as a result of the intention's playing its proper causal role. Hence, we can put the position this way, where the variables are as previously defined:

*Duff's View*: D has the intention required for an attempt to C *if and only if* $\forall$ i (If ((X) & (D's intention plays its proper causal role)), then Ei.)

In contrast to the Guiding Commitment View, Duff's View is intended as an account only of the necessary and sufficient conditions that an intention must meet if it is to serve as the intention involved in a particular attempt; it is not an account of what it is to try to do something, as the Guiding Commitment View is. In our terms, we might say that Duff's View is an account of the Commitment Criterion, and so we can imagine it conjoined with additional conditions needed to constitute an attempt.

Both Duff's View and the Commitment Criterion in the Guiding Commitment View are efforts to systematically capture the intuitive idea that trying involves an intention to do something that would amount to success if done intentionally, and thus involves a commitment to each of the components of success. However, the two positions are different. They are clearly *logically* distinct.[7] The logical difference arises from the fact that on the Guiding

---

[6] Duff (1991), 112–13. Duff expresses the same position in Duff (1996), e.g. 22.

[7] The Commitment Criterion, the condition that must be met by the agent's intention for attempt under the Guiding Commitment View, is of the form $\forall$ i((p → Ei) OR (q → Ei)). Duff's View is of the form $\forall$ i((p&q) → Ei). These two statements have different truth conditions, as we can see by imagining that both of the following are true for some k: (p → not-Ek) and (q → Ek). In that case, $\forall$ i((p&q) → Ei) is false, while the Commitment Criterion is true. Conversely, "pigs fly" when conjoined with "this is a pig" entails "this flies", but neither "pigs fly" nor "this is a

Commitment View, thanks to the Commitment Criterion, *each* of the individual components of success must be planned for by the attempter by either being included in the intention's content, or implied by its playing its proper causal role. In Duff's View, by contrast, *the conjunction* of all of the components of success must be planned for by *the conjunction* of the intention's content and its playing its proper causal role. But for our purposes here what is more important is how the conditional in Duff's View is to be interpreted, in contrast to the way in which the conditional in the Commitment Criterion is to be interpreted.

Recall that, for the purposes of the Commitment Criterion, to assess the relevant conditional we consider *all* possible worlds in which the intention plays its proper causal role, and determine if the relevant component of the completed crime is present in *all* such worlds. If not, then the relevant conditional is false for the purposes of the Guiding Commitment View. The proper causal function of the intention must, itself, and not thanks to other things, bring with it the relevant condition's occurrence. By contrast, Duff has us consider only possible worlds in which the antecedent is true *and* the world is in other respects like the actual world. He thus allows that an intention could commit one to a condition even though the condition is not supplied by the intention's playing its proper causal role, per se, but supplied only by the proper causal role of the intention *given that the world is already in that condition*. So, for instance, under the Guiding Commitment View, if the defendant intends [to take something]—if that description truly exhausts the content of his intention—and he lacks consent, we find that his intention fails to constitute the commitment needed for attempted theft, since the absence of consent is not in the content of his intention and there are possible worlds in which his intention plays its proper causal role and he has consent. (As we will see in section 3, there are additional conditions such that when those conditions are met, a person who intends [to take something] and lacks consent is nonetheless committed by his intention to his lacking consent. But for now let's imagine those conditions are not met.) By contrast, under Duff's View, we hold fixed the fact that the defendant lacks consent, and so consider only possible worlds in which he lacks consent and takes something. Assuming the other conditions involved in the completed crime are met in all such worlds, he commits theft. Thus, under Duff's view, such a person has the commitment to the absence of consent required for attempted theft.

The point here is that Duff's approach to the conditional involved in his position—we are to confine our gaze to the "closest" possible worlds in which the antecedent is true, and hence we are to hold fixed the actual circumstances that the defendant faces in so far as they are consistent with him doing as he intends—encodes a theory of the commitment to circumstances that is

pig" entails "this flies". So it is possible also for $\forall i((p\&q) \rightarrow Ei)$ to be true and the Commitment Criterion false.

constituted by a particular intention. According to the theory, the defendant is committed to such circumstances by his intention if (a) they are actually present, or (b) they appear in the content of his intention, or (c) they would be caused by the intention were it to play its proper causal role. What's peculiar is that (a) should be sufficient. Consider, for instance, someone who intends [to take his neighbor's car], lacks permission, and has no idea one way or the other whether he has permission: he doesn't believe that he has it, but nor does he believe that he lacks it; perhaps his wife was to ask the neighbor for permission, but our defendant hasn't heard the outcome of that discussion. According to Duff's View, this defendant is as committed to lacking permission as he would need to be for an attempt, while he would not be sufficiently committed to that if the neighbor had given permission. On Duff's View, that is, we have a change in commitment without any change in mental state. What follows is that *under Duff's View the commitment in question is not intention-based*. But, as we saw in chapter 2, the commitments involved in trying are necessarily intention-based. And thus it seems that there is something wrong with Duff's View.

Two points need to be made about this line of objection. The first concerns the way in which the problem with Duff's View is hidden by his account's treatment of the attitude of the attempter to the mental state elements of the completed crime. The crime of rape is often defined so as to require recklessness with respect to the victim's non-consent. Duff does not think that an attempted rape requires an intention [to be reckless with respect to non-consent].[8] Rather, the fact that recklessness is required for the completed crime imposes a requirement on the attempter that can be met in one of two ways: the attempter can have intent with respect to non-consent—he can aim at having *non-consensual* sex—or he can simply be reckless with respect to the victim's non-consent. The first condition suffices for roughly the reasons offered in connection with the Guiding Commitment View's handling of the commitment with regard to the mental states involved in the completed crime discussed in chapter 4: were an intention that includes non-consent in its content to play its proper causal role, the defendant would meet the completed crime's mental state requirement. The second condition, namely that the defendant is reckless with respect to non-consent, meets the requirement imposed by the completed crime's mental state element because of the way that the conditional in Duff's View is to be treated: if the defendant *is* reckless, then we are to hold that fixed in determining what would be true were he to do as he intends; we thus find that were he to do as he intends, he would be reckless with respect to non-consent, just as the completed crime requires. In other words, just as in the case of circumstantial elements, it is possible, under Duff's View, to be committed to a mental state element of the completed crime thanks merely to the fact that one *has* that

---

[8] In fact, Duff thinks that such an intention is impossible. See the discussion of this issue in chapter 6.

mental state, and not thanks to anything about the intention one has. These, too, then, are commitments that are not intention-based.

Now notice that Duff's View will not *convict* the person of whom the following is true: he intends [to have sex with Victim], Victim does not in fact consent, but the defendant falls short of recklessness with respect to non-consent. Such a person, on Duff's View, has the needed commitment with respect to non-consent—Victim is non-consenting, and that's all that's required—but does not have the needed commitment with respect to the recklessness involved in completion: her lack of consent is not in the content of his intention, will not be caused by his intention playing its proper causal role, and, most importantly, is not present since he is not, in fact, reckless. What this means is that Duff's View reaches the right verdict about this kind of case, but it reaches it for the wrong reasons. In particular, Duff's View fails to accommodate the fact that this defendant is not sufficiently committed *to the lack of the Victim's consent* to warrant enriching our description of what he is trying to do with reference to it, as we would were we to describe him as attempting *to rape Victim*. The view implies that the problem is, instead, that the defendant is inadequately committed to *the mental state* needed for the completed crime. This is an inaccurate depiction of the situation. The fact that Duff's View's treatment of the circumstances, when working with the view's implications about the mental states involved in completion, reaches the right verdict in many cases, then, can conceal from us the fact that it involves an inadequate account of the commitment to circumstances of completion needed for attempt.

Now, and this is the second point to be made about the objection to Duff's View being offered here, it is possible to conceive of Duff's View a bit differently from the way in which it has so far been conceived. So far, we have conceived of Duff's View as involving the assertion that *even though* a circumstance can fail to be in the content of a person's intention, he can be sufficiently committed to it for attempt; this is so when the circumstance is actually present. We might, instead, conceive of Duff's View as an account of the conditions under which an account of the content of a person's *intention* can be expanded so as to include conditions that figure into other mental states. Perhaps, that is, Duff's View should be understood as claiming, for instance, that a person who intends [to have sex with Victim] and knows that Victim does not consent, actually intends [to have non-consensual sex with Victim]. On this construal, such a person has an intention-based commitment to the Victim's non-consent.

However, if we are to construe Duff's View in this way, then we need to see whether the position encodes an *adequate account* of the conditions under which it is proper to expand our description of an agent's intention's content so as to include a circumstance. In fact, it does not. To see this, consider the following example. D intends [to take *Guernica*] and is negligent with respect to the fact that it was painted by Picasso; any reasonable person (especially one educated at Oxford, as D was) would know that, but D does not since he believes it was painted by Braque. Now imagine that the legislature, out of a desire to give extra protection to the works of Picasso, defines the crime of stealing a Picasso painting; the completed crime's *mens rea* with respect to the circumstantial element of *having been painted by Picasso* is negligence. Under Duff's View, D has the intention needed for an attempt of this crime: the painting is actually by Picasso and he is actually negligent with respect to that fact. But it is plain that he does not intend [to take a Picasso painting]. There's an argument to be made that he intends [to take a Braque painting], but that's a different intention, and not one that would put him 'on the hook' for an attempt of the crime in question. The point is that negligence with respect to a circumstance is simply not sufficient to expand our description of what a person intends so as to include the circumstance.

What is really going on here is that, construed in the way just suggested, Duff's View involves a commitment to the following false principle, which is intended to identify a sufficient condition for expanding our account of the content of a person's intention with reference to a circumstance. Here, A is an action, P is a property and it is a circumstantial element of the crime that the thing A'd is P (for example, that the property received is stolen):

If ((D intends [to A]) & (D has the mental state needed for the completed crime with respect to the condition that the thing he A's is P)), then (D intends [to A the thing that is P]).

The problem with this principle is that the mental state with respect to the thing A'd being P required for the completed crime might very well be a mental state that does not allow enrichment of our description of the content of D's intention through appeal to that, even if the thing really is P. The Picasso example illustrates this for the case of negligence. In fact, we can see the problem also for the case of recklessness. Imagine that D intends [to sell cocaine] and believes that there is a 25 percent chance that the building he is standing in front of is an elementary school, and, indeed, it is. The relevant completed crime is the crime of selling cocaine near an elementary school—a crime, we can imagine, that requires recklessness with respect to the circumstance of being near an elementary school.[9] Is D reckless? That's a hard question. If he is, then under the principle just articulated, D intends [to sell cocaine near an elementary school]. That is, if the principle is correct, then it turns out that whether D intends [to sell cocaine near an elementary school] turns on whether awareness of a 25 percent chance amounts to recklessness. That's very odd. What kinds of risks amount to recklessness is a normative and legal question. What conditions need to be met for the content of one's beliefs to be properly appealed to in a characterization of the contents of one's intention is a conceptual question in the philosophy

---

[9] A typical state statute under which a much greater penalty is given for selling drugs near a school is Arizona's. See §13-3411 of the Arizona Criminal Code. In fact, such crimes are typically strict liability with respect to such elements.

of mind. It would be more than a little bit strange if it turned out that the two questions had to be answered in lock-step, as implied by the principle on offer.

I believe that Duff's View is intended to be interpreted in the first way, as an account under which the mere presence of a circumstance is sufficient for commitment to that circumstance. I do not believe that it is intended to be understood as an account of the conditions under which it is proper to enrich our description of the content of a person's intention with reference to a circumstance. Interpreted in the first way, however, the view falters by failing to give an account of the commitment of the attempter to circumstances which is intention-based. Interpreted in the second way, however, the view answers the right question—it just gives the wrong answer to it. The key to understanding circumstances in attempt, that is, is to provide an answer to the following question: "Under what conditions is a person who intends [to A] thereby committed to A-ing the thing that is P?" This is the right question, since if we had an answer to it, we would know the conditions under which a person can be rightly said to have an intention-based commitment to a circumstance, and it is that commitment that is needed for attempt. It is this question, and the answer's implications to the two problems with which this chapter began, that will be considered in the next section.

## 3. The Solution

The strategy undertaken in this section can be summarized, schematically, like so: first, the section identifies two different things that someone might be asserting when he says of himself that he has a particular intention, as when he says, "I intend to A the thing that is P." For now, call one of these "the *de dicto* interpretation" and the other "the *de re* interpretation", saving for later the description of what these interpretations involve, and why they are labeled as such. Correlatively, the intention the agent has, when such an assertion is true, is to be called "a *de dicto* intention" or "a *de re* intention", depending on how the assertion is to be interpreted. It is then argued that a *de re* intention to A the thing that is P, commits the agent who has that intention *to the thing he A's being P*. It is further argued that this is the minimal commitment to that which is needed for the *mens rea* of attempt. If the thing's being P is one of the circumstantial elements of the completed crime, then it suffices for the *mens rea* of attempt with respect to that circumstantial element that the defendant has a *de re* intention to A the thing that is P. Thus, the *de re* interpretation of assertions of sentences in which people attribute intentions to themselves gives us what we need in order to construct the *mens rea* standard that we seek. The rest of the section considers the implications. It is argued that given the *mens rea* standard identified, belief that the circumstance obtains frequently suffices for attempt.

And it is further argued that, given the *mens rea* standard identified, there are conditions under which a defendant meets the *mens rea* standard for the attempt only if the circumstance actually obtains.

## 3.1 *The* De Dicto *and the* De Re

Sentences attributing mental states to people, including intentions, are frequently subject to an ambiguity that is best illustrated by a somewhat complicated analogy. Consider the following sentence:

(a) The governor of California makes more than $1,000,000 a year.

Under one interpretation, the sentence expresses the same proposition as that expressed by one of the following two sentences:

(b1) Anyone who is governor of California makes more than $1,000,000 a year.

(b2) Someone who is governor of California makes more than $1,000,000 a year.

Someone who asserts (a) and expresses the same proposition as that expressed by (b1) is making a claim to the effect that two properties—namely being governor of California and making more than $1,000,000 a year—are always found together. This is the kind of thing that someone might say who believes (falsely, as it turns out) that the state of California pays the governor more than $1,000,000 each year to do the job. Someone, by contrast, who asserts (a) to express the same proposition as that expressed by (b2), makes an existence claim. Say that I have not yet heard the outcome of the election and you assert (a) in order to give me a clue about who won. I learn from your assertion that there is a person who has the two properties in question and so, if I know that only one of the candidates makes more than $1,000,000 a year, I am able to determine who won. However, your assertion will be false if the person who is governor does not make more than $1,000,000 a year. Therefore, if (a) is to be interpreted as expressing the same proposition as either (b1) or (b2), it is true only if at least one person who makes $1,000,000 a year is also the governor of California.

However, these are not the only ways of interpreting (a), nor are they the most important for our purposes. If, for instance, we assume that the speaker of (a) is using the phrase "the governor of California" in just the way in which he uses the proper name "Sylvester Stallone"—he mistakenly thinks Stallone is governor—then (a) expresses the same proposition as the following sentence:

(c) Sylvester Stallone makes more than $1,000,000 a year.

When so interpreted, (a) asserts something about the income of the person referred to by the speaker with the phrase "the governor of California". When

(a) is understood in such a way that it expresses the same proposition as (c), the properties referred to in the description "the governor of California" are not used to determine whether or not the sentence is true. After all, (c)'s truth value does not turn on whether or not Sylvester Stallone is governor, so if (a) is interpreted as expressing the same proposition as (c), then neither does (a)'s truth value turn on that. What this implies is that when a person asserts (a) and is rightly taken to express the proposition that (c) expresses, he can be mistaken in his belief that the description he uses applies to the object he refers to with it, and still assert something true. The person who asserts (a) while falsely believing that Sylvester Stallone is governor of California might be asserting no more than that Sylvester Stallone makes more than $1,000,000 a year, which is perfectly true, despite the fact that he is not governor of California.

Philosophers of language frequently draw the distinction between *de dicto* interpretations of referential descriptions, like "the governor of California", and *de re* interpretations. Although there is controversy about how, exactly, that distinction is drawn, for our purposes, to interpret (a) as expressing the same proposition as either (b1) or (b2) is to interpret the description as it appears in (a) *de dicto*, while to interpret (a) as expressing the same proposition as (c) is to interpret that description *de re*. When a descriptive phrase is interpreted *de re*, it contributes only its referent to the truth conditions of the sentence. When it is interpreted *de dicto*, by contrast, the properties referred to in the description contribute to the sentence's truth conditions independently.

A sentence like (a) is, when asserted, usually correctly construed as an expression of a belief that the speaker holds. How we characterize what the speaker believes will depend at least on whether we interpret the phrase "the governor of California" *de dicto* or *de re*. Let's say, however, that we interpret the description *de re*. Further, let's imagine that the speaker, as in the case just mentioned, falsely believes that Sylvester Stallone is governor of California, and uses the phrase "the governor of California" to refer to Stallone. By asserting (a) he expresses the belief that Stallone makes more than $1,000,000 a year, and this belief has a particular kind of primacy: the question of whether what he said is true or false turns only on the question of whether this belief is true or false. However, typically we learn more about his psychology from his assertion of (a) than merely that he believes that Stallone makes more than $1,000,000 a year. If the circumstances cooperate—say he's watching Stallone give an interview on television and pointing at the screen when he utters (a) and circumstances are otherwise normal—we also learn, perhaps among other things still, that he believes that Stallone is governor of California.

Is there a psychological difference between the person who asserts (a), understood *de re*, and the person who asserts (c), assuming that both falsely believe that Stallone is governor of California? There are, to be sure, differences between what we would need to do in order to reconstruct each one's beliefs. In order to reach the conclusion that the person who asserts (a) believes that

Stallone makes more than $1,000,000 a year, we need to learn, somehow, that he uses the description "the governor of California" in the same way that he uses the name "Stallone". No such step is required in order to determine that the person who asserts (c) believes that Stallone makes more than $1,000,000 a year. But does a difference of this sort speak to a difference in the psychology of these two people, or only a difference in what we need to do in order to reconstruct their psychologies? Happily, we do not need to answer this very difficult question. As stated, this question concerns *de re belief*, while our ultimate concern here will be with *de re* intention. Further, as we are about to see, the question is easier in the case of *de re* intention.

To see this, consider what is involved in intending [to A the thing that is P], where A is an act and P is a property. Imagine that the person who has an intention of this sort asserts the following sentence:

(d) I intend [to pay the governor of California $1,000,000].

Like (a), (d) admits of a *de dicto* or *de re* interpretation. Under its *de dicto* interpretation (and assuming that the speaker envisions a one-time payment, rather than a payment to all who will ever be governor of California), it expresses the same proposition as the following sentence:

(e) I intend [that someone is both the governor of California and paid $1,000,000 by me].

However, if (d) is interpreted *de re*, it expresses the same proposition as the following sentence, assuming that the speaker falsely believes Stallone to be governor and so is using "the governor of California" in the same way in which he uses "Stallone":

(f) I intend [to pay Stallone $1,000,000].

The parallel question to the one asked above is this: "Is there a psychological difference between the person who asserts (d), understood *de re*, and the person who asserts (f), assuming that both falsely believe that Stallone is governor of California?" There must be. The reason is that the world does not match the intention of the person who asserts (d) unless Stallone is governor of California, while that is irrelevant to the question of whether the intention of the person who asserts (f) matches the world. Notice, and this is important, for this to make sense there must be a difference between the world matching an intention, on the one hand, and the person doing as intended, on the other. Both the person who asserts (d), *de re*, and the person who asserts (f) *do as intended* when each gives the money to Stallone. But only the latter's intention matches the world. Thus, the person who asserts (d) is *not* aptly characterized as having a belief that Stallone is governor and an intention to give Stallone $1,000,000. If that were correct, then his *intention* would match the world in all respects when he gives the money to Stallone (although his belief would not). So whatever we ought to say about the belief case—perhaps there is no psychological difference there— we must not say that there is no psychological difference between the person who asserts (d), *de re*, and the person who asserts (f). The psychological difference consists in the fact that a role is played by the description in the first's intention, but that description plays no role in the intention of the second. Put, perhaps, more intuitively, the person who asserts (d) can point to the fact that Stallone, to whom the money is given, is not governor and say, "In this respect, things have not turned out as I intended." The person who asserts (f) can only say, "That's not what I believed", for there is no sense in which the fact that Stallone is not governor indicates a failure of his intention to match the world.

Intentions set two different standards of success by which the future world can be judged. They set a standard for the agent's act, and they set a standard for the world as a whole, including, but not limited to, the act. In the typical case, if the world lives up to the first standard, it also lives up to the second. This is the case when the person asserts (d), *de re*, believes Schwarzenegger to be the governor of Calfornia, and gives $1,000,000 to Schwarzenegger who is, indeed, the governor of California. His act has succeeded in meeting the standard set by his intention, since he gave the money to the person he had in mind, namely Schwarzenegger. And the world has lived up to his intention as a whole because the person to whom he gave the money met the description that he used, in his intention, for thinking of that person—namely, "the governor of California". In the case, however, in which the person asserts (d), *de re*, but falsely believes Stallone to be governor, and gives the money to Stallone, the world has lived up to the first standard set by his intention, but not the second. He has given the money to the person he had in mind, but in doing so he has not given the money to someone who meets the description included in his intention. And there is a third case to consider too, namely, the case in which the person asserts (d), *de dicto*, falsely believes that Stallone is governor, and gives the money to Stallone. In that case, the world has fallen short of both of his intention's standards because, in essence, the standards collapse into one another. In such a case, his act succeeds only if the person to whom he gives the money is, in fact, the governor of California, and the second standard is met only if this same thing is true.

## 3.2 *The Commitments Constituted by* De Dicto *and* De Re *Intentions*

As indicated earlier, for convenience, the term "*de dicto* intention" will be used to refer to the intention of the person who asserts a sentence like (d) *de dicto*, and the term "*de re* intention" to refer to the intention of the person who asserts a sentence like (d) *de re*. The difference between *de dicto* and *de re* intentions marks a difference in the commitments of the people who have those intentions. To see this, consider the difference between an event's occurring, on the one hand, and the defendant being the cause of the event's occurring, on the other. The latter includes the former plus more. Typically, as mentioned earlier, including a reference to an event in the content of one's intention is sufficient for generating two commitments: a commitment to the event's occurring, and a commitment to being the cause of the event's occurring (since one would be the cause were the intention to play its proper causal role). In a large class of cases, we are to interpret *de dicto* the description of the relevant event employed in a sentence stating that the defendant includes the event in the content of his intention. In fact, it is so natural to give the *de dicto* interpretation of the descriptions of acts and results that appear in the contents of intentions that it sometimes takes some mental gymnastics to even see what it would be to interpret them *de re*. What this indicates is that when a description appearing in the content of an intention is to be interpreted *de dicto*, the agent has two commitments: (1) a commitment to its being the case that the object with respect to which he acts falls under the description, and, also, (2) a commitment *to causing* this to be the case. For instance, when (d) is interpreted *de dicto*, the intention that it asserts the speaker, D, to have brings with it two commitments: a commitment to its being the case that the person who receives $1,000,000 from D is the governor of California, and a commitment to causing this to be the case. As we saw in chapter 3, D can cause this to be the case in one of two ways. He could, in theory, cause a particular person to be the governor of California—perhaps by fixing the election—and then give that person $1,000,000; or, more likely, he could see to it that he only gives $1,000,000 to the person who is, in fact, the governor of California when the money is given. If he follows the latter strategy, then he would switch the target of his money when he learns that the person at whom it is aimed is not, in fact, the governor of California. If (d) is true, then, and the description is interpreted *de dicto*, the person who asserts it has an intention that commits him to doing one of these two things.

By contrast, the agent with the *de re* intention has merely the first of the two commitments. The *de re* intention, that is, commits the agent to its being the case that the object with respect to which he acts falls under the description, but does not commit the agent to causing this to be the case. This is why, when (d) is to be interpreted *de re*, and the person who has the relevant intention gives $1,000,000 to Stallone, falsely believing him to be the governor of California, the right way to diagnose the failure of the intention to match the world is to say that although the act succeeded, the intention misrepresented the world in which that success was to take place. The intention represented the world in which success of the act takes place as a world in which the governor of California is given $1,000,000, when, in fact, in one such world someone, namely Stallone, who is not the governor of California, is given the money.

The very idea of being committed to a condition's obtaining, without being committed to causing that condition can seem quite puzzling. You are not really committed to it, we might say, if you are not willing to take steps to see to it that it obtains. You need to at least *be ready* to cause it should that be needed, and so you need to be committed to causing it. The very idea of *commitment to the condition*, the thought is, brings with it the idea of commitment *to causing* the condition. But the puzzlement is dissolved when we recognize the range of ways in which a person can be committed to a condition by his intention. Although there may be further senses yet, consider two different ways in which one can be committed by one's intention to the world being a certain way, without being committed thereby to causing it to be that way:

*Commitment to Non-Reconsideration:* The commitment to not reconsider one's intention on the grounds that one believes the condition to hold.

*Commitment to Not Complaining:* The commitment to not complaining that the world fails to be as intended in light of the fact that the condition holds.

In both of these cases, to fail to live up to what one is committed to is to be in violation of a norm of rationality to which one is subject thanks to the fact that one has the intention. (As we will see later, a person can have a commitment to not complaining with respect to a condition, while lacking a commitment to non-reconsideration with respect to that same condition.) Commitments to non-reconsideration involve norms of rationality that apply to agents after intention formation and before what we might call "plan's end", the moment at which the world has come to match their intentions in all respects. Commitments to not complaining, by contrast, involve norms of rationality that apply to agents at and after plan's end. Consider a person, for instance, who has the *de re* intention [to receive stolen cloth] but reconsiders that intention. When asked why he reconsiders he says, "Well, I think the cloth I intended to receive is stolen!" This explanation falls flat because the fact that the agent cites in explanation was already represented by his intention. He can no more cite the fact that he thinks the cloth is cloth in explanation of his decision to reconsider, than he can cite the fact that the cloth is stolen. He is equally irrational to reconsider *for that reason* in both cases. He might rationally decide to reconsider on the grounds that the cloth's being stolen is a weightier consideration than he thought at the time of intention formation; or he might rationally decide to reconsider on the grounds that he just learned that it is illegal to receive stolen cloth. But what he cannot do in full rationality is to reconsider merely on the grounds that he believes the cloth is stolen. Similarly, if he succeeds in receiving the cloth, he cannot without irrationality complain that the world is not as he intended it to be in light of the fact that the cloth he received is stolen: that is part of what he intends and so the world has not fallen short of being as he intended in light of that fact.

A person with a *de re* intention [to A the thing that is P] has both a commitment of non-reconsideration with respect to the thing he A's being P, and a commitment not to complain with respect to that same condition. Since one can have either or both of these commitments without being committed to causing the thing to be P, or to selecting a thing to A that is P, these commitments are independent of any commitment to cause the thing one A's to be P.

## 3.3 *The* Mens Rea *Standard and Beliefs About Circumstances*

Recall that under the Guiding Commitment View to try to do something is to be committed by one's intention to each of the components of success and to be moved by those commitments. Circumstantial elements of crimes are components of success. But since success does not require that the defendant cause them, an attempt requires no more than an intention-based commitment to their occurrence that falls short of commitment to causing their occurrence. When we put this together with the view of *de re* intention just offered, we reach the following result: *to have the commitment to the circumstantial elements involved in an attempted crime, it is sufficient for the defendant to include the circumstantial elements of the completed crime in the content of his intention as part of a* de re *description. De dicto* descriptions will do, but since such intentions constitute a commitment to causing the circumstances to obtain, they are more than is required for attempt. We, therefore, have identified the *mens rea* standard that we sought.

When we add to this the idea that an intention that includes a *de re* description (such as the intention [to pay the governor of California $1,000,000]) involves a commitment of non-reconsideration and a commitment to not complaining, we are tempted to hold that a person who merely believes a circumstantial element of the completed crime to be in place, and has the relevant accompanying intention, is sufficiently committed to that circumstance for attempt. This isn't quite true, although there is a live possibility, to be discussed shortly, that it is close enough to being true for the government's work of assessing the *mens rea* of attempt. To see why it is not strictly true, consider (d) again, together with the following two sentences:

(g) Arnold Schwarzenegger is the star of *The Terminator*.
(h) I intend [to pay the star of *The Terminator* $1,000,000].

Now imagine that (d) is true when "the governor of California" is interpreted *de re*, and that the person who asserts it, D, uses the phrase "the governor of California" in the same way he uses the name "Schwarzenegger". He would point to the man at the podium, who is Schwarzenegger, and say things like, "There's the governor of California!" And imagine that (g) could be asserted by this same person in order to express his belief. The question is whether, in such a case, we can, without exception, conclude that (h) is true (or, rather, would be if uttered by D). We cannot.

There are at least three kinds of cases in which (d) and (g) are true and (h) is false. First, there are so-called "Frege Puzzles":[10] imagine that D believes that Arnold Schwarzenegger and the governor of California are different people. In that case, (h) does not follow from (d) and (g), even though (d) and (g), both of which are to be interpreted *de re*, concern the very same person, namely Arnold Schwarzenegger. Second, there are failures "to put two and two together": imagine that D's belief that Arnold Schwarzenegger starred in *The Terminator* is entirely dispositional. He pays little attention to the movies, and a great deal of attention to politics, and just never has occurrent thoughts about movies except in special circumstances. Were you to ask him if Schwarzenegger starred in that film he would assert (g), but he would not have an occurrent thought that it would be proper for him to express by uttering (g) in the absence of prompting. In having the intention [to pay the governor of California $1,000,000], D simply is not thinking about the movies that the governor of California starred in. But if he is not thinking about that, then he very well may not have the intention [to pay the star of *The Terminator* $1,000,000]. Perhaps he has it in some purely dispositional sense, but he does not have it occurrently. Such an intention includes an occurrent thought about the movies that a particular person has starred in, and we are stipulating that D just isn't thinking about that when he has the intention he attributes to himself with (d). But on the assumption that it is occurrent intentions, and not dispositional ones, that actually motivate token actions, it follows that (h) is not true in the sense of relevance to the criminal law.

There is a third category of cases in which sentences like (d) and (g) are true and a sentence like (h) is false, and it is in some ways the most important of the three for legal purposes.[11] For reasons that will become clear, call these cases "insalience cases". To appreciate this category, consider someone who has the *de re* intention [to pay the governor of California $1,000,000], the occurrent belief that the governor of California has an Austrian accent, and the belief that the person whom he intends to give the money and the person he believes to have an Austrian accent are one and the same person, namely Arnold Schwarzenegger. His is neither a Frege puzzle case, nor a failure to put two and two together. Now let's further imagine that this person could not care less that Arnold Schwarzenegger has an Austrian accent. He takes this fact to give him no reason whatsoever to refrain from giving him the money, nor a reason to give him the money, nor does he see it as in any way a salient fact about Arnold Schwarzenegger in any other respect pertaining to the act he intends to perform. Does this person have the *de re* intention [to pay the Austrian-accented

---

[10] The term refers to Gottlob Frege, who introduced puzzles of this sort in his famous Frege (1948).

[11] Robin Jeshion helped me to recognize this third category and its importance. Many of the examples that I use to illustrate it are thanks to her, as well.

150

person $1,000,000]? He does not. In asking about the *de re* intention, we are assuming that a person who has this intention uses the description "the Austrian-accented person" analogously to a proper name in order to refer to Arnold Schwarzenegger. The man in the example might very well be willing to use that phrase in that way. But even if he is, that does not mean that he has the relevant *de re* intention. In having the intention that he attributes to himself in asserting (d), he is not thereby thinking of Arnold Schwarzenegger *as* an Austrian-accented person, despite the fact that at that very moment he has another thought, namely his occurrent belief that Arnold Schwarzenegger has an Austrian accent, that does involve thinking of Schwarzenegger in that way. The intention and the belief remain distinct thoughts that represent the same object in different ways. Only the belief, in this case, represents Schwarzenegger as having an Austrian accent. In this case the insalience of the fact that Schwarzenegger has an Austrian accent blocks the inference from the intention and belief to the further intention [to pay the Austrian-accented person $1,000,000].

Frege puzzle cases, failures to put two and two together, and insalience cases are cases in which the agent falls short of a commitment to not reconsider the intention in the face of the belief that the relevant condition holds. In Frege puzzle cases, the agent could without irrationality reconsider his intention at the moment that he discovers that the object of his intention and the object of his belief are one and the same. D might without any form of irrationality give up his intention [to pay the governor of California $1,000,000] when he realizes that the person he has in mind is the very one who is drawing large sums every year from the residual income that he gains thanks to having been the star of *The Terminator*. Because he would not be irrational in any sense in such a case, he does not have the intention he would ascribe to himself with (h). The same is true if the case is a failure "to put two and two together". The agent in such a case lacks the commitment to non-reconsideration constituted by the *de re* intention [to pay the star of *The Terminator* $1,000,000]. At the point that he puts two and two together and comes to have an occurrent belief that the man to whom he intends to pay the money is the star of *The Terminator*, he can without irrationality reconsider his intention [to pay the governor of California $1,000,000]. And, similarly, the person for whom the movies the governor has starred in is completely insalient can, nonetheless, reconsider an intention [to pay the governor of California $1,000,000] on the grounds that Schwarzenegger starred in *The Terminator*. In some such cases, the person will have come to recognize this fact as providing him with reason not to pay Schwarzenegger the money. But even if he does not change his mind about that, *his intention* is not rationally stable in the face of the relevant belief. It might be *factually* stable in the face of that belief—perhaps he will not, in fact, reconsider his intention in the face of the belief—but he would not be in violation of a commitment constituted by his intention were he to do so. This is the sense in which *his intention* does not place him under any rational pressure to not reconsider in the face of the belief, and hence he does not have a commitment of non-reconsideration with respect to the condition that the person he gives the money to starred in *The Terminator*.

Still, despite the fact that sentences like (d) and (g) do not entail sentences like (h), it is also the case that the truth of sentences like (d) and (g) can provide powerful evidence in favor of the truth of a sentence like (h), especially when conjoined with other evidence to the effect that the case is not a Frege puzzle case, a failure to put two and two together, or an insalience case. To see this, consider again *United States v. Crow* (164 F.3d 229 (5th Cir. 1999)), in which the defendant falsely believed himself to be chatting with a 13-year-old girl whom he asked to send him sexually explicit photographs of herself; he was actually chatting with a detective. Crow has the *de re* belief that the person he is chatting with is a minor. He also appears to have the intention [to sexually exploit the person he is chatting with]. It is a little unclear whether this intention is *de dicto* or *de re*—does it matter to Crow whether the person he sexually exploits actually chats with him, or not? Is it part of what he is after that he *convinced* the minor whose photos he enjoys to send them, or would it be enough for success merely that, at the end of the day, he has her photo? We do not know enough about Crow to know the answers to these questions. But let's assume that the relevant intention is *de re*. The question is whether we can infer that Crow intends [to sexually exploit a minor]. If he does have that intention, then he is sufficiently committed to his target's being a minor for an attempt to sexually exploit a minor.

We cannot *deduce* that Crow has the intention [to sexually exploit a minor]. It is possible that his is a Frege puzzle case: perhaps he falsely believes that the person he intends to sexually exploit and the person he believes to be a minor are different people. We would need a complicated story to make this plausible, but imagine that we have it: perhaps he mistakenly thinks that he is chatting with two different people, one of whom is a minor and one of whom is not, who happen to be using the same screen name. Or perhaps he is like the person whose relevant belief is dispositional. Perhaps, that is, although he believes that the person he is chatting with is a minor he doesn't have an occurrent thought to that effect, and so cannot have formed the intention [to sexually exploit a minor]. These things are *possible*, but they are highly unlikely. They are so unlikely, in fact, that the doubt that their possibility supplies could hardly be thought reasonable in the absence of compelling evidence in their favor. It seems much more likely that Crow believes that the person he intends to sexually exploit and the person that he believes to be a minor are one and the same. And, given that the detective explicitly claimed to be a minor, it is hard to imagine that Crow did not have the occurrent belief that the person he was chatting with was a minor. Further, there is little reason to think that the person's status as a minor was not extremely salient to Crow. He knows, for instance, that there are criminal penalties for the sexual exploitation of minors that do not apply to the sexual exploitation of adults. And there may be reason to think that he is positively in search of sexually explicit photographs of minors, and so, assuming that he has reason to believe that the pictures he hopes to receive are of the person he is chatting with, that person's minor status is important to Crow. Given all of this, chances are that he intends [to sexually exploit a minor]. At the least, it seems that if the prosecution has proven beyond a reasonable doubt that the defendant has a *de re* intention [to A a thing] and a *de re* belief that the thing he intends to A is P, then the burden switches. At this point, it seems, we are justified in assuming that the defendant has a *de re* intention [to A the thing that is P], and is thus committed by his intention to its being P, unless the defendant is able to provide us with compelling reason for thinking that we ought not to reach this conclusion. What this implies is that we ought to hold that *proof beyond a reasonable doubt that the defendant has the* de re *belief that the circumstantial element of the crime is in place, together with a relevant intention, creates a rebuttable presumption that he has an intention that commits him to the circumstantial element of the completed crime.*

Although it is an empirical question, it seems that insalience cases are likely to be far more commonly found in courtrooms than are the other sorts of conditions that block the inference from the belief to the intention that commits the defendant to the circumstantial element of the completed crime. For instance, imagine an 18-year-old defendant who tries and fails to have sex with a 15-year-old in a jurisdiction in which the age of consent is 16. Let's imagine that the defendant has a *de re* intention [to have sex with Victim], and an occurrent *de re* belief that Victim is 15. And let's further imagine that the two are of comparable emotional maturity when it comes to sex. If this is an attempted statutory rape, the defendant must, at least, have a *de re* intention [to have sex with a minor]. But does the defendant have this intention? We need to know much more about him in order to answer this question. The question is whether he takes the minor status of his would-be partner to be at all salient. Given the small age difference between them, the stipulated small difference in emotional maturity, and, even, perhaps, some rather foggy-headed ideas on his part about what his legal obligations are, it is perfectly possible to imagine that the victim's age just isn't salient at all and so prevents the content of his belief from making its way into the content of his intention. This is why, when he says, on the stand, "But I really love her!" what he says is of relevance to his case. What he is saying is that her age was not relevant to him. It was as irrelevant to him as was Schwarzenegger's accent in our example earlier. But irrelevant facts, even those which one believes to be present, often do not make their way into the contents of our intentions, even in the face of occurrent belief that they are present. By contrast, if the facts are the same except that the defendant is 50 years old, then our perception of the case changes radically. Here we are much more likely to see him as having intended, *de re* [to have sex with a minor]. The reason is that it is hard for us to imagine that the minor status of one's partner would be entirely insalient to a person of that age. It *could* be so: the conceptual possibility remains. But it seems extremely unlikely, given a few basic assumptions about human psychology.

There is a fourth way in which a defendant could rebut a presumption to the effect that he has the intention needed for attempt given that he has a relevant belief and a *de re* intention. He could show that his belief is *de dicto*. In the case in which Crow's belief is *de dicto*, he might not intend [to sexually exploit a minor]. The *de dicto* belief that the person he is chatting with is a minor amounts to the belief that two properties co-occur—the property of being the person he is chatting with and the property of being a minor. It is awkward, although possible, to imagine having this belief. Other similar beliefs are more familiar. Consider, for instance, a woman who has the *de dicto* belief that the man she is dating resembles her father. She may not see the resemblance herself. She may, in fact, have the *de re* belief that the man she is dating does not resemble her father. But she also might know herself well enough to know that she always ends up dating men who resemble her father. She believes that two properties co-occur: the property of being dated by her, and the property of resembling her father. Imagine that Crow's belief is like that. He believes that it so happens that he always finds himself chatting with minors. There is little reason to think that Crow, in such a case, intends [to sexually exploit a minor]. Note that it is clear that even if the woman in our example intends [to marry the man she is dating], she does not intend [to marry a man who resembles her father]. How could she intend that, given that she has the *de re* belief that the man she is dating does not resemble her father, and it is *he* that she intends to marry? Similarly, there are reasonable grounds for doubting that Crow, when he has the *de dicto* belief, intends [to sexually exploit a minor]. Of course, given that StephieFL *told* Crow she was a minor, it seems very unlikely that his actual belief is *de dicto*.

What we have shown, then, is that the position enshrined in *Model Penal Code* §5.01(1), and accepted in many jurisdictions, is too strong. Under that section, belief that a circumstantial element of a crime is present suffices for the *mens rea* of the attempt with respect to that element. Under such a position, the relevant *mens rea* is present, even in cases in which the defendant lacks an intention that commits him to the circumstantial element of the completed crime because of one of the conditions that would block the relevant inference. The correct policy is that such a belief creates a rebuttal presumption that there is *mens rea*, provided that the defendant has been shown to have an appropriate intention. The defendant can rebut this presumption by showing that his case is a Frege puzzle case, a failure to put two and two together, an insalience case, or, even, by showing that his relevant belief is *de dicto*. These are all hard roads for any defendant to follow, and so typically all the prosecution will need to show is that the defendant had a relevant belief. But law should not close possible roads to a showing of innocence, no matter how unlikely they are to be open to any given defendant.

## 3.4 Disjunctive Descriptions of Circumstances

So far we have no reason to think that the circumstantial elements of the completed crime need actually to be in place for the attempted. We have identified a minimal condition for the commitment to circumstances involved in attempt: the defendant has a *de re* intention that includes the circumstantial element. We have also identified a distinct condition that creates a rebuttable presumption that this is the case: the defendant has a *de re* belief that the circumstance obtains, together with an intention that serves for commitment to performing the act involved in the completed crime. But, in fact, there is one class of cases in which a defendant charged with attempt probably has an intention that incorporates a circumstantial element of the completed crime only if that circumstance is actually present. These are cases in which the property included in the *de re* description in his intention is a disjunctive property, one of the disjuncts of which includes the circumstantial element. I explain.

Say that I'm offered a choice between two boxes. One of the boxes contains $5, the other contains either $100 or a small amount of marijuana with equal probability, although I'm not certain which it contains. I see no attraction to possessing marijuana and recognize that were I to possess it, I would incur, let's say with certainty, a fine of $50. Assuming my only motive is profit, I calculate the expected value and act accordingly, thereby forming the intention to take the box containing either $100 or marijuana; that box has an expected value of $25. So, were I to utter the following sentence it would be true:

(i) I intend [to take the $100-or-marijuana box].

Let's assume that "the $100-or-marijuana box" is to be interpreted *de re*: I have in mind a particular box—the very one that I occurrently believe contains either $100 or marijuana, and I intend to take it. Imagine that I act on this intention, although I fall short of taking the box I have in mind because I am arrested and charged with an attempt to possess marijuana. Whether I have committed this crime turns on whether or not the intention I report with (i) committed me to the following condition: the box I intended to take contains marijuana. Did my intention commit me to that?

The first thing to see is that I do not have a commitment of non-reconsideration with respect to the box's containing marijuana. After all, imagine that before I can take the box I come to believe that it contains marijuana. At this point, I know that the box I intend to take promises nothing but a $50 fine, while the other box promises me $5. There is no irrationality in reconsidering my intention in the face of this belief. In fact, rationality may even require reconsideration in this case. Hence, I am not committed *in the sense involved in a commitment of non-reconsideration*, to the box containing marijuana.

But this does not show all by itself that I am not sufficiently committed to the box's containing marijuana for the attempt to possess it. Recall that an intention might also constitute a commitment to not complain about a particular condition; one might be irrational, that is, were one to cite the fact that a condition is met in order to support a complaint to the effect that the world is not as intended. I would be sufficiently committed to the box containing marijuana if my intention constitutes a commitment to not complain with respect to that condition. As I will now argue, I do have this commitment *if the box contains marijuana*. Appreciating this requires further reflection on the nature of commitments not to complain about conditions.

Start with the following observation: a reasonable complaint is, by its nature, about some actual fact. A person's complaint can always be neutralized by noting that the world is not actually the way that the person is complaining about its being. If I complain that I repeatedly am given the short end of the stick, my complaint has no bite in the face of the fact that I am not, in fact, repeatedly given the short end of the stick. So, each and every one of us is committed to not complaining about unactualized conditions. We all have that commitment simply because of what complaints are. Any complaint about an unactualized condition is, by its nature, misplaced, and therefore we are all committed to not offering such complaints. But it is possible for people to have commitments to not complaining that go beyond this. People can have commitments to not complaining that are special to them, and, in particular, that are special to them thanks to their intentions. It is natural to characterize their situation as involving some kind of conditional commitment. A person who is committed to not complaining about condition K, in the sense of interest, is someone who is committed to not complaining *if K*.

The claim that D is committed to not complaining if K admits of scope ambiguity. Is that to which D is committed conditional in its nature, or is the presence of D's commitment conditional? We find, that is, that there are two kinds of conditional commitments, which the recent philosophical literature has labeled "wide scope" and "narrow scope".[12]

*Wide Scope Commitment to Not Complaining*: The commitment to not complaining that the following conditional is true: If K, then the world fails to be as intended.
*Narrow Scope Commitment to Not Complaining*: If K, then one is committed to not complaining that, in light of K, the world fails to be as intended.

---

[12] The terminology appears to have been introduced in Schroeder (2004). The concept of wide and narrow scope was present in the philosophical literature far before the introduction of those terms. Sometimes, for instance, philosophers would refer to the Wide Scope cases as "internally conditional" and the narrow scope as "externally conditional".

The first thing to see is that a Wide Scope Commitment to Not Complaining with respect to condition K does not amount to any kind of commitment *to K*. The commitment involved there is a commitment to the conditional of which K is the antecedent, but it is not a commitment to K itself. However, those who have Wide Scope Commitment to Not Complaining with respect to a particular condition also, typically, have Narrow Scope Commitment to Not Complaining with respect to that very condition. However, Narrow Scope Commitments to Not Complaining also fall short of commitment to K all by themselves. To say that a person *would* be committed to something *if* a particular condition were met is not to say, *ipso facto*, that he's committed to anything at all, given the way things actually are. After all, the condition might not be met. But those who have the Narrow Scope Commitment are committed by their intentions *to K itself* under one particularly important circumstance: the circumstance in which K is realized.

So, this is what we have learned: a person who has the *de re* intention [to A the thing that is P] has, at least, a Narrow Scope Commitment to Not Complaining with respect to the following condition: the thing he A's is P. He may also have the Wide Scope Commitment to Not Complaining. In fact, that he has that Wide Scope Commitment might be why he has the Narrow. But, whatever the reason he has the Narrow Commitment to Not Complaining, nothing of interest yet follows about his commitment to the thing he A's being P. However, if the thing he A's *is* P, then he is committed by his intention to not complaining about that. Hence, his intention commits him to that condition *when the thing he A's is P*, and it does not commit him to that if that is not so.

Now return to our example involving the *de re* intention [to take the $100-or-marijuana box]. In having this intention, I am not committed to not reconsidering with respect to the condition that the box I take contains marijuana. But I do have the Narrow Commitment of Not Complaining with respect to that condition. Thus, if the box contains marijuana, I am committed by my intention to not complaining that the world has, on those grounds, fallen short of being as intended. Whether I am committed by my intention to that condition, then, turns on whether or not that condition is actually in place. Notice that if the box turns out to contain methamphetamine, I am not committed by my intention to its containing methamphetamine. In that case, I can without irrationality complain that the world has failed to be as intended since my intention did not represent the box, even disjunctively, as containing methamphetamine.

Notice, and this will turn out to be of some importance when applying what we have learned to cases like *Dlugash*, it is perfectly possible for the disjuncts involved in the disjunctive representation of the object on which one intends to act to fill logical space. A person can intend [to receive the stolen or unstolen cloth], for instance. To have such an intention is to represent the cloth one intends to receive as having some relevant legal status or other, without representing it as being stolen, and without representing it as being unstolen. The property of being stolen or unstolen, despite being possessed by every object, might or might not be included in the representation of the object in one's intention. Every object is made in China, or not made in China; every object has that disjunctive property. But for someone for whom the belief that the object is or is not made in China is entirely dispositional, or for someone for whom the fact that the object possesses that property is entirely insalient, this property is unlikely to be included in the intention to receive the object, or to steal it, or to act in some other way with respect to it. That is, everything that we learned above about the ways in which the properties of an object are and are not found in an agent's intention when he has the belief that the object possesses that property, apply to disjunctive properties in which the disjuncts fill logical space.

As we saw, the fact that a person's case is a Frege puzzle case, a failure to put two and two together, or an insalience case defeats the otherwise safe inference from the fact that he believes *de re* that a thing is P, and has a *de re* intention [to act on it], to the conclusion that he has a *de re* intention [to act on a thing that is P]. Similarly, in the absence of one of these same defeaters, a person who believes *de re* that a thing *might* have a property and has a *de re* intention [to act on that thing] has a disjunctive *de re* intention [to act on a thing that has or lacks the property]. For instance, if a defendant has a *de re* belief that the cloth might be stolen and might not be, and intends [to buy the cloth], then chances are that he intends [to buy the stolen or unstolen cloth]. This further intention is not *entailed* by the relevant intention and belief: the case might be a Frege puzzle case, a failure to put two and two together, or an insalience case. But we are nonetheless safe in assuming that the person has the relevant disjunctive intention in the absence of evidence supportive of the claim that his case is of one of these three sorts. As before, the intention and belief support a rebuttable presumption that the agent has the relevant further intention.

### 3.5 *The Position in Action*

In the preceding parts of this section, we have reached the following four, interconnected results. Here A is an act involved in crime C, P is a property such that some thing's being P is a circumstantial element of C, and Q is an alternative property that is incompatible with P. So, for instance, A might be the act of receiving goods, while P might be the property of being stolen, and Q the property of not being stolen. In that example, the circumstantial element of C is that the goods received are stolen.

(1) If D intends [to A the thing that is P], then D has the *mens rea* with respect to the thing being P needed for an attempt to C, whether his intention is *de re* or *de dicto*.

(2) If D has the *de re* intention [to A] and the *de re* belief [that the thing that he intends to A is P], then there is very good evidence that D intends [to A the thing that is P]. There is, therefore, very good evidence, given (1), that D has the *mens rea* with respect to the thing being P needed for an attempt to C.

(3) If D has the *de re* intention [to A the thing that is P or Q] and the thing is P, then D is committed by his intention to the thing's being P. Therefore, given (1), D has the *mens rea* with respect to the thing's being P needed for an attempt to C.

(4) If D has the *de re* intention [to A] and the occurrent *de re* belief [that it is at least likely that the thing is either P or Q], then there is very good evidence that D has the *de re* intention [to A the thing that is P or Q]. Therefore, given (3), if the thing is P there is very good evidence that D has the *mens rea* with respect to the thing's being P needed for an attempt to C.

These results provide us with sufficient resources to resolve both the *Jaffe* case and the *Dlugash* case, and others like them. Jaffe has a *de re* belief that the cloth that he is buying is stolen. And he intends [to buy the cloth]. His is not a "Frege Puzzle" case. He does not falsely believe that the cloth he intends to buy and the cloth that he believes to be stolen are distinct. Nor is his likely to be a case of failure "to put two and two together". Further, given the salience of the status of the cloth as stolen or unstolen, it seems very likely that he has its status in mind when he buys it. Further evidence, such as evidence that he took precautions to avoid detection, would support this contention. His case, in other words, is to be handled in exactly the same way as the *Crow* case discussed above. In both, the defendant has a *de re* belief (that the cloth is stolen, that the person he is chatting with is a minor) and a relevant intention (an intention [to buy the cloth], an intention [to sexually exploit the person he is chatting with]). And in both there is no reason to think that the special conditions that defeat an inference to the conclusion that the defendant has the intention needed for attempt (the intention [to buy stolen cloth], the intention [to sexually exploit a minor]) are present. Because of these defendants' *de re* beliefs about the presence of the circumstantial element, we are in a position to say that they are suffi-ciently committed to those elements for attempt *without any inquiry into the question of whether those elements are in fact present*.

To resolve the *Dlugash* case we must draw on the lesson provided by reflection on the hypothetical involving the box containing either $100 or marijuana. Start with a prior question: "What, exactly, did Dlugash intend?" Given what little we know of the case, the answer to this question is surely indeterminate. But the answer to a closely related question might not be: "Consistent with what we do know, what characterization of Dlugash's intention will paint him in the best possible light?" It is tempting to characterize Dlugash's intention as conditional. Perhaps he intended [to kill Geller, if Geller was alive and to mutilate Geller's corpse, if Geller was already dead]. If this was Dlugash's intention, then the case is a relatively easy one to resolve, although not through appeal to the principles presented here, but, instead, through principles for determining the conditions under which a conditional intention serves to meet an unconditional intention *mens rea* standard. That is, if this is Dlugash's intention, then the question is just whether an intention [to kill if Geller was alive] should serve to meet the *mens rea* standard for a crime that requires intent to kill. I have developed an account of how to answer such questions elsewhere.[13] Under both the account that I advocate, and under the rival account to be found in the *Model Penal Code*,[14] the conditional intention under consideration would suffice for *mens rea* for attempted murder. So if that was Dlugash's intention, he is guilty of attempted murder. This is why a showing to the effect that Dlugash was firing insurance shots—a showing to the effect that he was seeing to it that Geller was dead while recognizing that he might be wasting ammunition—would be enough to show that he had the intention needed for attempted murder.

So the characterization of Dlugash as possessing the conditional intention [to kill if...] does not paint him in the best possible light. There is, in other words, a characterization of his intention that is less bad and is consistent with what we know of Dlugash. To see this, let's assume that Dlugash takes shooting Geller to be a necessary means to some end of his, and let's further assume that the end is not, itself, killing Geller. For instance, perhaps Dlugash believes that shooting Geller is the necessary means to impressing Bush. Let's further assume, as seems plausible, that Dlugash occurrently believes Geller to be alive or dead and his is not a Frege puzzle case, a failure to put two and two together, or an insalience case. Assume, yet further, that Dlugash intends the consequences of his act. He does not merely foresee, for instance, that Geller will be in some condition following the shooting: he positively intends that Geller be in that condition. So understood, it seems that Dlugash intends [to put the person who is dead or alive into the condition that results from his shooting him several times in the head]. This is different from the conditional intention discussed above, since Dlugash is not under pressure from his intention to do one thing if Geller is alive and another if Geller is dead. There is just one thing that Dlugash's intention commits him to doing: that is to bring about a further condition in Geller by shooting him in the head. What he does not know is *what* condition that will be; but he intends it either way. So characterized, Dlugash's intention is similar to that of the person who intends [to take the $100-or-marijuana box]. Both such a person and Dlugash intend an act (shooting, taking) and intend a result of that act (putting Geller into the resulting condition, placing oneself in possession of the box's contents). But both think of the result under a

---

[13] Yaffe (2004).    [14] §2.02(6).

disjunctive description. In Dlugash's case, and not in the other case, the disjuncts fill logical space, since Geller is either alive or dead. But that difference needn't detain us.

So, for our purposes, Dlugash intends [to put the person who is dead or alive into the condition that results from his shooting him several times in the head]. But it follows, then, for the reasons discussed above, that Dlugash's intention commits him to Geller's being alive at the time he is shot if Geller *is* alive at the time he is shot. In representing Geller as dead or alive in his intention, Dlugash has a narrow scope commitment to not complain with respect to Geller's being alive; he is thus committed to not complaining that Geller is alive *if he is alive*. Thus whether or not Dlugash is committed to Geller's being alive at the time of the shooting—whether he is committed by his intention *to shooting someone living*—turns on whether or not Geller was, in fact, alive when Dlugash shot him. Thus, the question of what Dlugash's intention commits him to turns on the facts. It follows, then, that Dlugash attempted murder only if Geller was alive. Since the prosecution cannot show this beyond a reasonable doubt, they cannot show beyond a reasonable doubt that Dlugash attempted murder. In this case, because Dlugash's intention is disjunctive, and only some of the disjuncts represent the property (being alive) that figures in the circumstantial element, the actual presence or absence of that element is crucial for determining whether or not Dlugash had the intention required for the attempted crime. At least, so it is, provided that we are willing to ascribe Dlugash with the disjunctive intention and not a conditional intention that would inculpate him for the crime.[15]

## 3.6 *Glanville Williams's View Formalized?*

It is important to see that the approach recommended here for resolving the Dlugash case, and other cases like it, may, in the end, amount merely to making satisfying philosophical sense of the view offered by the great criminal law theorist Glanville Williams.[16] After describing the problem of *mens rea* with respect to circumstances in attempt, Williams writes,

The solution is found simply by saying that a man who attempts to have a woman willy-nilly does intend to commit rape, and so can be guilty of an attempt to rape, even though he is not certain whether she is rejecting him or not. His intention may be analysed as

---

[15] Notice that, for parallel reasons, the prosecution cannot show that Dlugash attempted to mutilate a corpse without showing beyond a reasonable doubt that Geller was dead when Dlugash shot him. Does this imply that Dlugash is guilty of no crime? No. The reason is that when a person can be shown beyond a reasonable doubt to have committed either crime 1 or crime 2, he has been shown to be guilty of the lesser crime. This is a principle governing guilt attribution independently of proof of commission of a crime.

[16] In fact, we see signs of a similar view in Fletcher (1986). For ideas in the neighborhood see, also, Alexander and Kessler (1997).

being an intention to copulate with the woman *nolens* or to copulate with her *volens*—to commit rape, or to enjoy consensual sex—as matters may turn out. He does not care which. The first of these two intents make him guilty of an attempt to rape, which is not erased by the fact that he has an alternative lawful intent.[17]

If taken literally, Williams seems to be saying that someone with a disjunctive intention [to have nonconsensual sex or to have consensual sex], is thereby committed to having nonconsensual sex, and so has the intention needed for an attempted rape, *whether or not the victim consents*. If this is what Williams means, then he is mistaken. After all, the person who intends [to take the $100-or-marijuana box] is not committed by his intention to the box he takes containing marijuana when it actually contains money. Nor does the person who intends [to have nonconsensual sex or to have consensual sex] thereby commit himself to having nonconsensual sex when the victim, unbeknownst to our defendant, consents. However, what Williams is sensing is that there are conditions under which a person who intends [to have nonconsensual sex or to have consensual sex], or equivalently, intends [to have sex with consenting or non-consenting Victim] is thereby committed to Victim's non-consent. Williams is right about this. What has been offered above is an account of the relevant conditions: the disjunctive description must be *de re*, and Victim must actually be non-consenting.

Duff has offered a criticism of Williams's position,[18] and it is important to see why the criticism fails when directed at the view offered here. Duff considers what Williams's view implies about a person who moves towards sex with Victim while acting on an intention [to have sex with a consenting person] and while unsure whether or not Victim consents. This defendant, Duff imagines, would desist, were he to come to believe that Victim does not consent, but he does not have this belief. Thus, the description "consenting person" that appears in the content of this defendant's intention is to be interpreted *de dicto*: the defendant is committed by his intention to causing it to be the case that the person he has sex with consents; he is committed to choosing a different target should he discover that the person at whom he aims is not consenting. So far, there is no pressure at all from any quarter for taking this person to have committed attempted rape. He seems to have merely the mental states of many a hopeful suitor who arrives at the front door, roses in hand. But Duff adds that this person is willing to take the risk: if he receives no clear sign that consent is absent, he will go ahead and have sex with Victim. Now there seems to be pressure to see this person as attempting rape. Notice that, in adding the further feature that the defendant will go ahead and have sex with Victim if he does not come to believe that she does not consent, Duff is tacitly implying that

---

[17] Williams (1991), 121–2.    [18] Duff (1996), 16.

the defendant has another intention, namely an intention [to have sex with Victim]. Add to this that the defendant is reckless with respect to non-consent—he thinks Victim might not consent—and, assuming that the case is not a Frege puzzle case, a failure "to put two and two together", or an insalience case, and it appears that this defendant has the *de re* intention [to have sex with consenting or non-consenting Victim], then, under the view on offer here, this defendant is committed by his intention to Victim's non-consent, if Victim does not consent, and has much less sinister commitments if she does consent. Therefore, if she does not consent, this defendant may very well be attempting rape. If all he has done is arrive at the door, roses in hand, then we may acquit him on the grounds that the act element of the attempt is absent. But, still, even in this case, he has the intention needed for attempted rape. So far so good. The view proposed here accounts for both the fact that there is no pressure to take this to be a case of attempted rape until it is said that the defendant will go ahead with sex unless he comes to believe that Victim does not consent, and it explains why there is such pressure when that is added.

At this point, Duff makes the following remark:

[I]f Williams convicts such a man, by insisting that (in some extended sense) he intends 'to copulate with the woman *nolens* or to copulate with her *volens'*, he must also convict others whom he rightly wishes to acquit: agents who are only reckless as to the possible occurrence of some criminal result. He wants to acquit of attempted assault a stone-thrower who intends to break a window, realizing that this might also injure someone in the room: she 'does not intend to assault a person, even as an alternative intent'. If the man is guilty of attempted rape, however, because he intends 'to copulate with the woman *nolens* or to copulate with her *volens*...as matters may turn out', why should the stone-thrower not be guilty of attempted assault, because she intends 'to break the window without causing injury, or to break it and cause injury, as matters may turn out'?[19]

Duff's challenge is to distinguish the case in which the disjunctive description pertains to a circumstance, from the case in which it pertains to a result. However, we have the resources to make that distinction. Note that, as the case is set up, the injury cannot appear in the content of the intention through a *de dicto* description. If it did, then our defendant would be committed by his intention to causing injury which, by hypothesis, he is not; he would not, for instance, select a different window if he came to believe that no one was behind the one at which he is taking aim. So, the stone-thrower has a *de re* intention [to cause an injuring or non-injuring window-breaking]. That is, there is a particular event that she intends and represents in her intention *as* an injuring or non-injuring window-breaking. If she causes *that* event, and no other event than the one she has in mind, her act will have been successful. But the world will not match her intention, unless the event she causes is either injuring or

---

[19] Duff (1996), 16.

non-injuring. On the view offered here, such a person is committed by her intention to perform an injuring window-breaking, and so has the intention needed for attempted assault, *if the particular event she intends to cause is, indeed, injuring*. In short, she has the intention needed for attempted assault, only if *she completes* an assault. If she does not, in fact, cause an injury with the throw of her stone, then she was never committed to an injury of another in the first place. In fact, unless she breaks the window—and the window-breaking is the very event that she intended to cause—neither is it the case that she was committed by her intention to the occurrence of a non-injuring window-breaking. All we can say, in the absence of the occurrence of the relevant event and subsequent injury or non-injury, is that she intended [to cause an injuring or non-injuring window-breaking], which is not the intention that she needs to have in order to have attempted assault. So, if she has completed an assault, then she has attempted one, but the attempt is irrelevant, since the crime we care about in that case is the completed assault. And if she has not completed an assault, then she has not attempted one. Thus we reach the desirable result that in the only relevant case, namely that in which no one is injured by the throw of the stone, she has not attempted an assault. Duff's challenge is, therefore, met.

## 3.7 Missing Objects

Another kind of case which is often raised in discussion of these issues is that in which some object that would have to exist for the completed crime to take place does not exist at all. What should we say, to use the standard example, of the person who, intending [to pick a pocket], reaches into a pocket and finds it empty? Here the relevant circumstantial element of the crime is that there is something in the pocket. This is a circumstantial element of the crime since to show that the completed crime took place, the prosecution must show beyond a reasonable doubt that something was stolen from the pocket, and so must show beyond a reasonable doubt that the pocket held something; but the prosecution need not show that the defendant caused the pocket to hold something, or would have selected a different pocket to put his hand into had he known the one he did choose was empty. This last is quite likely to be true. But the prosecution need not show it to be true in order to establish that the crime was completed: it is not a component of the completed crime. The consensus view is that the mere fact that the pocket is empty is irrelevant to the question of whether there was an attempt. The view offered here has that same implication in the standard case. In the standard case, the defendant has an intention [to take something from the pocket]. Whether the intention is *de re* or *de dicto*, that there is something in the pocket is, in this case, something to which the defendant's intention commits him. So the fact that the pocket is empty is no obstacle to his commission of an attempted theft.

However, not all missing object cases are like the standard ones in this respect. Imagine, for instance, that the defendant has the *de re* intention [to take the contents of an empty or not-empty pocket]. Such a person is intent on taking the contents of this very pocket, the one he reaches into, and he thinks of it through the disjunction "empty or not empty". This might be the mental state of the person who, for instance, is just as interested in the thrill of "taking" the contents of an empty pocket as he is in taking something of value from a pocket. For him, knowing that he would have taken something of value, had there been anything of value in the pocket, is good enough for success. If, in such a case, the pocket is empty, there is no attempted theft because the person is then committed by his intention to the pocket's being empty and so does not intend to take anything of value at all. Notice, however, how very peculiar such cases are. To be convinced that a particular defendant met this description, one would have to be convinced that the defendant's act would have succeeded, even if the pocket were empty. To learn, for instance, that the person would not have reached into the pocket had he known that it was empty would support the claim that he had, instead, the *de dicto* intention [to take something from the pocket], which is sufficient for an attempt even if the pocket is empty.

## 4. Conclusion

It was suggested in the introduction to this chapter that the source of the thought that attempts in which a circumstantial element of the completed crime are absent cannot possibly be completed comes from extending too far the analogy between what one takes as given for practical purposes and what cannot be otherwise. What has been argued here is that taking a condition as given for practical purposes, while close to sufficient for the kind of commitment to a circumstance needed for attempt, is not quite there. The reason is that it is possible to take a condition as given, without thereby setting a standard of success for the future world, a standard that has been met when one acts as intended in a world in which the condition is met. Many conditions, that is, that we take to be given, are nonetheless conditions that we are not committed to. Once we recognize this, it becomes equally evident that the relevant place to look for principles to resolve cases of absent circumstantial elements is in principles governing the impact of their absence on the commitments constituted by the agent's psychology, rather than on the impact of their absence on the possibility or impossibility of completion. After all, the analogy between what we are committed to and what cannot be otherwise is thinner, even, than the analogy between what we take to be given and what cannot be otherwise.

But with the move towards consideration of the commitments constituted by psychological state and away from issues of modality comes the risk of ignoring the world outside the agent's head. The temptation to conceive of the commitments constituted by an agent's psychology as established, without exception, independently of the facts is powerful. And so the temptation to conclude that we ought to judge defendants charged with attempt always by appeal to the world as they believe it to be, and never by appeal to the world as it is, is powerful too. But both temptations must be resisted. As has been shown here, sometimes what a person is committed to by his intention depends on what is actually so. And so sometimes what a person is trying to do is determined, also, by how things actually are. How things are, then, can sometimes decide whether a person is attempting a crime.

# APPENDIX: LADY ELDON AND HER CHILDREN, MR FACT AND MR LAW

A famous hypothetical, posed in 1932 by Francis Wharton and popularized by Sanford Kadish, can be resolved using tools developed in this chapter and the last.

Lady Eldon, when traveling with her husband on the Continent, bought what she supposed to be a quantity of French lace, which she hid, concealing it from Lord Eldon in one of the pockets of the coach. The package was brought to light by a customs officer at Dover. The lace turned out to be an English manufactured article, of little value, and of course, not subject to duty. Lady Eldon had bought it at a price vastly above its value, believing it to be genuine, intending to smuggle it into England.[1]

It is extremely tempting to hold, as some have, that Lady Eldon has not attempted a crime since what she was trying to do—namely bring this lace into England without paying duty—was not a crime, given that *this lace* was not subject to duty. So construed, we are to assimilate the case to that of the repentant attempted adulterer, discussed in chapter 4, who falsely believes adultery to be a crime and attempts it. There is no attempt in that case because there is no crime of which the repentant adulterer's attempt is an attempt. Similarly, we might say, in the case of Lady Eldon.

The analogy with the repentant attempted adulterer breaks down quickly, however, for there is a crime that Lady Eldon is attempting to commit: namely, the smuggling of French lace. Noting this, but determined to find a lesson in the comparison between the repentant attempted adulterer and Lady Eldon, we might suggest that what the case of the repentant attempted adulterer shows is that if one thinks one is attempting a crime as a result of a mistake of law, as in that case, then one is not guilty of any kind of attempt, while a mistake of fact, as in the Lady Eldon case, does not similarly exonerate. And so we can find ourselves thinking that there is some important difference between "legal" and "factual" "impossibility".

Sanford Kadish, objecting to this line of thought, offers the following hypothetical:

Two friends, Mr. Fact and Mr. Law, go hunting in the morning of October 15 in the fields of the state of Dakota, whose law makes it a misdemeanor to hunt any time other than from October 1 to November 30. Both kill deer on the first day out, October 15. Mr. Fact, however, was under the erroneous belief that the date was September 15, and Mr. Law was under the erroneous belief that the hunting season was confined to the month of November, as it was the previous year.[2]

---

[1] Wharton (1932), 304 n. 9.
[2] Kadish and Schulhofer (2001), 599.

The hypothetical shows, to my mind decisively, that the fact-law distinction isn't the one to be worried about when trying to figure out what to say about Lady Eldon. It also shows that impossibility, per se, isn't the issue. After all, it *could have been* September 15 and it *could have been* out of the hunting season. But, despite helping us to see what roads *not* to follow in resolving the Lady Eldon case, the Mr Fact–Mr Law hypothetical does not show us, immediately, what road we should follow. However, the tools developed so far can help us to do so.

The intuition the hypothetical invokes is that Mr Fact and Mr Law ought to be lumped together, rather than split. Intuitively, they either both attempted a crime, or neither did. But, as we will see, whether this is correct depends on what, exactly, the completed crime involves; this is true under one construal of the completed crime and not under two others. As it happens it is much harder to see the three different possible construals of the completed crime when the relevant condition of the completed crime is the date—or any other condition of the world as a whole—as opposed to when the relevant condition concerns the properties of some particular object; more on this shortly. But to help to clear the fog, consider the following hypothetical:

Two friends, Mr. Elk and Mr. Deer, go hunting in the fields of the state of Dakota, whose law makes it a misdemeanor to hunt elk, but whose laws allow one to hunt deer. Both kill deer on the first day out. Mr. Elk, however, was under the erroneous belief that the animals he killed were elk, and Mr. Deer was under the erroneous belief that it was illegal to hunt deer.

To show that a defendant *completed* the crime of hunting elk, the prosecution must show that the defendant hunted and that the animals he hunted were elk. But there are three importantly different ways of construing the crucial mental state element of the crime. Under the first, the prosecution must show only that the defendant had some mental state with respect to the following:

(a) The animals hunted were elk.

Perhaps, for instance, the prosecution must show that the defendant knew or intended that the animals he hunted were elk, or perhaps recklessness or negligence would suffice. (The case of strict liability will be discussed shortly.)

On the second construal, the prosecution must show only that the defendant had some mental state with respect to the following:

(b) It is legally prohibited to hunt the animals hunted.

Perhaps, for instance, the prosecution must show that the defendant knew or intended to hunt something that it is illegal to hunt, or perhaps recklessness or negligence would suffice. Under the first construal of the completed crime, a person could be guilty even if he did not know that it was illegal to hunt elk, so long as he had the required mental state with respect to the animals being elk. On the second construal, a person could be guilty even if he did not know that what he was hunting were elk, so long as he knew it was illegal to hunt what he was hunting. Imagine, for instance, that the defendant has no idea what kind of animal it is that his gun is pointed at, although it is an elk. Right before he fires the gun, and kills the elk, his guide, whom he trusts completely, says, "It's illegal to hunt that animal." Assuming that he believed the guide, such a defendant would be guilty under the second construal of the completed crime, but not under the first.

On a third construal, the prosecution must establish that the defendant had appropriate mental states with respect to both (a) and (b). On such a construal, it is not enough to know that what you are hunting is elk, nor is it enough to know that what you are hunting cannot be legally hunted; both mental states are required (or if not knowledge, then some other mental state).

Even though these three construals seem to differ only with respect to the mental state elements of the crime, they actually differ with respect to the non-mental state element that the animals hunted are elk. Under the first construal, the prosecution needs to show that the animals are elk because their being elk is the relevant element of the crime. Under the second, however, the relevant element of the crime is that the animals are illegal to hunt. Since the judge, and not the jury, determines what animals it is legally prohibited to hunt, it is sufficient *for showing* that the animals are not legally hunted to show that they are elk. But, it is not that fact itself that is the element of the crime. Under the third construal, the prosecution needs to show both that the animals are elk and that it is illegal to hunt them, but it can meet this dual burden through one showing: a showing to the effect that they are elk.

Once we see that a difference in the mental state elements tracks an underlying difference in the non-mental state elements of the completed crime, we can see, also, that we can have three different construals of the completed crime, even when the crime is strict liability in all relevant respects. In such a case, the prosecution can meet its different burdens in exactly the same way: by showing that the animals are elk. No showing about the mental states of the accused with respect to either the animals being elk, or its being illegal to hunt them is required. Still, despite the fact that the prosecution can meet its burden in precisely the same way, no matter how we construe the strict liability crime, the different construals are very important. In particular, they are very important to understanding what must be shown in order to show *an attempt* of the crime, where mental state is crucial.[3] If (b), for instance, is an element of the completed crime, the prosecution can meet its burden by showing (a). But it cannot meet its burden in showing *attempt* merely by showing that the defendant had an intention-based commitment to (a). It must show, instead, that the defendant had an intention-based commitment to (b).

Now under the Guiding Commitment View, recall, a person has attempted a crime only if there is a crime each of the components of which he is committed to by his intention. So, to attempt the crime of hunting elk, under any of these three construals, a defendant must be committed to hunting. Under the first construal he must, in addition, be committed to the animals he hunts being elk; under the second, to their being animals it is illegal to hunt; and under the third he must have both commitments. Mr Elk is committed to the animals he hunts being elk. He has at least the *de re* intention [to hunt elk]. He may even have the *de dicto* intention. (Would he have switched his target had he realized that what he was hunting were deer? If so, then his intention was probably *de dicto*.) Further, he has the *de re* belief that the animals he is hunting are not legally hunted. And, given that his is not a Frege puzzle case, a failure "to put and two together", or an insalience case, which we can assume, it follows that he has the *de re* intention [to hunt animals that it is illegal to hunt]. And, in fact, he has the *de re* intention [to hunt elk that it

---

[3] These three different construals will also have differing effects on what must be shown to establish solicitation, conspiracy, and accomplice liability.

is illegal to hunt]. The first of these three intentions suffices for the attempt when the crime is construed in the first way, the second in the second, and the third in the third. It follows, as it should, that he is trying to hunt elk, that he is trying to hunt animals that it is not legal to hunt, and that he is trying to hunt elk that it is not legal to hunt. So, however we construe the completed crime, Mr Elk has attempted it.

The situation is different with Mr Deer. Mr Deer is not committed to the animals he hunts being elk. He has neither the *de re* nor the *de dicto* intention [to hunt elk]. He also lacks both the *de re* and the *de dicto* intention [to hunt elk that it is illegal to hunt]. Of the three intentions possessed by Mr Elk, Mr Deer shares only the intention [to hunt animals that it is illegal to hunt]—the intention required for an attempt to complete the crime under the second construal, in which the prosecution bears a burden only to show that the animals hunted are legally protected from being hunted. Hence it follows that if the completed crime is to be construed in the second way, then Mr Elk and Mr Deer are not to be split, but lumped together: both attempted the crime. But if the completed crime is to be construed in either of the other two ways, then Mr Elk has attempted it and Mr Deer has not. The intuition, then, that the two are to be lumped together is veridical if the crime is defined in the second way, and not if it is defined in either of the other two ways.

Now return to Mr Fact and Mr Law. The equivalents of (a) and (b) are, respectively:

(c) The day of the hunt is not between October 1 and November 30.
(d) It is illegal to hunt on the day of the hunt.

Under the first construal of the completed crime, the prosecution needs to show (c), but not (d). On the second, (d) but not (c). And on the third, the prosecution needs to show both. As before, we would find a difference in what the prosecution needs *to do* to meet its burden in the case of the completed crime only if the crime is not strict liability. If the crime is not strict liability, then there would be corresponding differences in the defendant's mental states that would need to be shown. If the crime is strict liability, then, even though the prosecution's burdens differ, they can be met in all three cases simply through a showing to the effect that the date of the hunt was not between October 1 and November 30.

Analogously to Mr Elk, Mr Fact is committed by his intention to (c) and to (d). He has an intention [to hunt on September 15], an intention [to hunt illegally] and an intention [to hunt illegally on September 15]. Hence, he has the intention needed for an attempt, no matter how the completed crime is construed. Mr Law, by contrast, has only the second of these three intentions. He intends [to hunt illegally], but lacks any intention that involves reference to a date not between October 1 and November 30 since, after all, he believes it to be October 15. Hence, Mr Law has attempted the crime only if it is construed in the second way and not if it is construed in either the first or third way.

Why is it harder to see the various construals of the completed crime in the Mr Fact–Mr Law hypothetical than it is in the Mr Elk–Mr Deer hypothetical? The reason is that we don't ordinarily think of the date, or of any properties of the world as a whole, as properties of the acts in which we engage or the objects with respect to which we act. We don't ordinarily take the date to figure into one's intention as a property of one's act—the act of hunting on September 15, for instance—but think of it, instead, as a property of the world in which we act. Contrast with the property of being an elk. But it is because conditions of the world, like the date, supply properties of the acts and objects involved in completed crimes that they are elements of those crimes, and so in legal contexts properties of the world—like the date—ought to be construed as properties of the acts and objects involved in crimes.

Now return to Lady Eldon. How ought we to construe the crime of smuggling French lace? The conditions corresponding to (a) and (b), and (c) and (d), respectively, are as follows:

(e) The object carried is French lace.
(f) It is illegal to pay no duty on the object carried.

Lady Eldon is committed to both (e) and (f). She intends [to pay no duty on French lace], intends [to pay no duty on something on which duty is owed] and intends [to pay no duty on French lace on which duty is owed]. Hence, no matter how we construe the completed crime, she has attempted it.

So far, in all of the hypotheticals we have considered, the protagonists are flatly certain in their beliefs. Lady Eldon is sure the lace is French and subject to duty. Mr Fact is sure the date is September 15 and out of the hunting season. Mr Law is sure the date is October 15 and out of the hunting season. And so on. But imagine that in each case, instead, there is significant doubt. Lady Eldon, imagine, is uncertain if the lace is French or British, and uncertain whether it is subject to duty in either case. Mr Fact is unsure if the date is September 15 or October 15, and uncertain about whether either date is out of the hunting season. And so on. Lady Eldon, so construed, intends [to pay no duty on French or British lace on which duty may or may not be owed]. Mr Fact intends [to hunt legally or illegally on September 15 or October 15]. And so on. Now, under the analysis offered in this chapter, whether the relevant facts are in place matters. If this is Lady Eldon's intention, then she is committed by her intention to paying no duty on French lace on which duty is owed *only if the lace is indeed French and only if duty is indeed owed on it.* If this is Mr Fact's intention, then he is committed by his intention to hunt illegally on September 15 *only if it is indeed illegal to hunt today and only if today is indeed September 15.* Where there is doubt, then, the facts matter because they matter to the proper characterization of the commitments constituted by the agent's intention. And that matters to the question of what he is trying to do and, hence, to the question of whether he is attempting a crime.

The hypotheticals discussed in this appendix, then, can all be resolved only given a particular account of what the relevant completed crime involves. To know both what a person who attempts the crime must and needn't be committed to, we must know what the completed crime must and needn't involve. This is not always clear, in part because in crimes like those involved in the hypotheticals, differences in the burdens that the prosecution bears are not always reflected in differences in what the prosecution needs to do to meet its burdens with respect to the completed crime. Since the hunting season is between October 1 and November 30, a showing to the effect that the day is October 15 just is a showing to the effect that it is illegal to hunt on that day. The result is that the hard normative question of what we want and have good reason to criminalize, which is, in the end, the question that one needs to answer to decide what is involved in the completed crime, is not one which a court adjudicating only with respect to charges of completion need face. But the question of what the completed crime involves arises when the charge is attempt. Still, what the analysis of attempt offered here implies is that courts and legislatures cannot duck the hard normative questions if they are to adjudicate attempt charges on principled grounds.

# 6

# If it Can't be Done Intentionally Can it be Tried?

## 1. Introduction

It is quite common to find criminal law theorists and judges saying that it is not possible to attempt crimes essentially involving the absence of intent, such as crimes of negligence, like negligent homicide. In fact, to date I know of no one who has denied it. A person who commits a negligent homicide necessarily fails to intend to kill; if he had intended to kill, his homicide would not have been negligent, but of some other sort. Negligent homicide, we might say, is an "intent-excluding" crime. However, as argued in chapter 2, attempt necessarily *includes* intent. To some, this has seemed to imply that negligent homicide, along with all other intent-excluding crimes, cannot be attempted. On occasion this thought has been a defendant's salvation. The employees of a hotel chased John Hembd away for loitering there drunk, and while they followed him down the block he lit a donut wrapper on fire and dropped it next to the building. It was a pointless and spiteful act analogous in motive and effect to spitting on the hotel. The fire was put out by employees without causing any damage and probably would have gone out on its own had the employees not intervened. No damage, no arson, and since there was no intent to damage, it was not a typical attempted arson. He was convicted of misdemeanor attempted *negligent* arson. In overturning his conviction for that offense, the court offers the following line of reasoning:

It is possible to purposely attempt to start a fire. The crime of negligent arson, however, requires purposely or knowingly starting a fire and negligently placing property in danger. To purposely attempt to be negligent is a contradiction in terms ... Attempted negligent arson, felony or misdemeanor, is a nonexistent crime.[1]

---

[1] *State v. Hembd* (197 Mont. 438, 643 P.2d 567 (1982)).

Attempts to commit intent-excluding crimes are a "contradiction in terms" and so there cannot possibly be any, but if there can't be any such crimes, then Hembd certainly didn't commit one.

Now, if this argument works, it is quite important, and not just for defendants like Hembd. It might have seemed that for every completed crime there is an attempted crime. But if the argument works, this isn't so; there are many crimes that simply cannot be attempted under any circumstances. Now in chapter 1, a rationale for a fairly broad principle of criminalization was offered. The Transfer Principle says that if a type of conduct is legitimately criminalized, then so is an attempt of it. The Transfer Principle provides us with a license to extend criminality from harmful behavior to a particular class of non-harmful behaviors, namely attempts to engage in harmful behaviors. But if the argument works, if there can be no attempts of intent-excluding crimes, then at least one road to the criminalization of non-harmful behavior is closed. We cannot criminalize *as attempts* even a subset of those reckless or negligent behaviors that fail to cause harm. This does not imply that we cannot legitimately criminalize such behavior, as we do when, to take just one example, we criminalize the endangerment of a child even when there is no injury to that child. It implies only that we cannot criminalize even some such behaviors on the grounds that they are attempts.

Important as it would be, however, the argument fails. It is perfectly possible to attempt crimes of negligence, and any other intent-excluding crimes. The result, as we will see, however, is not sweeping. Attempts of intent-excluding crimes, while possible, and encountered in court rooms, are still rare creatures indeed. Thus the vast majority of reckless and negligent acts that fail to cause harm cannot be criminalized under the Transfer Principle. Most of them are not attempts. If such acts are legitimately criminalized, as some almost undoubtedly are, it will not be because they are attempts, but for other reasons. Still, if we want to stem the tide of the criminalization of non-harmful behaviors, we cannot legitimately do so on the grounds that it is not possible to attempt intent-excluding crimes. And, in fact, by holding on to the idea that intent-excluding crimes cannot be attempted, we close our eyes to the morally salient fact about a class of acts that put defendants into courtrooms, namely, that they are attempts to engage in reckless or negligent behavior.

The argument against the possibility of attempts of intent-excluding crimes can be understood in two importantly different ways. Section 2 discusses the first construal, section 3 the second. As we'll see, the failure to recognize the flaw in the first version of the argument derives from a failure to appreciate a simple fact about trying to act, namely that it is (usually) perfectly possible to try to do the impossible, even the logically impossible. Interestingly, many who have advocated the claim that intent-excluding crimes cannot be attempted, also advocate abandoning the old rule according to which the impossibility of completion was a defense to a charge of attempt. What is to be argued in section 2, therefore, is that anyone who holds, as I do too (with qualifications to be discussed in chapter 9), that impossibility should not be a defense, ought not to justify that claim through appeal to the idea that we cannot attempt the impossible; some other reason for rejecting impossibility defenses must be found.

The failure to see the flaw in the second argument intended to show the impossibility of attempts of intent-excluding crimes derives from a very natural error in thinking about the content of the intention involved in attempt. It is natural to think that when one tries to act, one intends something that would amount to success (or would were one's beliefs true) were one to do it intentionally. This is false. The problem with the principle, as we'll see, is that it does not allow for legitimate efforts that involve self-management. Often, that is, we try to act by, among other things, taking steps to ensure that we will be in the right mental state when the time for action arrives. In employing such self-management techniques, we sometimes try to act recklessly or negligently, even unintentionally. The principle in the neighborhood of this false claim which is correct is the claim implied by the Guiding Commitment View of trying, introduced in chapter 3—namely, that when one tries to act one has an intention that commits one to each of the components of success, including those components that are mental states. But, as we will see in section 3, the true principle will not serve to support the argument against the possibility of attempts of intent-excluding crimes. Quite the reverse: it implies that it is possible to attempt intent-excluding crimes.

Before considering the details of the arguments for the claim that intent-excluding crimes cannot be attempted, a word about the nature of such crimes is in order. As noted in chapter 4, under the *Model Penal Code* _§2.02(5), a person can be guilty of a crime even if he lacked the mental state required, provided that his mental state was as bad or worse than that required. If negligence is required, then recklessness, knowledge, or intent will serve; if recklessness is required, then knowledge or intent will serve, and if knowledge is required, intent will serve. The *Model Penal Code*'s rule has some important practical implications for crimes like negligent homicide. Say, for instance, that a defendant wakes up early and makes herself tea before leaving for work; she leaves the gas on and her sleeping husband dies as a result. She's charged with a negligent homicide. If a member of the jury is convinced that the defendant actually intended to kill—it was no accident that the gas was left on, he thinks—then a vote to convict is appropriate. To be convinced beyond a reasonable doubt that a person is guilty of negligent homicide, it is enough to be convinced that she committed intentional homicide. Similarly, a prosecutor who strongly suspects that the homicide is intentional—the defendant stood to inherit a large amount of money, she was having an affair, the neighbors overheard ugly fights, etc.—might still legitimately charge only negligent homicide, if he thinks he'll have grave difficulties proving intent to kill beyond a reasonable doubt. So what is meant by the claim that negligent homicide is intent-excluding? It is strange that a person *who intends to kill* could be guilty of such a crime.

Now it was noted in chapter 4 that under the *Model Penal Code's* rule, there can be guilt without commission. If the woman in our example really did intend to kill her husband with gas as he slept, then she *committed* an intentional homicide, but because she was charged with a negligent homicide, she is guilty only of that crime, a crime that she did not commit. She didn't commit it because she was not negligent, and negligence is an element of the crime. But she is plainly still guilty. As in previous chapters, it is important to keep the distinction between guilt and commission in mind in what follows. To say that a crime is intent-excluding is not to say that a person with intent cannot be guilty of it: he could. It is to say, instead, that a person with intent cannot have committed it.

## 2. The Argument from the Incompatibility of Attempt and Success

The argument against the possibility of attempting intent-excluding crimes is usually offered all in a rush. And, in fact, its appeal derives in part from its hasty presentation, a presentation that conceals false premises. Consider J. C. Smith's statement of the argument as applied to involuntary manslaughter—for our purposes, this is reckless or negligent homicide[2]—in his classic article "Two Problems in Criminal Attempts":

[T]here can be no attempt to commit involuntary manslaughter. The consequence involved in that crime is the death of the victim and an act done with intent to achieve this, if an attempt at all, is attempted murder. It is of the essence of involuntary manslaughter that the consequence be produced either recklessly or negligently, but not intentionally.[3]

Although there is some lack of clarity here, it appears that Smith thinks that the impossibility of attempted involuntary manslaughter derives from an incompatibility between the occurrence of the attempt and the occurrence of the completed crime: the first necessarily involves an intention that must be absent if the second is to occur. So he seems to be offering the argument set out below. Here D is a defendant, C is an intent-excluding crime, and X is that which is necessarily intended by anyone who attempts C.

---

[2] Some reckless homicides—namely so-called "depraved heart" reckless homicides—will typically be classified not as manslaughter, but as murder.

[3] Smith (1957), 534.

(1.1) If D attempts to C, then D intends [to X].[4] (p → q])

(1.2) If D commits C, then D does not intend [to X]. (s → not-q)

(1.3) ∴ D does not attempt to C. (not-p)

If they are to have a chance of being true, the premises here would need to be formulated in a way that accomodates time. (1.2), for instance, is not generally true: a person can intend to kill someone and then, many years later, kill him negligently. What he can't do is to *kill someone intentionally*, where the act is intentional in virtue of its relation to the intention involved in the attempt, and also commit a negligent homicide, the act element of which is the intentional act of killing the person. But we can put these issues aside, for it is quite plain that the conclusion here fails to follow from the premises, even if the premises are formulated so as to accommodate these problems. Even if premises (1.1) and (1.2) are true, the argument shows only that when the crime is intent-excluding there is never *both* an attempt to C *and* the commission of C. That is, the argument shows at best only that attempts to perform intent-excluding acts always fail. Perhaps that's true, but given that all of the attempts of legal interest are those in which the defendant fails to complete the crime, this fact alone does not show that defendants necessarily fail *to attempt* intent-excluding crimes. Perhaps they only manage to attempt them when they also fail to succeed, as in all the cases of legal interest.

The argument as it stands is missing a premise linking attempt and success. There is an appealing idea to insert here: it must be logically possible for any given attempt to blossom into completion. A person isn't attempting, the thought is, if he's realizing a condition that necessarily, non-contingently, undermines success. This idea should be distinguished from the thought that we cannot attempt what is, in fact, impossible. Both of the following can be true: we cannot attempt things that are necessarily incompatible with the attempt of them; and, we can attempt things that can't be done (as when I try to open a locked door). It is the former claim, and not the latter, that might be used to support the argument here. According to this line of thought, then, the problem with attempts of intent-excluding crimes is that the attempt of them necessarily undermines their completion. If we add this claim as a premise, we get the following argument:

(2.1) If D attempts to C, then D intends [to X]. (p → q)

(2.2) If D commits C, then D does not intend [to X]. (s → not-q)

(2.3) If D attempts to C, then it is logically possible that D both attempts to C and commits C. (p → ◊(p&s))

(2.4) ∴ D does not attempt to C. (not-p)

---

[4] The argument is here formulated with respect to an intention *to*. It could just as easily be formulated with an intention *that*, or some more complicated intention.

The conclusion follows from the premises since, after all, it is not possible to both have an intention and lack it (assuming that temporal issues are accomodated in the formulations of the premises). However, despite its appeal, premise (2.3) is false. The most obvious counterexamples derive from consideration of acts that it is logically impossible to complete, but perfectly possible to attempt. Someone who sits down to construct a counterexample to a true but unproven mathematical theorem is *trying* to construct such a counterexample. But it can't be done. In this example, the logical impossibility of *both* attempting and succeeding derives from the logical impossibility of succeeding. Of course, in every example of legal interest it is logically possible to complete the crime in question; plenty of people have committed negligent homicide, for instance. What would be of legal interest, then, are examples in which it is logically possible to complete the crime and logically possible to attempt it, but not logically possible to *both* attempt it and complete it. The question then is whether any such crimes can be attempted. If they can, then (2.3) is false.

Imagine a criminal code that defines "first degree carjacking" as a car theft that involves, also, a kidnapping. The code defines "second degree carjacking" as a car theft that involves, also, an attempted kidnapping. And the code specifies that no first degree carjacking is also a second degree carjacking. Such legislation, we can imagine, has two motivations. First, the legislature aims to give a greater penalty to someone who steals a car, and tries unsuccessfully to kidnap the driver, than would be given to someone who fails both in his endeavor to steal the car and his endeavor to kidnap the driver. Second, the legislature aims to prevent overcharging by preventing a prosecutor from charging both a second degree carjacking and a first degree carjacking. It is clearly possible to complete a first degree carjacking: one merely needs to steal a car and kidnap someone in the process *without trying to commit a kidnapping*. Say, for instance, that the defendant points a gun at a driver of a car and tells him to get out, which the driver does, leaving the keys in the ignition. The defendant, who is in a great hurry, then drives off even though he recognizes that there's someone in the backseat of the car. He knows that he's kidnapping this person, but does not intend to. And since he does not intend to, he does not attempt to. Thus, his is a first degree carjacking: he steals a car, kidnaps someone, and does not attempt to kidnap anyone.

Now it is also possible to attempt a first degree carjacking. One can, for instance, try to steal a car and try, thereby, to kidnap someone, failing in both endeavors. But one can also attempt a first degree carjacking by successfully stealing a car while failing in an attempt to kidnap someone; second degree carjacking is a form of attempted first degree carjacking. But, and this is the crucial point, it is not logically possible to attempt a first degree carjacking and to complete one; were one to complete the kidnapping one attempted, one would have committed second degree carjacking, and so by definition would have failed to commit first degree. One of the necessary conditions of a first degree carjacking, after all, is that one has not attempted a kidnapping. This is a counterexample to premise (2.3): a first degree carjacking can be attempted, and completed, even though it is not logically possible to both attempt one and complete it.

There are ways of trying to respond to this example. One might, for instance, insist that despite what this imagined criminal code says, it *is* possible to both attempt a first degree carjacking and complete one: the code cannot simply stipulate that it is not possible to commit both a first and second degree carjacking. But why can't the code stipulate that? In making that stipulation, the code may be stipulating the impossibility of something that was, prior to that stipulation, logically possible. But, still, a crime can be defined in any way that the legislature sees fit to define it. If the legislature defines first degree carjacking as a car theft plus a kidnapping *which is not a second degree carjacking*, then that is what a first degree carjacking is. If it follows from that definition that first degree carjacking cannot be both completed and attempted, then so be it. At this point, the defender of premise (2.3) might admit that this is true but insist that a first degree carjacking cannot be attempted. The problem is that it is hard to think of any motive for insisting on this, other than a desire to maintain premise (2.3). After all, there is at least one obvious way in which first degree carjacking can be attempted: through the commission of a second degree carjacking.

Notice that a similar argument to that summarized in steps (2.1)–(2.4) could be offered for *any* necessary condition of attempt, the absence of which is necessary for completion. That is, it is of little importance to the argument that something must be intended for attempt and must not be for completion. To see the point, imagine that a criminal code proclaims that no public officials can commit a crime of attempt; every attempt has as an element that the defendant is not a public official.[5] And imagine further that crime C can only be completed by a public official: one of its elements is that the defendant is a public official, as in certain crimes involving receipt of a bribe. Then "intends to X" could be replaced in the above argument by "is not a public official", and the argument would go through. That is, this argument against the possibility of attempts of intent-excluding crimes has little to do with the mental states involved in attempt. The argument, that is, has little to do with the fact that intent-excluding crimes are *intent-excluding*. It is time, then, to turn to another more powerful argument for that conclusion that does require consideration of the mental state involved in attempt.

---

[5] Given the Transfer Principle, such a code would clearly mandate unequal treatment. It is legitimate to criminalize attempts, both by public officials and by those who are not, but only the behavior of the latter is criminalized. But let that pass.

## 3. The Argument from Intention Content

For some, the impossibility of attempts to commit intent-excluding crimes derives from the impossibility of the intention that a would-be attempter of such a crime would need to have. So, one court makes the following remark about the idea of attempted involuntary manslaughter:

[T]he crime of attempted involuntary manslaughter requires a logical impossibility, namely, that the actor in his attempt intend that an unintended death result.[6]

The court sees the problem with attempts of intent-excluding crimes as deriving from the intention, considered in itself, that such attempts require. But the court's thought here needs to be sharpened.

Consider the following appealing principle concerned with the intention involved in attempt:

If D attempts to C, then: If D X's intentionally, then D commits C.

Or, in other words, trying requires intending acts that would amount to succeeding were they performed intentionally. The principle captures the intuitive idea that trying to do something means pointing oneself towards a goal that would amount to success. This principle is false, although a principle similar to it, and capturing the same intuitive idea, is true. (The true principle is the Commitment Criterion in the Guiding Commitment View, offered in chapter 3. More on this shortly.) This appealing false principle can form the basis of an argument for the claim that intent-excluding crimes cannot be attempted.

A person who hopes to use this principle for this purpose has in mind the following argument: since to attempt one must intend, and since every time one has an intention one intends *something*—there are no content-less intentions—the would-be attempter has to intend *something*. Further, the thing that he intends would have to meet the demand described in the principle: it would have to be such that if he did it intentionally, he would commit the crime. The problem is that nothing meets this condition. Attempt requires him to have an intention. But no intention will do, given that the crime is intent-excluding. So, the problem is not that the person who attempts realizes a condition that undermines success, as in the argument discussed in section 2, but, instead, that the would-be attempter can't even get an attempt off the ground in the first place, since he can't form an intention that serves as an essential part of the attempt; no intention would do, even in principle.

---

[6] *State v. Almeda* (189 Conn. 303, 455 A.2d 1326 (1983)).

Put more formally, this argument proceeds as follows:[7]

(3.1) If D attempts to C, then (If D X's intentionally, then D commits C). ($p \rightarrow (q \rightarrow r)$).

(3.2) If D X's intentionally, then D does not commit C. ($q \rightarrow$ not-r).

(3.3) ∴ If D attempts to C, then (If D X's intentionally, then it is not the case that D X's intentionally). [$p \rightarrow (q \rightarrow$ not-q)].

(3.4) ∴ D does not attempt to C. [not-p].

The conclusion here follows from the premises. (3.2) follows trivially from the definition of an intent-excluding crime, and (3.3) follows logically from (3.1) and (3.2). So if this argument fails, it must be because premise (3.1) is false. Is it? Yes.

Before explaining why (3.1) is false, it is important to head off one possible, but flawed line of objection to it. The principle claims that, if acted on, the intention involved in attempt would lead to commission of C, not merely to guilt for C. This implies that if A intends to hold Victim while B rapes her, but does not intend to have sex with her himself, then he lacks the intention needed for attempted rape when, for instance, Victim struggles free and escapes. The reason is that, even if A had intentionally held her while she was raped, he would not have *committed* rape, but would merely have been guilty of the crime. Some will see examples of this kind as reason enough to reject the principle. However, we should not be hasty. After all, in a case like this, the defendant is clearly attempting *to be an accomplice* to rape, and that might be enough for *guilt* for attempted rape, even if it is not enough for *commission* of attempted rape.[8] The distinction between guilt and commission does not apply just to completed crimes, but to attempts, as well. That fact should be obvious once we reflect on the fact that a person can be guilty of an attempted crime merely because he helps someone else to attempt the crime, a paradigm instance of guilt without commission. Hence we can reach the normatively correct outcome here—punish A for attempted rape—without having to say that A *committed* attempted rape. We merely have to accept the further appealing claim that commission of an attempt to be an accomplice to a crime is sufficient for guilt, although not for commission, of an attempt to commit the crime.

The problem with premise (3.1) is not that it invokes commission, rather than guilt. The problem is that it fails to accommodate cases in which people try to act by planning to take steps to assure that they will be in the right mental state when the time for action comes. To see this, first consider the following example offered by Alfred Mele while discussing a somewhat different issue:

---

[7] R. A. Duff appears to offer precisely this argument. Duff (1996), 22–4.

[8] *Model Penal Code* §5.01(3) establishes that a defendant like the one in our example is guilty of an attempt. The Code thereby establishes yet another condition under which a person can be guilty of a crime he did not commit.

Ann is promised $10,000 for offending Bob unintentionally, and she knows that there is no reward for intentionally offending him. Wanting the money, Ann wants to offend Bob unintentionally... Ann knows that she tends to offend Bob unintentionally when she is extremely busy: when she is preoccupied with her work, for example, she tends, without then realizing it, to speak more tersely than she ordinarily does to people who phone her at the office; and, when Bob calls, her terse speech tends to offend him. Knowing this, Ann decides to undertake an engrossing project (writing a paper on intentional action), believing that her involvement in it will render her telephone conversations at the office sufficiently terse that, on at least one occasion when Bob calls (as he frequently does), she will unintentionally offend him... She intends to bring it about that she offend Bob unintentionally by implementing the strategy just described.[9]

If given one natural interpretation, the example is a counterexample to (3.1). The interpretation consists of a series of claims:

(a) Ann is trying to offend Bob unintentionally.
(b) Ann intends to offend Bob unintentionally.
(c) If Ann intentionally acts as she intends, then she will *not* offend Bob unintentionally (although she will offend him).

Given (b) and (c) it follows from premise (3.1) that Ann is not trying to offend Bob unintentionally. But given (a), she is. Therefore (3.1) is false. I will now defend (a), (b), and (c).

Consider (a). Is Ann trying to offend Bob unintentionally? Notice first that Ann is trying to offend Bob. After all, she's trying to get the money, and she believes quite correctly that she can't get it if she doesn't offend Bob. And so she intends to offend Bob, and is adopting a course of conduct that she hopes will culminate in her doing so. That surely is enough for trying to offend Bob. So far, however, there is no incompatibility with the principle described in (3.1). Her intention to offend Bob meets the condition that the intention included in an attempt to offend Bob must meet according to the principle: if she intentionally offends Bob, then she, *ipso facto*, offends him. However, notice that once we agree that she is trying to offend Bob, it becomes quite difficult to deny that she is trying to offend him unintentionally. After all, she knows full well that she will not get the money unless her act of offending him is unintentional. That's the reason why she elects this complicated course of conduct in which she becomes engrossed in a project before tersely answering the phone; if she was merely trying to offend Bob, and didn't care whether her doing so was intentional, it would have been much easier for her to just call him up and offend him.

Some might deny (a) because they accept (c)—the claim that if Ann intentionally does as she intends, then she will not unintentionally offend Bob. But the acceptance of (c) does not commit one to denying (a). It only commits one

---

[9] Mele (1999), 420.

to that if one also holds that it is not possible to attempt the impossible. Since plainly it is possible to do that, (a) and (c) are consistent.

Some will wish to deny (b). Consider the following remark from R. A. Duff:

[T]he legal definitions of most offences include some explicit or implicit fault requirement: but the content of the agent's intention cannot sensibly be required to include such fault elements. Attempted criminal damage would require an intention [to damage property intentionally]: but it is either otiose or nonsense to talk of intending [intentionally to damage property]; nor can I intend [to damage property recklessly], since one who intends [to damage property] is more than merely reckless as to whether property is damaged.[10]

Duff holds that nothing about the mental states involved in the action one intends *can possibly* be included in the content of the intention involved in attempt, and so an attempt need not involve an intention that includes them in its content.[11] We could agree with Duff's conclusion without agreeing with his premise. As we saw in chapter 4, not all attempted crimes require intentions with regard to the mental states needed for completion. In crimes that can be completed with intent, it is sufficient to have an intention-based commitment with respect to the act, results, and circumstances involved in the completed crime. Further, and of relevance to our purposes here, there is no reason at all to think that one *cannot* have intentions with regard to one's later mental states. Interestingly, it is widely held by philosophers of action not just that it is neither "otiose" nor "nonsense" to intend to act intentionally, but that *all* intentions to act are, in fact, intentions to act intentionally. Carl Ginet is explicit on the point, writing, "If I intend to do a certain thing, I intend to do it intentionally."[12] George Wilson uses just such a claim to argue against any effort to analyze intentional action as causation of behavior by intention.[13] Others, such as Gilbert Harman, take the claim for granted in an argument for the further claim that intentions to act are necessarily self-referential in content: they are always intentions [to act as a result of this very intention].[14] Michael Bratman holds that a certain species of intention with regard to one's later motives for action constitute what it is to value something.[15]

All of these philosophers are aware that intentions with regard to one's further mental states are an important and common part of self-management, and play a crucial role in much of the planning that we do every day. A person who locks the liquor cabinet and throws away the key intends that later he will

---

[10] Duff (1996), 6–7.
[11] There is a whiff of the same idea in the remark made by the *Almeda* court quoted at the beginning of this section.
[12] Ginet (1990), 35–36.
[13] Wilson (1989), esp. 275ff.
[14] Harman (2000). See also Velleman (1989).
[15] Bratman (2007c).

involuntarily fail to open the cabinet; he anticipates that he will struggle with it, in an effort to get it open, and fail, and this is precisely what he wants to take place. A person who takes a pill for clinical depression intends to bring it about that he, later, will have some mental states to the exclusion of others. A person who has an extra drink on a date might intend to be more spontaneous, to act later with less reflective deliberation. A person who practices, over and over, a certain move on the basketball court intends that, in the game, he will perform that move without making any explicit or conscious decision to do so, since such conscious decisions would delay performance when speed is of the essence. A person who decides to "cross that bridge when he comes to it" intends to, later, form an intention one way or another with regard to some particular question. It is not only possible to intend to act intentionally, unintentionally, recklessly, or even negligently, such intentions are a common and essential part of the way in which we manage our behavior over time.

What other reason could we have for denying that Ann intends to offend Bob unintentionally? Given that we have set aside worries about intending one's later mental states, it seems that the best reason we could have is that it is not possible for her to conceive of the act she envisions as, at once, unintentional, and envision it to be, if all goes as planned, the product of an intention that she has to perform it. But why can't she conceive of her act that way? She would tell you that this is precisely how she conceives of it: she takes herself to be intending to do something that will, when she does it, be done unintentionally. Forming such an intention, that is, is what she takes to be the first step in her plan to earn the money. Further, if we admit, as we must, that she is trying to offend Bob, then we have to admit that she has the intention required for *that* attempt. But she only has one plan for winning the money. So if she doesn't have an intention to unintentionally offend Bob, then it seems implausible that she has an intention to offend him. Insistence that, despite what she thinks, she lacks an intention to offend him unintentionally sits uncomfortably with the concession that she intends to offend him, which is undeniable.

Turn now to (c): the claim that were she to do as she intends intentionally, Ann would not unintentionally offend Bob. Is it possible to intentionally do something unintentionally? I believe that the answer is "no", for a reason to be explained in a moment. However, it is important to see that the argument on offer for the claim that intent-excluding crimes cannot be attempted would fail either way. If it were possible to intentionally act unintentionally, then Ann clearly unintentionally offends Bob when she intentionally acts as she intends, and her intention can serve for attempt under the principle in (3.1). However, if it is possible to intentionally act unintentionally, then premise (3.2) is false. For instance, under that assumption, the fact that negligent homicide is necessarily unintentional homicide does not entail that X is not done intentionally; if X is the act of negligently killing another person, then it could be done intentionally while a negligent homicide is committed.

But, in fact, it is not possible to intentionally do something unintentionally. We can see this by following Davidson in thinking of acts as events that are intentional under some description. In other words, to say that an event e, such as a bodily movement, is an act, is to say that of all the descriptions d1, d2 . . . dn that can be given of e, under at least one of them e is intentional. So, the event referred to with the description "Ann's offending Bob" is an act just in case there's a description of it under which it is intentional. What this implies is the entity possessing the property of being intentional or being unintentional is not an event; it is, instead, *an event under a description.* Formally, that which is intentional or unintentional is an ordered pair of the form <e, d>, where d is a description and e is the token event picked out by that description. The term "intentional" refers to a property possessed by that which is formally represented as this ordered pair. So, in the case of Ann's act of offending Bob, that which is intentional or unintentional can be represented as the ordered pair <Ann's offending Bob, "Ann's offending Bob">, where the first term is the event (which we pick out here using the description), and the second is the description that refers to it. To say that this was done unintentionally is to say something not merely about the event that "Ann's offending Bob" refers to, but something about that event under the description "Ann's offending Bob"; it is to say something about that which is represented by the ordered pair <Ann's offending Bob, "Ann's offending Bob">. So the entity referred to in "Ann's offending Bob unintentionally" is exactly the same as the entity referred to by "Ann's offending Bob". The entity in question is just the one formally represented as <Ann's offending Bob, "Ann's offending Bob">. The description "Ann's offending Bob unintentionally" predicates something of that entity that the description "Ann's offending Bob" does not: it assigns the property of being unintentional to it. So, to say that Ann intentionally offended Bob unintentionally, then, is to say that the event under the description possesses incompatible properties, which is impossible. Formally, we would represent that claim as follows: Intentionally <Ann's offending Bob, "Ann's offending Bob"> & not-intentionally <Ann's offending Bob, "Ann's offending Bob">. But since nothing, including objects formally represented as ordered pairs, possesses incompatible properties, it is not possible to intentionally act unintentionally. To put the point another way, we might be tempted to say that the statement "Ann intentionally offends Bob unintentionally" asserts that Ann's act of offending Bob is unintentional under the description "Ann's offending Bob", but is intentional under the description "Ann's offending Bob unintentionally". The trouble is that "Ann's offending Bob unintentionally" is not a distinct description of the act of Ann's offending Bob. Rather, it is a predication of an event under a description, namely <Ann's offending Bob, "Ann's offending Bob">, and it is precisely the same event under a description that is asserted to be intentional when we say that Ann intentionally offended Bob unintentionally.

Note, however, that we cannot conclude without further argument that when Ann offends Bob, she offends him, when all goes as planned, *intentionally.* Maybe, instead, she offends him, in such a case, *unintentionally.* Perhaps those acts that are falsely described as "intentional unintentional offendings" are actually merely unintentional. If that were true, then the case of Ann and Bob would not be a counterexample to (3.1). We would have to say, instead, that Ann manages to try to offend Bob unintentionally, thanks to having an intention that meets the standard imposed by (3.1). If she were to intentionally offend Bob unintentionally, on this view, then she would, in fact, merely offend him unintentionally, which is precisely what needs to be true for her intention to offend him unintentionally to serve for attempt under (3.1). As noted above, this would be to give up on the argument against the possibility of attempts of intent-excluding crimes since, under this approach, it is perfectly possible to have the intention that one would need to have in order to attempt an intent-excluding "crime" like unintentional offending; premise (3.2) would turn out to be false. But, still, since our interest here is not merely in responding to the argument against the possibility of intent-excluding crimes, but also in determining what intention is needed for attempt, it is important to consider this defense of (3.1). If it turns out, that is, that Ann can have the intention needed for attempt according to (3.1) then intent-excluding crimes are not shown to be unattemptable by the argument under discussion in this section. But what would be shown is that (3.1) can accommodate cases that would appear to be counterexamples to it.

However, this effort to save (3.1) by showing that under it Ann has the intention needed for an attempt to offend Bob unintentionally fails. The reason is that, when all goes as planned, Ann *intentionally* offends Bob. The truth in the claim that Ann's act, when she tersely answers the phone thereby offending Bob, is the act of intentionally offending him unintentionally is just this: although the act is intentional it is not intentional in virtue of the mental states that immediately cause and precede it, as most intentional acts are. It is intentional, instead, in virtue of its relation to the prior intention to offend Bob unintentionally. But then the true claim that we might misleadingly express by saying that Ann intentionally offends Bob unintentionally implies that the act is *not* unintentional. I explain.

It is well known that an act can fail to be intentional even though it is caused by an intention to do it. There are many different kinds of defeaters. One set of defeaters involves deviant causal chains, as in Davidson's mountain climber example: the intention to drop his partner makes the climber so nervous that he drops his partner. Perhaps under the same banner are lucky execution cases: the agent thinks he knows the ten-digit code for diffusing the bomb; in fact, the code he has in mind has a 3 as its third digit while the real code has a 2; intending to diffuse the bomb, he enters the code he has in mind but mistypes, putting in a 2 where he means to put in a 3; the bomb is diffused, but not intentionally. Another set involves cognitive confusions: the sharp-shooter intends to assassinate the president but believes that he must first shoot the secret service agent standing next to him; in fact, the man he thinks is the secret service agent is the president; he shoots that man dead, acting on his intention to kill the president, but he has not thereby killed the president intentionally; he may even think that he's failed to kill the president if he doesn't manage to take a second shot. Yet another set of cases exploits the gap between mental representations that we would express by using the first person pronoun "I" and those that are expressible by using proper names that refer to oneself: Christopher Robin intends to stop the heffalump from wandering in the Hundred Acre Wood, and so follows its tracks; little does he know that he's following his own tracks; when he discovers this, he stops wandering the Hundred Acre Wood, and so stops the heffalump from wandering the Hundred Acre Wood, since he is the heffalump; so he stops the heffalump as a result of his intention to stop the heffalump, but he does not intentionally stop the heffalump thanks to the fact that his intention led to that result; if his act of stopping the heffalump is intentional, it is so in virtue of the intention to stop that he forms on discovering that he is the heffalump and not thanks to the prior intention that prompted him to follow the tracks.

Now, Ann has an intention that brings it about that the world comes to be a certain way: the intention causes her to offend Bob. But there is no reason to think that any of the defeaters of the sort just listed are present in her case. It is not a case of deviant causation: she has the intention to offend Bob throughout and she offends him as a result of that intention in precisely the way that she anticipates when she forms the intention. In fact, she forms the intention in part because she anticipates that it will cause her to offend Bob in precisely the way in which it does, indeed, lead to that result. This is, at least, a sufficient condition for non-deviance (although it is surely not necessary). Further, it is not a case of lucky execution or cognitive confusion: all happens precisely as she believes it will and while accompanied by true beliefs about the identities of all the relevant objects and parties involved. Similarly, it is not a case in which her intention represents her future self under a description that she fails to recognize to apply to herself. She knows that it is *she* who will offend Bob, assuming all goes according to plan; we could aptly use the first person pronoun in the active voice to capture the content of her intention: she intends [that *I* offend Bob].

Are there other possible ways in which the intention-action relation present in Ann's case undermines the claim that Ann intentionally offends Bob when all goes as planned? Perhaps the action that executes the intention is not sufficiently responsive to the prior intention for it to count as intentional. In the typical case of intention execution, the act would be interrupted were the agent to change his mind, give up the intention, before execution is complete: the person who intends to eat an ice-cream sundae puts his spoon down halfway through when he finds that he's full. However, when Ann answers that phone and is in the midst of offending Bob, she will not stop even if she changes her mind and decides that offending him is not worth the money. Perhaps this fact defeats the intentionality of her act of offense.[16] However, this objection seems to me to have bite only by exaggerating the sense in which responsiveness to one's intention throughout execution is a necessary condition of the intentionality of action. When I swing the hammer intending to hit the nail, I will hit the nail even if I abandon my intention halfway through the swing. To be sure, if I abandon my intention halfway through, I may not be rightly said to hit the nail intentionally. But the fact that the counterfactual "If I change my mind, I will still hit the nail" is true does not defeat the intentionality of my act of hitting the nail in the instance in which I do not change my mind. Similarly, it is probably true that Ann will go through with offending Bob even if she changes her mind halfway through doing so. But the fact that this counterfactual is true does not defeat the intentionality of the act of offending him when she does not, in fact, change her mind.

It is worth sealing the case for (c), the claim that Ann intentionally offends Bob when she does as she intends, by making the following general point. The claim that is required to defeat (3.1), and thus the argument on offer for the impossibility of attempts of intent-excluding crimes, is only that *it is possible* to attempt to do something while lacking an intention that would result in success if what is intended is done intentionally. A single counterexample will do. So, although none of the known defeaters of the intentionality of acts caused by intention are present in the case of Ann, the objection to (3.1) will succeed even if a new defeater, present in that case, is discovered, provided that it is possible to adjust the case so that it is absent. What I hope to have shown is that, given the present state of knowledge about the intention-action relation when the act is intentional, there is no reason to take Ann's act of offending Bob, when all goes as planned, not to be intentional: it bears the needed relation to the intention that causes it to warrant that conclusion. But I suspect that the ultimate conclusion sought will hold even as knowledge of that relation expands, and even if it expands in such a way as to impugn my claim about the case of Ann.

Since (a), (b), and (c) are true, premise (3.1) is false. However, the Guiding Commitment View, offered in chapter 3, implies that a principle similar to (3.1), namely the Commitment Criterion, is true. Recall how the Commitment Criterion is formulated. Here, as before, D is a defendant, C is a crime, X is the content of D's intention, and E1, E2...En are those conditions that must be shown beyond a reasonable doubt for commission of C:

---

[16] Thanks to Kory DeClark, Joseph Raz, and Mark Schroeder for pushing this point in different ways in conversation.

*Commitment Criterion*: D attempts C *only if* ∀Ei, ((Ei is included in X) OR (If D's intention plays its proper causal role, then Ei)).

Although Ann's intention to unintentionally offend does not serve for an attempt to do so under the earlier principle, expressed in premise (3.1), it does serve under the Commitment Criterion, as it should. Four conditions are involved in Ann's unintentionally offending Bob: (1) Bob is offended, (2) Ann is the cause of Bob's offense, (3) the agency-involvement factor is present, (4) the act of offending Bob is unintentional. Since Ann intends [to unintentionally offend Bob], conditions (1), (3), and (4) are included in the content of her intention. And since she would cause Bob's offense were her intention to play its proper causal role, the Comitment Criterion is met with respect to all four conditions. Ann, that is, has an intention that commits her to all of the conditions involved in success. Now it is also true that were her intention to play its proper causal role, she would offend Bob *intentionally*. But the fact that her intention commits her to offending him intentionally does not erase the fact that it also commits her to offending him unintentionally. She has a role-based commitment to intentional offense and a content-based commitment to unintentional offense; therefore, she has an intention-based commitment to unintentional offense.

If we were to substitute the Commitment Criterion for premise (3.1) we would not have a valid argument for the conclusion that it is not possible to attempt intent-excluding crimes. To see this, consider how the argument so altered would look:

(3.1') If D attempts C then ∀Ei, ((Ei is included in X) OR (If D's intention plays its proper causal role, then Ei)). (p → (s ∨ t))

(3.2) If D X's intentionally, then D does not commit C. (q → not-r)

(3.3) ∴ If D attempts to C, then (If D X's intentionally, then it is not the case that D X's intentionally). (p → (q → not-q))

(3.4) ∴ D does not attempt to C. (not-p)

Here, the conclusion does not follow from the premises. The reason is that under the Commitment Criterion, a person can be committed to each of the components of success in the way needed for trying, despite the fact that were he to do as he is committed *in every respect* he would not do as he is trying to do. Ann, after all, has an intention-based commitment both to intentionally offending Bob and to unintentionally offending Bob. She cannot do all of the things that her intention commits her to doing. But, still, it commits her to all that is involved in unintentionally offending.

Are examples in which intent-excluding crimes are attempted so rare as to be beyond anything that the criminal law should care to accommodate? After all, a defendant like Hembd (the man who lit the donut wrapper on fire and whose conviction for attempted misdemeanor negligent arson was quashed) still did not attempt any intent-excluding crime. Hembd probably did not intend to damage any property at all, and so did not intend to do so negligently or in any other way; he just intended to insult the hotel employees. The outcome of that case, anyway, does not change in the face of the discussion here, and it might be thought that the same is true of virtually every other case in which the issue of the attempt of intent-excluding crimes arises. Maybe they are possible, but for practical purposes, we might say, things are just as if they were not.

But, in fact, there is reason to think that cases analogous to Ann's are not so far removed from real cases as to be safely ignored. Consider *State v. Norman* (580 P.2d 237 (Utah 1978)). Norman went to the victim's home on Christmas Eve for a celebration. Some time into the gathering "the Spirit of Christmas merged into that of Bacchus", as the court puts it, and Norman and the victim, who had been arguing throughout the evening, were sitting around a table drinking and playing a game with several other people. Norman went into the other room and returned with a pistol, which he concealed. He sat down at the table and, unbeknownst to the victim, pointed the gun at him under the table and cocked it. Norman then demanded that the victim give him a knife that he had. The victim, not aware that he was in any serious danger, gave Norman the knife. Norman then tried to uncock the pistol, which caused it to fire. The victim was severely injured, although not killed. The court rules that Norman cannot be convicted of an attempted reckless homicide, since there is no such crime.

Now we do not know, on these facts alone, exactly what Norman had in mind when he cocked the pistol under the table and demanded the knife.[17] But one possibility is that Norman was trying to kill the victim recklessly. Asking the victim for the knife was a way of baiting him, as Norman surely knew. It's quite possible that Norman expected that if the victim refused to hand over the knife, then he, Norman, would have become so angry as to fire the gun at the victim; he would especially have expected this if he knew himself to be an angry drunk. If, in addition, he knew that he really couldn't bring himself to shoot the victim if not very angry, and also knew that he would be incapable of acting on an intention to kill, then it appears that in demanding the knife, Norman was acting on an intention to recklessly kill. His aim, that is, might have been to bait the victim into acting in a way that would put Norman into the mental state that he would need to be in to fire the gun at him while falling short of an intention to kill, but aware of a good chance that in firing the gun he would cause the victim's death. Of course, given the arguments already offered, he

---

[17] The act of uncocking the pistol, the act that immediately caused the injury, is also of significance to the case. But since it was clearly not performed in furtherance of an intention to injure or to kill, but, instead, in furtherance of the intention *not* to do so, it cannot serve as the act element of any attempt on Norman's part. That act might form the basis of a defense of abandonment. For discussion of abandonment and change of mind, see chapters 10 and 11.

would necessarily have failed to kill recklessly as a result of that intention's playing its proper causal role: one cannot intentionally kill recklessly. But still, this very well may be what he intended. In fact, there is some evidence in support of the contention. If Norman had cocked the pistol with the straight-forward intention of killing the victim, the request for the knife and the ensuing effort to uncock the pistol would make no sense at all. Norman did not have the intention typically involved in an attempted murder. On the other hand, if Norman was not preparing for a scenario in which he shot the victim, why would he have cocked the pistol and aimed it at the victim? But if he planned for such a scenario, then he was planning for a scenario in which he killed the victim, since he knew that there was a good chance that shooting the victim would kill him. Whether this is really what happened would have to be determined by a jury. But by denying that there is a crime of attempted reckless homicide, the court precludes the possibility that a jury could judge these to have been the facts.

Far from being a mere philosopher's counterexample to an abstract principle, the case of Ann, instead, distills what we find frequently: efforts to commit crimes in part through intentional efforts to manage and induce our later mental states. Many such efforts are attempts to commit crimes negligently or recklessly and such efforts find their way into courtrooms, even if they are not recognized there as what they are.

## 4. Conclusion

One line of resistance to the claim that it is possible to attempt intent-excluding crimes like negligent homicide comes from the observation that the intention involved in such attempts constitutes all of the commitments constituted by the intention involved in attempts of similar crimes involving intent, such as intentional homicide. If one can attempt negligent homicide, as has been suggested here, then it seems that one who does so is committed by his intention to all of the conditions involved in intentional homicide. To put the point a slightly different way, it would seem to follow from the possibility of attempts of intent-excluding crimes that attempts are individuated less finely than completed crimes. Completed crimes C1 and C2 might be of different types, despite the fact that an attempt to perform C1 and an attempt to perform C2 are of the same type.[18] If this is true, then the claim that it is possible to attempt intent-excluding crimes has precisely the same relevance to criminali-zation as the claim that they cannot be attempted. After all, if in criminalizing attempted intentional homicide we criminalize all the same behavior, and no

---

[18] In fact, at an earlier point I embraced this consequence. See Yaffe (2006).

less, as would be criminalized were we to criminalize both attempted intentional and negligent homicide, then nothing about the scope of criminalization of attempts turns on the claim that intent-excluding crimes can be attempted.

However, despite appearances, it does not follow from the possibility of attempts of intent-excluding crimes that they are no different from attempts of similar crimes involving intent. The reason is that for an intention to serve as the intention involved in an attempt to C, its content must meet certain conditions that are determined by the features of C that distinguish C from other similar crimes, including its mental elements. The intention involved in an attempt to commit negligent homicide will have to meet different conditions from those that need to be met by the intention involved in an attempt to commit intentional homicide. So, although the two attempts involve an intention with similar content, they do not involve precisely the same intention. Hence attempts are individuated no less finely than completed crimes. Where there are distinct completed crimes there are distinct attempts, as well.

In chapter 4, in discussing the sense in which an attempter's intention must commit him to the mental elements of the completed crime, it was noted that there are two importantly different kinds of case: those involving crimes that can be completed with intent, on the one hand, and the intent-excluding crimes, on the other. It was argued in chapter 4, that when the crime can be completed with intent, when it is not intent-excluding, an intention that commits one appropriately to the act, result, and circumstantial elements of the completed crimes suffices. However, what we have learned here is that such an intention does not suffice when the completed crime is intent-excluding. In such cases, the mental states that are required to the exclusion of intent must figure into the content of the intention involved in the attempt. The fact that a person with such an intention thereby is committed both to acting with intent and to acting without intent should puzzle us no more than it puzzles us to find people intending to do things that are, in fact, impossible, even logically impossible.

The treatment in the law of attempts to perform intent-excluding crimes, and the general consensus that there can be no such attempts, is one of the places in which theorists and practitioners have been misled about what the law is—about what is actually proscribed by law—through faulty but seductive inferences employing the elusive concept of trying. The law can put a name to any collection of elements and call it a crime, but it cannot, thereby, limit what can be attempted. Our capacity to try is greater than has been assumed by those who have accepted the arguments discussed here against the possibility of attempts of intent-excluding crimes. We can see this in part by recognizing the important role that is played in conduct by our efforts, not just to act, but to prepare ourselves to be in the mental states that such action requires.

# 7

# Trying by Asking: Solicitation as Attempt

## 1. Introduction

Ronald Decker wanted his sister Donna dead. She owed him money, and had no intention of paying it back. But Decker was smart enough to know that he shouldn't try the crime himself. Instead, he made some inquiries and eventually found Wayne Holston, whom he offered $25,000 for the job. Holston agreed and Decker paid him $5000 as a downpayment, with the balance to be paid when the murder was complete. When Holston asked Decker if he was sure this is what he wanted, Decker replied, "I am absolutely, positively, 100 percent sure, that I want to go through with it. I've never been so sure of anything in my entire life." Much to Decker's surprise he was soon after arrested, for *Detective* Holston had recorded and videotaped the entire conversation. Decker sought out Holston because he did not want to *try* the murder himself. But in asking Holston to kill his sister, did Decker, despite his efforts, try to commit murder? What he did is a crime, to be sure. It is, at least, the crime of *soliciting* another to commit murder, a crime that, in California, where Decker and his sister lived, could bring a prison term of nine years.[1] But soliciting a murder is a much less serious crime than attempting one.[2] If Decker attempted to murder his sister, then he could face a life sentence.[3] Whether Ronald Decker is to have a life outside of prison, then, turns on the question of whether a person who asks another to do something is thereby trying to do it.

---

[1] Cal.Penal Code § 653f(b).

[2] Quite often those who solicit murders are shown to be guilty of much more serious crimes thanks to additional facts beyond those used to establish the solicitation itself. If, for instance, the party solicited agrees to do the murder, and really intends to follow through with it, then the solicitor is guilty of conspiracy to commit murder, a crime that often carries as severe a sentence as murder itself. But, still, solicitation itself—considered independently from attempt or conspiracy—is a much less serious crime than attempt.

[3] Cal.Penal Code § 664(a).

In 2007, the Supreme Court of California announced that Decker was, in fact, attempting to murder his sister (*People v. Decker* (41 Cal.4th 1 (2007))).[4] In making this announcement, the court thereby overturned a case from the 1970s, *People v. Adami* (36 Cal.App.3d 452 (1973)), another case in which the defendant paid an undercover police officer to kill someone, but in which the court ruled that a solicitation did not amount to an attempt. In fact, there is no standard view across jurisdictions on the matter. Pay someone to kill in Idaho, Nevada, or South Dakota, for instance, and you've committed only the lesser crime of solicitation;[5] pay someone to kill in Georgia, New York, or Ohio and you've attempted the murder.[6] We find even greater variation when we consider crimes other than murder. If you ask a minister to marry you to your niece, have you tried to marry someone incestuously?[7] If you ask someone to bribe a witness, have you attempted to bribe a witness?[8] If you ask someone to burn down a barn have you attempted arson?[9] Courts have to answer questions like this quite often and they answer them differently in different places and in different times, and give different answers when one crime is involved than when another is. The problem is that courts have very little idea what *principles* to employ in answering questions of this kind. In fairness to the courts, it is not easy. The issue stands at the intersection of three independently thorny parts of the criminal law: attempt, solicitation, and complicity, and, if we aren't careful, we find ourselves embroiled in all but intractable questions about causation, as well.[10]

As we'll see in what follows, the Guiding Commitment View, and the accompanying Elemental Conception of the intention in attempt (described in chapters 3 and 4) can help us to identify the crucial questions that need to be answered in a principled solution to the problem of the sort that we would like to see from our courts. The solution proposed here is this: in the most difficult cases, if the defendant has asked another to bring about an event that is a result element of the completed crime, then the defendant may have, thereby, attempted the crime; if, however, the result the defendant has asked another to bring about figures into the definition of the act element of the completed crime, then the defendant has not attempted through his solicitation. Thus, a distinction that seems to be merely formal—the distinction between act

---

[4] More carefully, the court reached the conclusion that a reasonable jury could so find and so reached the conclusion that a solicitation like Decker's could be an attempt under California law.

[5] See *People v. Otto* (102 Idaho 250 (1981)), *Johnson v. Sherriff* (91 Nev. 161 (1975)), *State v. Disanto* (688 N.W.2d 201 (S.D. 2004)).

[6] See *Howell v. State* (157 Ga.App. 451 (1981)), *People v. Sabo* (179 Misc.2d 396 (N.Y.Sup.Ct. 1998)), *State v. Group* (98 Ohio St.3d 248 (2002)).

[7] Cf. *People v. Murray* (14 Cal.159 (1859)).

[8] Cf. *State v. Baller* (26 W.Va. 90 (1885)).

[9] Cf. *State v. Taylor* (47 Or. 455 (1906)).

[10] Cases of this sort have less to do with conspiracy since that crime requires all parties to be planning to commit a crime. In cases like *Decker*, there's no meeting of the minds.

elements and result elements of crimes—turns out to be of substantive importance. As we will see in what follows, not all cases are hard, and so not all cases require this approach. More importantly, we will also see what principles underly this approach, and imply that it is the right one to adopt.

Section 2 describes a few different kinds of cases in which it is possible for a court to reach a resolution on principled grounds without engaging with the difficult question of the conditions under which someone who solicits thereby attempts. The section ends, however, by noting that a set of cases remain where that issue cannot be ducked. In fact, the *Decker* case is one such case. Section 3 explains how such difficult cases ought to be resolved.

## 2. Easy Cases, Hard Cases

In all the cases that concern us, Defendant, intending that a crime C should be committed (either by himself or by another person), asks another person, Solicited, to perform some act A, where Defendant believes that if Solicited performs A, then the intended crime C will either thereby be committed, or be closer to being committed. The question before the court in every such case is whether Defendant has attempted C. As it turns out, there are three kinds of cases of this sort that are easy. This is to say that there are three kinds of cases of this sort in which clear-headed application of well-defined criminal law principles can tell us whether Defendant is criminally liable for an attempt to C without any sojourn into subtle questions about the nature of trying to act. As we'll see, not all of the cases that interest us fall into one of these three categories; there are hard cases too. Further, as indicated below, some cases fall into more than one of the categories of easy cases. Still, it will be helpful in corralling the problem to identify those cases in which it is not a problem at all.

### 2.1. Type 1: Accomplice to an attempt

In cases of this first type, Solicited responds to Defendant's solicitation by attempting C. For this to be the case, Solicited must have the intention required for an attempt of C, and must engage in conduct sufficient for the act element of attempt. Solicited has then committed a crime—not C, but the crime of attempting C—and the question then arises whether Defendant is Solicited's accomplice in the attempt of C. If the solicitation is sufficient for the act required for accomplice liability, as it almost always is,[11] then Defendant will be guilty of an attempt to C.

---

[11] *Model Penal Code* §2.06(3)(a)(i) makes solicitation itself sufficient for the act needed for accomplice liability, and the commentary makes clear that this is so even if the solicitation had

For instance, in *People v. Berger* (131 Cal.App.2d 127 (1955)), the defendant, a doctor, was asked by a pregnant undercover police officer to help her to procure an illegal abortion. The defendant asked Inez Brown to do the procedure. Brown came to the police officer's home bearing various medical tools and prepared the police officer for the procedure which she clearly intended to perform. Brown was then arrested and Berger was charged as Brown's accomplice. Here the hard question is whether Brown did enough to be said to have attempted the abortion; the court says she did and then convicts Berger for the attempt simply by applying standard rules of accomplice liability under which the kind of solicitation that Berger made to Brown is enough to hold Berger to be Brown's accomplice.

In a case like *Berger*, then, the court need not address the question of whether the defendant committed an attempt of the crime because he is rightly held guilty for an attempt even if he did not commit one; the question of commission, then, has no practical importance.[12] In Type 1 cases, that is, we have *guilt* for an attempt, an attempt made by Solicited, but we do not know if we have *commission* of an attempt by Defendant at all.[13]

---

no actual influence on the principal's performance of the crime (see *Model Penal Code*, Commentary on §2.06, p. 314). However, sometimes courts have required, not just a showing of solicitation, but also a showing to the effect that the principal was motivated to act by the solicitation. See, for instance, *Workman v. State* (216 Ind. 68, 21 N.E.2d 712 (1939)).

[12] At various times, courts faced with solicitation-as-attempt cases have turned to the question of whether Solicited intended to commit the crime. It can seem puzzling why this should matter; one court even says of other courts' fixation on that question that it "baffles reason" why the mental states of Solicited should help to exonerate Defendant (*State v. Hayes* (78 Mo. 307 (1883))). After all, if the question is whether Defendant attempted the crime, the inquiry would appear to be entirely about the acts and mental states of *Defendant* and not about those of the person Defendant tried to enlist. But a court trying to determine if Defendant is Solicited's accomplice in the attempt needs to know if Solicited actually attempted the crime, and so needs to know if Solicited intended to commit it. I suggest, then, that reason need not be baffled for long in the search for an explanation for why the Solicited's intention might be of importance to the question of the Defendant's criminal liability.

[13] Type 1 cases differ from standard cases of accomplice liability in two respects. First, in the standard accomplice liability case, the defendant performs some act that aids or encourages the principal in the completion of the very crime for which the defendant is charged. By contrast, in Type 1 cases, Defendant does not ask Solicited to attempt the crime: he asks him to do something that would complete the crime, and yet he is to be held liable as an accomplice to the attempt. Second, in standard accomplice liability cases, the defendant *intends* that the principal complete the very crime for which Defendant is charged as an accomplice. By contrast, in Type 1 cases, Defendant does not intend that Solicited attempt the crime, but intends that it be completed by him, even though Defendant is charged as an accomplice to the attempt. Discrepancies of this sort between Type 1 cases and standard cases of accomplice liability should not give us pause, however: they are to be explained by appeal to principles governing accomplice liability in cases that involve neither solicitation nor attempt, but in which there is some mismatch between the precise conduct the accomplice was aiding and intending to aid, and the conduct for which he is charged as an accomplice.

## 2.2. Type 2: Soliciting Another's Aid

In *People v. Coleman* (350 Mich. 268 (1957)), the defendant learned that a man who was to be a witness against him in a trial for another crime was cheating on his wife. The defendant asked Charles Goldsborough to deliver a letter to the witness threatening to reveal the affair to the wife should the witness testify. Goldsborough did not deliver the letter but instead told the police of the plot. Coleman was charged with attempting to obstruct justice. This is clearly not a Type 1 case: Goldsborough did not attempt to obstruct justice, and so Coleman cannot be an accomplice to any attempt to do so. In cases like this, the combination of the particular crime in question and the circumstances are such that if Solicited acts in the way Defendant asks him to, then Defendant will be closer to completing the act element of the completed crime *himself*. This is the distinctive feature of Type 2 cases. Solicited's performance of A, in these cases, would bring the world closer to *Defendant's* commission of C. Typically, this is because what Defendant is really asking is for Solicited to help Defendant *himself* to perform C. The proposal might appear on its face to distance Defendant from performing the acts involved in the crime, but, in cases of this kind, this is only an appearance. Coleman might *seem* to be asking merely that Goldsborough threaten the witness; he seems to be asking for something that would keep him, Coleman, out of it. But, in fact, were Goldsborough to act as asked, it would be *Coleman himself* (and probably Goldsborough too) who would threaten the witness. This is true since to arrange for the delivery of a threatening letter that one writes oneself is a way of threatening another person.

Type 2 cases can be thought of analogously to single-agent cases in which the agent's progression towards performance of an act depends on events that are entirely out of his control. When a dart leaves a person's hand on its journey towards a dartboard, the dart's progress is the agent's progress towards the act of hitting the bull's eye. The closer the dart gets to hitting the bull's eye, the closer *the agent* gets to hitting the bull's eye. Similarly, the closer that Goldsborough gets to delivering the letter, the closer that *Coleman* gets to threatening the witness. Whether Solicited's behavior can be analogized to the behavior of the dart in this way will depend on several factors. However, one crucial factor is the concept of action employed in assessing defendant's behavior. In the *Coleman* case, the relevant concept of action is threatening, or maybe obstructing justice. We look at Coleman's plan—namely that Goldsborough deliver the letter—and we ask whether the concept of action in question is such that it would apply to Coleman's behavior were things to go according to plan. Goldsborough's delivery of the letter is a way for Coleman to *threaten* the witness. It is probably also a way for Coleman to *obstruct justice*. It is not a way for Coleman to *deliver* a letter; the concept of delivery would not apply to Coleman's act were Goldsborough to do as Coleman asks. In short, to determine if the case before one is a Type 2 case, one must first identify the relevant action concept in play, and then determine if it is the sort of concept that would apply to the defendant's act were things to go according to plan. If so, then the case is a Type 2 case.

The question in Type 2 cases is the same question that is before the court in any attempt case, even those in which no solicitation is involved: did Defendant's behavior bring him far enough down the road toward the crime to qualify for the act element of the attempt? (This question is addressed in chapter 10.) The fact that another agent was involved, much less that the other agent was asked to act in a particular way, is irrelevant, in cases such as this, to the normative and conceptual question of whether Defendant's behavior went far enough. For instance, the court in *Coleman* chooses to use a "*res ipsa loquitur*" test, or "unequivocality" test, to determine if Coleman did enough for the act element of the attempt. Under such a test, if the defendant's action cannot be reasonably construed in any way other than as an effort to further an intention to commit the crime, then the act is sufficient for the attempt. Concluding that there is no other reason why Coleman would have given the letter to Goldsborough to deliver, the court convicts Coleman of the attempt. Notice that it is completely irrelevant to the court's reasoning that Goldsborough knows of Coleman's plans and was, in fact, asked to threaten the witness. Even if Goldsborough had been a courier, ignorant of the contents of the letter, or even if Coleman had elected to use a carrier pigeon to deliver the letter, the court's reasoning would have gone through. The fact that the "unequivocal" act is a solicitation is of no importance to the case.

In cases of this kind, whether a solicitation is enough for the act element of the attempt depends on two things: on the nature of the crime and the circumstances, and on the test that the court in question employs for determining whether the defendant's act was enough for the act element of the attempt. Imagine that the so-called "dangerous proximity" test were applied in *Coleman*. According to that test, the defendant's act is enough for the act element of the attempt if it is close enough to completion of the crime to make such completion dangerously likely. Although there are a whole series of hazy concepts involved here, one can imagine a court applying this test and concluding that Coleman had not done enough to warrant an attempt. After all, how likely it was that Coleman would succeed in obstructing justice depended on, among other things, how likely it was that Goldsborough would deliver the letter. If that wasn't very likely, then it wasn't very likely that the crime would have been completed. This shows that, given an appropriate test for the act element of attempt, such as the dangerous proximity test, a court that is conceiving of its case as a Type 2 case might care about how much Solicited did following the solicitation by Defendant. Solicited's progress is, itself, Defendant's progress in such cases since, if Solicited does all that is asked, Defendant will have succeeded in acting as he intends.

197

In many cases of this kind the completed crime consists of a transaction between two parties. Consider *Metler v. State* (697 N.E.2d 502 (1998)). The defendant left a letter for his adult daughter soliciting sex and was charged with attempted incest after the daughter took the letter to the police. If Metler is to do as he intends, the daughter must acquiesce, and so the question is only whether the solicitation takes Metler far enough towards his goal; the court felt that it did not. The reason that it is easy to get confused in a case like this is that the crime of solicitation, of which Metler is clearly guilty, is not predicated on the fact that were he to have sex with his daughter, then *Metler* would be committing a crime, but on the fact that were he to have sex with his daughter, *his daughter* would be commiting a crime, a crime that he asked her to commit.[14,15] By contrast, the fact that Metler himself would be committing a crime were his daughter to acquiesce is clearly the pertinent point when it comes to attempt. But, as in the Coleman case and all other Type 2 cases, the fact that the step that the defendant took was to solicit something from another is of no direct relevance to the question of whether or not he attempted. What matters, instead, is whether the act went far enough, a question which is settled in different ways in different jurisdictions, and which must be settled in every attempt case, and not just in those involving solicitation. These are "easy" cases, then, not because they are easy, but because they are hard in a way which has nothing to do with solicitation, per se, but is endemic to attempt generally.

Type 2 cases are a proper subset of cases sometimes described as "perpetration by means".[16] Cases of perpetration by means are ordinarily defined as those in which one person's act is merely the means through which another's aims are advanced. However, the category is broad enough to conceal distinctions that are important to the question of when a solicitation amounts to an attempt. In

---

[14] Getting past this confusion and seeing that the real issue has little to do with solicitation, and only to do with whether or not defendants like Metler have gone far enough towards fulfillment of their intentions to have attempted, the Indiana courts have made the error of thinking that the *only* kinds of solicitation that can amount to attempt are those in which "the cooperation or submission of the person being solicited is an essential feature of the substantive crime" (*Ward v. State* (528 N.E.2d (1988))). This amounts to the assertion that all cases in which solicitors have attempted are of Type 2, a claim which is clearly false.

[15] Notice that had Metler's daughter been a child, then his act of solicitation would have differed from standard cases of criminal solicitation in which what one asks another to do is itself a crime. A minor daughter who has sex with her father has committed no crime; it is the father, rather, who has committed the crime in such a case. There are two ways to handle the problem, assuming that we think that soliciting a child for sex should be a crime. First, solicitation of this sort can be specifically criminalized by statute, as it is in many jurisdictions. (In Indiana, the jurisdiction of the *Metler* case, the relevant child solicitation statute is Ind.Code § 35-42-4-6.) Alternatively, it can be enough for solicitation that the following is true: if the solicited party does as asked, then the defendant will be party to a crime; this is true in the case of solicitation of a minor for sex, and is true also of the standard cases in which the solicited party will have committed a crime if acting as asked.

[16] Although the concept of perpetration by means is very old, the term was coined in Fletcher (2000), 639.

particular, a person's aims can be advanced because *he advances them*, or they can be advanced because somebody else advances them. Type 2 cases are those in which were Solicited to act, Defendant himself would be advancing his own aims. As we will see, there are both another kind of easy case and hard cases that fall into the category of perpetration by means.

### 2.3. *Type 3: Act Substitution*

In cases of this sort, in response to Defendant's solicitation, Solicited does something that is sufficient for the *act element* of an attempt to C, but falls short of an attempt to C for one of a variety of reasons. For instance, Solicited might fall short of an attempt because he is a child, as when Defendant tells a child to place poison in someone's coffee, which the child does, and the coffee is never drunk. Even if the child knows that it is poison in the coffee, the child lacks the capacity to form the needed intention to kill (or, anyway, lacks the capacity to do so in a way that would count as such for legal purposes), and so did not attempt murder. Still, in such a case, Defendant is criminally liable for an attempted murder. Or Solicited might fall short of an attempt to C because, although equipped to form the intent needed for attempt, Solicited simply doesn't form it; perhaps Solicited acts merely to comply with Defendant's demand and hopes that the result that Defendant intends will not come to pass, or perhaps Solicited lacks information that one would need to have to attempt to C, as when the courier delivers a threatening letter, ignorant of its contents.[17]

The *Model Penal Code* would not call Type 3 cases cases of "accomplice" liability by Defendant at all, but would, instead, consider them to be cases in which Defendant is "legally accountable for the conduct of another", reserving the term "accomplice" for cases in which the offense is actually committed by the party solicited.[18] But the terms are not important. What matters is only that to motivate conduct that is enough for the act element of the crime can be equivalent, for legal purposes, to engaging in such conduct yourself. The law here has a substitution rule: we treat Solicited's act as though it were Defendant's in assessing Defendant's criminal liability. This substitution rule is a

---

[17] There are also cases in which Solicited attempts C but has an affirmative defense against the charge. Whether these are Type 1 cases or Type 3 cases will depend on the nature of the affirmative defense. If, for instance, Solicited has the defense of voluntary abandonment—he gave up his plan to C before completing the crime—then it will be a Type 1 case: there's been an attempt, but Solicited is not criminally liable for it because he abandoned. If, however, Solicited has a mistake defense in a jurisdiction that still treats mistakes as affirmative defenses, then it will be a Type 3 case: Solicited has acted as required for an attempt, but lacks *mens rea*.

[18] *Model Penal Code* §2.06(2)(a). There are other differences between those who are "legally accountable for the conduct of another" and those who are "accomplices". Most importantly, the *mens rea* requirements for the former are the same as those required for the completed crime, while they are less than those for accomplices.

principle allowing guilt in the absence of commission. So, as in Type 1 cases, courts are able to bypass the question of whether Defendant has committed an attempt through his solicitation since, whether he committed one or not, he is guilty of one.

Still, despite this similarity, Type 1 cases differ from Type 3 cases. Type 3 cases require from Defendant the mental states that are required for an attempt *by him*, while, in Type 1 cases, the Defendant could, for instance, merely intend to help, and not intend that the crime or the attempt be completed, in order to be sufficiently closely associated with the attempt to warrant holding him criminally liable for it. Further, Type 1 cases require an intention to complete the crime by Solicited; without it there is no attempted crime for Defendant to be an accomplice to. However, Type 3 cases require only action by Solicited that could serve as the act element of an attempt, even in the absence of appropriate mental states on Solicited's part.

Type 3 cases are "easy", only given a solution to a hard problem: under what conditions is Defendant's role in motivating Solicited's act enough to take that act to count as Defendant's for purposes of assessing guilt? This is a normative question, not a descriptive one. It is not the case that Defendant's volition can be related to Solicited's bodily movement in such a way as to make that bodily movement Defendant's voluntary act. Type 3 cases do not involve commission of an attempt by Defendant. The normative question, that is, concerns how to specify the content of the guilt-without-commission principle that is appealed to in the resolution of such cases. In fact, the normative question here has broad scope. The issue arises most often in cases in which neither attempt nor solicitation is at issue, as when, for instance, one party baits another into assaulting a third, or when a religious leader marries a child to an adult knowing full well that this will result in the rape of the child. So although Type 3 cases are not easy, like Type 2 cases they are not hard in a way which should give us pause here. Resolution of the problems involved in such cases, that is, is not special to cases of solicitation as attempt.

Like Type 2 cases, Type 3 cases are examples of perpetration by means. Solicited's act is merely the means through which Defendant's aims are advanced. However, these cases are different from Type 2 cases in that the solicitation does not contribute in Type 3 cases to *Defendant's* performance of an act that would serve for the act element of the crime, or the act element of the attempt. Rather, Defendant, thanks to his solicitation, becomes associated with Solicited's act in a way that makes it equivalent, for purposes of assessing guilt, to an act of his own. Since, as we will see, some hard cases are also cases of perpetration by means, the mere fact that a case is one involving perpetration by means gives us little guidance about how to come to a principled resolution of it.

Notice that some cases fall into more than one of the easy categories. Had Goldsborough gone to the house of the witness, intending to threaten him while delivering the letter, then, assuming Goldsborough thereby did enough for an attempt to obstruct justice, the case would have been both Type 1 and Type 2. It would have been Type 1 since Goldsborough would have attempted to obstruct justice and Coleman would have been his accomplice in that crime, and it would have been Type 2 since, had Goldsborough succeeded in doing what Coleman asked, then Coleman would have obstructed justice himself. Add that, for instance, Goldsborough has an affirmative defense for his crime—perhaps he's insane—and the case is of all three easy types. When the question at issue is whether Defendant is criminally liable for an attempt to C, the fact that the case is of any one of the easy types is enough to guide us in its resolution. But, as we will see, there are some cases that fall into none of these three categories.

## 2.4. Hard Cases

The Decker case is not of any of the three easy types. It is not a Type 1 case, for Holston was far from attempting to kill Decker's sister; among other things, he had no intention of doing so and intention is required for attempt. Nor is it a Type 2 case since, had Holston done as Decker requested and killed Decker's sister, it would not have been true that *Decker* killed his sister. We might speak that way in some metaphorical sense, but we recognize that it is only metaphorical. What we mean when we say that, is only that had the sister been killed by Holston, Decker should be held responsible for the killing: we don't actually mean that *he* killed her, in such a case. Nor is it a Type 3 case, for Holston did nothing that could serve as the act element of an attempt. Accepting money for a job is not undertaking a means to doing the job; such behavior is clearly on the "mere preparation" side of the relevant line. It is different, for instance, from accepting money to cover materials needed to do the job, since in that case acceptance of the money brings one over a hurdle that one must pass to do the job. And this is so even if we grant that Holston did accept money *for the job*, which is, itself, a questionable claim, given that he had no intention of either keeping the money or doing the job. Further, even if Holston's conduct were sufficient for the act element of attempt under some "test" for the act element, it would be possible to construct a case in which Defendant's conduct does not differ from Decker's, but in which Solicited's conduct falls short of the act element of attempt even under the relevant test.

There is some evidence to suggest that the court mistakenly takes the case to be a Type 2 case. Consider the following remark:

> The issue ... is not whether "solicitation alone" is sufficient to establish an attempt, but whether a solicitation to commit murder, combined with a complete agreement to hire a professional killer and the making of a downpayment under that agreement [is].
>
> (*People v. Decker* (41 Cal.4th 1 (2007) at 428))

The court, recall, is overturning an earlier case, *Adami*, in which a defendant who hired an officer posing as a professional killer was ruled not to have attempted murder on the grounds that "solicitation alone" cannot constitute an attempt. The court overrules that case by noting that the defendants in *Decker* and *Adami* did more than merely solicit: they also reached an agreement and made a downpayment. But why does the court care about this additional conduct? If one is conceiving of the case as a Type 2 case, then one might care about the additional conduct because one thinks that it took *Decker*, and not merely Holston, closer to performance of the act element of the crime. If this is what the court has in mind, then the court is mistaken, since the reaching of the agreement and making of the downpayment took *Decker* no closer to *killing his sister*; at best it took Holston closer to that. What is really going on in *Decker* is that the court is convinced that Decker's solicitation did indeed amount to an attempt. The court simply does not see what principles would justify that conclusion, and so it engages in some rather convoluted reasonings to assimilate the case to those in one of the easy categories, in which principled reasoning could lead to that conclusion. And, of course, given the court's role one can see why it would do this: despite its conviction about *Decker*, the court senses also that there will be cases in which a solicitation does not amount to an attempt (more on this below), and cannot see how such cases would be distinct from *Decker*. Lacking principled grounds, then, on which to draw the needed lines, the court searches for a way to convict Decker without damaging future defendants whose solicitations do not amount to attempts.

*Decker* is a hard case. But what makes it so? Hard cases have two related features that distinguish them from the three types of easy cases. First, if we set aside the solicitation itself, nothing that either Defendant or Solicited did could serve as the act element of an attempt. Second, Defendant's intention is not to act himself by inducing Solicited to act (as in Type 2 cases), but, instead, to bring about some desired result of which he will not be the agent.[19] Thus, hard cases are different from ordinary single-agent attempts both in action and in mental state. In the ordinary single-agent case, there is an act that is not an act of solicitation which serves as the act element of the attempt. And in ordinary single-agent attempts, the defendant has an intention to act himself in a way that would be enough for the completed crime. Unlike in the easy cases, in hard solicitation-as-attempt cases we have neither of these things.

---

[19] In his dissent in *Decker*, Justice Werdegar makes the following remark:
[F]or attempt it must be 'clear from a suspect's acts what *he* intends to do'... In this case, what defendant intended to do was have his sister killed *by someone else*... That he hired another, supplied him with information, and paid him a downpayment only highlights his intention not to perform the act himself. (*People v. Decker* (41 Cal.4th 1 (2007) at 432)).
Werdegar is noticing the second feature of a hard case, and so noticing the flaw in the majority's efforts to treat the case as though it were easy.

Intuitively, it seems that some hard cases are, and some of them are not, attempts.[20] For instance, say that Defendant is holding a quantity of heroin and asks Solicited to take it—maybe Defendant wants to kick the habit but just can't bring himself to destroy the stuff; Solicited refuses. In such a case, Defendant has solicited possession of heroin. But he obviously hasn't attempted possession of heroin by so doing. After all, what Defendant is trying to do is to *dispossess* himself of the heroin he is possessing. Imagine, to give another example, that Defendant asks Solicited to try heroin and in doing so Defendant does not just think that Solicited will enjoy it, he really intends that Solicited should use; Solicited refuses. Did Defendant attempt to use by soliciting Solicited? Of course not. Imagine that Defendant asks Solicited to drive himself home, knowing full well that Solicited is far too drunk to drive legally; Solicited refuses. Defendant has clearly not attempted to drive drunk in such a case.

By contrast, imagine that Defendant asks Solicited to carry a quantity of heroin across the border into the United States; Solicited refuses. Has Defendant attempted to smuggle drugs into the United States? It seems so. Imagine that Defendant asks Solicited to deface a piece of public property; Solicited refuses. It seems that Defendant, in such a case, has attempted to deface public property. If examples fitting facts of these sorts are constructed with sufficient care, all will be hard cases. So, intuitively, some hard cases are, and some are not, attempts. What facts are being tracked by our intuitions? What principles ought a court to use to decide a hard case?

## 3. The Solution

The solution to our problem can be reached by first looking at the second of the two distinctive features of hard cases: the fact that in such cases, Defendant's intention differs from that of the paradigmatic attempter. As we'll see, despite this difference, sometimes Defendant's intention commits him to all of the

---

[20] The *Model Penal Code* has a provision designed to solve a different problem, but which appears at first glance to allow us to deal with hard cases: "A person who engages in conduct designed to aid another to commit a crime that would establish his complicity...if the crime were committed by such other person, is guilty of an attempt to commit the crime, although the crime is not committed or attempted by such other person." (§5.01(3)) Although Defendant would be complicit in Solicited's crime, were Solicited to do as asked, Defendant, in a hard solicitation as attempt case, does not "engage in conduct designed *to aid*" Solicited; solicitations aren't ordinarily designed to help others to do as asked. Note the difference in the *MPC's* language here in comparison to its language in defining the *mens rea* required for accomplice liability as a "purpose of *promoting or facilitating*" the commission of the offense (§2.06(3)(a)). In hard cases, Defendant has the *mens rea* needed to be an accomplice, but not the *mens rea* needed to fall under §5.01(3). Also, if we interpret §5.01(3) more broadly than this, then it follows that under it *all* solicitations are attempts. If that's what the *Model Penal Code* says, then one starts to wonder what point there is in having crimes of solicitation at all, given that they always warrant lesser sentences than attempts.

components of the completed crime, and sometimes it does not. Thus sometimes Defendant's intention suffices for the attempt, and sometimes it does not. The further question of whether an act of solicitation is good enough for the act element of the attempt can be settled using standard attempt principles designed for the single-agent case, principles that will be discussed in chapter 10.

As noted, in hard solicitation-as-attempt cases, like *Decker*, Defendant's relevant intention is not an intention *to* perform any act that would serve as the act element of the completed crime; Decker does not intend [to point a gun at his sister and pull the trigger], for instance. This is part of what distinguishes these cases from the easy ones. But in all such cases, Defendant does intend [that Solicited A's], where A is an act that could serve as the act element of the completed crime were it performed; Decker intends [that Holston kill Decker's sister]. A crucial question, then, for determining if Defendant's solicitation amounts to an attempt, in a hard case, is this: under what conditions is an intention with that content sufficient for the intention required for the attempt? We can use the answer to this question offered in chapter 4 to solve our problem.

As noted in chapter 3, while crimes have distinct act elements and result elements, the acts that the criminal law cares about are virtually always described by reference to their results. The California murder statute of relevance to Decker's crime, a statute which is perfectly typical of jurisdictions that have not adopted the *Model Penal Code*, reads, "Murder is the unlawful killing of a human being... with malice aforethought."[21] Should we characterize this as a crime with the act element of killing, or a crime with the result element of a death? Criminal law students are taught to characterize it the first way. So such students are taught that among the things that must be proven in a murder trial in California is not just that the defendant caused a death, but also that the agency-involvement factor was present. (Recall from chapter 3 the definition of the agency-involvement factor: whatever it is that, when present, allows us to move from "D caused an A" to "D A'd", or would allow that if there were an appropriate verb in our language.) By contrast, the *Model Penal Code* defines one form of "criminal mischief" like so:

A person is guilty of criminal mischief if he purposely or recklessly causes another to suffer pecuniary loss by deception or threat.

*(Model Penal Code §220.3(1)(c))*

Here it seems that the act element is deception or threat—a guilty defendant deceived or threatened another—while pecuniary loss is a result element. A guilty defendant caused pecuniary loss, but it need not be the case that his agency is involved in that result in a way that would make it appropriate to say that the defendant *lost* the other's money. To show a defendant guilty of

---

[21] Cal.Pen.Code §187(a).

criminal mischief under the *Model Penal Code* he must be shown to have caused another to be deceived or threatened *with the agency-involvement factor present*, and to have caused another to lose something of pecuniary value *where the agency-involvement factor is irrelevant*—it will be present in some guilty defendants, absent in others. The broker who, through deception, takes control of another's money and *loses* it, is guilty of criminal mischief; the agency-involvement factor is present in both the deception and the loss in such a case. But the person who deceives another and thereby leads him to make an investment whereby the victim loses his own money has also committed the crime; such a person has committed criminal mischief, even though the agency-involvement factor is absent with respect to the loss of money.

The divide between act elements and result elements is not merely formal: it is of normative significance. It is something about which legislators ought to debate when defining a crime by statute. To criminalize the causation of a fetus's death, for instance, would be to criminalize a much larger number of acts than would be criminalized were the crime to require, instead, the killing of a fetus. If a defendant is at fault in a minor car accident with a pregnant woman that results in the death of the fetus, then he has caused a fetus's death, but has probably not killed a fetus. We can imagine adding details, that is, implying that the agency-involvement factor is absent despite the fact that there is causation. Whether we want to criminalize this under a particular statute will depend on our normatively significant goals in writing the statute and will influence what penalty we take to be appropriate for the crime we are defining. Although this is not the only relevant factor, when an event, like a fetus's death, figures into the description of the act required for the crime—when what is criminalized is "the killing of a fetus"—the *mens rea* requirement for the act and the result cannot be different. A person who recklessly kills a fetus is also reckless with respect to the death of the fetus. By contrast, when an act element is separately defined from the result element—when what is criminalized is, for instance, any act that "causes the death of a fetus"—then there is room for the *mens rea* with respect to the act and result to diverge; it is possible to intentionally run a red light and only negligently thereby cause a fetus's death. So the act-result distinction makes a difference to what is criminalized and so, although it is a formal distinction, it is a formal distinction of normative importance.

As discussed in chapter 4, whether a particular event figures in the completed crime's act element or result element is of importance for the characterization of the intention needed for an attempt of that crime: an attempter must have the intention *to* act, but only the intention *that* a result comes to pass. An intention [*to* A] constitutes a commitment to both A's occurrence and to the presence of the agency-involvement factor in its occurrence. Commitment to the defendant's causing A is present in such an intention also, since were the intention [to A] to play its proper causal role, the defendant would cause A. However, because the agency-involvement factor need not be present with respect to the occurrence of a result element, R, of the completed crime, an intention [*that* R] suffices for an attempt. After all, were such an intention to play its proper causal role, the defendant would cause R, and when R is a result element, all that the attempter need be committed to is R's occurrence and the causation of R. So an intention [to R] would suffice, but only an intention [that R] is necessary.

Now return to the second of the two features that make hard cases hard: Defendant does not intend that he act himself, but only that Solicited perform an act that would serve as the act element of the completed crime. Under what conditions does this show that Defendant lacks the *mens rea* of attempt? *Defendant's intention is sufficient for the* mens rea *of attempt when the event that Defendant intends Solicited to cause is a result element of the completed crime, but his intention is insufficient for the* mens rea *of attempt if that event figures in the specification of an act element of the completed crime.* This follows immediately from the account of the intention needed with respect to acts and results offered in chapter 4 and just summarized.

So does Decker have the intention needed for an attempt to murder his sister? Assuming that California's homicide laws are read literally, and thus that in California the other's death figures into the definition of an act element of the crime—assuming that one must have *killed* another in order to have committed murder in California—the answer is "no". Under this assumption, an attempt to murder requires an intention [to kill], something that Decker lacks; his intention [that his sister die] is not enough for attempted murder under California law. However, consider the *Model Penal Code's* alternative definition of homicide:

A person is guilty of criminal homicide if he purposely, knowingly, recklessly or negligently causes the death of another human being.

(*Model Penal Code* §210.1(1))

Here the act element is left undescribed: any act at all could serve for the act element of the completed crime, even an act that was not a killing. The death of a human being is a result element of the crime. As such, a person should be able to try to commit criminal homicide, as defined by the *Model Penal Code* by intending [to perform some act] and intending [that another dies].[22] Decker has these two intentions, for he intends [to solicit Holston] and intends [that his sister dies]. So, Decker has attempted a murder under the *Model Penal Code's* definition of that crime.[23]

---

[22] The two intentions in question here would have to be linked somehow. A person who intends [that another dies], but is engaged in some entirely separate activity—and is thereby acting on an intention [to perform some act]—is not thereby trying to commit murder. However, the best way to understand this link is not through consideration of what is in the mind of the person trying to do something, but rather through consideration of the act of the person trying. The acts of such a person must be in furtherance of *both* the intention [to perform some act] and the intention [that another die]. (Thanks to Michael Bratman for pushing me on the point.)

[23] Decker has not attempted *to kill*; but just as one can murder without killing, under the *Model Penal Code*, one can attempt murder without attempting to kill.

Although I will not defend the claim here, it seems to me that the *Model Penal Code*'s definition of homicide—with the death of another as a result element rather than killing another as an act element—is superior, on normative grounds, to definitions, like that in California, under which a killing is required.[24] But the important point for our purposes is, rather, that the question of whether a soliciter has the intention needed for an attempt has to be settled by a normative argument over how to define the completed crime. Now one can imagine the *Decker* court having reached the verdict it sought, even given the language of California's murder statutes, by claiming that, despite appearances to the contrary, the death of another is a result element of the crime of murder in California. To do this, they would have had to abandon the most natural interpretation of the explicit language of the statute, but there may be an argument for doing so. After all, the court might have reasoned, common law homicide definitions were formulated using language that was developed before criminal law theorists and legislators had the act-result distinction firmly in mind, and so it would be no surprise if some statutes were drafted with language misleadingly suggesting that a result element figures, instead, into the description of an act element. The fact that, on normative grounds, it is better for death to be considered a result strengthens the case for this form of argument.[25]

Notice that this way of determining if the defendant in a hard case has the intention needed for an attempt does not require us to take any stand on the question of whether Defendant is the cause of the result when Solicited does as asked and brings the result about. That is, we need not take a stand on the following controversial and well-known principle:

*The Voluntary Intervention Principle*: If event A is brought about voluntarily[26] by agent S1, then it is not caused by agent S2 (even if it would not have occurred but for some act of S2's).[27]

---

[24] The *Model Penal Code* does not provide much by way of a normative defense of this claim, but says only, "It seems clear that causing death purposely, knowingly, and recklessly ... must in the absence of justification and excuse establish criminality." (*Model Penal Code*, Commentary on §210.1, 5.) I quite agree. The important point for our purposes is that it is not so under homicide laws like those in California.

[25] A court faced with a statute that specifies "causing A" as an element must consider whether there is an appropriate verb that would have allowed "A-ing" instead of "causing A". If so, then that is powerful reason to take A to be a result element. However, if there is no such verb, then the statute is ambiguous for, recall, the agency-involvement factor can be present even when there is no relevant verb. In such a case, the court may have no choice but to ask whether the normatively relevant category of conduct is the one in which the agency-involvement factor is present or the one in which it is absent.

[26] "Voluntarily", in this formulation of the principle, has a somewhat different meaning from "voluntarily" when used in formulations of the act requirement under which it requires only bodily movement guided by volition. For our purposes, it will be enough to note that, in the principle, "voluntarily" should be understood to mean what it means in ordinary language.

[27] The principle was first named in the classic Hart and Honore (1959), 129. Hart and Honore's formulation is only cosmetically different from this one.

Recall the example introduced in chapter 3 of the owner who calls his dog from across the street, and the dog is crushed by a car while running to the owner. According to the Voluntary Intervention Principle, the owner who calls his dog, in this example, causes the dog to be crushed if the driver of the car that hits it simply cannot stop in time, but if, instead, the driver seizes the opportunity to voluntarily crush the dog, then the owner is not the cause of the dog's being crushed. The principle also implies that there is no causal link to the result when, in contrast to this case, one person causes another to voluntarily bring about a result, as in solicitation cases in which the solicited party follows through. This principle has intuitive appeal, but it is not clear that it captures a truth about *causation*, especially given that causation is transitive.[28] It may, instead, derive its appeal from some closely related principle that concerns, not causation, but responsibility. In accepting an appropriately formulated version of this principle, that is, the criminal law may be registering merely that there are good reasons not to hold a defendant responsible for results that others voluntarily bring about, quite independently of the question of whether the defendant actually caused those results. Be that as it may, what has been said so far with respect to solicitation as attempt does not require that we take a stand on this issue. The approach works if the principle is false, and works in a slightly different way if it is true.

To see this, assume first that the Voluntary Intervention Principle is false; assume that causation does pass through voluntary interventions. Now imagine that Defendant, on facts similar to those involved in *Decker*, is charged with attempted murder under the *Model Penal Code*'s definition of murder, in which the death is a result element and killing is not required for murder. Defendant intends [that Victim dies]; our question is whether this intention is enough for the *mens rea* element of the attempt. So, according to the approach proposed, we are to imagine that this intention plays its proper causal role and brings it about that Solicited follows through with Defendant's request to kill Victim; we then check to see if Defendant causes the death in that event; if not, then Defendant's intention is not sufficient for the *mens rea* of the attempt, since he fails to be properly committed to causing the death. Given the falsity of the Voluntary Intervention Principle, which we are assuming, if the intention plays its proper causal role, Defendant causes Victim's death when Solicited kills Victim. It follows that Defendant is properly committed by his intention to the causation of Victim's death. And, given that the death is included in the content of the intention, from this it follows that his intention is sufficient for the *mens rea* element of the attempt.

Now assume that the Voluntary Intervention Principle is true, and let's make the same suppositions as before: Defendant solicits Solicited, intends [that

---

[28] For discussion, see Moore (2009), esp. chapters 11–13.

Victim dies] and is charged with attempted murder under the *Model Penal Code*'s definition of murder. Our question, again, is whether Defendant's intention is sufficient for the *mens rea* element of the attempt and, again, we are to answer that question by checking to see if Defendant causes Victim's death when his intention [that Victim dies] plays its proper causal role. Now, if the Voluntary Intervention Principle is true, as we are assuming, then an intention that causes another to act and which, in turn, causes the world to match the content of the intention *does not play its proper causal role*. After all, in such a case, given the Voluntary Intervention Principle, the intention is not the cause of the fact that the world matches its content; that fact must be imputed, instead, to the intervening agent who voluntarily acted so as to make the world that way. So, in assuming that the intention plays its proper causal role in bringing it about that the world matches its content, we are assuming that this occurs in some other way, perhaps by leading Defendant to actually kill Victim himself. But under that supposition, Defendant does indeed cause Victim's death. And it follows that the intention is sufficient for the *mens rea* of the attempt.

The point is that the Voluntary Intervention Principle, like any principle discriminating between cases in which there is and there is not causation, has implications for our characterization of the proper causal role of our intentions. Our intentions have the role of causing it to be the case that the world matches their content. But then what needs to happen for them to play that causal role depends on what kinds of chains of events, beginning with the intention and ending with the world matching its content, are such that the intention causes the world to match its content in those chains. This, in turn, depends on whether principles like the Voluntary Intervention Principle are true. What follows is that the proposed way of determining, in a hard solicitation-as-attempt case, if a Defendant's intention is sufficient for the *mens rea* of attempt—it is if the relevant event figures into a result element of the completed crime, and not if it figures into an act element—can accommodate either rejection or acceptance of principles like the Voluntary Intervention Principle.

So we now have a principled way of handling the second feature of hard solicitation as attempt cases in virtue of which they are hard, namely that Defendant has a different intention from that of the paradigmatic single-agent attempter. But what about the first feature of such cases, namely, that in such cases the only act that could possibly serve as the act element of the attempt is the solicitation itself? Given that we have learned that in a hard solicitation-as-attempt case Defendant lacks the intention needed for attempt when the event Defendant asks Solicited to bring about figures in a description of an act element of the crime, we can limit ourselves to the other kind of case, namely those in which the event is a result element of the crime. In those cases, is the act of solicitation sufficient for the act element of the attempt? Here the answer depends on what the act element of the crime is, and on what test the court in question uses to determine if defendants have gone beyond "mere preparation". Under the *Model Penal Code*'s definition of homicide, for instance, it is quite clear that Defendant's act is sufficient, for any act at all could serve as the act element of the crime. If any act can serve, then a solicitation could, itself, serve as the act element of the completed crime, and so is certainly sufficient for the attempt.

Things are a bit more complicated when it comes to crimes that have defined act elements and also have result elements, as does criminal mischief under the *Model Penal Code*, mentioned earlier. If the question is whether Defendant has attempted criminal mischief by soliciting Solicited, Defendant must be shown to have intended [to deceive or threaten a third party] and to have intended [that the third party suffer a pecuniary loss]; the former is the act element of the crime, the latter the result element. If this is shown, then we have two questions: first, did the solicitation take Defendant far enough towards deceiving or threatening the third party *himself* to warrant the claim that he was attempting to do so? And, second, did it take Defendant far enough towards fulfillment of his intention [that the third party suffer pecuniary loss]? Both of these questions will need to be answered by employing the test for the act element of attempt used in the relevant jurisdiction. However, it is virtually certain that the answer to the second question will be "yes"; if all that is at issue is a result element, a solicitation is surely enough.

The approach that I am recommending for the resolution of hard cases, then, can be thought of like so: the analysis of whether Defendant has the mental state needed for the crime requires a careful determination of the elements of the completed crime, and a clear separation between the act and result elements. The analysis of whether the act of solicitation is enough towards fulfillment of an intention *that* a result come to pass is easy: it is enough. But the analysis of whether Defendant's act of solicitation is sufficient for the act element of the attempt to fulfill an intention *to* proceeds, functionally, as though the case were an easy Type 2 case. Either it is possible for Defendant to act himself as required by the completed crime by first soliciting another, or it is not. If it is not, then there is no attempt. If it is, then the question of whether the act of solicitation is enough must employ the going resolution to the problem of where to draw the line between acts that are and are not sufficient for the act element of an attempt.

## 4. Conclusion

In attempt and solicitation, not to mention conspiracy, we recognize a sense in which the criminality of the act is diluted in comparison to that from which its criminality derives, namely the completed crime attempted or solicited. If completed crimes are blood red, attempts and solicitations seem to be shades of pink. This metaphor tempts one to imagine that the more we stack attempts and solicitations on one another, and the more attenuated the relation to the completed crime thereby becomes, the more diluted is the criminal liability. However, this is only a metaphor and one by which we should not be misled. In attempted crimes we do what we can to extend our agency into the world in objectionable ways. In solicitations we do what we can to extend another's agency into the world in objectionable ways. What has been shown here is that one way to do what one can to extend one's own agency into the world is to do what one can to lead another to extend his. This is so when all that is required to extend one's own agency into the world in an objectionable way is to cause a result. To try to cause a result, it is enough to ask another to bring it about. Others cannot act for us, but they can alter the world on our behalf, and sometimes to ask someone to do so is enough to thereby try to do so oneself. Since where they can, our laws should follow our ordinary concepts, they should follow them also in this. And this fact should guide our legislators when deciding on the formal but normatively important question of whether to place a bad result that we want to minimize into the definition of the act or result element of a crime.

Part 3

# The Evidential Conception of the Act Element and Its Implications

# 8

# The Need for an Act

## 1. Introduction

In 1678, Matthew Hale, the Lord Chief Justice of England, said that to hold a person criminally liable for a failed attempt to commit a crime would be to accept a flawed maxim of Roman law according to which the intention to act was, for legal purposes, no different from the action itself.[1] Out of a concern about the possibility of pure thought crimes, that is, Hale claimed that a just criminal code could not punish failed attempts. But, in 1784, in the case of *Rex v. Scofield* (Cald. 397 (1784)) Lord Mansfield, by then himself Lord Chief Justice, ruled that there could indeed be criminal liability for a failed attempt. The defendant had tried and failed to burn down a house, but Mansfield took the fact of his failure to be insufficient for excuse saying, "*completion* of an act, criminal in itself, is not necessary to constitute criminality".[2] Mansfield, however, was just as concerned as Hale about the spectre of crimes of pure thought. In his opinion he wrote, "So long as an act rests in bare intention, it is not punishable by our laws; but immediately when an act is done, the law judges."[3] Mansfield ruled, that is, that a legitimately proscribed attempt necessarily involves an act: some kind of act is an element of every attempted crime. And so stands the law to this day.

Mansfield's decision was surely the right one. But why? Why must an attempted crime include an act if it is to be justifiably punished? This chapter answers this question. (Left until chapter 10 is the question of how, exactly, to distinguish acts that do serve for the act element of attempt from those, such as "mere preparations", that do not.) The answer to the question defended here is deceptively simple: without an appropriate act we necessarily lack the kind of evidence that the defendant is trying to commit a crime that we must have if we are to be justified in punishing. Thus, attempts ought to have an act element for

---

[1] Hale (1736), 532. The Latin maxim is "Voluntas reputabitur pro facto", or, literally, "the will is to be taken for the deed".
[2] Cald. at 400 (emphasis in original). This remark is quoted, also, by Fletcher (2000), 134.
[3] Cald. at 403.

reasons that go beyond the general reasons that one might have for thinking that all crimes ought to have act elements. Trying is the sort of thing that can only be evidenced through action.

Section 2 explains the challenge that one faces in trying to justify the practice of requiring an act for criminal attempt by explaining the tension between that practice and the intuitive claim that when two agents differ only with respect to things that are under the control of neither, they do not differ in a morally significant way. Section 3 describes the formidable obstacles that are encountered by anyone hoping to argue that an act is required for criminal attempt because of the evidence that it provides. The *Model Penal Code*'s evidentialist approach, for instance, is shown to be unsatisfactory. Despite the difficulties, however, section 4 argues for an evidentialist approach. By reflecting on the account of trying to act offered in chapter 3, the Guiding Commitment View, we learn that trying to commit a crime is something that can only be adequately evidenced when the defendant has performed some actions, actions that he may not have performed were it not for various events entirely out of his control.

## 2. The Problem: Moral Luck, Equality, and the Means Requirement

It is justified to criminalize attempts under the Transfer Principle—the claim that if it is legitimate to criminalize a certain type of behavior then it is also legitimate to criminalize attempts to engage in such behavior—because there are two important commonalities between completers and attempters. They recognize and respond to reasons in the same way, and they are both guided by their resulting conception of their reasons for action. So goes the argument of chapter 1. If we add that the criminal law ought to strive towards equality, that we ought as far as we can to treat as criminal the behavior of those who are equally deserving of such treatment, then we can reach the further conclusion that a *failure* to criminalize the attempt of a crime, completion of which is legitimately criminalized, is a failure worth criticizing. In criminalizing attempts, we are solving a problem of inequality: since both the person who completes the crime and the person who tries but fails have engaged in criminalizable conduct, and since there is often no other good reason to treat one but not the other as a criminal, there ought not to be a difference in the state's treatment of them in this respect. A system that does not criminalize attempts to commit crimes treats differently citizens equally deserving of the title of "criminal", and for no good reason.

To accept this line of thought is to make what many see as a salutary commitment to the denial of moral luck. Those who take there to be moral luck, in the sense in which the term is to be used here, hold that it is possible for two actions to differ morally in virtue of the fact that they differ in some respect that was entirely out of the control of the agent of either action.[4] In fact, the intuitive thought that there can be a moral difference between an action, on the one hand, and a failed attempt to perform the very same action, on the other, is often cited as support for the contention that some moral intuitions point towards the existence of moral luck.[5] After all, often the difference between succeeding and merely trying is nothing but a difference in the air currents wafting through different parts of the casino. Yet, it seems intuitively that this difference can make a moral difference. So, it is no surprise that those who take the intuition to be flawed also think that one of the points of criminalizing attempts is, precisely, to correct for the influence of this flawed intuition in our legal system.

People who take this line are also often disturbed by the sentencing practices that we find in many jurisdictions, practices which seem to involve a commitment to moral luck. Many jurisdictions provide lesser penalties for attempted crimes than for completed; under the common law, for instance, an attempted felony is a misdemeanor.[6] In response, a number of theorists,[7] and the drafters of the *Model Penal Code*,[8] have claimed there to be no adequate justification for a discrepancy between sentences for attempted and completed crimes, and they have done so on the grounds that there is no moral luck, and so often no difference in moral desert between those who try and fail, on the one hand, and those who succeed in committing a crime, on the other. Such theorists accept the idea that the proscription of attempts corrects for morally irrelevant luck, and so moves us a step closer to a system in which equally deserving citizens are treated the same. This line of reasoning, they think, should also be reflected in our sentencing practices.[9]

The sentencing of attempts will be discussed at greater length in chapters 11 and 12. However, for now it is worth noting that there is room for a view, to be defended in chapter 12, according to which by criminalizing attempts we

---

[4] Thus, for the purposes of this book, my concern is with moral luck as it applies to the assessment of actions, and not to the assessment of agents, except in so far as assessment of actions is a form of assessment of agents. My concern then is not with so-called "constitutive" luck: luck that influences what sort of person an agent is. My concern is, however, with "consequential" luck and, to some degree, with "opportunity" luck. What one does often depends both on what consequences flow from what one does and on what opportunities one had to act. If either can make an action morally worse or better, even when the consequence or opportunity is out of the agent's control, then there is moral luck.

[5] Cf. Nagel (1979), 24–38.

[6] States use various methods for calculating the sentence for an attempt, but most offer a lesser penalty for the attempt than for the completed crime. California, for instance, gives half the penalty of the completed crime for the attempted (see Cal. Penal Code §664). This remains the most common formula.

[7] See, for instance, Kadish (1994), Morse (2004).

[8] *Model Penal Code*, Commentary on §5.05, 490.

[9] Lewis (1989) is probably the most sophisticated effort to respond to this sort of argument while still allowing that there is no moral luck.

correct for a form of inequality for which we ought to correct, but we are still justified in imposing different sentences on those who attempt and complete crimes. Such a position is supported by the following view: distinguish between censure-luck and sanction-luck. The believer in censure-luck thinks that two people can differ only with respect to something under the control of neither, and still differ in their desert of censure. The believer in sanction-luck thinks they can differ in their desert of sanction. There is no censure-luck. But for reasons to be explained in chapters 11 and 12, there is sanction-luck: two people differing only with respect to something out of either's control can nonetheless morally deserve different sanctions. The argument for sentencing attempts and completions equivalently requires the denial of sanction-luck. In what follows, however, only the denial of censure-luck will be assumed. Our concern for the rest of this chapter, then, will be with censure, and not with sanction.

To accept that there is no censure-luck is to accept that the criminalization of attempts solves a problem of inequality: there is often only a lucky difference between the attempter and the completer; when this is so, there is no difference in desert of censure, so both of their acts should be criminal. But if the criminalization of attempt solves an inequality problem, then we ought not to define attempt in the law in such a way as to simply reintroduce the very same problem. That is, we ought not to allow that there are those who do less than attempt a crime and who do not differ in their desert of censure from those who attempt it, and who are for no good reason nonetheless censured differently by the state from those who attempt. If attempt law allows for this, then we would find that proscribing attempts solves a problem only by reintroducing the very same problem. And, in fact, as we're about to see, there is reason to think that in the legacy of Mansfield—in, that is, the inclusion of an act among the elements of an attempted crime—we have reintroduced just the problem that we might have thought the criminalization of attempts solves.

To see this, consider the class of actions believed by the agent to be means to doing as he intends and performed, in part at least, because of that belief; call that class of actions "the class of means". Many actions that an agent performs, even if required in order to do as he intends, do not belong in this class. Much that is necessary to successfully climbing the staircase is not performed by me in part because I believe it to be so; I can't climb the staircase if I don't breathe, but (without telling some special story) it doesn't appear that I breathe *because* I believe it to be a necessary means to climbing the staircase, and so breathing is not in the class of means. I do, however, both tie my shoes and ascend the first stair, in part because I believe those acts to be means to doing as I intend. Now, there is an important distinction between actions in the class of means: some are sufficient for the act element of attempt, others are not. Tying my shoes is, clearly, "mere preparation", and so insufficient, while walking up the first fifty stairs of a fifty-one stair staircase is clearly enough of an act for an attempt to climb the staircase. However we are to distinguish those acts in the class of means that are sufficient for the act element of attempt and those that are not, this much is clear: the class of acts that are sufficient for the act portion of an attempt is a proper subclass of the class of means. *A defendant has committed a criminal attempt only if he has performed an act in the class of means.* Call this "the Means Requirement".

If we were constructing a law that involved a wholehearted rejection of censure-luck, and wholehearted commitments to both a moral justification for the censure involved in punishment and to equal censure of the equally deserving, there would seem good reason to reject the Means Requirement. As we saw in chapter 3, since it is possible to attempt even basic actions, it is possible to be guided by one's intention-based commitments without thereby performing any *action* in furtherance of one's intention. Thus, it is possible to try to commit a crime without performing any act that is in the class of means. The difference between an agent who tries without performing an act in the class of means, and the agent who tries while performing such an act, is often only a matter of luck. Whether one's intent makes its way into even simple physical action is always, in part, a matter of luck: we need well-wired bodies and curare-free bloodstreams to accomplish the trick. Thus it seems that the gap between meeting the minimal conditions required for trying to act, on the one hand, and undertaking an act in the class of means, on the other, will involve at least some luck. If there's no censure-luck, it would follow that the Means Requirement draws a distinction in censure—we censure only if the defendant has performed an act in the class of means—that is unjustified; in light of the Means Requirement, we censure only one of two equally deserving agents.

Despite this concern, the Means Requirement is justified. There are several different approaches one might take to reach this conclusion. A first approach sees the Means Requirement as arising from what is known as "the voluntary act requirement", the legal stricture resting on the idea that criminal punishment is never justifiably applied simply in virtue of the thoughts or dispositions of its recipient; *some* kind of action is needed for criminal responsibility. This requirement imposes a restriction on the definitions of crimes: no crime can be defined in such a way that all of its elements can be present despite the defendant having performed no voluntary action.[10] The easiest way to meet this demand, in crafting a definition of a crime, is to include an act among the elements of the crime.[11] The voluntary act requirement is undoubtedly

---

[10] This is a bit weaker than the claim that every crime must have an act as an element. It leaves open the possibility that a definition of an offense meets the act requirement if some result or circumstantial element requires that the defendant performed a voluntary act. However, for our purposes this distinction is of little importance.

[11] Another way would be to include a result or circumstance among the elements that can only be present if the agent performs some voluntary act. See the previous footnote.

justified.[12] Further, it seems that it should be justifiable independently of any view about censure-luck; whether one accepts or denies censure-luck, that is, one would still have sufficient reason to accept the voluntary act requirement. Thus, the Means Requirement, on this view, is purely formal: it's required for the definition of attempt to meet the voluntary act requirement, but it is not intended to sort the morally deserving of censure from the morally undeserving, nor is it intended to lump together defendants who differ only with respect to luck. Since the voluntary act requirement is not intended to do either of these things, on this view, neither is the Means Requirement. Hence the tension between the Means Requirement, on the one hand, and the denial of censure-luck and commitment to equality of censure, on the other, is merely apparent.

There is something right about this first approach, but it is not sufficient to solve the problem. The reason is that a requirement much weaker than the Means Requirement could serve to satisfy the demands of the voluntary act requirement. A law of attempts, for instance, that took action expressive of intent, but not taken by the defendant to be a means to the execution of his intention—such as, for instance, a verbal report by the defendant of his intention—would also satisfy the voluntary act requirement's demand.[13] But it would not be justified to use the Transfer Principle to criminalize the behavior of someone who did nothing at all to further his criminal intention, but merely confessed to having it. Indicating why the Means Requirement is justified requires more than can be provided by an appeal to the need not to criminalize mere thoughts and dispositions. Or, to put the point another way, when Mansfield requires that the defendant be shown to have performed an act *in the class of means* if he is to be guilty of an attempt, he adds an ingredient that is not strictly necessary in order to respond to Hale's concern about the criminalization of mere thoughts and dispositions. But what this shows is that if we are to have a satisfactory rationale for the Means Requirement we need to appeal to more than the need to satisfy the voluntary act requirement.

A second approach appeals to the nature of trying to act and insists that trying to act involves (at least) two components: a mental state such as an intention, and some further act performed by the agent in furtherance of the intention. The idea is that in proscribing trying to act criminally, we are, necessarily and because of the very nature of trying to act, proscribing more

---

[12] For discussion see, for instance, Morris (1965); Dworkin and Blumenfeld (1966); Moore (1993), esp. chs 2 and 3.

[13] There is logical space to deny this claim. One who does so, however, would need to provide a justification for the act requirement, consistent with the denial of moral luck, which had the implication that only acts taken as means to doing as one intends could satisfy the act requirement. To provide such a justification is just as hard as it is to provide a justification of the Means Requirement; in fact, the two tasks are the same. Hence someone who chooses to occupy this bit of logical space doesn't evade the problem that this chapter is trying to solve.

than just a mental state; the mental state must be manifested in the form of mental or bodily action. While there may be intention, there will have been no *attempt*, on this view, unless and until there has been some act in the class of means. Hence, the Means Requirement is justified for roughly the same reasons that our law is justified in holding that there has been no murder if there has been no death; the very nature of murder requires a death and the very nature of attempt requires action.[14]

As we saw in chapter 3, this view of trying to act overlooks the fact that it is possible to try, and fail, to perform a basic act; hence, it is possible to try without acting at all. But even overlooking this problem, as so far formulated the approach fails to meet the stricture on a justification imposed by those who think there is no censure-luck. After all, just as the question of whether or not a person commits a murder is often in part a matter of luck—if the paramedics had arrived just moments earlier, there would have been no death and so no murder—under the view that takes a component of trying to act to be an act undertaken as a means, trying to act will, itself, be partly a matter of luck. Compare two agents who have the relevant mental state but only one of whom is lucky enough to have that mental state cause the action component of trying to act; nothing but luck distinguishes them, but if trying to act is legally proscribed, then this lucky difference makes a moral difference. Perhaps it will turn out that trying to act includes action undertaken as a means to furthering one's intention, as proposed. But even if it is true, it cannot be this fact that justifies the Means Requirement without that justification relying on the existence of censure-luck as a premise. The mere fact that trying to act includes action doesn't justify censuring those who try, and not those with the same intentions who, because of luck, fail to try, unless there is censure-luck.

A third approach, one version of which is the centerpiece of the discussion here, appeals to special purposes of legal punishment that are furthered by sometimes censuring only one of two equally deserving defendants. Views in this category differ from one another in appealing to different special purposes that are so furthered. For instance, if our aim in punishing—and thereby both censuring and sanctioning—is to threaten just enough unpleasantness, and no more, as is needed to lower the incidence of the peculiar forms of damage that crimes cause, then we might hold, with Oliver Wendell Holmes,[15] that we should punish only attempts that impose a severe risk of completion, or are in "dangerous proximity" to the completed crime. Since only acts taken as means to doing as one intends are candidates for dangerous proximity to completion, the Means Requirement is justified. On this view, the censure

---

[14] This is, essentially, the form of argument offered in chapter 2 for the claim that legitimately proscribed attempts necessarily have intent as an element. This is so, it was suggested there, because of the nature of trying to act: trying necessarily involves intending.

[15] Holmes (1881), 68–9.

that is necessarily involved in punishment is to be applied, like the sanction, only when the costs of doing so are worth the deterrent effect of censure. This approach to justifying the Means Requirement, while accepting that there is no censure-luck, essentially involves abandoning the commitment to equal censure of the equally deserving. Two defendants equally deserving of censure, on this view, are never to be equally censured *for that reason*; even if they are to be, it is only because censure has deterrent value in both cases. Such a view is exactly as defensible or indefensible as the view of the justification of criminal punishment that it presupposes, a view that has been extensively explored.[16] This chapter says nothing to suggest that this approach is flawed, although I believe it to be.[17] For our purposes here it is enough, perhaps, to lay bare one of the assumptions of the ensuing discussion: if the Means Requirement can be justified in a way that does not require us to cleave legal censure away from moral desert, such a justification is to be preferred to alternatives. Such a justification is provided here, and so there is no need to huddle behind the need for social order as justification for giving unequal treatment to equally deserving defendants, as this second approach does.

An alternative way to follow the third approach is to conceive of the Means Requirement as a form of free speech protection. Such an approach proceeds from the idea that any government policy that has a chilling effect on speech— including expressions of intention in the form of speech, such as confessions of intent to one's friends—requires special justification; and any government policy that authorizes the punishment of people for their speech might be all but impossible to justify but is, in any event, in particularly powerful need of special justification. Were there no Means Requirement, those intending to commit crimes would be given powerful incentive, in the form of the prospect of punishment, not to confess their intentions. In the absence of a Means Requirement, such confessions, together with the intention confessed, would be sufficient for criminal liability for attempt. Since there is no pressing need for such a policy, the advocate of such a view takes there to be sufficient reason against instituting it. Hence, the Means Requirement is justified.[18]

While there is something to this way of pursuing the third approach—the law has a legitimate interest in avoiding policies that interfere with speech—it would be peculiar if this were the right way to justify the Means Requirement. It seems unlikely, that is, that the strong view of the value of the expression in speech of criminal intention, or the right to engage in such speech, that such an approach requires is really essential to the justification of the Means Requirement. It seems

---

[16] For an entrance into the vast literature on this topic, see Feinberg (2008).

[17] I say a word or two about such an approach as applied in another context in Yaffe (2005), esp. 18–19.

[18] Thanks to Seana Shiffrin for pushing me to engage with this line of thought. I give it a lengthier treatment in Yaffe (2008a).

more likely that the Means Requirement ought to be accepted even by those who have a laxer view about the protection of speech and would be willing to tolerate policies that discouraged speech expressive of criminal intention.

The view advocated in this chapter, which is a version of the third approach, starts by identifying a legal interest furthered by the Means Requirement that competes with the interest in censuring the deserving, but which is distinct from the interests already mentioned, namely, the interest in discouraging bad behavior, and the interest in avoiding policies that have a chilling effect on speech. Under this alternative view, the Means Requirement serves the interest of censuring *only those who have been shown adequately by the evidence to have committed the crime for which they are censured*. There might be reasons for thinking that only when a defendant has undertaken a means to doing as he intends do we have the right kind of *evidence* that he has committed an attempted crime, and so only then are we justified in holding him criminally responsible for an attempt. So, although we recognize that there are equally deserving agents who differ only in luck from those whom we convict of attempted crimes, the lucky difference does not speak to a difference in desert of censure, but, instead, to a difference *in our evidence*. There's no inconsistency in a legal regime that convicts only the thief whose theft is proven by the admissible evidence, and not the thief who, through a lucky break could not be proven to be one, perhaps because crucial pieces of evidence were inadmissible; similarly, a commitment to the Means Requirement does not require one to either accept that there is censure-luck, or weaken one's commitment to equal treatment of the equally deserving. The difference between the attempter who fails to perform an act in the class of means, and the attempter who gets at least this far, is not a difference in desert of censure—they are equally deserving of censure, but we have adequate evidence only that the latter actually attempted a crime.

Evidentialist approaches of this sort can be divided into at least two kinds, distinguished by what, precisely, they take action in furtherance of intention to be evidence *of*. Recall that under the Guiding Commitment View, there are two distinct parts of an attempt: an intention, and guidance by the commitments the intention constitutes. One might take action in furtherance of intention to be essential evidence of either one of these two things. Call views according to which action performed as a means to the satisfaction of a criminal intention is essential evidence of *intent*, "intent-based evidentialist approaches". Under such views, without the Means Requirement, we would find ourselves convicting people of attempted crimes despite lacking adequate evidence that they had the objectionable intentions in virtue of which they are deserving of censure. Alternatively, one might take action performed as a means to be essential evidence of the *guidance* by intention-based commitments involved in attempt. Call these "guidance-based evidentialist approaches". The next section argues that intent-based evidentialist approaches, such as that found in the *Model Penal Code*, are indefensible. The section following offers an argument for a guidance-based evidentialist approach.

### 3. Intent-Based Evidentialist Approaches

The *Model Penal Code* adopts an intent-based evidentialist approach to the justification of the Means Requirement in its test for determining if a defendant's acts constitute what the code calls "substantial steps". "Substantial steps" is the *Model Penal Code*'s name for acts that are sufficient for the act element of attempt in non-last act cases in which completion would have required further conduct on the part of the defendant. The relevant section of the code reads as follows:

Conduct shall not be held to constitute a substantial step...unless it is strongly corroborative of the actor's criminal purpose.

(Model Penal Code §5.01(2))[19]

Under the *Model Penal Code*'s attempt provisions, the prosecution must meet two burdens in non-last act cases. First, the prosecution must show beyond a reasonable doubt that the defendant had the intention required for the crime of attempt. Second, they must show that the acts which the defendant took constitute very good evidence of his intention on their own. To meet the first demand, the prosecution can appeal to acts undertaken as means, but they can appeal to much more than just those acts; they can appeal, for instance, to the defendant's verbal reports of his intentions, to other acts that are expressive of his intent but are not performed as means to doing as he intends, and even to things other than his actions that might serve to evidence his intent, such as the judgments of psychiatrists and other experts. But to meet the second demand, the prosecution must argue, even if it has already met the first demand, that the acts which the defendant took as means to doing as he intended constitute, themselves, non-trivial evidence of his intent. So, the prosecution has to provide adequate evidence of intent, *and* a large part of the prosecution's case for the claim that the defendant had the requisite intent must derive from the acts the defendant performed in furtherance of his intention.

In virtually every real case, the evidence of the defendant's intention is a mixed bag, only some of which is action that may have been performed in furtherance of the relevant intention. Consider the case of *State v. Duke* (700 So. 2d 580 (Fla. App. 1998)). The defendant had a series of conversations in an internet chat room with someone going by the name of "Niki" and claiming to be a 12-year-old girl. "Niki" and Duke discussed having sex, and then arranged to meet for that purpose in a parking lot on a particular night. They agreed that

---

[19] The *Model Penal Code*'s formulation does not make explicit that the conduct in question must be believed by the defendant to be a means to doing as he intends. For all the text says, a verbal report that was "strongly corroborative" of the defendant's intention would serve for the act element. However, despite what the text says, it is clear that the *Model Penal Code* requires that the conduct in question is in the class of means.

Duke would signal by flashing his lights and then take "Niki" back to his home. Duke went to the parking lot at the appointed time and flashed his lights, at which point he was arrested by the detective who had posed as "Niki". He was charged with attempted sexual battery. For all we know, some of the things that Duke says to "Niki" are expressive of his intention, but are not acts performed in furtherance of it. Duke might tell "Niki" his fantasies, for instance, without taking himself to be thereby undertaking means to making them a reality. But when he suggests a place for them to meet, and when he actually travels to that location and flashes his lights, he is performing acts in furtherance of his intention.

In Duke's case, conduct expressive of intent, but not performed in order to further his intention, seems likely to have been insufficient to establish intent. Plenty of people confess fantasies in chat rooms that they have no intention whatsoever to act on. Notice, however, that the acts he performed in order to further his intention were probably also insufficient: without knowing about his chat room conversations we can imagine a variety of reasonable explanations for the act of driving to the parking lot and flashing his lights that don't involve ascribing him with any criminal intention, much less the intention to commit acts that would constitute sexual battery in particular. Are the acts that Duke performed in furtherance of his intention of greater probative significance than the acts that were merely expressive of intent? So long as we take acts in furtherance of intention to be important because they are evidence of *intent*, the answer is no. Imagine replacing each act that Duke performed in furtherance of his intention with an act merely expressive of intention, but with the same probative significance. If, say, his driving to the parking lot raises the probability by x that he has the intention, then imagine that the record shows, instead, some act expressive of intention, but not performed in furtherance of it, which raises that probability by precisely x. Perhaps we imagine that he's had conversations with a friend in which he's mentioned his intention to have sex with a child; "No," he said, in response to questioning, "I really do intend to do it. I'm not just talking here." Or perhaps we imagine that he's purchased pornography depicting the very acts that he has described himself as having an intention to commit.

The problem is that intent-based evidentialist approaches fail to identify any special evidential significance to action taken in furtherance of intention, and so fail to explain the Means Requirement. Acts performed as means to doing as one intends provide good evidence of intent, granted, but evidence of equal quality could be provided through an alternative route.

Now, we can imagine a position, different from the *Model Penal Code's*, according to which action in furtherance of intention is essential evidence, not of intent, period, but of a special kind of intention, such as *a resolute* intention. Without action in furtherance of intention, we might say, we lack evidence that the defendant *really* intends to commit the crime, or is *genuinely willing* to do so. Such a position has precisely the same problem, however: there is no reason to deny that something other than action in furtherance of intention could have exactly the same, or even greater, probative value. True, we might not take first-person reports of the defendant's resolute intention to be very good evidence of it. We don't necessarily trust the person who says, confidently, "I'm resolved to jump from the plane when the hatch opens." "Talk is cheap," we say, implying that the real test of such resolution is action: no mere report of one's own degree of resolve will serve as evidence of resolute intention. However, there are other forms of evidence of resolute intention besides either first-person reports or action performed in furtherance of it. Applicants to various jobs that require resolve can be given psychological tests in order to determine if, for instance, they would really, when it came to it, leap in front of the bullet shot at the president. It seems quite likely that people who pass such tests really are more likely, maybe even *much* more likely, to have not just the intention to do the thing the job might require, but the *resolute* intention. To pass such a test, however, is not to take steps towards furthering the intention. Still, the results of such tests would serve as useful evidence of resolute intent. Further, the fact that a person has been habituated in certain ways can serve as strong evidence of the resoluteness of his intention. Someone who has undergone a certain kind of military training is more likely to be resolute in his intention to kill the enemy than someone who has not. Thus it seems that evidence of such training, or, more generally, such habituation, can serve as quite good evidence of resolute intent, and not just intent. Relatedly, we often think that a person's emotional reactions in a variety of contexts speak to the resoluteness of certain intentions on which he has not acted. The fury felt by a person on reading about new legislation permitting more abortions, might, itself, serve as evidence—not decisive evidence, but evidence still—of the resoluteness of his intention to bomb an abortion clinic, an intention that he may have taken no steps towards executing.

Even if we shift away from resolute intention directly, the problem persists. For instance, imagine a view according to which what we are really seeking is evidence that the defendant with the criminal intention will not change his mind and abandon the plan before completion. What we need, that is, is evidence that the defendant has a not-to-be-abandoned intention. The resulting intent-based evidentialist justification of the Means Requirement would then involve asserting that action taken by the agent as a means to doing as he intends is an essential form of evidence of the fact that the agent would not abandon his plan. The problem with this is that if the adoption of means is to count as evidence that the defendant would not reconsider, then it must be true that people are more likely to abandon their plans if they don't adopt means than if they do. It is true that to adopt means is to sink costs into an enterprise that one hopes to recoup by succeeding in the enterprise. To abandon a plan after sinking costs, then, is to assure a loss. Perhaps people are more likely to follow through, then, if they've already adopted means, because they want to avoid wasting their efforts. However, it seems unlikely that reasoning of this sort will extend smoothly to the kinds of cases that concern the criminal law. Consider just one example that would seem, at first glance, to be amenable to this form of analysis. In a British case, *Regina v. Gullefer* (1 WLR 1063 (1990)), the defendant had bet on a dog race. In the middle of the race, seeing that his dog would lose, he ran onto the track in the hope that the race would be voided and he could reclaim his money from his bookmaker. He was charged with attempted theft of the bookmaker's money.[20] There were, obviously, losses associated with his running onto the track: public embarrassment and permanent expulsion from the dog track, for instance. Now compare Gullefer to someone who, like Gullefer, has the intention to steal from the bookmaker, but who has yet to adopt any means. Is there any reason to think this person less likely to abandon his plan than Gullefer is? It doesn't seem that the question turns on the investment in stealing that Gullefer, in contrast to this person, has already made, and so it doesn't seem likely that the adoption of means really serves as evidence of the truth of the relevant counterfactual. It just seems silly to imagine that Gullefer would reason like so: "I don't want to waste the effort of having run onto the track, so I'll ask the bookmaker for my money back." He might or might not ask the bookmaker for the money back, but the issue doesn't seem to have anything to do with his having run onto the track, but depends, instead, on other aspects of his temperament that he might or might not share with the person who intends to steal from the bookmaker, but who has yet to act on that intention. In fact, Gullefer's conduct is sufficiently bird-brained that we might think him *less likely*, rather than more likely, to follow-through with the plan than the person who intends to steal but has yet to take any steps.

More importantly, even if we grant that actions in the class of means are very good evidence that the defendant's intention is of the not-to-be-abandoned variety, there is no reason to think that we cannot have equally good evidence that the intention is in that category without the defendant having performed any actions in furtherance of it. Learning, for instance, that Gullefer is a stubborn person who persists with his intentions even when it becomes abundantly clear that he will fail to do as he intends would be far better evidence that he would not abandon his intention than is his running onto the dog track. Thus, we have the same problem here as we had with the *Model Penal Code's* approach and with the approach that appeals to resolute intention. To justify the Means Requirement on evidentialist grounds, action in furtherance of intention must be *irreplaceable* evidence. No intent-based evidentialist

---

[20] The case is discussed in Duff (1996), 58–9.

approach can meet this demand, and so no such approach provides an adequate justification of the Means Requirement.

## 4. The Solution: A Guidance-Based Evidentialist Approach

As we have seen, under the Guiding Commitment View, to try is to be committed by one's intention to each of the components of success and to be guided by each of those commitments. To be guided by one's intention-based commitments is for one's intention to cause something as part of motivating action believed by the agent to be, or to be a means to, that which is intended. This leaves the difficult question of how to distinguish causing something as part of motivating action from causing something without such motivation. In chapter 3, where the Guiding Commitment View was initially explained, it was suggested that the following counterfactual conditional, when correctly interpreted, is true just in case D's intention's causal influence at time t1 is of the motivational sort:

*The Completion Counterfactual*: If (1) from t1 to t2 D has the ability and the opportunity to C and does not fall prey to "execution failure", and (2) D does not (at least until after t2) change his mind, then D would C.

The underlying idea behind the claim that this counterfactual must be true if D is guided by the commitments constituted by his intention is this: motivation is a kind of causal influence that will result in performance if nothing interferes.

In assessing this counterfactual, we follow a multi-step process: first, we consider possible worlds which are different from the actual in the four respects specified in the Completion Counterfactual's antecedent. We imagine, for instance, that Duke (the man who met the undercover detective in a chat room, believing the detective to be a 12-year-old girl) was not apprehended by police after flashing his lights; that the person whom he contacted in the chatroom really was a 12-year-old girl; that he was perfectly capable of overcoming such a child's efforts to prevent him from committing sexual battery; and that the causal sequence launched by his intention to commit sexual battery is not interrupted either because he gives up his intention, or because he decides not to act on it. Second, we ask if, in that remaining set of worlds, the defendant performs the crime. If there are possible worlds in which the defendant fails to perform, we check to see whether he fails to perform in those worlds because of something that defeats the inference from the falsity of the counterfactual to the conclusion that the intention's influence is not motivational; if so, we exclude those worlds from consideration. So, for instance, if we find that Duke fails in one of the possible worlds merely because, in that possible world, "Niki" is a blonde and he is only interested in brunettes, that possible world is excluded from consideration (assuming that his aversion to blondes was not operative in the actual world). Failure to perform the crime in any of the remaining worlds is definitive of a failure to actually try to act, and conversely, performance of the crime in all of those worlds is definitive of trying to commit the crime, assuming that the defendant's intention commits him to each of the completed crime's components.

A guidance-based evidentialist justification of the Means Requirement would be aided by an argument for the following pair of claims. First, if the defendant has undertaken means, there is evidence in support of the Completion Counterfactual, and, second, nothing else besides action in furtherance of intention would be likely to supply such evidence. Towards the end, then, of providing the needed argument, start with the following question: "What are acts performed as means to doing as one intends evidence of?" They are, at least, evidence that the defendant was trying to perform *those acts* and was trying to perform them *as means*: they are evidence, that is, that the defendant tried to adopt means to furthering his criminal intention. The defendant didn't just perform an act that was, in fact, a means to C; he performed the act *under the description*, "a means to C", or for the reason that the act was a means to C. Buying a screwdriver might be a means to killing someone with it. Of course, one can buy a screwdriver for various innocent purposes, as well. However, if there is evidence that a particular defendant bought the screwdriver *for the purpose of killing someone with it*, then there is evidence that the defendant was trying to undertake means to killing someone. So, what's required is a link between trying to perform a means to C, on the one hand, and trying to C, on the other. If we can show further that if an agent is trying to perform a means, then he is trying to complete the crime, then we have reason to think that taking a means is evidence that the Completion Counterfactual is true. And if we can show that nothing else could serve as evidence of the Completion Counterfactual, then we will have shown that nothing other than acts taken as means could provide adequate evidence of guidance and so of attempt, and then we will have justified the Means Requirement on evidentialist grounds.

Now consider the following argument: it is irrational for a person who intends to perform an act, and who tries to take some means to the action, to fail to try to perform the other acts that he believes to be necessary means to it. Such a person invests himself in a course of conduct, expending energy and resources to do so, but doesn't invest himself to the degree necessary to reach his intended end. Thus, a rational person, intending to reach an end, who tries to perform one means to it, tries to perform all necessary means to that end. But a person who tries to perform all the necessary means to an end and also has the ability and the opportunity to reach that end, and doesn't suffer from "execution failure" and doesn't change his mind, will reach it. After all, if he has the ability and opportunity to reach the end, he must have the ability and opportunity to take all necessary means. If he also tries to take those means, then he does all that's necessary for reaching his end, assuming he doesn't suffer from "execution failure" and doesn't change his mind. What this shows is that if we have evidence suggesting that a person who intends to act criminally is trying to take a means to the performance of the intended crime, we thereby, *ipso facto*, have evidence that he would have completed the crime had he had the ability and opportunity to do so and neither suffered "execution failure" nor changed his mind. But then we have reason to think the Completion Counterfactual is true, and so we have evidence for thinking that he's trying to act criminally. What this shows is that actions taken as means to satisfying a criminal intention provide a very special form of evidence that a rational defendant is trying to act criminally.

More formally, the argument just offered can be put like this, where t1 is some time at or preceding the moment at which crime C would be begun, and t2 is the time at which C would be completed:

(1) If (at t1 ((D intends to C) & (D tries to M) & (D believes M to be a means to C and performs M for that reason) & (D is rational))), then at t1 D tries to perform all the acts that are necessary means to C.

(2) If ((at t1 D tries to perform all the acts that are necessary means to C ) & (from t1 to t2 D has the ability and the opportunity to C and does not fall prey to "execution failure") and (D does not (at least until after t2) change his mind)), then D C's.

(3) ∴ If ((D intends to C) & (at t1 D tries to M) & (D believes M to be a means to C and performs M for that reason) & (D is rational) & (from t1 to t2 D has the ability and the opportunity to C and does not fall prey to "execution failure") and (D does not (at least until after t2) change his mind)), then D C's.

(4) ∴ If ((D intends to C) & (at t1 D tries to M) & (D believes M to be a means to C and performs M for that reason) & (D is rational), then the Completion Counterfactual is true.

(5) If the Completion Counterfactual is true, then D is guided by his intention to C.

(6) ∴ If (at t1 ((D intends to C) & (D tries to M) & (D believes M to be a means to C and performs M for that reason) & (D is rational))), then at t1 D is guided by his intention to C.

If this argument succeeds, it brings us much of the way towards supporting an evidentialist justification of the Means Requirement. The conclusion says that a rational defendant who has a criminal intention and was trying to adopt means to doing as he intended, was guided by his intention; given that the intention together with guidance by it amounts to trying to commit the crime, under the Guiding Commitment View, it follows that if we have adequate evidence that a defendant has the relevant intention and has performed an act in furtherance of it, then we have adequate evidence that he attempted the crime. What this shows is that at the very least performance of an act in furtherance of a criminal intention by a rational agent is sufficient for trying to act criminally, even though acts taken as means to doing as one intends are nothing more than evidence of something else, namely of one's efforts to take such means, efforts which are guaranteed (in a rational agent) to be found with an effort to complete the crime.

As noted, the argument does not show, full stop, that the defendant who performs some means to doing as he intends is trying to commit the crime. Rather, it shows that this is true of *rational* defendants. Even assuming the argument is valid, does this additional requirement undermine its import? The answer is "no". The reason is that the Means Requirement is merely a necessary condition for the act element of attempt: a defendant's act does not serve unless it is performed as a means to fulfilling his criminal intention. To justify this requirement on evidentialist grounds, we need to argue that an act performed as a means is a necessary condition of having adequate evidence that the defendant is trying to act. So, even if such an act provides *sufficient* evidence only when other conditions are met—such as that the defendant is rational—it can still be necessary for the adequacy of evidence of attempt. In fact, as we will see in chapters 9 and 10, the mere fact that a defendant has undertaken means to C is not sufficient evidence that the Completion Counterfactual is true; other conditions, including that the defendant is rational, must be met. This is just to say that this chapter's aim is not to supply an account of the act element of attempt; that task is saved for chapter 10. Such an account will offer necessary *and sufficient* conditions that a defendant's conduct meets if the defendant is to be justifiably convicted of attempt. The aim of the argument on offer is merely to justify one particular necessary condition, namely the Means Requirement.

Premise (1) requires some clarification. To understand it, it is important to distinguish between the following two claims:

(a) $\forall m$ (m is a necessary means to C $\rightarrow$ D tries to m)

and

(b) D tries to perform the following act: performing all the acts that are necessary means to C.

The consequent of premise (1) is (b), not (a). To see the difference between (a) and (b), consider an example:[21] say that D intends to rob a bank three months from now in New York. Right now D is trying to book a plane ticket to

---

[21] Thanks to Michael Bratman for the example, which he offered, originally, as a counterexample to premise (1) when I had not yet formulated it in such a way as to avoid the ambiguity noted here.

New York. D believes that booking the ticket is a necessary means to robbing the bank. D also believes that opening the bank's safe three months from now is a necessary means to robbing the bank, and this belief is true. And D is rational. It is manifest, however, that D is not trying *right now* to open the safe; after all, right now D is merely sitting at his computer browsing airline websites. And let's stipulate that, in fact, D will never try to open the safe: perhaps his plan will be foiled before he gets that far, or perhaps he'll give up his intention before the time to open the safe arrives. Thus, in this case (a) is false. Since the conditions specified in the antecedent of premise (1) are in place in this example, it follows that premise (1) would be false if (a) were its consequent. But notice that in the example (b) very well might be true: the fact that D is not right now trying to open the safe does not imply that he is not trying to perform all the acts necessary to robbing the bank. If someone were to ask D if he was trying to do everything necessary to rob the bank he might very well say that he was, and the fact that he is not right now trying to open a safe would not invalidate his claim. Trying to do, at a particular time, everything that's necessary doesn't require trying to do, at that time, each of the individual acts that are necessary.[22]

What this implies is that premise (1) is not a claim to the effect that a rational person who is trying to take one step towards doing what he intends is thereby committed to not changing his mind. Premise (1) would have that implication if (a) were its consequent. But, since (b) is its consequent, premise (1) has no implications whatsoever for what the rational agent will do after time t1, the time at which he is trying to undertake means to doing as he intends. Premise (1) can be thought of as a coherence constraint on the set of things which a rational agent is trying to do at a particular time. Just as it would be irrational for an agent to try to A while, at the same time, trying to refrain from A, it would be irrational for an agent to try to undertake a means without also trying to undertake *all* the necessary means.

The success of the argument being offered turns on premises (1) and (2). To see why premise (1) is true, consider, first, what the purpose of trying is. That is, consider what good is served by our being agents that have the capacity to try to do things. (The same question is considered, and the same answer to it given, in chapter 2 in arguing that trying to act entails intending to act.) It is a contingent fact that we have the capacity to try. It's possible to engage in purposive behavior, end-directed behavior, without ever trying to do anything. Perhaps bees do this. Bees are not architects: they do not frame a conception of the hive

---

[22] The point here is really no more than the well-known point that co-referential action descriptions cannot be substituted for one another in sentences while preserving the truth values of those sentences: "is trying to _____" is an opaque context. The sentence "D is trying to do all that is necessary to rob the bank" is true even though the sentence "D is trying to open the bank's safe" is false, and this is so despite the fact that among the acts D believes to be necessary to robbing the bank is the opening of the safe.

before they build it and endeavor to bring it about that the world matches their conception of it. Yet they build hives. But human beings do do this. We don't just plan: we also execute our plans. And the execution of our plans is itself an exercise of agency. Our plans don't simply translate themselves into conduct. Instead, we *try* to do as our plans direct. The point of trying is acting; we are trying creatures precisely because we are not the sort of creatures who, in many aspects of life anyway, will pursue ends except by actively doing so. Given the sorts of creatures we are, we need to have the capacity to try to do things if we are to reach our ends. What this suggests is that trying is an activity that is governed by certain norms of instrumental rationality. To be trying to do something is to be subject to norms that, in general, need to be obeyed if one is to thereby succeed in acting. To take the obvious example already mentioned above: an agent who is trying to A is irrational if he is also trying to refrain from A-ing. The reason is because, generally, an agent who both tries to act and tries to refrain fails to act; since the point of trying to act is to act, an agent whose tryings are inconsistent in this way is irrational.

To reach premise (1), however, we need more than this. We need to show that the point of trying is generally undermined when an agent tries to take a means to an end without also trying to take all necessary means to that end. What is the point of trying to take a means to an end? Part of the point is to, in fact, take that means. One of the goods that is served by trying to pull a trigger is that one, thereby, pulls the trigger. But the point of trying to do something under the description "a means to an end" is not just to do it: it is also to reach the end. Thus an agent who tries to take a means to an end—who endeavors, for instance, to pull a trigger not simply because he would be pulling a trigger, but also because pulling a trigger is one step in a course of conduct that he hopes will culminate in him killing another person—is under rational pressure to do all those things that he believes to be necessary to reach the end. But if he's under rational pressure to do these things, he is also under rational pressure to try to do them. Premise (1) follows: a rational agent who performs one act as a means to his end tries to perform all the necessary means to his end.

The argument for premise (2) depends on the idea that *all* failures to do as one intends when one is motivated by one's intention derive from inability, inopportunity, "execution failure", or change of mind. The assumption is that this list is exhaustive. It is obviously not always the case that performance of all the necessary means to an end is sufficient for reaching it: there might be some obstacle to reaching the end that the agent cannot hope to evade, or the agent might suffer "execution failure", or change his mind before completion. However, in such cases one of the conditions that we are assuming away is met. Premise (2) follows. Further, if this list of the causes of failure is not exhaustive, the argument can be amended by merely adding the missing category to the antecedent of both the Completion Counterfactual and premise (2).

So, to summarize, acts taken as means provide evidence that the defendant was trying to perform a means to the crime. Add to this the idea that the function of trying—namely, to lead to action—places a constraint on the set of things that a rational agent who is trying to perform a means to commit the crime is trying to do: he also tries to perform all the acts that are necessary means to committing it. Add further that an agent who is trying to undertake that act—the act of performing every necessary means—and who has the ability and the opportunity to commit the crime, does not suffer from "execution failure" and does not change his mind, will commit it. It follows that acts undertaken as means provide evidence for thinking that the agent would have committed the crime had the antecedent of the Completion Counterfactual been true; they thus provide evidence for thinking the Completion Counterfactual true. This is the mark of guidance by one's intention. Thus, acts taken as means to doing as specified by one's criminal intention provide evidence that the defendant was, in fact, guided by his intention to commit the crime. Since it is precisely that that we are criminalizing in criminalizing attempts, acts taken as means provide precisely the kind of evidence we need to justify conviction.

Recall that in the last section it was argued that while acts taken as means are construed as evidence of the intention involved in attempt, we lack an adequate justification of the Means Requirement; intent-based evidentialist approaches are doomed to failure. The primary problem is that other things besides acts taken as means would serve as adequate evidence of intention (or even of any special class of intentions), and so it seemed that there was no acceptable justification for constraining the evidential route through which the defendant's guilt is to be established in the way that the Means Requirement does. Does the proposed explanation for the evidential import of acts taken as means evade this concern? Yes.

There are good reasons to think that nothing other than action in further-ance of intention could serve as evidence that the agent's intention is *motivating* such action. To see this, imagine two different agents, both of whom have a criminal intention that causes something, but neither of whom performs an act in furtherance of his intention. Agent One's intention causes his temperature to rise by two degrees. Agent Two's intention causes the release of acetylcholine to the nerve animating a muscle in his arm. Both causal sequences are halted after these respective effects. Are both motivated by their intention? Are neither? Do they differ in this regard? To answer such questions we would need to know what causal sequences are involved in motivating an act believed by the agent to be a means to doing as intended. However, the problem is not merely that we don't know whether or not the rise in body temperature, or the release of acetylcholine, is part of such a sequence. *That* problem could be remedied. In fact, what we know about the mechanics through which brain states are translated into bodily movements tells us that the release of acetylcholine is far more likely to be part of a sequence leading to action than is the rise in body temperature. The problem is that *any* causal sequence, no matter how different from the normal person's, might be of the sort involved in motivation. Perhaps *this* man's intentions motivate by first raising his body temperature. The fact that no one else's intention's motivate in that way is irrelevant. Similarly, perhaps *this* man's intentions do not motivate by the release of acetylcholine; perhaps the bodily movements that result from such release are mere twitches that accompany his conduct but are not part of it. The idea of an intention motivating, as opposed to merely causing, is the idea of its causing something in a certain normal or characteristic way that results in action. But whether the particular sequence leading to a bodily movement is of this normal and characteristic sort is determined in large part by whether or not the resulting bodily movement is indeed action. If the sequence that begins with the rise in body temperature concludes in action, then the rise in body temperature was caused as part of the motivation of the act. So we cannot hope to distinguish between causation of the kind involved in guidance, and causation of the sort that is not, in the absence of action in furtherance of intention. This is not to say that there is no difference—for all we know Agent Two is motivated and not Agent One— but only that we cannot make the needed discrimination.[23]

The guidance-based evidentialist approach requires two claims: that acts in furtherance of intention provide evidence of guidance (and so evidence of attempt), and that the evidence they provide cannot be provided by anything else. This section suggests that the first claim follows from the fact that rational agents trying to take means are trying to take *all* the means, and that the second follows from the fact that the only observable mark of guidance by one's intention, in contrast to other kinds of causal influence of intention, is culmination in action. Put these ideas together and we are left with the view that, although it is possible to try without acting, we can know someone is trying only if he does.

## 5. Conclusion

The elements of crimes are treated by the law as constitutive of those crimes; they are treated as necessary, and not just causally necessary, for performance of the crime. This is what makes an evidentialist justification of the Means

---

[23] Notice that the agents themselves are in no better position than we are to say whether they are motivated or merely caused. Both intend the crime. Both fall short of action and so both feel that they have gone no distance towards doing as intended. Neither is in a better position than we are to assess whether the Completion Counterfactual is true of himself. No level of introspective perspicacity would remedy the problem. To know whether what their intentions caused were events on the way to performance of an act believed to be a means, both agents would need to know whether the relevant causal sequences would have led to action had they not been halted. Neither is in a better position to know that than we are.

Requirement difficult, for acts undertaken as means are an element of the crime of attempt, and evidence is, except in rare cases, merely correlated with that which it is evidence of; evidence is not ordinarily necessary for the fact that it evidences. But the case of attempt, the case of trying, is not ordinary in this regard. Undertaking means to an intended act is evidence of trying to undertake such means, and a rational agent's trying to undertake means is sufficient for trying to perform the intended act. The Means Requirement is justified precisely because of the evidence that actions undertaken as means provide. In this case, the evidence is so closely related to the fact that it evidences, that it makes sense for the law to treat it as an element of the crime. And it is because this is so that the Means Requirement can be justified, even by those who deny that there is censure-luck. Those, then, who deny censure-luck should be happy with the standard doctrine of criminal attempt inherited from Mansfield; it enshrines in law deep features of our ordinary conception of trying and does so in a way which is consonant with both the thought that there can be no difference in desert of censure where there is only a lucky difference, and the thought that a commitment to equality requires us to strive towards equal censure of the equally deserving.

# 9

# Stupid Plans and Inherent Impossibility

## 1. Introduction

Richard and Shirley Elmore's house in Pontiac, Illinois, burned down and more than $11,000 of property in the house was destroyed. The Elmores itemized the property for their insurance company and included on the list a $290 stereo that had not been destroyed in the fire. In fact, the Elmores had sold the stereo to a neighbor well before the fire and pocketed the cash; listing the stereo was not an inadvertent error. Their insurance policy covered only $7,000 worth of losses, so the Elmores would have received the same amount of money from the insurance company whether or not they listed the stereo as destroyed. Still, looking at the list, the insurance company smelled a rat and brought the case to the district attorney. While it is a crime to make a false statement of this sort to an insurance company,[1] that is not the crime with which the Elmores were charged. They were charged, instead, with an attempted theft by deception and convicted at trial. On appeal, the Elmores argued that they should be acquitted since even if the insurance company had been deceived, they would not have managed to steal any money. Given the ceiling on the insurance policy, that is, it was impossible for them to steal any money from the company by inflating the estimate of their losses as they did. They didn't know this at the time, they admit. They thought they could get $290 more from the insurance company by listing the stereo. But the fact that the means they chose for stealing the money could not possibly have led to success, they claim, is enough to undermine their guilt no matter what they happened to think. The court rejects the argument and the guilty verdict stands.[2]

*Elmore* is a case in which the question of impossibility's relevance to attempt is raised, but it is importantly different from the kinds of case discussed in

---

[1] See 720 ILCS 5/46-1.
[2] *People v. Elmore* (129 Ill.App.2d 312, 261 N.E.2d 736 (1970)).

chapter 5—cases in which a circumstantial element of the completed crime is absent—in which that issue is frequently brought up. In *Elmore*, no circumstantial element of the completed crime is absent. A defendant who successfully deceives his insurance company into giving him money that he is not otherwise owed is guilty of the completed crime of theft by deception regardless of the limits on his policy. It is true that it is more difficult to deceive an insurance company into paying what is not owed when one's losses exceed the policy's ceiling; perhaps one would also need to deceive the company, somehow, about that. But a person who manages to do so, despite the difficulty of it, has succeeded in committing the crime. That the ceiling on the policy exceeds what one asks for, that is, is not a condition that must be met for success in completing the crime. Compare to missing object cases of the sort discussed in chapter 5. If the pocket one picks is empty, or if the object one shoots at out of hunting season is not a deer but a mannequin, then a necessary condition of completion is absent. It is part of the very concept of picking a pocket that there is something that one takes from it; it is part of the very concept of hunting out of season that there is an animal that one hunts. By contrast, it is not part of the concept of deceiving an insurance company into paying money that is not owed that one's policy's limit is higher than what one asks for. But if it is not part of what completion involves, then we need not concern ourselves either with its presence or with the nature of the defendant's commitment to its presence when adjudicating an attempt.

Two elements of the completed crime are indeed missing in *Elmore*: the Elmores didn't deceive anyone and they didn't manage to take any money. These are both things that the Elmores were committed to causing, although they failed to do so. In a case like *Elmore*, that is, success is precluded by the facts about what will and will not cause what: asking for more than is allowed already by your insurance policy will not ordinarily cause an insurance company to give you any more. What this suggests is that the Elmores' case does not appear, at first glance anyway, to be any different from that of the person who tries and fails to open a safe, intending to take its contents. The missing elements of the completed crime are, in such a case and in *Elmore*, elements that the defendants are committed to causing, and they are guided by those commitments.[3]

So far, then, it appears that the right result was reached in *Elmore*. The Elmores are to be lumped together with that vast group of defendants who

---

[3] In fact, even if the policy's ceiling were an element of the completed crime, the Elmores would still have committed an attempt under the analysis offered in chapter 5. After all, the Elmores believed that their actual losses fell short by more than $290 of the maximum covered by their policy, and so it seems very likely that they intended [to deceive the insurance company into paying more than was owed]. Such an intention is sufficient for commitment to each of the elements of the completed crime and so, assuming these commitments guided, which they seem to have, the Elmores attempted theft by deception under the Guiding Commitment View.

are moved by commitments to cause various events involved in the completed crime, but fail. But our discussion of cases like *Elmore* should not end here. The reason is that although *Elmore* bears important similarities to cases of failed attempts in which it is simply obvious that the defendant attempted a crime and is rightly punished for the attempt, it also bears important similarities to cases in which this is not true. For instance, in 1989, in the town of Tupelo, Mississippi, Leroy and John Henry Ivy bought a lock of Judge Thomas Gardner's hair and a photo of him from his housekeeper, intending to kill the judge using the hair and the photo as part of a voodoo ritual. The Ivys were arrested for conspiracy to commit murder, although never tried.[4] Like the Elmores, the Ivys were trying to commit a crime, and count as such under the Guiding Commitment View. And like the Elmores, the Ivys adopted a hopeless plan for accomplishing their objective. In the case of the Ivys, it seems absurd to convict of an attempted murder, or even of a conspiracy to commit a murder, crimes that bring prison terms of at least ten years in Mississippi.[5] After all, it is hardly progress past witch trials to limit withcraft convictions and punishments only to those who *think* they are witches. And, importantly, the fact that the means chosen by the Ivys are so hopeless is the crucial fact for explaining the absurdity of convicting them for attempt. The Elmores and the Ivys should be split, not lumped together. But why?

Cases like the Ivys' are often referred to in statutes and by judges as involving "inherent impossibility". The idea is that the means chosen are inherently, or by their very nature, useless for reaching the criminal objective. In many jurisdictions, inherent impossibility is a defense to an attempt charge, or at least mitigates the sentence, as under the *Model Penal Code* §5.05(2). In fact, in Illinois, the court's opinion in *Elmore* set the precedent that inherent impossibility provides a defense to an attempt charge, even though the court ruled that the Elmores' attempt was not inherently impossible. The practice of acquitting or mitigating where attempts are inherently impossible seems right, as far as it goes, but it provides us with little to go on when trying to adjudicate cases like *Elmore*. Properly described, every stupid choice of means is "inherently" incapable of leading to success. Just as saying incantations over some hair and a photo is a hopeless way to kill someone, asking an insurance company for a payment over one's policy's limit is a hopeless way to get the company to pay more than is owed. The term "inherent" gives only the illusion of substantive guidance. It amounts, merely, to saying that there is a category of attempts in which the means chosen are so stupid that it makes no sense to convict, but the term provides us with no direction about what features distinguish such stupid attempts from the rest. When does the inept and the stupid cross the line into the "inherently impossible"?

---

[4] Grimm (1989).
[5] Miss. Code Ann. § 97-1-1, § 97-1-7.

It might appear that to insist, as I am, that the Ivys ought not to be convicted of attempted murder, and at the same time to admit that what they did counts as an attempted murder under the Guiding Commitment View, also accepted here, is to embrace a contradiction. But in fact there is no contradiction. To see why not, it is important to be reminded, once again, of the distinction between commission and guilt. The Guiding Commitment View is a theory of attempt *commission*: under it, it is necessary and sufficient to commit an attempted crime that one has an intention-based commitment to each of the conditions involved in the completed crime and is guided by those commitments. As we have seen, it is possible to be guilty of a crime without committing one, as in cases of accomplice liability in which the accomplice is guilty of a crime that the principal committed. In fact, as was suggested in chapter 4, there can be guilt for an attempt without commission in cases in which the defendant foresees an unintended result element of the completed crime, as when the defendant intends [to crush Victim's brain] but does not intend [to kill Victim]. But, and this is what matters for our purposes here, it is also possible to commit a crime without being guilty of one, as is true of the person who commits a crime but is acquitted, or is never even charged, or is granted an executive pardon. In fact, it is even possible to commit a crime without it being also true that one could be *legitimately* found guilty of it, given the facts, as when a person commits a crime, but there is insufficient evidence that he did. Thus, in saying that the Elmores and the Ivys attempted crimes we leave open the possibility that they are not rightly held guilty for their attempts. Consistent with the Guiding Commitment View's implications that the Elmores committed an attempted theft by deception, and that the Ivys committed an attempted murder, we can ask whether the fact of impossibility undermines the case for *guilt* for those attempts. Perhaps, that is, as in the Ivys' case, there is good reason to think that the Elmores are not rightly taken to be guilty of an attempt even though it is also true that they did commit one.

As we saw in chapter 5, impossibility, all by itself, never prevents *commission* of an attempt. People attempt the impossible frequently. In fact, they even sometimes attempt the impossible while believing that what they are attempting *is* impossible, as when a person tries in earnest to find a counterexample to a mathematical theorem that he believes to be true in order to help himself to see why it is true. Even when the absence of a circumstantial element of the completed crime undermines commission of an attempt—as in those cases, like *Dlugash*, discussed in chapter 5, in which the defendant has a disjunctive *de re* intention—it is not impossibility per se, but rather the absence of the needed mental state, that prevents commission. But all of this is consistent with impossibility undermining *guilt*. Does it? And, if so, under what conditions? The distinction between a stupid attempt, certain to be a failure, and an "inherently impossible" one is a distinction in the appropriateness of guilt. Both stupid attempts and inherently impossible attempts are commissions of attempted crimes, but the former, and not the latter, are appropriately convicted.

It is tempting to hold that a defendant's stupid plan crosses the line into "inherent impossibility" when it is so stupid that there is no danger at all of completion of the crime. This suggestion, offered in, among other places, the *Model Penal Code*, is discussed and rejected in section 2. Section 3 offers an alternative way of construing the line between the merely hopeless attempt and the inherently impossible one. There it is suggested that in a certain class of cases, the stupidity of the plan undermines the sufficiency of *the evidence* for attempt. These are cases in which the defendant has a diminished capacity to determine what abilities he actually has and to adjust his choice of means accordingly. In such cases, it will be argued, even if we stipulate that the defendant intends to commit a crime and is undertaking means to do so, we necessarily lack the kind of evidence of attempt that warrants a finding of guilt. To have that kind of evidence, we need to have evidence that the defendant would have completed the crime given ability and opportunity and no change of mind on his part. But defendants who are extremely bad at determining what their abilities actually are might not commit the crime even under such ideal circumstances. Thus, a defense of inherent impossibility is, like the act element of attempt itself (as we saw in chapter 8), justified on evidentialist grounds. In fact, as we will see in chapter 10, where a more careful account of the act element of attempt is given, in cases of inherent impossibility, the act element of attempt is absent. In such cases, the defendant is trying to commit a crime, but he is not *doing* anything that adequately evidences that. This is true even though he is doing something that he believes will get him closer to completing the crime. But, when construed correctly, the act element of an attempt is action that *does* supply adequate evidence of this, and so it follows that people like the Ivys, while they are trying to commit crimes, are not rightly held guilty of any criminal attempt.

## 2. Inherent Impossibility as Absence of Dangerousness

As was discussed in chapter 1, the framers of the *Model Penal Code* take attempts to be legitimately criminalized on the grounds that those who undertake them are dangerously likely to complete the crime on that or some other occasion. It is then no surprise that the code offers us the following test for determining if a defendant's attempt was "inherently impossible":

If the particular conduct charged to constitute a criminal attempt...is so inherently unlikely to result or culminate in the commission of a crime that *neither such conduct nor the actor presents a public danger*...the Court shall...impose sentence for a crime of lower grade or degree or, in extreme cases, may dismiss the prosecution.

(*Model Penal Code* §5.05(2), emphasis added)

The controlling question, on this view, is whether the choice of means was so inept as to show that the defendant was very unlikely to have completed the crime on the particular occasion on which he tried it (his "conduct" did not present "a public danger"), and very unlikely to complete it at some other past or future time (the "actor" does not present "a public danger"). Recognizing that dangerousness of this sort is a matter of degree—there might be a 20 percent chance that one defendant will complete the crime, a 60 percent chance that another will—the code recommends treating "inherent impossibility" as a mitigating factor for sentencing, rather than grounds for an affirmative defense, where it would provide all-or-nothing support for acquittal. Still, the code recognizes the possibility of "extreme cases" in which the defendant's choice of means was so inept as to undermine any justification for a finding of guilt. Presumably, the Ivys would fall into this category. Some commentators, drawn to the idea that the "inherently impossible" attempts are those in which there is no danger of completion, take the unflinching position that they should all be acquitted, and not merely mitigated.[6]

There are several problems with an appeal to lack of dangerousness in order to justify acquittal, or even mitigation. The first is that one would turn to the question of dangerousness of this sort only if one already accepted that as the justificatory basis for criminalizing attempts. As we saw in chapter 1, the dangerousness of those who attempt cannot serve to justify the Transfer Principle, according to which an attempt is legitimately criminalized if completion is legitimately criminalized, which is the principle to which we in fact appeal when we follow the practice of automatically criminalizing an attempt whenever we define a completed crime. Sometimes the conditional probability of completion given attempt is high, sometimes it is not, but attempts are criminalized under the Transfer Principle independently of this consideration. The point for our purposes here is that we cannot disentangle the suggestion that a defendant's attempt is "inherently impossible" if there's no danger of completion, from the suggestion that attempts are properly criminalized since they pose such dangers. The first view stands only if the second does; and so since the second falls, so does the first.

Second, and more importantly for our purposes here, notice that to distinguish cases like the Elmores' from cases like the Ivys' we would need to appeal not to the dangerousness of the *act*, since both acts are equally unlikely to result in commission of the completed crime: the probability of success was, in both cases, functionally zero. We must appeal entirely to the dangerousness of the actors if we are to distinguish the cases. However, when we turn to that consideration, it seems that we get the cases backwards: from the point of view of the dangerousness of the actors, there is a better case for convicting

[6] E.g. Spjut (1987), Strahorn (1930). The state of Minnesota follows this line, allowing a statutory defense of inherent impossibility. See Minn. Stat. Ann. §609.17(2) (2007).

the Ivys of attempted murder than there is for convicting the Elmores of attempted theft by deception. After all, the Ivys were surely aware of a variety of perfectly good ways in which one can kill another person. Had the voodoo trick failed, as we can suspect it would have, they may well have resorted to more prosaic measures, such as shooting the judge as he walked up the courthouse steps one morning. By contrast, the Elmores were attempting to exploit very special circumstances for stealing: they were trying to take advantage of the fact that the insurance company was going to pay for, as they saw it, anything plausible that they listed as destroyed in the fire. It seems very unlikely that the Elmores would make some other effort to steal by deception on some other occasion, since they were unlikely to face such special circumstances again. In any event, there is certainly less reason to expect them to do so than there is to expect the Ivys to adopt some other means for killing the judge. It is not as though the Elmores were running a deceptive scam on passers-by, or even seeking opportunities to bilk large companies. The case might be different if there were evidence that they had burned down their own house as their first step in the scheme, but there is no reason to think that they were doing anything other than trying to take advantage of what were, for them, singular circumstances. But then the probability that they would commit the crime on some other occasion is a function, in part, of the probability that they would face such circumstances again, which is very low indeed.

Third, the *Model Penal Code*'s approach overlooks the fact that crimes differ radically in how difficult they are to complete. Hence, whether or not a particular defendant's inept effort to complete it will show him to be likely to complete the crime, or to have completed it on some other occasion, will turn not just on facts about the defendant and the means that he chose, but on facts about the completed crime itself that shouldn't matter to the question of whether guilt for attempt is appropriate. While this is an extreme example, consider the crime of assassinating the president of the United States. This is very hard to do. While it is difficult to know how many times it has been attempted—hundreds? thousands?—we do know that it has been completed only four times. The success rate is extremely low. But we wouldn't want to say that someone who attempts to kill the president by, for instance, sending a box of poisoned candy to the White House with a card that says, "For the president" is to be acquitted on the grounds of "inherent impossibility". In fact, there is virtually no chance at all of assassinating the president in this manner. Someone who even tries to commit the crime in that manner is virtually certain to lack the criminal imagination necessary to actually pull off an assassination. Such a person might be dangerous in some way, but he is not dangerous in the relevant respect: he is not likely to assassinate the president on some other occasion. But that fact just doesn't seem relevant in such a case.

Finally, it is important to be reminded that ineptitude is rampant among those who try and fail to commit crimes. But in very few cases in which the defendant is so inept as to be of little danger are we tempted to suggest that mitigation or acquittal on grounds of "inherent impossibility" is appropriate. The defendant who tries and fails to run a confidence game with a stranger is still rightly held guilty of attempted theft by deception even if, given his lousy acting skills, he really is incapable of ever convincing any random stranger to trust him enough to hand over money. The aged and weak defendant whose hands shake badly is still rightly held guilty of attempted assault when he wildly swings a kitchen knife at his wife intending to cut her. This is so even if we can be confident that his young and nimble wife would not have been injured this time, that he never has succeeded in injuring anyone in such a way, and that he never will do so in the future. There are also defendants who attempt crimes out of pure desperation and in extraordinary circumstances, very unlikely to recur, in which it is certain that they will fail. Think of the impoverished teenager who tries to secure an illegal abortion. Are none of these sorts of defendants rightly held guilty of attempted crimes?

It would clearly be an abuse of the *Model Penal Code*'s provision to use it to mitigate the sentences of those who attempt crimes that are inherently very hard to complete or to mitigate the sentences of all those who are, for some reason or another, very unlikely to succeed in completing the crime, or to have succeeded in the past. The framers of the *Model Penal Code* intend this provision to have very narrow scope. But what that suggests is that they intend for judges to inform their sentences by more than just whether "the conduct or the actor presents a public danger". But then whatever more is relevant remains unspecified in the *Model Penal Code*. What this suggests is that the *Model Penal Code* has not gotten to the bottom of inherent impossibility. We still don't know what the fundamental grounds are for holding back on conviction of a defendant who adopts a stupid plan for committing a crime.

## 3. Inherent Impossibility and Evidence of Attempt

### 3.1 *Practical Competence and a Proposed Account of Inherent Impossibility*

Recall the argument of chapter 8. That chapter addressed the question of why it is justified to convict for an attempted crime only if the defendant has performed an act as a means to completing the crime. It was suggested that this is justified because without an act performed as a means to completing the crime, we lack adequate evidence that the defendant was trying to commit the crime. The reason is that in order to have adequate evidence of that, we must have evidence that the following counterfactual is true (for some times t1 and t2):

*The Completion Counterfactual*: If (1) from t1 to t2 D has the ability and the opportunity to C and does not fall prey to "execution failure", and (2) D does not (at least until after t2) change his mind, then D would C.

It was argued that we have adequate evidence that the Completion Counterfactual is true only if the defendant has performed an act as a means to completing C. Such an act provides evidence that the defendant was *trying* to engage in such an act, and, given a presumption of rationality, this shows that he was engaging in conduct such that, had he had ability and opportunity to complete the crime and did not change his mind, he would have completed the crime. So, the act of undertaking means provides evidence of guidance, and so of attempt, and it is probably the case that nothing else could.

Notice that this argument helps us to identify a class of cases in which a defendant commits an attempt but is not rightly held guilty for an attempt: those in which although the defendant is committed to each of the conditions involved in completion and is moved by each of those commitments, he is not moved by them so far as to make it true that he is undertaking an act as a means to completion. As was suggested in chapter 3, since it is possible to attempt a basic act, it is possible to attempt without performing any act that is, or is believed to be, a means to completion. Hence it is possible to be trying to commit a crime without performing any act as a means to committing the crime. Such a person is committing an attempt but, assuming the argument of chapter 8 succeeds, we necessarily lack the necessary evidence that he is, and so he is not rightly held guilty for the attempt. In such a case, the Completion Counterfactual is true, but we lack adequate evidence that it is. Put another way, we know that the Completion Counterfactual is true only because we are *stipulating* in this example that the agent is trying to C; without that stipulation we have no good reason for thinking that the Completion Counterfactual is true at all. But if we are to have adequate evidence of attempt we need *independent* evidence; we need to know that the Completion Counterfactual is true without stipulating that the defendant has attempted.

But there is another class of cases in which there may be an attempt but, because of lack of evidence of guidance by the relevant intention, it would be inappropriate to take the person to be guilty of an attempt. To see this, first consider the thirsty cow that is led to water, but instead of drinking, continues to lick a saltlick, which makes her thirstier and thirstier. It is tempting to reconstruct the cow's psychology like so: the cow wants water, but also wants salt; the second of these desires is more powerful than the first, and so it is that which motivates her action. If this is what is happening then the cow, when licking the saltlick, is not trying to satisfy her desire for water; instead, she's trying to satisfy her desire for salt. But there is another possible way of construing the cow's psychology through appeal only to the desire for water. Perhaps, that is, the cow wants only water, but for some reason the desire for water functions causally in a self-defeating way. It causes her to lick the saltlick and thus to engage in behavior that is certain if it persists to lead to failure. In this case, is the cow's desire for water motivating her conduct, or causing it in some way undeserving of that title? Put in the language of the Guiding Commitment View, is her desire *guiding* her behavior?

The answer is this: we cannot know. The reason is that we cannot know whether the Completion Counterfactual is true. There are two things that are defeating the cow from having water: the fact that licking a saltlick won't get her any, and the fact that her desire is causing her to lick the saltlick. In possible worlds in which the antecedent of the Completion Counterfactual is true there is some means to having water, call it M, that is no less attractive intrinsically to the cow than licking the saltlick is and which will actually lead to the cow having water. So in these possible worlds, the first cause of failure is functionally absent, not because licking saltlicks somehow magically leads to having water in those possible worlds, but, instead, because there is something else that does, namely M, which is no less rational from the cow's point of view than licking the saltlick. But is the second cause of failure still present? In the relevant possible worlds, does her desire, continuing to animate her behavior as it does in the actual world, lead her to take M, or not? We cannot answer this question because we do not know why the desire for water is functioning in the peculiar way it is. For instance, one possibility is that the desire causes the cow to lick the saltlick because the desire itself causes her to *believe* that licking saltlicks is a good way to get water. If that's her problem, then in the relevant possible worlds she'll continue to lick the saltlick, rather than taking M, the means to having water. It could be that whenever M is available to her, the cow's desire for water, if it continues to function as it does, will lead her to perform some different act instead by leading her to the false belief that that act will get her what she wants. This possibility would seem very unlikely were there some good reason to think that a cow whose desire was functioning normally would think that licking a saltlick would get it water. If, for instance, the cow had been trained to lick the saltlick in order to fill a bucket with water, then we would have no reason to think that her desire for water was interfering in some pathological way with her beliefs about what the best means to her ends were. But without some special story of that kind, we can't rule out that possibility.

The lesson to take from this example is this: when an agent takes hopeless means to doing as he intends, to be convinced that he is nonetheless trying to do as he intends we must be convinced that his intention itself is not causing him to believe those hopeless means to be a good way to reach his end. If the intention is functioning in that way, then providing him with ability and opportunity, and insulating him against "execution failure", will not be enough to lead him to success because, even in those ideal conditions, his intention will still send him down a path to failure.

In general, the Completion Counterfactual is true only of those agents who are disposed to adjust their choice of means to their abilities and opportunities. Call this "practical competence". If D, an agent with an intention [to kill] for instance, is practically competent, then if he has the ability and opportunity to kill by shooting, and is actually undertaking means to kill, then he undertakes means to kill *by shooting*; if he has the ability and opportunity to kill by poisoning, then he undertakes means to kill *by poisoning*; and so on. The practically competent agent ordinarily *gets it right* about what abilities and opportunities he actually has, and chooses action as means that accord with that judgment. If an agent who is in fact undertaking means to kill is not practically competent, then, when we consider the possible world in which he has the ability and opportunity to kill by poisoning, and does not change his mind, we do not know what act he will actually perform. Since we are stipulating that he does not change his mind, and that he is in fact undertaking an act that he takes to be a means to killing, we know he will perform some act that he believes to be such a means. But what act will that be? Perhaps, in such a possible world, he will shoot at Victim even though it is poisoning, and not shooting, that will get the job done in that possible world. We cannot say whether the Completion Counterfactual is true of the agent who is not practically competent. To return to the cow example, her problem is that, for all we know, her desire is inducing practical incompetence when it comes to having water. She may be practically competent in many domains, but given that her desire for water is causing her to lick the saltlick, we cannot rule out the possibility that her desire is causing her to have false beliefs about what the means are to her ends.

Practical competence is not the same as what is sometimes referred to as "know how". A practically incompetent agent might have perfect know how; he might know how to shoot a gun, know how to hit a bullseye. The practically incompetent agent might be no more subject to "execution failure" than the rest of us; he might be even somewhat less likely than we are to simply miss, despite having the ability and opportunity to hit, and despite trying his hardest. There is one and only one thing that the practically incompetent agent cannot be trusted to do: choose to perform the act that will lead to his doing as he intends. When an agent is not practically competent, we are in doubt about whether the Completion Counterfactual is true of him. The fact that he intends to do something, actually took what he believed to be a means towards doing it, and is in a position to recognize that some other means is just as supported by reasons as that which he did choose, is not enough for us to predict with confidence that he will choose to perform that means.

It is the usual presumption of practical competence that is thrown into doubt in cases like the Ivys'. For all we know, the Ivys' intention to kill the judge is functioning in a pathological way and systematically inducing in them false beliefs about what will help them to reach their end. If, for instance, the Ivys are of the belief that dark acts require for success the cooperation of dark spirits and cannot be performed directly by mortal men, then their intention to kill the judge will always motivate them to undertake means that will induce such cooperation, and will never motivate them to perform acts that will actually kill the judge. To determine if the Completion Counterfactual is true of the Ivys, on the assumption that they are in fact performing an act as a means to killing the judge, we consider possible worlds in which the Ivys have the ability to kill the judge *somehow*; in some they have the ability to kill the judge by shooting him, in others the ability to kill him with voodoo, etc. In each possible world, the Ivys have the opportunity to kill the judge through the exercise of the ability to kill the judge which they have in that possible world. So, in possible worlds in which the Ivys have the ability to kill the judge by shooting him, they also have the opportunity to shoot him; in possible worlds in which they have the ability to kill him with voodoo, they also have the opportunity— nothing prevents them from saying the needed incantations, for instance, in such possible worlds. And in each of the relevant possible worlds, the Ivys are still, as they are in the actual world, undertaking an act they believe to be a means to killing the judge. But in the world in which the Ivys have the ability and opportunity to kill the judge by shooting him, are they shooting at him, or are they still persevering with incantations? We can only say that they are shooting him in that world if we take the Ivys to be practically competent. But we cannot say for certain that they are: for all we know their intention is functioning in a way that undermines their practical competence with respect to dark acts like the murder of a judge. Hence we cannot say that the Completion Counterfactual is true. The result: we lack necessary evidence that the Ivys are guided by their intention to kill the judge, and so we lack necessary evidence that they are attempting murder.

Now consider the Elmores. In assessing whether the Completion Counterfactual is true, we consider possible worlds in which the Elmores have the ability and opportunity to steal from the insurance company by deception because their policy limit is higher than their losses, but we also consider possible worlds in which, although the policy limit is lower than their losses, they also have the ability and opportunity to keep the insurance company from noticing this. And we consider possible worlds in which they have radically different abilities and opportunities to steal by deception, such as those in which they have an "inside man" at the insurance company. Since the Elmores are undertaking what they take to be means to steal by deception, we imagine them doing so in each of these possible worlds. Now, if we have no doubts about the Elmores' practical competence, then we will imagine that they undertake, in each relevant world, an act that is, indeed, a means to stealing by deception in that world. But do we have any reason to doubt their practical competence? It does not seem so. Failing to know about the limitations on one's insurance policy is compatible with a disposition to get it right most of the time about what one's abilities and opportunities are, even in matters pertaining only to insurance. And so it follows that we do not encounter the obstacle in assessing the Completion Counterfactual that we encountered when considering the Ivys. So, unlike the Ivys, we have adequate evidence of an attempt on the part of the Elmores.

From this we can conclude that, even if it is stipulated that both defendants are committing an attempted crime, we are justified in holding only the Elmores guilty of one. In general, if we have evidence sufficient to throw a defendant's practical competence into doubt—if we have evidence to suggest that, when it comes to the intended crime, the defendant is not disposed to get it right about what he does and does not have ability and opportunity to do—then we have a case of "inherent impossibility". A case of "inherent impossibility", then, is a case in which the means chosen are so hopeless as to throw into doubt our usual presumption of the agent's practical competence. In some of these cases, the intention, itself, is, for all we know, undermining success by inducing false beliefs about how the agent can do what he intends.

### 3.2 Two Putative Counterexamples

Consider two seemingly problematic kinds of case for the view just presented. The first involves agents who are practically incompetent but who nevertheless will succeed in completing the crime if given ability and opportunity and no change of mind. The second concerns agents who are practically incompetent only in a highly specific way. For an example of the first sort of defendant, consider Carole Hargis and her lover Teri Depew, who decided to kill Hargis's husband David for the proceeds from his life insurance policy.[7] They made no fewer than ten failed attempts, almost none of which had any chance whatsoever of success. On one occasion, they buried a non-venomous tarantula in a blackberry pie, hoping that David Hargis would eat it and be poisoned to death (he didn't). Other poisoning efforts included lacing his French toast with LSD (it made him a bit ill) and putting sleeping pills in his beer (they did not dissolve). They also filled his car's carburetor with bullets hoping the car would explode (it did not). However, despite their ineptitude, they eventually succeeded. One night after David Hargis returned from taking his stepsons to a Boy Scout meeting, Depew and Carole Hargis beat him to death with a heavy curtain weight.

It might appear that this example is problematic for the analysis of inherent impossibility offered here. After all, we know that Hargis and Depew were sufficiently practically competent to take advantage of at least one opportunity to kill David Hargis: they had the ability and the opportunity to beat him to death and did it, after all. But imagine that Hargis and Depew had made only one of their attempts before being arrested for attempted murder; imagine they had done nothing other than put the tarantula in the blackberry pie and offer it to David Hargis. Granting that the Completion Counterfactual is true, how would an inherent impossibility defense fare? Under the analysis on offer,

---

[7] The case is described in Rule (2001), 305–24. Thanks to Larry Alexander for alerting me to it.

Hargis and Depew ought to be acquitted, in this hypothetical, on grounds of inherent impossibility. The reason is that if all they did was to bake a tarantula in a blackberry pie, we have insufficient evidence supporting the claim that, even if invested with ability and opportunity and shielded from "execution failure", they would have adopted the means necessary for killing David Hargis. In fact, on the basis of the tarantula stunt alone, we have no reason to believe, even, that they would beat David Hargis to death if given ability and opportunity. Our evidence is consistent with the possibility that they would not have recognized the opportunity to beat him to death as an opportunity to kill him; anyone who thinks that baking a tarantula in a blackberry pie is a good way to kill another might not recognize other better means as such. It is true that Hargis and Depew would have beaten him if given ability and opportunity—they did do so—but it is not true that, in the hypothetical under consideration, there is sufficient evidence in support of this claim. In fact, we would even lack sufficient evidence in support of this claim if Hargis and Depew had confessed their plan to beat David Hargis to death should other means fail.

We can imagine a different kind of problematic case. Consider a defendant who is practically incompetent in only one quite specific domain.[8] He has a phobia about knives, say, and will complete the crime if given ability and opportunity *provided that completion does not require him to use a knife*. The result of his phobia is that he simply fails to recognize that he can do as he intends by using a knife: his phobia invariably directs his attention elsewhere. It is not that he recognizes that he can do as he intends by using a knife but would elect not to do so; it is, rather, that thanks to his phobia he would sooner judge himself to have no way to do as he intends than he would judge himself capable of doing so by using a knife. But, acting on an intention to kill another person, he fires a gun at him and misses. Will this defendant complete the crime if given the ability and opportunity to do so *using a knife*? No. Is this result problematic for the view proposed here? It can appear that it is. After all, if the possible world in which the defendant has the ability and the opportunity to kill with a knife is among those that need to be assessed when we assess the truth of the Completion Counterfactual, then we must conclude that the counterfactual is false. And if it is false, then we lack sufficient evidence that the defendant is guided by his intention-based commitments, and so lack sufficient evidence that he is, actually, trying to commit murder. The trouble is that it is patently absurd to acquit this defendant on grounds of inherent impossibility, or on any other grounds: firing a gun at someone is simply not an "inherently impossible" attempt at murder.

However, the example is not a counterexample to the view on offer, despite appearances. The reason is that possible worlds in which this defendant can kill

---

[8] Thanks to Steve Finlay for pressing me to accommodate such cases.

by using a knife are not among those that need to be surveyed when assessing the Completion Counterfactual. In chapter 3, it was suggested that when the failure to complete the crime in a given possible world is explicable by reference to some facts that distinguish the possible world from the actual in a way that shows the failure to complete, not to speak to the question of whether the defendant is actually motivated by his criminal intention, then the possible world in question is not to be considered. After all, we care about the Completion Counterfactual because we are trying to assess whether the intention's actual influence is motivational. Is the defendant in fact being moved by the criminal intention towards completion of the crime? If the defendant would fail to complete in some possible world for reasons that don't speak to this question, then that possible world is not relevant to our purposes in assessing the Completion Counterfactual in the first place. Such is the case in this example. The knife phobia explains the failure to complete in possible worlds in which a knife must be used. But since the phobia wasn't operative in motivating the defendant to fire the shot, such possible worlds are not similar to the actual in the way that matters. The fact, for instance, that the defendant does complete the murder in possible worlds in which he can do so with a gun, a rope, with poison, and even with a shove off a bridge, is enough to show that he is actually guided by his intention to kill. The Completion Counterfactual is true in this case because the possible worlds in which the defendant has ability and opportunity and fails are possible worlds that are not relevant to assessing it.

### 3.3 *Alternative Approaches and the Relevance of Common Knowledge*

Some courts have suggested that the right test for inherent possibility is this: would a reasonable person have recognized that the means the defendant chose were hopeless?[9] Under the view presented here, this is close to the right way to tackle the problem, but not quite the right way. The reason it is not quite the right way is that it is defensible only if we massage the notion of the reasonable until it aligns with practical competence. Hence the view is misidentifying the crucial notion. For instance, if the reasonable person would have known the limits on the Elmore's insurance policy, then he would have recognized that their means of stealing from their insurance company were hopeless. Why should we say that the reasonable person would not have known this? Perhaps because the Elmores did not know it. But neither did the Ivys know that saying incantations over a lock of the judge's hair would not cause death. Why should we ascribe the defendant's state of false belief to the reasonable person in the one case and not in the other? The reason is that the false belief about the policy's limit is compatible with practical competence on behalf of the Elmores,

---

[9] E.g. *State v. Bird* (285 N.W.2d 481 (Minn. 1979)). This case is quoted in Dressler (2009), 406.

while the false belief about the power of voodoo is not. That is, what really guides our intuitions about what means a reasonable person would have recognized as hopeless is not anything about *reasonableness* per se, but, instead, something about the practical competence of the agents whom we are assessing. Ultimately, that is, appeal to what a reasonable person would recognize as hopeless will solve the problem of inherent impossibility only if it collapses into the view proposed here.

Peter Westen has recently proposed an account of "inherent impossibility" which bears affinities with the view offered here. According to Westen, no attempter is to be held guilty of an attempted crime unless he "would have committed the offense under counterfactual circumstances that [informed citizens] fear could have obtained".[10] People like the Ivys, then, are to be acquitted because the counterfactual circumstances in which they would have completed the crime—such as those in which voodoo works—are circumstances that informed citizens do not fear they might have faced. The problem with the proposal, as it stands, is that informed citizens do not fear that, for instance, the Elmores might have had an insurance policy with a higher limit, a circumstance under which their attempt would have led to completion. At least, it is difficult to see why informed citizens would fear that possibility independently of a desire to reject the Elmores' defense of inherent impossibility. But there are, nonetheless, a pair of insights contained in Westen's position that, I hope, are captured more fully in the proposal made here. The first is the insight that what actually matters in cases like the Elmores' or the Ivys' is not future dangerousness. What matters, instead, is something about the facts at the moment of the attempt. As we've seen, what really matters is whether the criminal intention is animating the defendant's behavior in the distinctive way that we label as "motivating", a way that leads many to completion of crimes. The second insight is that the facts in question track the truth or falsity of a particular counterfactual. Whether the defendant is being moved by his intention in the distinctive way that is involved in attempt depends on whether a particular counterfactual is true of him. As I see it, Westen misidentifies the relevant counterfactual slightly, since what really matters is the Completion Counterfactual.

Both the approach that appeals to what reasonable people would recognize to be hopeless and Westen's approach are able to accommodate a seemingly puzzling fact, namely that common knowledge about what will and will not succeed in helping one to reach one's end seems relevant to the question of whether what one does is "inherently impossible". The point is illustrated nicely by a number of cases, spread over the last thirty years or so, involving HIV-positive defendants who make inept efforts to infect others with the virus. Is, for instance, the HIV-positive defendant who spits on another, intending to

---

[10] Westen (2008), 558.

kill by infecting the other with the virus and believing falsely that the virus can be transmitted through saliva, rightly held guilty of attempted murder?[11] Or, should we acquit such a defendant on grounds of inherent impossibility? There is a powerful intuition to the effect that the question turns in part on what the state of general knowledge about HIV was at the time of the crime. In the early 1980s, for instance, it was not widely known that HIV could not be transmitted through saliva. By the late 1990s, and probably well before, this was common knowledge. But why should it matter what other people knew or didn't know when the defendant acted? Shouldn't the question turn entirely on the facts—particularly the fact that the virus cannot be transmitted that way—and the *defendant's* state of belief? If what is crucial is what a reasonable person would have taken to be hopeless, then common knowledge matters since, presumably, the reasonable person believes what we all believe. Similarly, if what is crucial is what the defendant would do in circumstances that we fear he would have faced, then common knowledge matters again: what circumstances we fear he might have faced is a function, in part, of what we all believe about which circumstances can lead to completion of the crime.

But under the view offered here, also, what is and is not common knowledge can matter to the question of inherent impossibility. The reason it matters is that it gives us evidence about the defendant's practical competence in the relevant domain. A person who knows less than is common knowledge about what his abilities and opportunities are, is more likely to be practically incompetent. One of the main ways in which we learn what we can and cannot do is by observing what others do and do not believe themselves to be capable of doing. Someone who has failed to soak up from others a belief about what can and cannot be done is less likely to be able to correctly make such determinations. By contrast, someone who believes what everyone falsely believes is not, on those grounds, any less likely to get it right when he is presented with alternative means to his end. Whenever everyone falsely believes that HIV can be transmitted through saliva, the fact that the defendant believes this does not suggest that he will fail to take an opportunity to shoot another dead when he can. When he's normal in his beliefs of this sort, there is no reason to think him less than normal in his practical competence. The result is that when adjudicating cases in which defendants adopt hopeless means, courts ought to consider whether the hopelessness of the means was common knowledge at the time of the crime. The state of common knowledge is not the fundamental question—the fundamental question concerns the defendant's practical competence—but its answer can nonetheless give us some evidence about how the fundamental question is to be answered.

[11] E.g. *Weeks v. State* (834 S.W.2d 559 (Tex. App. 1992)).

253

## 4. Conclusion

The view presented in section 3 of this chapter helps us to see what the framers of the *Model Penal Code* were on to in suggesting that the reason not to find defendants like the Ivys guilty is that they aren't really dangerous. As we saw in section 2, this isn't literally true: some of them are very dangerous, and some who are rightly convicted are not terribly dangerous at all. It seems likely that the probability that the Elmores would commit theft by deception on this or another occasion is, if anything, lower than the probability that the Ivys would commit murder, and it is perfectly possible that the probability in both cases is zero, or very close to it.

However, in turning, as we have in section 3, to practical competence, we have identified something as crucial to understanding cases like the Ivys and the Elmores which is found alongside a particular sort of dangerousness. The danger that a person will complete the crime *if he has ability and opportunity and does not change his mind* is far greater if the person is practically competent. Those who are not, very well may, in such circumstances, choose some means to the intended criminal end that is no more effective than the one actually chosen. Put a gun in the hands of the Ivys and place a target on the head of the sleeping judge, and for all we know they will still choose incantations. We have reason to think that they are like the thirsty who, even when led to water, do not drink. We have no reason, by contrast, to think that the Elmores would have failed had they had ability and opportunity and not changed their minds. They are good enough at figuring out what they can and cannot do to support the expectation of their success in such ideal circumstances.

The conditional probability of completion given ability, opportunity, and no change of mind is, in the case of the Elmores, one, while it is less than one in the case of the Ivys. However, this conditional probability matters to guilt for attempt not because the Elmores are more dangerous than the Ivys in the sense of "dangerous" invoked in the *Model Penal Code*. Since the Elmores were virtually certain never to encounter ideal circumstances, the chances of their commission of the crime remain close to zero. Rather, the conditional probability of commission given ability, opportunity, and no change of mind matters for evidential reasons. We care about whether there would be success in such ideal circumstances because the truth of the relevant counterfactual (namely, the Completion Counterfactual) is the only evidence that we can hope to have that the defendant is trying to commit the crime, that he is guided by his intention-based commitments to each of the elements of the completed crime. We should acquit on grounds of "inherent impossibility", then, because where there is good reason to doubt the agent's practical competence, there is reasonable doubt that he is actually attempting the crime. There are not good grounds for guilt for attempt, in such cases, even if the defendant did indeed commit one.

# 10

# The Act in Attempt

## 1. Introduction

The skeptical student, when told that we punish people, not just for doing bad things, but also for trying to, usually says, "But doesn't that mean that we punish people for their bad thoughts?" Many such skeptical students are silenced by the rejoinder, "No, for we only punish people for attempts when they have *acted* on those bad thoughts." As we saw in chapter 8, there is good reason for this practice even if, contrary to the student's assumption, the fundamental facts in virtue of which a person is deserving of punishment for an act are facts about his mind. Action in furtherance of intention is indispensable evidence of trying, and there are good reasons not to punish even the deserving in the absence of adequate evidence.

However, to say that action in furtherance of intention is indispensable evidence of trying, and to say that it is sufficient evidence are two different things. For all that was said in chapter 8, it is possible that not all acts performed as means to accomplishing an intended criminal objective provide sufficient evidence that the defendant is trying to act. Perhaps any such act is sufficient, but nothing has been said so far in support of that claim. The aim of this chapter is to provide an account of the act element of attempt. The aim, that is, is to provide not just necessary *but also sufficient* conditions that an act must meet if there is to be adequate evidence that the defendant is guided by his intention-based commitment to each of the components of the completed crime—guidance which is necessary, under the Guiding Commitment View, for trying to complete the crime.

If we were to judge the importance of questions about attempted crimes by considering either the number of pages that have been published offering answers, the number of thinkers who have weighed in on them, or by the number of decades or even centuries that the questions have been occupying those with an interest in attempt, we would find a virtual tie between two questions: "Does the impossibility of completion undermine criminal liability for attempt?" and "What, exactly, must someone with an intention to commit a crime *do* in order to be justifiably held criminally liable for an attempted crime?" Further, theorists have frequently seen the questions as linked. They have offered accounts of the act element of attempt—answers to the second question—that imply that impossibility does, or does not, prevent a person from engaging in an act that would serve for guilt for attempt, and so they have thought that they could resolve the question of impossibility simply by explaining what a person needs to have done to attempt a crime. The approach here is importantly different, but resonates with this one. The question of impossibility has been answered already, and it has been answered in the absence of an explicit account of the act element of attempt. Still, the account offered in this chapter fits nicely with the view of impossibility presented already.

As we saw in chapters 5 and 9, cases in which the question of impossibility arises are of two overlapping sorts: there are those in which a circumstantial element of the completed crime is absent in the attempt, and there are those in which the defendant adopts a hopeless plan for completing the crime.[1] The first sort are, as suggested in chapter 5, best understood through consideration of the mental state required for commission of an attempt. Although they are rare, there are conditions in which a person has an intention that includes an event in its content only if that event actually occurs, and so there are rare conditions in which a person has the intention needed to commit an attempt only if a circumstantial element of the completed crime is actually in place at the time of the attempt.[2] The second sort are, as suggested in chapter 9, best understood through consideration of the indispensable evidence required for guilt for an attempted crime. We have adequate evidence of attempt only if we have adequate evidence that the defendant is guided by his intention-based commitment to each of the components of the completed crime. We have adequate evidence that he is so guided if his intention is causing some kind of behavior, and if a particular counterfactual is true of him: he would complete the crime if he had ability and opportunity and did not change his mind. As it turns out, this counterfactual is true of a person only if he is practically competent—only if, that is, he can be counted on to select means to his ends that align with his abilities. In certain cases, a person who selects a wildly hopeless plan for doing as he intends throws our belief in his practical competence into doubt, and thus undermines one of the necessary conditions that must be met if we are to have adequate evidence that he is guided by his intentions in the way distinctive of

[1] The two categories overlap since, for instance, a person might adopt a hopeless plan for receiving some property that is not, in fact, stolen, even though he thinks it is.

[2] In chapter 5, *People v. Dlugash* (41 N.Y.2d 725 (1977)) was given as an example. To review the reasoning offered there: Dlugash has a disjunctive *de re* intention [to put living-or-dead Geller into the condition that results from shooting him]. As was argued in chapter 5, such an intention commits Dlugash to killing Geller only if Geller was alive when Dlugash shot him. Since the attempted murder of Geller requires such an intention, Dlugash attempted to murder Geller only if Geller was alive when Dlugash shot him.

attempt. As we will see here, this approach to problems of "inherent possibility" influences the account of the act element of attempt offered here.

No discussion of the act element of attempt can proceed without consideration of at least some of the many and various "tests" that have been proposed by courts and theorists for determining whether a particular bit of conduct serves for guilt for an attempted crime. The tests that have been proposed can be divided, roughly, into two broad kinds. In the first category are tests motivated by a geographical metaphor. The thought is that doing as you intend is much like traveling from one geographical point to another. The starting point is the formation of intention and the end point is completion of the crime. How far must you go from the start point to the end point to be justifiably held guilty of an attempt? The great nineteenth-century criminal law theorist, historian and judge James Fitzjames Stephen's test is of this sort. He holds that you must go far enough to warrant the conclusion that you would not have stopped had you not been interrupted. In the second category are tests that take the crucial feature of conduct to be what that conduct expresses about the agent's intention. The *Model Penal Code's* test, according to which an act suffices for the act element of attempt just in case it is "strongly corroborative" of the defendant's criminal intention, is one example. It will be argued that a version of Stephen's test that captures its basic insight, and a version of the *Model Penal Code* test that captures its basic insight are both adequate and, in fact, both express the very same position, in different ways. Whether we follow the geographical metaphor, on the one hand, or the approach that appeals to expression of intention, on the other, so long as we correct our position to accord with the facts about trying to act, we end up in the same place. This implies that, where some have seen a deep divide in thinking about attempt, there is in fact only a superficial divide. Both those who take the really bad thing about attempted crimes to be the acts they involve, and those who take the really bad thing to be the mental states they involve ought to agree, in the end, about what conduct suffices for guilt for attempt. Section 2 discusses the first category of tests and develops Stephen's position, although the discussion is by no means limited to Stephen's way of developing the geographical metaphor. Section 3 considers tests in the second category and develops the *Model Penal Code's* tests. In section 3, an argument for the claim that these two lines of thought converge is also offered. Section 4 offers a word about the concept of "mere preparation" and indicates why acts that intuitively fall into this category are insufficient for the act element of attempt under the account proposed here.

## 2. The Geographical Metaphor

When you decide to take a trip right now, you form the intention to travel from wherever you are at the moment of intention formation to some other place. In such cases, you will have done as you intend when you get to the place that you intend to go. We could place an arrow on an ordinary map of the world pointing to the spot where you formed the intention, and another arrow pointing to the spot you intend to go. If you are stopped on your way, we can look at our map to see what path you traveled—how far you went and in how much time, what route you took—and what path remained to be traveled. The geographical metaphor that informs many tests for the act element of attempt involves analogizing every case to this kind of case. The picture is that at the beginning of a road is a mere intention to complete a crime and at the end of the road lies completion of the crime intended. When the defendant forms his intention to complete the crime, he stands at the road's beginning. When he performs some act as a means to doing as he intends, he embarks down the road. How far down the road need he have gone before he is rightly held guilty of an attempt to commit the crime? Of course, the problem with the metaphor is that the distance in question—the distance from the formation of the intention, at one end, and completion of the crime, at the other—is not generally of the sort that can be measured in miles or kilometers. Without some guidance about how this "distance" is to be measured, the metaphor is no more than a metaphor.

Typically, tests motivated by the geographical metaphor fail in one of two ways: either they involve no specification of the relevant metric, and are thus hopelessly vague, or else they specify a metric of distance that is not of normative relevance: it fails to make distinctions in guilt on the basis of facts that are relevant to that issue. Still, there's no harm in employing the geographical metaphor so long as we remind ourselves to avoid two gaping pitfalls: the metaphor is empty unless coupled with a precise specification of how the distance in question is to be measured, and it is harmful unless coupled with a metric of distance under which the greater the distance between the defendant's act and the act involved in completion, the weaker the grounds for guilt for attempt.

When the metric is not specified, judges typically employ whatever unarticulated notion of distance they take to be relevant. They then often cloak this by suggesting, for instance, that the defendant's act was "a direct movement towards" the completed crime, or "immediately connected with" the completed crime, or they use some other similar phrase. Such terms simply reassert the geographical metaphor without explaining at all how distance (not to mention direction) on the relevant "map" is to be measured. Courts that specify the metric—that tell us how distance from intention to completion is to be measured—often take the metaphor too literally and find themselves employing a metric that is either of no normative relevance or of relevance only because it is a sign of some other unarticulated thing that is of normative relevance. Some courts, even, have adopted a *physical* proximity test. The court in the famous case of *People v. Rizzo* (246 N.Y. 334, 158 N.E. 888 (1927)), for instance, acquit the defendants in part on the grounds that although they were driving around looking for a particular payroll person to rob, they were in fact nowhere near where the man actually was at the time. Since the defendants' act took place a large physical distance from the place where completion would have taken place—namely where the intended victim was—the court claims the act to be insufficient for attempt. This kind of frank appeal to physical distance does not generalize, even if we grant for the sake of argument that it matters in *Rizzo*. After all, to give just one obvious counterexample, imagine someone who sends a dishonest letter to another, intending to defraud, and the letter is intercepted. Such a person is not more appropriately taken to be guilty of attempted fraud if the intended recipient lives next door than if he lives across the country, nor if the letter traveled half the distance before being intercepted rather than only one-quarter.

In many cases, it is far from clear how one would even start to identify an appropriate metric of distance. Say that the defendant steals blank checks from someone's mailbox, intending to use them to draw funds from the person's bank account. How "far" has such a person gone? How "far" does he have to go? If we insist on numerical answers to such questions, it is difficult to know where to start in thinking about them. Even in those rare cases where a natural metric of distance presents itself, the geographical metaphor can mislead badly. Imagine two defendants both of whom plan to kill another person with as many daily doses of arsenic in the morning coffee as is required. Both are stopped after administering three doses and before the intended victims have died. Now imagine that the first's victim was much heartier than the second's. The first's victim would have required one hundred doses, while the second's would have died after only fifty. Does it follow that the first has traveled half as far down the road to success as the second? Or, since both have administered three doses, have they traveled equally far? In cases of this kind, two natural metrics of distance—number of doses required to kill, or, alternatively, number of doses actually administered—are at best *indicators* of crucial normative facts; they are not the crucial facts themselves. A similar point can be made about the total amount of poison administered, as well as its potency. It is far from clear that someone who administered more or less poison per dose would differ in any significant way from the two imagined defendants, nor that someone who administered the same amount of poison but in more doses or in fewer would, nor that any of these cases differs significantly from that of someone who used a poison that was much more or much less potent. In these cases, we might have different evidence for the crucial normative facts; but the differences imagined are not the crucial normative facts themselves. If any of these metrics of distance mattered, then that would make little sense. Such measures appeal because they are easy to apply and not because they capture what ought to matter to criminal liability for attempt.

The geographical metaphor is one of the factors that leads to confusion in thinking about impossible attempts. The thought is that if the defendant embarks down a road that does not lead, even in a circuitous way, to completion of the crime—think of efforts to kill with voodoo (discussed in chapter 9), or of attempts to pick empty pockets (discussed in chapter 5)—then his conduct has not reduced the amount of time needed to complete the crime: no amount of time would do, so nothing one does can reduce the time needed. But if the defendant's act suffices for attempt only if it brings him closer to completion, it follows that the act is always insufficient in cases of impossibility. As attractive as this line of reasoning is, however, it only follows if the relevant metric of distance obeys the rules that measures of physical distance obey. In physical distances, travel towards a point ordinarily reduces the time it will take to get there. But when the point cannot be reached, there is no way to reduce one's travel time and so nothing one does gets one closer, in the sense of travel time, to the objective. But since it is clear that in attempts, the analogue of travel time, namely time from intent formation to crime completion, is of no normative relevance—some crimes take a long time to complete, others almost no time at all—we need pay no attention to facts about travel time, such as the fact that one cannot reduce it by travel, when there's no way to reach the end point. To conclude from the geographical metaphor that the act element of attempt is absent wherever completion is impossible is to place weight on the geographical metaphor that it cannot bear.

Oliver Wendell Holmes' dangerous proximity test is motivated by the geographical metaphor, but it appeals, at least, to a metric of distance that is of some normative relevance. Holmes holds that the defendant's act is sufficient for attempt if it is in "dangerous proximity" to completion. The term "dangerous proximity" provides no guidance in itself; it simply invokes the geographical metaphor. But Holmes puts some meat on the bones by suggesting that it is a probabilistic notion: an act is in dangerous proximity to success if the conditional probability of success given the act is dangerously high.[3] On such a view, the administration of three doses of poison in a slow poisoning case might or might not serve for the act element of attempt, depending on how likely the death is, given the doses. Hence the number of doses, the number required to kill the victim, the amount of poison in each dose, and the potency of the poison administered, would all be relevant factors to consider, but not because they are the fundamental facts relevant to measuring the distance between intention and completion, but because they each provide some evidence of what the crucial conditional probability is. The more potent the poison, for instance, the greater chance of death (ordinarily).

As was suggested in chapter 1, the dangerous proximity test is adequate only if attempts are criminalized because they increase the probability of completion. But this view is consistent neither with our practice of automatically, by

---

[3] Holmes (1881), 68–9.

default, criminalizing a corresponding attempt whenever we criminalize a form of completed conduct, nor with our practice of failing to criminalize as attempt, conduct that increases the probability of a completed crime but is not, itself, an attempt (such as reckless conduct unaccompanied with an intention to complete a crime). Further, and importantly, the degree to which an act increases the probability of a completed crime does not align with the degree to which it is deserving of censure, nor with the severity of the censure that it deserves. The problem with the dangerous proximity test, then, is not that it appeals to something for measuring distance that is normatively irrelevant—conditional probability of completion, given action, matters for a variety of purposes pertaining to the maintenance of social order which are relevant to questions of punishment—but that it appeals to something that is not of normative relevance *to attempt* in particular.

Some, moved by the metaphor of a road from intention formation to crime completion, have focused, not on how "far" intention is from completion but, instead, on whether or not the defendant would travel the distance. So, for instance, James Fitzjames Stephen defines the act involved in an attempt as "an act . . . forming part of a series of acts which would constitute [the crime's] actual commission if it were not interrupted".[4] As I'll argue here, suitably modified, this is the correct test for the act element of attempt. However, as stated by Stephen, the test is misleading in some ways and insufficiently precise in others.

First, note that as the test is stated, a person's *act* could fall short of what is required for attempt even though it would be enough for the act element *of completion* in the absence of interruption. Consider, for instance, the person who is stopped just before taking possession of property that is not stolen but which he believes to be stolen. Such a person would not have received *stolen* property even if he had taken possession of the property in question. So, under Stephen's test, the person's act does not suffice for an attempt to receive stolen property. But the problem for completion of receipt of stolen property in such a case is not that the act was interrupted, but, instead, that the property was not stolen. Cases of receipt of unstolen property believed to be stolen are charged as attempts, rather than completions, not because the act is less than that involved in completion, but because the circumstances are less than that involved in completion. It is nothing but confusing to take absent circumstantial elements of crimes to bear on the question of whether the act is sufficient. Yet in its explicit formulation, Stephen's test does exactly that.[5]

---

[4] Stephen (1883), §49, 37.

[5] This point forms the basis of H. L. A. Hart's critique of Stephen's test in the form offered by the House of Lords in 1978. See Hart (1981). Hart notes that by thinking of all attempts as interrupted completed crimes we lose sight of a large class of attempts that are not, namely those in which a circumstantial element of the completed crime is absent. Hart uses the point to argue that impossibility ought not to be a defense to a charge of attempt, since he takes it to be

This problem is easily remedied, however. A better way to formulate Stephen's test is like so:

D's act A serves as the act element of an attempt to C *if and only if* If D had not been interrupted, then D would have performed an act that can serve as the act element of C.

Under this formulation, unlike Stephen's explicit formulation, the person who is prevented from receiving unstolen property has still performed an act sufficient for attempt, for had he not been stopped, he would have received the property, and receipt of property serves as the act element of the crime of receipt of stolen property, even though the crime would not have been completed in the absence of interruption.

However, Stephen's test still requires refinement. To see this, consider the concept of "interruption". What, exactly, would Stephen consider to be an "interruption"? What, exactly, are we imagining away when we consider what would be true in the absence of "interruption"? To see the problem, consider *People v. Mahboubian* (74 N.Y.2d 174, 543 N.E.2d 34 (1989)). The defendant hired some people to break in to a secure storage facility and take Persian artifacts that he owned and was storing there. His plan was to file an insurance claim of approximately $18.5 million with Lloyds of London for the loss, while secretly keeping his property. The hired hands succeeded in taking the artifacts from the facility, but because of police intervention, the defendant never had the property returned to him and never had the opportunity to file an insurance claim. He was charged with attempted grand larceny of $18.5 million from Lloyds of London. Now consider various things that might be true but for the actual intervention of the police:

(a) Mahboubian would not have filed a claim out of fear of getting caught.

(b) Mahboubian would not have filed a claim because he would have come to renounce the entire enterprise as wrong.

(c) Mahboubian would have filed a claim but the police would have intervened before Lloyds of London paid Mahboubian any money.

(d) Mahboubian would have filed a claim but Lloyds of London would have rejected it, challenging Mahboubian to sue for the payment and risk bringing the criminal enterprise to the attention of the police; Mahboubian would have accepted their decision rather than sue.

---

clear that the person who has done enough for completion, but fails because circumstances he believes to be present (e.g. the property being stolen) are actually absent, ought still to be held guilty for attempt. We can agree with Hart without throwing the baby out with the bath water. In cases in which the defendant's act does fall short of the act needed for completion, it is because he was interrupted. And in such cases we need to know what would have happened if he had not been interrupted.

It is clear that in applying Stephen's test we are to imagine away the actual intervention of the police in considering what would happen. But even imagining that to be absent, (a)–(d) each offers a scenario in which Mahboubian still fails to take any money. Since taking something is the act element of grand larceny, it seems that whether or not Mahboubian has done enough for an attempt of the crime under Stephen's test depends on what other "interruptions" we are to imagine away when considering what he would have done in the absence of police intervention. Are we to assume that he does not change his mind out of fear of getting caught? Does not have a true change of heart about his criminal ways? Does not get caught after he has taken further steps falling short of taking the money? Does not get stopped by someone other than the police? We can imagine a wide variety of answers to these questions and, given facts supporting each of (a)–(d), such answers will yield different verdicts in the case.

In fact, the various variants of the so-called "probable desistance" test are functionally identical to Stephen's test, supplemented with various answers to such questions. In its simplest form, according to the probable desistance test, the defendant's act suffices for attempt if the defendant "would commit the crime but for the intervention of another person or some other extraneous factor".[6] Although there is ambiguity about what factors are "extraneous", this test would appear to acquit Mahboubian if either (a) or (b) is shown. By contrast, under this version of the probable desistance test, Mahboubian's act is sufficient for the act element of attempt even if either (c) or (d) is true. The future interruptions that would occur in scenarios (c) or (d) had Mahboubian not been arrested, are themselves to be imagined away under this version of the probable desistance test—we are to ask what would have happened had such interruptions *not* occurred—while the sort that would occur in scenarios (a) and (b) are not. In essence, this version of the probable desistance test is Stephen's test coupled with the claim that the "interruptions" to be imagined away are only those caused by others or by "extraneous factors"; we are not to imagine away interruptions caused by the defendant himself. We can also imagine versions of the probable desistance test that imagine away interruptions like those involved in (a)—why should the defendant get credit for being too scared to continue?— but not those in (b). Someone attracted to such a position might insist that the defendant has done enough for an attempt if he would commit the crime but for the intervention of another person, a complete renunciation of the criminal enterprise, or some other extraneous factor.

However we sort out the details, the accounts of "interruption" that we find in the probable desistance tests have a common problem. Under all of them, two agents who have exactly the same intention, exactly the same plan for doing as they intend, undertake exactly the same acts for exactly the same

---

[6] We find this phrase or variants of it in many cases, e.g. *Berry v. State* (280 N.W.2d 204 (Wis. 1979)).

reason, and are stopped in exactly the same way, might differ with regard to whether *their acts* are sufficient for the act element of attempt. This is more than a little bit strange given that if they have all these things in common, then they have engaged in precisely the same types of act. We can imagine good reason to take them to differ in their criminal liability for attempt; perhaps the person who would have renunciated his criminal plan had he not been arrested should not be held guilty for attempt. But we needn't try to accommodate such differences *in our account of the act element of attempt*. To do so is to create a legal fiction where none is needed. It is to posit a difference in the legal status of acts where there is no difference *in the acts*. It is better to, for instance, incorporate such ideas, if they have merit, into the affirmative defense of abandonment, or even to craft a new would-have-abandoned affirmative defense. Those approaches, in contrast to the probable desistance approach, do not involve any pretense.

Consider Robert Skilton's proposed test, which is quoted with approval by the majority in *Mahboubian*, and is often taken to be a version of the probable desistance test:[7]

No more definite rule of law can be suggested... than to say that the defendant's conduct must pass that point where most men, holding such an intention as the defendant holds, would think better of their conduct and desist.[8]

To apply Skilton's test in *Mahboubian*, we would have to imagine that an ordinary law-abiding citizen has formed the intention to steal $18.5 million from Lloyds of London by faking a burglary, and ask at what point such a person would look at himself in the mirror and say, "What do you think you are doing?!?" before giving up the plan. The idea is that we see whether the opportunities to abandon the plan *that the agent has actually forsaken* are such that an ordinary person with the same intention as the defendant would have taken them and abandoned the plan. There are probably insuperable problems of application with this test. Since an ordinary law-abiding citizen would never have formed such an intention, how are we possibly to know whether, for instance, an ordinary person *with such an intention* would have abandoned the plan before doing the things Mahboubian did? For instance, Mahboubian provided the thieves with a map of the storage facility indicating the location of his goods. Would an ordinary person with Mahboubian's intention have done this, or abandoned the plan? It is simply impossible to imagine on what basis one would reach an answer to this question, taken to be crucial by Skilton. It simply seems indeterminate whether an ordinary person with such an intention would, or would not, go as far as to supply such a map, given that in imagining this person to have such an intention we are imagining someone

---

[7] LaFave, for instance, lumps them together. See LaFave (2000), 548.
[8] Skilton (1937b), 309–10.

who is rather less restrained in the formation of his intentions than ordinary people are.

However, problems of application are not nearly as important as problems of principle. If Skilton has identified the normatively crucial question, then we should see what can be done in practice to make progress on an answer to it in particular cases. The normatively crucial facts, in this case, are those that distinguish between agents for whom guilt for attempt is appropriate, and agents who are otherwise the same but for whom it is not. However, even if Skilton's question is important for answering some normative questions, he has not identified the crucial normative question *for understanding the act element of attempt*. To see this, imagine a sequence of acts, A1, A2 . . . Am, each of which is a means to C, and where a person who performed all of them in order would thereby have performed acts that suffice for the act element of C. Further, imagine that an ordinary citizen intending to C would have abandoned the plan after performing Aj and before performing Aj+1, where j is some number less than m; it is between Aj and Aj+1 that the ordinary person would have his what-do-you-think-you're-doing moment. At what point has an agent who undertakes this sequence done enough to warrant guilt for an attempt? Skilton's answer to this question is "Aj+1". The attraction of this answer is that someone who performs Aj+1 has acted in a way which is worse than ordinary. The reason that this is attractive is that the following principle has great appeal (even though it would need to be revised to accommodate exceptions in order to be defensible): *"People should not be held criminally liable for behavior that is no worse than that of ordinary people."*[9] Skilton's view seems to follow from such a principle.

The problem is that people are appropriately expected not to form and act on intentions to commit crimes, even if not all such action can legitimately form the basis of a judgment of guilt for attempt. Hence someone who forms the intention to C, and goes as far as performing Aj before being stopped, has already fallen short of appropriate expectations in a crucial respect: he's formed and acted on an intention to C. But once we recognize that, appeal to the principle that people should not be punished for doing what ordinary people do loses its force. For all that principle says, it might be appropriate to hold someone who is stopped after performing Aj guilty for an attempt; after all, such a person is doing worse than is ordinary. This isn't to say that the point at which an ordinary person with the intention would abandon isn't of some normative relevance. The fact that someone goes past that point tells us some-thing about him that is of relevance to various normative questions. It tells us, for instance, that he is more determined than ordinary people. But it is far from clear that it tells us that he has crossed the line demarcating acts for which guilt for attempt is appropriate. To say merely that someone who is doing what is

---

[9] For discussion of this idea, see Husak (1996b).

ordinary has not crossed that line does not establish the conclusion Skilton seeks, since he does not ask us to compare the defendant to an ordinary person but only to an ordinary person *with a criminal intention*. Put another way, it is quite possible that it is appropriate to convict ordinary people *with criminal intentions* who are stopped after performing Aj, and before given the opportunity to either perform Aj+1 or abandon their plan. After all, such people have done worse than is ordinary.

Skilton takes the position that a defendant who is stopped before he reaches the point at which the ordinary person would abandon the enterprise has not done enough to warrant guilt for attempt *even if he would have gone past that point had he not been stopped*. Hence Skilton's view is not, precisely, a development of Stephen's. Such a person, after all, would have performed an act sufficient for completion had he not been interrupted. But we can imagine a view inspired by Skilton's, and more like the probable desistance views, that goes the other way on this point. According to such a position, the interruptions that we are to imagine away are all and only those "extraneous factors" that stop the defendant before he reaches the point at which an ordinary person would abandon. If, imagining those interruptions away, we find that he goes past the point at which an ordinary person would stop, then he has done enough to warrant guilt for attempt. On such a view, the relevant interruptions are only those that prevent us from determining merely from examination of what the defendant actually did whether he is worse than the ordinary person in his perseverance with action in furtherance of criminal intentions.

The problem with this Skilton-inspired position is the same as that which we found with the various probable desistance tests. Under it, two agents who have done exactly the same thing, for the same reasons, with the same mental states, and are stopped in the same way may nonetheless differ as to whether their actions suffice for attempt. Hence we still need to find a way to supplement Stephen's test with an account of the distinction between those interruptions that are to be imagined away when asking what the defendant would have done if not interrupted, and those that are not. How is that distinction best understood?

Notice that the various probable desistance tests, as well as the Skilton-inspired position, are all motivated by the thought that one or more of the following facts are relevant to the question of whether a defendant is appropriately held guilty for an attempt:

(a) The defendant changed his mind.

(b) The defendant would have changed his mind for some reason (e.g, fear of getting caught, renunciation of the criminal enterprise) but was stopped before he had the opportunity.

(c) The defendant would have changed his mind for good reasons (for example, not out of fear of getting caught) but was stopped before he had the opportunity.

(d) The defendant forsakes (what was for all he knew) his last opportunity to change his mind.

(e) The defendant did not change his mind at the point that an ordinary person would have changed his mind.

(f) The defendant would have changed his mind at the point that an ordinary person would have changed his mind, but was stopped before that point.

For any two of these conditions we can imagine circumstances under which one is true and the other is false. So, each captures something a bit different from the others. Which of these is normatively relevant and why will be discussed at some length in chapter 11, where the question of what to do with those who voluntarily abandon their attempts is considered. However, for our purposes here, a more modest observation is in order. If we craft the act element of attempt in such a way that whether or not a person has engaged in an act that suffices for attempt turns on whether or not one or more of (a)–(f) is true, then we are implying that action matters in attempt because of what it says about the firmness of the defendant's commitment. If one of (a)–(f) is true of an agent, then that does indicate that the agent is less firmly committed, over some time interval, to completing the crime than someone of whom the proposition is not true. However, given the arguments of chapters 2 and 3, we know what kind of commitment is required for attempt: an intention-based commitment to each of the components of the completed crime. All of the defendants under discussion, since they are assumed to intend to complete the crime, have that kind of commitment. There is, therefore, an error in trying to incorporate something about firmness of commitment into our account of the act element of attempt. Firmness of commitment might matter, but it doesn't matter for attempt commission, nor for evidence of attempt commission. So long as we have adequate evidence that the defendant has the intention needed for attempt, we have adequate evidence that he is committed in the way necessary for attempt. If the firmness of his commitment is important—and, as we'll see in chapter 11, it is—it is not for reasons that ought to lead us to suggest that whether or not the act element of attempt is present turns on it.

The presence of the act element of attempt does not help us to see that the defendant is firmly enough committed to the completed crime to warrant a finding of guilt. So long as we have adequate evidence of intent, we have all the evidence we need about his *commitment*. Instead, the presence of the act element of attempt helps us to see that the defendant is *guided* by his intention-based commitments in the way that is distinctive of attempt. But change of mind, whether actual or hypothetical, cannot speak to that question. A person can be guided by his commitments and then change his mind; but, still, when this happens he is indeed *guided* by his commitments, and so he is trying, even though he stops doing so as soon as he changes his mind.

It is important to see how this point is already present, in the background, in the Guiding Commitment View. As was discussed in chapter 3 and again in chapters 8 and 9, if a person's intention is animating his behavior in the distinctive way that is involved in trying—if it is motivating, or guiding his behavior—the following counterfactual is true:

*The Completion Counterfactual*: If (1) from t1 to t2 D has the ability and the opportunity to C and does not fall prey to "execution failure", and (2) D does not (at least until after t2) change his mind, then D would C.

The commonplace idea about trying to act which this counterfactual captures— the idea that to be trying to act at a time is to be such that you would act if you had ability and opportunity, did not fail to execute, and did not change your mind—implies that the fact that one would change one's mind after t1, or even that one did *in fact* change one's mind after t1, is irrelevant to the question of whether one is trying to C at t1. If one would change one's mind, or even if one did change one's mind, when assessing whether or not one is guided by one's commitments to the components of C *at t1*, we imagine what would be the case *if one does not change one's mind*. It is built into the very idea of guidance on which the Guiding Commitment View rests that whether or not one is guided by one's commitments at a particular time does not turn on any facts of the sort that (a)–(f) describe. Add to this the idea that the act element of attempt's function is to provide us with evidence in favor of thinking that the Completion Counterfactual is true of the defendant, and we reach the conclusion that there is a serious flaw in any test for the act element of attempt that makes the question of whether the act suffices turn on the truth of propositions like those described in (a)–(f).

These reflections help us to supply Stephen's test with an account of "interruption". They help us, that is, to determine what causes of incompletion need to be imagined away when determining whether or not an agent has engaged in an act sufficient for guilt for attempt: *we need to imagine away all and only those things that interfere with ability or opportunity, ensure execution failure, or prompt change of mind*. In essence, that is, Stephen's test should be understood to assert that a defendant has done enough, at time t1, for attempt of crime C just in case the Completion Counterfactual is true. However, the Completion Counterfactual could be *true* even if the defendant has done nothing at all. This is the lesson, emphasized first in chapter 3, of the fact that it is possible to attempt to perform basic acts. If my intention to raise my arm (which we can assume to be a basic act) causes the release of acetylcholine which, for some reason, fails nonetheless to be taken up by the nerve animating the arm muscle, the Completion Counterfactual is still true. In such a case what we lack is *adequate evidence* that the Completion Counterfactual is true. The crucial question for Stephen, then, must not be merely whether or not the Completion Counterfactual is true of the defendant, but instead whether *we have adequate evidence that it is*. This returns us, then, to the fundamental question that occupied us in chapter 8 in our discussion of the practice of holding defendants guilty of attempt only if they have performed some act as a means to doing as they intend. Under what conditions do we have adequate evidence that the Completion Counterfactual is true? A full answer to that question *just is* the account of the act element of attempt that Stephen was grasping for.

We've seen part of the answer already in chapter 8: the defendant must have performed the act as a means to doing as he intends. But an example that Stephen uses to illustrate his position can help us to identify another condition:

B is a contractor for the supply of meat to a regiment. [D] is B's servant, and his duty is to return the surplus meat to B, after weighing out a certain allowance to each mess. By using a short weight, [D] sets aside, as surplus, sixty pounds instead of fifteen pounds, intending to steal the forty-five pounds, and return the fifteen pounds to B. [D]'s fraud is discovered before he carries the meat away. [D] attempts to steal the forty-five pounds as soon as he sets aside the sixty pounds.[10]

At the point that he sets aside the sixty pounds, D still needs to separate the fifteen that he intends to return to the owner and needs to take possession of the forty-five pounds that remain. Stephen takes the act of setting aside the sixty pounds to suffice for attempt because, presumably, he thinks that there is no question that D would have performed these additional acts, and so would have completed the crime, had he not been stopped. But what is the source of Stephen's confidence about this on the strength, merely, of the few facts reported in his example? One source is his confidence that D is practically competent: Stephen must assume that D will recognize that he has to do these additional things if he is to do as he intends and steal the forty-five pounds of meat. Practical competence is a condition that must be met if the Completion Counterfactual is to be true of a person, as we saw in chapter 9. But this is not all. Someone who recognizes what more he needs to do in order to steal the meat might still fail to do what's necessary, even without changing his mind, if he is not rational.[11] Imagine, for instance, that he believes that he will not carry the forty-five pounds of meat away; perhaps he believes that he will be detected and stopped before he can do this successfully. So, he intends to steal forty-five pounds of meat, believes that carrying the forty-five pounds away is necessary for stealing it, and believes that he will not carry the forty-five pounds away. In such a case, he has an irrational set of intentions and beliefs. He either intends something (namely to carry the meat away) that he believes he will not do, or he fails to intend something (namely to carry the meat away) that he believes he must do if he is to do as he intends. If these are his mental states, is the Completion Counterfactual true? It is hard to see on what basis one would

---

[10] Stephen (1883) §49, 38.

[11] The sense of rationality of relevance here is the attitudinal sense, defined in chapter 2.

insist that it is. To insist on this is to insist that this agent will either find another way to take possession of the meat besides carrying it away, or else he will revise his belief that he cannot carry it away, or else he will do something else to bring his mental states into conformity with the norms of rationality and come to take possession of the meat. Rather, Stephen must be assuming that the agent in his example is rational. Without this assumption, Stephen's belief that the agent would have completed the theft if he had not been stopped, the belief on which the claim that his act suffices for an attempt rests, is groundless.

Now it is important to see that the prosecution generally has a right to assume the defendant's rationality. One reason for this is that all that we can hope to use as evidence of the defendant's mental state is the defendant's behavior, but inferences from behavior to mental states are mediated by a presumption of rationality.[12] Further, if the prosecution were required to establish the defendant's rationality prior to drawing inferences about his mental states from his behavior, the prosecution would have to have some means of providing evidence of his mental states in order to show that those mental states comported with each other and with the defendant's behavior in the way a rational agent's mental states would. But this would require the prosecution to have some means of evidencing mental states distinct from the behavior of the defendant: an evident circle. Still, to say that the prosecution has the right to assume the defendant's rationality is not to say that that this justified presumption could not be overridden, at least in theory, if not in practice. A defendant who provided evidence suggesting that he had formed a plan inconsistent with his beliefs, or with other plans of his, would throw into doubt our judgment to the effect that the Completion Counterfactual is true of him, even if there is no question that he intended to C and performed an act as a means to fulfilling this intention. In this way, the defendant's rationality is much like his practical competence (his ability, that is, to get it right about what needs to be done to do as he intends). The presumption of practical competence guides our judgments about what the defendant would do if he had ability and opportunity and did not change his mind. In rare cases—think, again, of those who try to kill with voodoo—the presumption is shaken and so, in turn, is our confidence in the truth of the Completion Counterfactual. Similarly, one can imagine rare cases in which a defendant's rationality is thrown into doubt sufficiently as to lead us to doubt that the Completion Counterfactual is true of him, even though he has undertaken an act as a means to fulfilling an intention to commit a crime.

Examples that would seem to fit this pattern—examples of agents whose capacity to conform to the norms of rationality seems to be sufficiently severely diminished to shake our ability to say in confidence what they would do if given

---

[12] Donald Davidson called this assumption the "principle of charity" or sometimes the "principle of rational accommodation". See, for instance, Davidson (2001a) and Davidson (2001b).

ability and opportunity and no change of mind—shade into examples in which the insanity defense seems appropriate. John Fischer and Mark Ravizza construct an example of a man who kills someone on the upper deck of a ship and, when asked why, insists that it was because someone on a lower deck was smoking a certain kind of pipe.[13] Further, let's imagine that there is simply no logic to this story: it is not that the smoking of the pipe was thought to signal some calamity that the killing was necessary to prevent, or anything like that. Imagine, instead, that this man simply takes it to be evident to anyone, as it is to him, that the smoking of the pipe provided a reason to kill a third party. Now imagine that this man had yet to strike the fatal blow when he was wrestled to the ground. The question before us, applying Stephen's test, is whether he would have gone through with it had he ability and opportunity and no change of mind. This man seems so radically out of touch with reality that it is difficult to say with confidence that he would have. Any change in this man's environment between the moment that he was stopped and the moment of completion might have been enough to lead him, without change of mind, to stop what he was doing, including changes in his environment that he anticipates at the moment he is stopped. Stopping would not make sense, given the mental states we imagine this man to have, but why assume that this man would do what makes sense? Where the presumption of rationality is shaken, we lose our ability to assess what people would go on to do even given ability, opportunity, and no change of mind.

It would be too quick, however, to suggest that an act in furtherance of a criminal intention suffices for the act element of attempt only if the defendant is practically competent and rational. The reason is that neither practical competence nor rationality is required in one class of cases: so-called "last act" attempts. The quintessential example of a last act attempt is firing a bullet at someone's heart, while acting on an intention to kill, but failing to kill because the victim is wearing a bulletproof vest. In such a case, the Completion Counterfactual is true *even if the defendant is not practically competent and not rational*. After all, to imagine that such a defendant has the ability and opportunity to kill is merely to imagine that the victim was not wearing a bulletproof vest. In that event, the defendant would have killed him, even if the defendant were not practically competent and not rational. Notice, however, that the presumptions of rationality and practical competence matter in those cases in which the defendant *falsely believes* that he has performed the last act, but would in fact need to do more in order to perform an act that would serve as the act element of the completed crime. Imagine, for instance, that the bullet missed, but, even if it had been aimed correctly it would not have killed the victim since he was wearing a bulletproof vest. In such a case, the defendant would have had to fire a second shot, but imagine that he is wrestled to the ground before he could do so. If the defendant is practically competent,

---

[13] Fischer and Ravizza (1998), 65.

rational, and fired the first shot as a means to killing the victim, then we can be confident that he would have killed him had he had ability and opportunity and no change of mind—he would have killed him, that is, had he not been wrestled to the ground, but had the opportunity to take the second shot, this time at the victim's head. Last acts suffice for the act element of attempt in the absence of practical competence and rationality only in cases in which they are *actually* the last act, and not in cases in which they are merely believed falsely by the defendant to be the last act required.

We are now in position to offer an account of the act element of attempt, an account that I take to be a development of Stephen's view. Here, as before, D is a defendant and C is a crime. $A_D$ is the token act actually performed by D, and $A_C$ is a type of act that suffices for the act element of C; $A_C$, that is, is the act involved in the completed crime:

$A_D$ suffices for the act element of an attempt to C *if and only if*

(1) $A_D$ is the "last act"; that is: (i) $A_D$ is a token of $A_C$, or (ii) if D had ability and opportunity to C, $A_D$ would have been a token of $A_C$,

OR

(2) $A_D$ is not the "last act", but (i) $A_D$ is performed as a means to C, & (ii) D is both practically competent and rational.

Clause (1)(i) captures those cases in which what the defendant did actually meets the description of the act required for the completed crime; the defendant receives property that is not stolen, for instance. In such a case, we have the act element of the completed crime, even if we do not have the completed crime because other elements are missing. In other examples, the defendant will have performed an act that would serve for the act element of the completed crime but falls short of completion because of an absent result element of the completed crime. Imagine someone who successfully deceives another person intending to cause that person pecuniary loss, but fails to cause pecuniary loss through the deception. Such a person has performed an act that suffices for an attempt to commit the crime of causing pecuniary loss through deception.

Clause (1)(ii) captures those cases in which the defendant would have performed an act that suffices for the act element of the completed crime had he had ability and opportunity *and even in the absence of practical competence and rationality*. If the act element of murder is "killing", but the defendant's act fails to fall under this description simply because his victim was wearing a bullet-proof vest, to return to that example, then the act suffices for an attempted murder, since if the defendant had had ability and opportunity (had the vest been missing) the act would have been one of killing.

Clause (2) is intended to capture those cases in which we reach the conclusion that the defendant would have performed the act involved in completion had he had ability and opportunity and no change of mind, only by assuming that the defendant is both practically competent and rational, assumptions that are false of some defendants. In these cases, we need to make a prior judgment to the effect that the act was performed as a means to committing the crime if rationality and practical competence are going to help us to reach the conclusion that the defendant would have done enough for completion had he had ability and opportunity and did not change his mind.

We have identified, then, both necessary and sufficient conditions that an act must meet if it is to serve as the act element of an attempted crime. The driving idea is that an act suffices just in case it provides us with adequate evidence that the defendant would complete an act that suffices for the completed crime given ability, opportunity, and no change of mind. This, it has been suggested, was the idea motivating Stephen's test, an idea that was lost through developments of that approach by the advocates of the probable desistance tests, including the version developed by Robert Skilton.

The geographical metaphor is extremely attractive. Like many metaphors, it seems to fit because it expresses some underlying valuable idea that is difficult to articulate without its help. But to rest with the metaphor, and not to find a way of expressing the underlying idea without it, is to risk inferring false conclusions about the act element of attempt from true conclusions about distances between geographical points. So what idea does the geographical metaphor express? The answer is that it expresses the idea that to be trying to act is to be engaging in action that would lead to completion given ability, opportunity, no "execution failure", and no change of mind. If the tank is full, the road is clear, and you don't turn back, the person who is trying will get where he is going. The metaphor is apt, not because the distance between attempt and completion, like geographical distances, is quantifiable, or even measurable in some other way, but because it is natural to represent plans graphically with start points, end points, and waystations. However, once we recognize the source of the metaphor's attraction, and are able to identify the crucial question, we find that the metaphor fades away. What matters is only what we can infer about what the agent would have done given ability, opportunity, no "execution failure", and no change of mind. As we will see in the next section, we reach the same conclusion by starting in a different place, namely in the view that the line between acts that are enough for attempt and those that are not is to be drawn by attending to what they express about the agent's intention.

## 3. Expression of Intention

A distinction is sometimes drawn between those who think of attempt liability in "objective" terms and those who think of it in "subjective" terms. The objectivists, on this line, conceive of attempts as wrong because they impinge in some way on the interests of others, perhaps by risking interference with legally protected interests. The subjectivists, by contrast, are thought to conceive of attempts as wrong because they express a willingness on the part of the defendant to make and act on objectionable choices. Construed from within this framework, the objectivists are likely to concoct tests for the act element of attempt that look to the relation between the defendant's act and the act involved in completion, both of which are to be considered independently of the agent's intention. By contrast, the subjectivists, on this view, are likely to concoct tests under which a defendant's act suffices for attempt if it tells us that the defendant has made and acted on an objectionable choice. Thus the sorts of tests under discussion in section 2—the various "proximity" tests, such as the dangerous proximity tests, the probable desistance tests, and Stephen's test—are all thought to fit in the objectivist camp: they are efforts to characterize the acts sufficient for the act element of attempt as those that are close enough to the act involved in completion to warrant guilt for attempt. From this point of view, then, choosing between tests for the act element of attempt is really a matter of settling the deep underlying dispute between objectivists and subjectivists.

One of the lessons of the present section will be that the objectivist–subjectivist divide is artificial when it comes to the act element of attempt. So long as both sides criminalize attempts because they are *attempts* (in contrast, for instance, to crimes of risk-creation), and so long as both sides accept that there can be no guilt for commission of an attempt in the absence of adequate evidence of commission of an attempt, the two sides should converge in their conception of the act required for an attempt. It is only when we fail to attend to the nature of trying to act—and, particularly, to the fact that trying to act involves *guidance* by one's commitments of the sort that guarantees completion given ability, opportunity, no "execution failure", and no change of mind—that we see that there is a difference of substance between a view that looks, in crafting a test for the act element of attempt, to the gap between attempt and completion, and one that looks, instead, to the expression of intention. In fact, they amount to the same thing.

Perhaps the first explicit appeal to expression of intention as marking the line relevant to the act element of attempt was the "unequivocality" test, or "*res ipsa loquitur*" test, which was the law for a period of time in New Zealand.[14] According to the unequivocality test, the defendant's act suffices for attempt if and only if it is "in itself sufficient evidence of the criminal intent with which it is done".[15] J. W. Cecil Turner, who is probably the most unflinching advocate of this approach, puts it this way:

---

[14] Such law was based on judicial interpretation of the New Zealand Crimes Act 1908, §93(2).
[15] *Barker* (NZLR 865 (1924)), quoted in Duff (1996), 49.

The *actus reus* of an attempt to commit a specific crime is constituted when the accused person does an act which is a step towards commission of that specific crime, and the doing of such act can have no other purpose than the commission of that specific crime.[16]

Turner's idea is that an act performed as a means to completing a crime suffices for attempt just in case it provides sufficient evidence of the defendant's criminal intention, even considered in the absence of other evidence of intent such as confessions and other acts expressive of intent but not performed in furtherance of it.

Glanville Williams presents a number of decisive counterexamples to the position. Consider two:

D presents a revolver at P and tries to pull the trigger. Apart from his confession it may not be clear whether he intends (a) to murder, (b) to wound, or (c) to frighten. Surely he can be convicted of attempting any one of these crimes if his confession shows the requisite *mens rea*.

D goes up to a haystack, fills his pipe, and lights a match. The act of lighting the match, even to a suspicious-minded person, is ambiguous. It may indicate only that D is going to light his pipe; but perhaps, on the other hand, the pipe is only a "blind" and D is really bent on setting fire to the stack. We do not know.[17]

Williams is right that these are counterexamples. Duff, adopting Williams's pipe example, points out that, under the unequivocality test, whether the man has done enough for an attempted arson when he lights the match might turn on whether or not he has a pipe in his mouth at the time, something that ought not matter to the question.[18]

But despite its flaws, it is important to see that the unequivocality approach is a response to a genuine evidential challenge. To see this, distinguish between the following two kinds of act:

*Is a Means*: An act falls into this category if it is a means to doing as one intends.
*Performed as a Means*: An act falls into this category if it is intentional under the description "a means to doing as I intend".

There are cases in which agents perform acts that are means to doing as they intend, but don't perform them for that reason, or under that description; there are acts, that is, that are in the "Is a Means" category, but not the "Peformed as a Means". Imagine that the man in Williams' pipe example does intend to light the stack on fire, but has lit the match, not for that purpose, but merely to light his pipe. He is committed by his intention to lighting the stack but is not guided by that commitment. Such a person has performed an act that is a means to doing as he intends, but he has not performed an act that is intentional under

---

[16] Turner (1935), 236.     [17] Williams (1961), 630.     [18] Duff (1996), 52–3.

the description "a means to doing as I intend". To have evidence that the Completion Counterfactual is true—to have evidence, that is, that the defendant would have completed the crime given ability, opportunity, and no change of mind—we need an act that is intentional under the description "a means to doing as I intend"; an act that is a means does not provide the necessary evidence of guidance without a showing to the effect that it was intentional under that description.

In practice, it is difficult to determine whether a person who has performed an act that is a means to doing as he intends has performed it under that description. Determining that the agent has the intention to commit the crime is not sufficient, since he might not be acting on that intention in performing the act. The unequivocality test exploits a condition that, when met, provides sufficient evidence that the act is intentional under the description "a means to doing as I intend": if there is no other reason why the defendant would perform the act, and the defendant did indeed intend to commit the crime, then it is beyond a reasonable doubt that he performed it for the reason that it is a means to committing the crime. The problem, which is illustrated by Williams' counterexamples, is that the equivocality test treats as a *necessary* condition for the act element of attempt a condition that is sufficient but not necessary: it is common enough for people to perform acts as means that *could* have been performed for some other reason, but were not *in fact*. The equivocality test acquits all such people, which is an error. But we can acknowledge this while still recognizing the difficulty of the problem. What more do we need, over and above the facts that (i) a person intends a crime, and (ii) performs an act that is a means to completion of it, if we are to have adequate evidence that he performed the act *as* a means to completion of the crime?

Perhaps more so when considering the topic before us than with respect to any other part of criminal law, judges express pessimism about the possibility of "hard and fast" rules for determining whether a defendant's act suffices for the act element of attempt. When faced with the present question, it is easy to see why. That a person's act is performed in furtherance of an intention that he has, and not for some other reason, is not the sort of thing that admits of direct evidence. However, it is nonetheless possible to make progress. Start by noting that inferring that a person is acting on a particular intention when he acts is very closely allied to inferring from his act that he *has* a particular intention. A man lights a match, and from this (together with facts about his circumstances and some background knowledge about his motives, perhaps) we infer that he intends to burn a haystack. A premise in our reasoning in this case is the fact that lighting a match is a means to burning a haystack. Once we reach the conclusion that the man intends to burn the haystack, we can reach a further conclusion: his act of lighting the match was intentional under the description "a means to burning a haystack" or, equivalently, he lit the match in order to burn the haystack. We can use the fact that the man's act is in the "Is a Means" category in order to first infer that he has a certain intention, and then we can go on to infer that his act is in the "Performed as a Means" category.

Contrast this kind of inference with another sort: inferring that a person has a particular intention from the fact that he performs an act that is merely expressive of intent. Imagine, for instance, that the man says, "I intend to burn the haystack." From this verbal act (together with facts about the man's circumstances, and background motives, etc.) we are able to infer that the man intends to burn the haystack. But having reached this conclusion we are not in a position to say that the act of reporting his intention was performed as a means to burning the haystack: it wasn't. The reason that we are not able to reach this conclusion in this case, but we are able to reach such a conclusion in the first case, is that the inference from lighting the match to intending to burn the haystack used the claim that lighting a match is a means to burning a haystack as a premise. No such premise was involved in the inference from the verbal report to the intention. To explain, notice that the first line of reasoning went like this:

1. D lit a match.
2. Lighting a match is a means to burning a haystack.
3. People who undertake acts that are means to doing things ordinarily intend to do those things.
4. ∴ D intended to burn a haystack.
5. ∴ D lit the match as a means to burning the haystack.

The second went like this:

1'. D said that he intended to burn a haystack.
2'. People who say that they have an intention ordinarily have that intention.
3'. ∴ D intended to burn a haystack.

Premise 2 in the first line of reasoning is part of what allows us to infer 4 from 3. But since there is no analogue to premise 2 in the second line of reasoning—the verbal report is not a means to burning the haystack—we cannot infer from 3' that D said that he intended to burn a haystack as a means to burning it.

What this shows is that where one is justified in reaching a conclusion about what a person intends on the basis of reasoning that uses the fact that his act was a means, one is also in a position to assert that the act was performed *as a means*. The equivocality test is a failed effort to solve the problem of specifying the conditions under which we can infer that a person performed an act as a means, from the fact that his act is a means. What these reflections tell us is that we can make such an inference whenever we can infer what his intention is from his action while using the premise that his act is a means to fulfilling such an intention. So we have a natural test for determining when an act that is a means to C was performed *as a* means to C: can we infer that the defendant intends to C from both the fact that he performed the act and the fact that the act is a means to C? If yes, then the act was performed as a means; if no, then it was not.

Although the framers of the *Model Penal Code* do not put it this way, I contend that they use precisely this idea in their account of the act element of attempt. Section 5.01 of the *Model Penal Code* distinguishes three types of attempts like so:

(1) *Definition of Attempt.* A person is guilty of an attempt to commit a crime if, acting with the kind of culpability otherwise required for commission of the crime, he:

    (a) purposely engages in conduct that would constitute the crime if the attendant circumstances were as he believes them to be; or

    (b) when causing a particular result is an element of the crime, does or omits to do anything with the purpose of causing or with the belief that it will cause such result without further conduct on his part; or

    (c) purposely does or omits to do anything that, under the circumstances as he believes them to be, is an act or omission constituting a substantial step in a course of conduct planned to culminate in his commission of the crime.

Section 5.01(1)(a) and Section 5.01(1)(b) identify the two types of "last act" attempts of the sort discussed in section 2 of this chapter. An attempt falls under §5.01(1)(a) if the defendant performed an act that would serve as the act element of the completed crime: there is no gap between the act involved in the attempt and that involved in completion. These are cases, for instance, of people who receive unstolen property that they believe to have been stolen. The act of receiving the property is sufficient for completion of the act element of the crime of receipt of stolen property. An attempt falls under §5.01(1)(b) if the defendant performed an act that would have sufficed for the act involved in completion had it caused results that it did not in fact cause. These are, essentially, those cases in which ability and opportunity would suffice for performance of the act involved in completion even if the defendant had changed his mind, since nothing is left for the defendant to do beyond what he in fact did. The case of shooting the person who is wearing the bulletproof vest is such a case. Section 5.01(1)(c) is intended to capture those remaining attempts in which the act falls short of that involved in completion, and the addition of ability, opportunity, and no "execution failure", would not suffice to make the act of the sort involved in completion; change of mind would defeat performance of such an act. So, we reach the conclusion from this that the following is the *Model Penal Code*'s test. Here, as before, D is a defendant, C is a crime, $A_D$ is the token act actually performed by D, and $A_C$ is a type of act that suffices for the act element of C:

$A_D$ suffices for the act element of an attempt to C *if and only if*

(1) $A_D$ is the "last act". That is: (i) $A_D$ is a token of $A_C$, or (ii) If D had ability and opportunity to C, $A_D$ would have been a token of $A_C$,

OR

(2) $A_D$ is not the "last act", but $A_D$ is a substantial step towards $A_C$.

The underlined portion distinguishes this test from the test proposed at the end of section 2, which was a development of Stephen's test. There the cases of action that were not "last acts" were taken to be sufficient for the act element of attempt when performed as means to C by a defendant both practically competent and rational. What I will now show is that an act counts as a substantial step under the *Model Penal Code* just in case these two conditions are met. The notion of a substantial step and the notion of an act performed as a means by a practically competent and rational agent are one and the same.

How are we to understand the notion of a "substantial step"? The next section of the *Model Penal Code*, §5.01(2), reads as follows:

(2) *Conduct That May Be Held Substantial Step Under Subsection (1)(c).* Conduct shall not be held to constitute a substantial step under Subsection (1)(c) of this Section unless it is strongly corroborative of the actor's criminal purpose.

What is meant by "strongly corroborative of the actor's criminal purpose"? The idea appears to be that, together with other evidence, we can infer that the defendant intends to C *from the act*. The approach differs from the equivocality approach since it allows the inference from the act to the intention to appeal to other facts about the defendant—background facts of the sort that must be appealed to in order for a line of thought such as that outlined in premises 1–5 above to go through. Further, it is clear that the framers of the code do not want to allow action merely expressive of intent to be "strongly corroborative" of the intent. We see this from the examples that the code provides of action that "shall not be held insufficient [for the act element of attempt] as a matter of law":

(a) lying in wait, searching for or following the contemplated victim of the crime;

(b) enticing or seeking to entice the contemplated victim of the crime to go to the place contemplated for its commission;

(c) reconnoitering the place contemplated for the commission of the crime;

(d) unlawful entry of a structure, vehicle or enclosure in which it is contemplated that the crime will be committed;

(e) possession of materials to be employed in the commission of the crime, that are specially designed for such unlawful use or that can serve no lawful purpose of the actor under the circumstances;

(f) possession, collection or fabrication of materials to be employed in the commission of the crime, at or near the place contemplated for its commission, if such possession, collection or fabrication serves no lawful purpose of the actor under the circumstances;

(g) soliciting an innocent agent to engage in conduct constituting an element of the crime.

These are all examples of actions that are means to completing a crime. So the idea that we find in the *Model Penal Code* is that wherever we find action that can support an inference to intent *while using the premise that the act is a means*, we find action that suffices for attempt even though it falls short of the act involved in completion. Or, in other words, the *Model Penal Code* is offering the following test for determining if an act is a substantial step, precisely the test that we reached through reflection on the flaws in the equivocality approach: can we infer that the defendant intends to C from the fact that he performed the act and while using the fact that the act is a means to C as a premise? If yes, then the act was a substantial step; if no, then it was not.

On this approach, our capacity to make an inference—namely an inference from the fact that D performed a means to C to his having the intention to C—serves as grounds for describing his act in a different way, namely as performed *as a* means to C. The approach then comports with Oliver Wendell Holmes's famous remark that even a dog can distinguish between being stumbled over and being kicked.[19] The thought is that we can rely on our capacity to judge intent from the consideration of action, even if we do not know how we do it. Typically, this is thought to be relevant to the question of how we determine a defendant's intent. But the *Model Penal Code* approach uses it in a different way. Where we have the capacity to infer intent from action we have a particular kind of *action*, namely action performed in furtherance of intent. But that kind of action is crucial for attempt. But once we recognize this, then the requirement that the defendant's action be "strongly corroborative" of criminal intent drops away. What matters is that the act is performed as a means to committing the crime. Very rarely, and perhaps never, are we able to conclude that this is true without being able to reach a conclusion about the defendant's intention on the basis of his conduct. But, still, in appealing to action "strongly corroborative" of criminal intent, the *Model Penal Code* has merely identified a proxy for action performed in furtherance of intention.

Now we have already seen why action in furtherance of intent is crucial to attempt. In chapter 8 it was argued that it is crucial because where there is action performed in furtherance of intent, there is indispensable evidence that the defendant would have completed the crime given ability, opportunity, no "execution failure", and no change of mind. And we have seen what else must be true if we are to have adequate evidence that this counterfactual is true: the agent must be both practically competent in the relevant respect and rational. When the *Model Penal Code*'s approach is revised to accommodate these facts,

---

[19] Holmes (1881), 3.

we find that it is precisely the same as the test that we reach when we develop Stephen's view in order to accord with the facts about trying to act and about indispensable evidence of trying to act. An act that is not the "last act" suffices for attempt just in case it is performed as a means to completing the crime by a practically competent and rational agent.

## 4. Mere Preparation

It is important to see how the account of the act element of attempt offered here aligns with the powerful intuition that some acts that are means to completion should nonetheless be understood as "mere preparation", and so as insufficient for the act element of attempt.[20] D, anticipating that he will need strength for the robbery that he is planning for later in the day, has an extra bowl of cereal for breakfast. Having an extra bowl of cereal is a means to committing the robbery, but it seems completely unacceptable to hold D guilty of an attempted robbery on the grounds that he had an extra bowl of breakfast cereal. Last acts, much less acts that are, themselves, sufficient for the act element of the completed crime, are never classified as "mere preparation", so the question is whether merely preparatory acts of this sort are classified as sufficient for the act element of attempt under clause (2) of the account offered here.

They are not. The reason is that there is reasonable doubt as to whether they are performed as a means. We can see this from consideration of such cases, either from the point of view of the geographical metaphor or from the point of view of the expression of intention. Take the expression of intention first. Can we infer from the fact that D has an extra bowl of cereal that he intends to commit a robbery? Even if D is practically competent and rational we cannot infer this from the act alone. So we need other evidence. That alone, however, does not show that the act is insufficient for the act element of attempt, since we need other evidence of intent, also, in the case of the man with the pipe who lights the match. But, unlike that case, in this one the other evidence must be sufficient all by itself to show that D has the intention to commit the robbery. Say, for instance, that D told a friend that he intended to commit a robbery, but the friend was unsure if he was joking. This bit of evidence, let's assume, is not sufficient to show intent. If the prosecution, in order to show that the defendant was not joking, brings forth the fact that D had an extra bowl of cereal, they will be laughed out of court. The problem is that we can think of many other intentions that would motivate that behavior, so, even if we have no reason to think that D has any of those other intentions, we still lack sufficient evidence from which to infer that he performs the relevant act as a means to

---

[20] The next few paragraphs have benefited greatly from discussion with Jacob Ross.

completing the robbery. This isn't to say that he doesn't, but only that the fact that the act is a means to committing the robbery does not license us to reach the inference that he is performing it as a means to doing so. Thus, the act of having the extra bowl of cereal does not suffice for the act element of the attempt.

Nothing just said depends on construing the view proposed here in the way preferred by those who place emphasis on action expressive of intention. We reach the same result by treating the test as a precise specification of Stephen's test, as in the previous section of this chapter. Even when we imagine away all of those things that interfere with D's ability or opportunity to commit the robbery, and imagine away "execution failure" and change of mind, the mere fact that the agent, even if he is practically competent and rational, is undertaking a means to the robbery—which he is, by hypothesis—he may not commit the robbery. To ensure that he commits it, it must further be the case that it is the intention to commit the robbery that is causing him to eat his extra bowl of breakfast cereal. But, as just noted, there are many different possible intentions that could be motivating that behavior. And this possibility supplies reasonable doubt that he is performing the act as a means to committing the robbery. Even if some of these intentions were formed precisely because the defendant intends to commit the robbery, it still might not be that intention that is causing him to eat his breakfast cereal. And so he might not be performing that act as a means to committing the robbery. "Mere preparations", then, ought to be construed as acts that are means to doing as intended, but which, for all we know, are not performed as means to doing as intended.

The view offered here is a hybrid of two well-known tests for the act element of attempt—namely the "first act" test and the "last act" test. Each of these tests is individually indefensible, but the test that results when they are combined, I suggest, captures the truth. Last acts are sufficient for the act element of attempt, but not necessary. Last act tests are usually criticized on this ground since, under them, *only* last acts suffice. But this is no criticism of the view proposed here since, under it, an act needn't be a last act to suffice for the act element of attempt. First acts, many have felt, are not enough to warrant criminal liability for attempt. But this concern is ameliorated by the remarks just offered regarding "mere preparations", as well as by the requirement that a first act suffices for guilt only if performed by an agent who is practically competent and rational. The counterexamples to the claim that first acts are insufficient, I contend, are all examples that are not classified as sufficient for the act element of attempt under the view on offer. This includes first acts performed as means by agents who are not both practically competent and rational, and acts such as "mere preparations" in which we lack sufficient evidence that they are performed as means, even though they are means. Thus, the view proposed here, in addition to uniting the two dominant approaches to the act element of attempt—namely those that appeal to the geographical metaphor and those that appeal to the expression of intention—also captures what is right about two of the simplest accounts of the act element of attempt, namely the "first act" and "last act" tests.

## 5. Conclusion

As indicated at the opening of section 3, commentators have sometimes said that there is a great divide in thinking about criminal attempts that is reflected in competing accounts of the act element of attempt. The objectivists think of attempts as dangerous acts to be minimized for the same reasons as any other dangerous acts. The subjectivists think of attempts as reflective of faulty commitments to objectionable principles. There is a divide here reflected in competing conceptions of the justification for the criminalization of attempt. (In chapter 1, I came out in favor of the subjectivist position on that issue.) Still, what has been argued here is that the divide is not reflected in a deep way in competing conceptions of the act element of attempt. When the haze before the eyes of those on both sides is cleared, we find them to be in fundamental agreement. When we recognize that "proximity" is just a way of capturing the idea that some would, and some would not, complete the crime given ability, opportunity, no "execution failure", and no change of mind, we come to see the view to which those who accept proximity to completion as the dividing line are committed. They are committed to the view that both "last acts" and acts performed as means to completion by the practically competent and rational suffice for the act element of attempt. And when we recognize that the capacity of an act to be used to infer an agent's intention is merely a proxy for the idea that the act was not merely a means to completion of the crime but was performed *as a means* to completion, then we come to see the view that those who take expression of criminal intention to mark the dividing line are committed to. They are committed to the very same position. When it comes to the act element of attempt, subjectivists and objectivists ought to get along.

# Part 4

# Sentencing Attempts

# 11

# Abandonment and Change of Mind

## 1. Introduction

To this point in this book various questions about attempted crimes have been answered using one of two approaches. Either the answer to the question has been derived from consideration of *what it is* to commit an attempt, or from consideration of *what evidence is* required to support the claim that a defendant committed an attempt. So, as an example of the first approach, it was argued in chapter 6, through consideration of what is involved in attempt commission, that, despite the law's resistance, it is perfectly possible to attempt a crime of negligence or recklessness, a crime that cannot be completed with intent. It follows, that is, from the Guiding Commitment view of trying that such attempts are perfectly possible. And, as an example of the second approach, it was suggested in chapter 8, that the requirement for guilt for attempt of an act in furtherance of a criminal intention derives from the need for adequate evidence of attempt commission, and not from what it is to commit an attempt; it is possible to commit an attempt without performing any act in furtherance of one's intention, but in such cases we necessarily lack adequate evidence of attempt. As the previous chapters of this book demonstrate, these two approaches are fruitful: several problems that courts have not known how to solve are soluble when approached in one of these two ways, and several practices that courts now engage in can be justified when considered in one or the other of these two ways. However, two long-standing issues concerned with attempted crimes cannot be addressed adequately through either of these two approaches.

The first issue, which is not to be discussed in this chapter, but in the next, concerns the broad issue of the relevance to sentencing of results, an issue that arises vividly in the sentencing of attempts. Should a person who falls short of causing a bad result be given a lesser sentence than one who, acting from the same mental states and in the same circumstances, does indeed cause it? This question is pressing when it comes to the consideration of the proper legal treatment of attempted crimes since it is common enough to find that the only difference between one who attempts a crime and fails, on the one hand, and one who succeeds, on the other, is in the results caused. If results matter to sentencing, we need to know why they do and how. We cannot answer this question through consideration of what it is to commit an attempt, or through consideration of what evidence of commission of an attempt is needed for guilt. After all, the question of the relevance of results to sentencing proceeds from the assumption that the defendant to be sentenced has committed an attempt and has been adequately shown to have done so by the evidence. Instead, the relevance, if any, of the absence of results to the sentencing of an attempt must be assessed by appeal to an account of the reasons for which the penal sanction is issued. It might turn out that in the absence of a bad result, we have one fewer reason to sanction than we have when there is a result. Or it might not. But answering the question requires examination of the variety of reasons that there are for sanctioning.

The second issue, linked to the first, as we will see in this chapter, through their common connection to the reasons for sanctioning, concerns the relevance of abandonment of one's attempt to the sentence for it. Consider the example, singled out in this context by Joshua Dressler,[1] of Arin Ahmed, a Palestinian who tried to kill a number of Jews in a public place through a suicide bombing, but changed her mind before the plan was complete. Here is how Ahmed describes how it came to pass that she stopped herself before anyone was hurt:

I got out of the car ... I saw a lot of people, mothers with children, teenage boys and girls. I remembered an Israeli girl my age whom I used to be in touch with. I suddenly understood what I was about to do and I said to myself: How can I do such a thing? I changed my mind.[2]

There is no doubting the prevalence and strength of the intuition that someone like Ahmed is importantly different, and ought to be treated differently under the law, from someone who got out of the car, intent on a suicide bombing, and was wrestled to the ground by police before any damage could be done. The fact of change of mind seems intuitively to be of tremendous ethical importance to responsibility for attempt. In fact, the *Model Penal Code* gives expression to this idea in its affirmative defense of abandonment. Under *Model Penal Code* §5.01(4), a person who abandons an attempt (under certain conditions that appear to be met in Ahmed's case) has an affirmative defense from the charge.[3] Twenty-six jurisdictions in the United States have adopted the *Model Penal*

---

[1] Dressler (2003), 800.

[2] Levy-Barzilai (2002), 17, 21.

[3] The *Model Penal Code* provides for abandonment defenses to conspiracy, and solicitation as well. See §5.02(3) and §5.03(6).

*Code*'s approach,[4] and even commentators who oppose it, mostly favor, instead, granting mitigation, rather than a complete defense, to those who, like Ahmed, abandon their attempts for laudatory reasons.[5] It is very hard these days to find anyone defending the common law position that abandonment is of no relevance to guilt for attempt. Even judges in jurisdictions that have never granted a defense or mitigation on the basis of abandonment tend to avoid asserting that none is to be granted, as a matter of law, in their jurisdiction. For instance, while there is officially no abandonment defense in the United States' federal law, federal judges faced with the question tend to do their best to avoid the issue by claiming that even if abandonment were a defense, or provided mitigation, the defendant before them provided insufficient evidence of abandonment of the sort that would provide defense or mitigate.[6] In fact, we see this even in cases in which the evidence of abandonment is as good or better than the evidence in many cases in other jurisdictions in which defense or mitigation has been granted on the basis of abandonment.

But many questions need to be answered if we are to be satisfied that those who abandon their attempts ought to receive no punishment at all, as under the *Model Penal Code*, or even if we are to be satisfied that they should receive less than those who do not abandon, as under the view of most of those commentators who oppose the *Model Penal Code*'s approach. Some of the questions that need to be answered arise from comparison with other defendants who change their minds. If there is an explanation for granting defense or mitigation on the basis of abandonment to those who attempt crimes, does that explanation extend, also, to those who complete crimes but are genuinely and wholeheartedly remorseful? What about the various "substantive" inchoate crimes such as burglary and larceny that include as an element an intention that never comes to fruition (an intention to commit a felony, an intention never to return a piece of property)?

Further, there is at least one important question to ask about abandonment that does not arise from comparing defendants who abandon attempts to other kinds of defendants who change their minds. Moral intuition (not to mention legal codes, like the *Model Penal Code*) supports the idea that the defendant's motive for abandoning his attempt is of crucial importance to the question of whether or not to punish or reduce the defendant's punishment. To give the most obvious example, a defendant who abandons his attempt because he discovers that if he goes through with the crime he will be caught—perhaps a police car happens to be passing by unexpectedly—does not deserve a defense or mitigation. There are other examples too. A defendant who stalks a victim

---

[4] Lee (1997), 120 n13.

[5] For example, Lee (1997).

[6] See, for instance, *State v. Patten* (489 A.2d 657 (1985)), *Hampton v. State* (468 N.E.2d 1077 (1984)), *United States v. Shelton* (1994 Fed. App. 0266P), and *United States v. Tanks* (978 F.2d 1260 (1992)).

intending a robbery, but decides to wait until later to complete it when he comes to believe that if he waits he can commit the robbery after the victim has visited an ATM machine, does not deserve a defense or mitigation. Broadly speaking, we recognize various impure motives for abandoning, motives importantly different from Ahmed's motives, that undermine whatever mitigating force the abandonment has. But why is this? Whatever rationale we give for granting a defense or mitigation on the basis of abandonment must support the idea that the motive for abandonment matters: a bad motive for abandoning can undermine abandonment's mitigating force.

It should be noted that one possible rationale for granting an abandonment defense—a rationale under which mitigation for abandonment would be insufficient and only a defense would do—has already been rejected in chapter 10 in a different guise. One might think that sometimes the fact that a defendant abandons his attempt shows that he fell short of performing an act that suffices for guilt for attempt. To take this approach is to accept an account of the act element of attempt under which absence of abandonment is a necessary condition for performance of an act that would serve as the act element. Accounts of the act element having this implication were rejected in chapter 10 on the grounds, primarily, that they imply that two agents can have performed precisely the same acts from the same mental states and in the same circumstances up to a particular time, while one and not the other has acted in a way sufficient for attempt. Here it is worth raising the further objection that such a view is powerless to explain why the motive for abandonment matters. If abandonment matters because when there's abandonment there's no act sufficient for the act element of attempt, then both those who abandon for bad reasons and those for good are equally undeserving of punishment for attempt: if the act element's missing then there is no attempt, whatever the motives for abandonment. Such a view, therefore, has unsatisfactory implications, independently of the objections offered against it in chapter 10.

Notice that an approach according to which only unabandoned attempts involve acts sufficient for attempt, were it to succeed, would derive the abandonment defense from the conditions that must be met if we are to have adequate evidence of attempt. After all, under the view presented in chapter 8, an act is necessary for attempt only because it is necessary evidence of guidance by one's commitments, guidance of the sort that is involved, under the Guiding Commitment View, in trying to act. If the fact that a defendant abandoned his attempt shows that he did not perform a relevant act, then it does so by showing that there is inadequate evidence of attempt. But such an approach fails. A person can be guided by his commitments to each of the components of success—he can be truly trying to commit a crime and evidence this through his behavior—and then, later, change his mind and abandon his plan. At the point that we recognize this, it becomes clear that the prospects for answering any of the various questions about abandonment through appeal to what is involved in committing an attempt, or through what evidence is needed of commission of an attempt, are dim at best. Abandonment, of the sort that seems to have independent normative significance, happens after an attempt has already been committed. Similarly, such abandonment seems to be of normative relevance even when we have adequate evidence that the defendant committed an attempt, and so it cannot be explained and justified through the second approach adopted earlier with respect to various attempt doctrines. We therefore need a new approach.

The approach developed in this chapter exploits the best rationale for the undeniable fact that the sanction for completion sets the ceiling for the sanction for attempt; it would never be appropriate to give a greater sanction to the attempter than would have been appropriately given to him if he had completed the crime. This is not to say that there are *no* attempted murders, for instance, that are not rightly sanctioned more heavily than *some* completed murders. Rather, it is to say that no attempted murder is rightly sanctioned more heavily than that very murder would have been rightly sanctioned had it been completed. The best rationale for this is that every reason to sanction attempt is a reason to sanction completion, even though there are additional reasons to sanction completion that are not reasons to sanction attempt. Only if there were reasons to sanction attempt that were not reasons to sanction completion would it be acceptable to give a greater penalty to an attempt than to completion of that attempt. It is argued here that abandonment of completion mitigates the sanction *for completion*: one of the reasons for sanctioning at a particular level, rather than at a lower level, does not apply when the crime was abandoned before completion. It is then argued that this ground for mitigation of the sanction for completion is also a ground for mitigation of the attempt. From this it follows that abandonment mitigates attempt. It is the burden of section 2 to make this argument in some detail and to address objections to it. It is also argued in that section that the rationale offered for abandonment-based mitigation for attempt explains why the defendant's motive for abandoning matters. Section 3 explains how the rationale for abandonment-based mitigation in attempt offered in section 2 extends, or fails to extend, to other cases in which defendants change their minds. It is argued that there are not the same reasons to mitigate for remorse, even wholehearted remorse that, had it occurred earlier, would have resulted in abandonment. Nor are there the same reasons to mitigate for abandonment of substantive inchoate crimes like burglary or larceny as there are for abandoned attempts.

## 2. A Rationale for Abandonment-Based Mitigation

This section argues that abandonment of an attempt mitigates; it does not excuse or justify and so should not be treated as an affirmative defense. An attempter who abandons has committed a crime—the crime of attempt—and this fact is not erased by his abandonment, nor are most of the reasons for punishing attempts negated by it.

What needs to be shown in order to show that abandonment mitigates? Mitigating and aggravating factors are never decisive. When such a factor is present, there is a reason for issuing a lower or higher sentence, or one fewer reason not to; the reasons in question rarely settle the question of what sanction to give. Hence a mitigating factor could be present and yet it might make sense to give the defendant a *greater* than typical sentence because there are several aggravating factors present also. Similarly, a mitigating factor might be present, but there may be a reason for sanctioning that is in no way lessened by the presence of the mitigating factor and which supports issuing a typically sized sanction. In such cases, a mitigating factor is present, but makes no difference to the final sentence. In this way, mitigating and aggravating factors are importantly different from either justifications or excuses. When a defendant has a justification—he injured another in the execution of a public duty, for instance—that settles the matter against punishment of the defendant. We do not weigh the justification against, for instance, the suffering of the victim, or the dangerousness of the defendant: a justification deflects criminal liability entirely. Similarly with excuse. Mitigating and aggravating factors, however, are different. They merely figure into the calculus of reasons for sanction and are therefore subject to all the vicissitudes of reasons; they can be present without changing the outcome, or absent even when the outcome is to be changed. The position advocated here is that when an attempt has been abandoned there is a change in the landscape of reasons that *ceteris paribus* supports lowering the sanction. Whether any given defendant should enjoy a final reduction in sentence as a result of this mitigating factor is yet another question not to be addressed by the argument offered here. An answer to *that* question would require a full normative theory of sentencing.

Mitigating factors (and perhaps aggravating factors too) function in at least two importantly different ways. First, they can provide positive support for giving a lower sanction. Considerations of mercy function in this way. If giving a lower sanction would be merciful, and if there are reasons to be merciful, then there is a positive reason to give a lower sanction than would otherwise be appropriate. Second, and more importantly for our purposes here, mitigating factors can cancel the force of a reason to give a particular sanction (say, a typical sanction) rather than a lower one. For instance, if the fact that a crime was the defendant's first offense mitigates at all, it mitigates in this way. Sometimes a reason in support of issuing a particular sanction rather than a lower one is the fact that the behavior punished is part of a pattern of criminal conduct by the defendant. This reason, if it is one, for issuing a particular sanction rather than a lower one is muted by the fact that the defendant's crime was not part of a pattern at all. It will be argued here that abandonment mitigates in this second way. The fact that the defendant abandoned does not provide positive support for issuing a lower sanction than would otherwise be appropriate; rather, it undercuts the force of one reason that might be given in support of issuing a particular sanction, rather than a lower one. Since other reasons for sanctioning the defendant remain, what is supported by the argument to be offered here is only mitigation. To grant a defense on the basis of abandonment, as under the *Model Penal Code*, is to mistake the absence of a reason to issue a particular sanction rather than a lower one for a sufficient reason to issue no sanction at all.

The argument for abandonment-based mitigation of *attempt* to be offered here starts with an argument for abandonment-based mitigation of *completion*. As we will see, it is because abandonment mitigates completion that it mitigates attempt. In fact, the argument for abandonment-based mitigation of completion would not support abandonment-based mitigation for attempt were it not for the fact that the sentence for completion sets the ceiling for the sentence for the corresponding attempt.

## 2.1 *Why Abandonment Mitigates Completion*

Some might wonder, and not without reason, how abandoned completions—completed crimes abandoned before completed—are even possible. But they are. D intends to blow up a building. He sets a bomb and lights a long fuse. Moments later, he sees the error of his ways and rushes to stamp out the fuse. If not interfered with, he will stamp it out. But before he can get to the crucial spot, he is apprehended. The police, however, do not manage to stamp out the fuse, and since they detain D, neither does he. The building explodes. D has completed the destruction of the building, but abandoned his efforts before completion.[7,8]

---

[7] The framers of the *Model Penal Code* discuss a similar example in the commentary to §5.01, 360. In that example, the fuse is stamped out by the defendant. The *Model Penal Code* grants an affirmative defense in such a case.

[8] What this example shows is that *some* crimes can be both abandoned and completed; it does not show that *all* crimes that can be abandoned can also be completed. Consider, for instance, abandoned rapes. Probably because of the tortured and ambivalent attitudes of many a would-be rapist—seeking violence, seeking affection—a disproportionately large number of cases of abandoned attempts are abandoned rapes. Consider, for instance, the case of *People v. McNeal* (393 N.W.2d 907 (1985)). The defendant abducted a 16-year-old from a bus stop and brought her back to his home, intending to rape her. The victim stayed calm, asked him questions about his life and his motives for abducting her, listened to his gripes about women, and eventually convinced the defendant to let her go, which he did, walking her back to the bus stop before saying goodbye. There was no way for the rape McNeal intended to have been completed after he abandoned it unless he reversed himself again and renounced his abandonment of it. In fact, this isn't special to the *McNeal* case. Rape is not the sort of crime that can be abandoned and then completed anyway without further change of mind. What does this fact show? For our purposes here, nothing of importance. The reason is that all the argument will ultimately require is the following: *were there such a thing* as an abandoned rape that was, nonetheless, completed, it would make sense to mitigate the sentence for it.

So, consider the class of abandoned completions. Why does abandonment mitigate in such cases? What is the reason for giving a particular sanction, rather than a lower one, that is undercut by the fact that the defendant abandoned? Imagine that a judge is asked why he issued sanction S to D for crime C, rather than the lower sanction S'? The judge might answer like so: "The benefits to D that C promised would not, from D's point of view, have been outweighed by S', but are outweighed by S. By issuing S, I make it true that committing C was not, from D's point of view, in his interests." In support of giving a particular sanction, rather than a lower one, in other words, a judge might note that were the sanction lower, then even if the defendant had foreseen it at the time he acted, he would not have recognized sufficient reason not to act criminally: were the sanction lower, the crime would still have seemed to the defendant to have been worth committing. If a day in jail is worth the thrill of drag racing, then there's a reason to give more than a day in jail to the drag racer. But, and here is the important point, this defense of the judge's decision to give a particular sanction rather than a lower one is not available when the defendant abandoned prior to completion. The reason is that the defendant who abandoned *already* recognized sufficient reason not to act criminally, and so would have recognized such reason even if he had anticipated a much lower sanction than the one the judge chose, or, perhaps, even if he had anticipated no sanction at all.

Someone who justifies his decision to issue sanction S, rather than a lower sanction, by noting that lower sanctions would not have made it worthwhile, from the defendant's point of view, to refrain, appeals to the following principle in justifying his decision to issue sanction S:

*The Principle of Prospective Reasons*: There is reason to issue sanction S, rather than a lower sanction, to defendant D for crime C, committed at time t, if: (1) If he had anticipated S, then D would have recognized at t sufficient reason not to C and would have been guided by that recognition, and (2) If D had anticipated a sanction lower than S, then it is not the case that D would have recognized at t sufficient reason not to C and would have been guided by that recognition.

The argument for abandonment-based mitigation just offered involves claiming that the Principle of Prospective Reasons, while true, fails to apply when the defendant abandoned C prior to completion since clause (2) is false: since the defendant abandoned, he would have recognized at t sufficient reason not to C even if he had anticipated a lower sanction. The abandonment, after all, involved the recognition at the time of the crime of sufficient reason not to commit it. Thus one kind of reason for giving sanction S, rather than a lower sanction, fails to apply. So, abandonment mitigates.

Why should we think that the Principle of Prospective Reasons is true? If it isn't, then there is no reason ordinarily provided under it in support of issuing a particular sanction rather than a lower one, and it would follow that the reason putatively muted by abandonment is no reason at all, and thus the argument offered here for mitigation on the basis of abandonment will falter. It is essential to the argument, that is, that the principle is true, but simply fails to apply when the defendant abandoned.

Whether or not the principle is true depends on what theory of the justification of criminal sanction is true. Consequentialist justifications of punishment fit easily with the Principle of Prospective Reasons: since one of the most important ways that punishment achieves optimal consequences is by motivating compliance, there is no point in punishing people less than would be needed to make compliance with the law worth their while. Sanction cannot serve its motivational function if the punishment is lower than that. While this consequentialist justification of the Principle of Prospective Reasons does provide an adequate rationale for it, it is important to see that retributivists, too, can accept the principle. This is not to say that all forms of retributivism are consistent with it: some are not. However, the retributivist theories that rule out the Principle of Prospective Reasons are very implausible. Take, for instance, an unflinching retributivism according to which the *only reasons* for sanctioning pertain to desert. Under such a theory, a consideration counts in favor of issuing a particular sanction only if that consideration counts in favor of the claim that such a sanction is deserved. But since it is perfectly possible for the harshest deserved sanction to be so low that the defendant would have taken himself to have sufficient reason to elect the package in which he commits the crime and suffers the deserved sanction, it follows that there could be no reason at all to issue a sanction S that the Principle of Prospective Reasons says there is reason to issue. If no more than a day in jail is deserved for drag racing, then, under the retributivist view imagined, there is no reason to give the drag racer more than a day in jail, even though a day in jail is worth paying for the thrill of drag racing.

Notice, however, how implausible such a retributist theory is. The retributivism just described says not merely that an undeserved sanction should never be issued, or even that desert of a sanction is sufficient reason to issue it. It says, much more strongly, that there are *no reasons* to issue an undeserved sanction, not even reasons that are outweighed by reasons pertaining to desert. Such a strong form of retributivism is surely false. Surely considerations of deterence, for instance, provide *some reason* to issue an undeserved sanction, even if those reasons are outweighed by considerations of desert. But as far as I know, such a strong retributist view has never been advocated, and so its inconsistency with the Principle of Prospective Reasons does not speak against the principle.

A retributivist who holds that a sanction S is justifiably issued if, and only if, it is deserved, might accept the argument for abandonment-based mitigation offered here. There are two ways to do so. First, such a retributivist might hold that a sanction is deserved only if no lower sanction would have provided the defendant with sufficient reason to refrain that he would have recognized as such at the time of the crime. I am not sure if a theory of desert having this implication would be defensible, although it might be.[9] Alternatively, such a retributivist might hold that a range of possible sanctions are deserved, and, therefore that although a sanction is justifiably issued if, and only if, deserved, considerations independent of desert are relevant to fixing the appropriate choice of sanction within the deserved range.

As will become important in chapter 12, I advocate a theory of this second variety, under which considerations of desert fix a range of possible sanctions. (How that range is fixed is discussed briefly in chapter 12. It is there suggested that the range is fixed by the demand that the sanction express the deserved level of censure; it turns out that a range of sanctions might express the same degree of censure, depending on the context in which they are issued.) It is unjustifiable to issue a sanction outside of the relevant range since such a sanction is, by definition, undeserved. Other considerations, independent of desert, then determine where in that range the sanction appropriate to a particular defendant lies. Such a view is consistent with the Principle of Prospective Reasons, and sits easily with it. Under this theory, a reason in favor of issuing a particular sanction that is, say, towards the top of the deserved range might be, precisely, that a sanction lower than it would not be such as to provide the defendant with sufficient reason not to commit the crime in the first place. Disputes of the sort that the Principle of Prospective Reasons might help us to resolve—disputes about where in the range to place the defendant—proceed in front of a background assumption that the sanctions being considered are all deserved.

## 2.2 Why Abandonment Mitigates Attempt

The argument for mitigating completion on the basis of abandonment just offered does not support, without supplementation, abandonment-based mitigation of attempt. We cannot simply think of the crime not as a completion, but as an attempt, and then hope to appeal to the argument in order to explain why abandonment mitigates attempt. The reason is that under the Principle of Prospective Reasons what is important are the reasons that the defendant would have had, in light of the sanction, *in prospect*, that is, *before* the crime for which he is punished was completed. Abandonment is thought to mitigate precisely because it took place *before* completion of the crime for which

---

[9] Perhaps it might be defended on the following grounds, inspired by Stephen Darwall's view of second-personal reasons. (See Darwall (2006). For some discussion see Yaffe (2008b)). If the issuing of sanction is an act of what Darwall calls "second-personal address of a second-personal reason", then it succeeds only if there is uptake on the part of the person to whom it is issued: that person must come to recognize that, thanks to the act of address, he now has a reason to act in a particular way. Perhaps, then, for a sanction to be deserved, the act of issuing it must be such that the person to whom it is issued would have recognized that, in light of that reason, he has sufficient reason to refrain from committing the crime.

punishment is being issued, and hence the fact of abandonment tells us something about the reasons that the defendant recognized *in prospect*. But abandonment of attempt, by definition, takes place *after* the crime *of attempt* has been completed: the defendant has done enough for an attempt, and did not abandon before doing so. So, we learn nothing from the fact that the attempter abandoned about what reasons he would have recognized *prior* to completing the attempt, which is the very crime for which he is to be punished. For all we know, *before* he changed his mind he might not have recognized sufficient reasons to refrain unless threatened with a typical, or even higher than typical sanction. (A closely related point will become important in discussion of remorse in section 3.)

But, still, the argument for abandonment-based mitigation of completion does support abandonment-based mitigation of attempt *when supplemented*. To see this, consider the fact that the sentence for completion sets the ceiling for the sentence for the attempt. A particular attempt is never rightly punished more heavily than it would have been punished had it been completed. While this is certainly true, why is it true? The answer is that there can be no reasons for punishing attempt that are not also just as powerful reasons for punishing completion. The reasons for punishing attempt, as we saw in chapter 1, derive from two commonalities between completion and attempt: both completer and attempter engage in the same faulty modes of recognition, weighing, and response to reasons, and both are guided by their commitments to the components of completion. Thus, to negate a reason to issue a particular sanction for completion that derives from these two facts about the completer is necessarily to negate a reason to issue that sanction for attempt. This is not to say that there are no reasons to sanction completion that are not also reasons to sanction attempt: there may be some. But when we restrict ourselves to reasons that are both reasons to sanction attempt and to sanction completion—reasons for sanctioning deriving from the commonalities between completion and attempt—we find the support that they give to a sanction of the two types of behavior to walk in lockstep: in that restricted class of reasons for a sanction, to negate a reason to issue a particular sanction for completion is, necessarily, to negate a reason to issue it for attempt.

The argument for abandonment-based mitigation of completion, then, supports abandonment-based mitigation for attempt when we add the following claim: *to negate a reason for issuing a particular sanction, rather than a lower sanction for completion is to negate a reason for issuing that sanction for attempt.* We find that this is true when we reflect on the rationale for the fact that the sentence for completion sets the ceiling for the sentence for attempt. Thus, we can present the argument for abandonment-based mitigation for attempt like so: had the crime been completed, one reason for giving it a particular sanction would have been negated, namely the reason supplied under the Principle of Prospective Reasons. Since to negate a reason to issue a particular sanction for

297

completion is *ipso facto* to negate a reason to issue that sanction for attempt, it follows that the same reason for issuing that sanction for an abandoned attempt is negated, given the fact that the defendant abandoned. Therefore, abandonment mitigates the sanction for attempt.

## 2.3 Why Does the Motive for Abandoning Matter?

The rationale for mitigation on the basis of abandonment supplied here explains the following fact, noted in the introduction to this chapter: if the defendant's motives for abandoning his attempt are objectionable—for example, he abandons because he recognizes that the crime will be more profitable to him if performed a bit later—then he does not deserve mitigation. In brief, the reason for this is that when the defendant abandons from some objectionable motive, the argument for abandonment-based mitigation offered here fails to go through. To see this, we need to consider each of the various types of objectionable motive for abandonment in turn.

The *Model Penal Code* offers an account of the various motives for abandoning that undermine abandonment's mitigating force. Under the *Model Penal Code*, the abandonment, what the code chooses to call the "renunciation of criminal purpose", must be both "voluntary" and "complete". But the code makes it clear that these terms are defined in such a way as to identify motives for abandonment that undermine abandonment's mitigating force. The relevant section of the code reads as follows:

[R]enunciation of criminal purpose is not voluntary if it is motivated, in whole or in part, by circumstances, not present at the inception of the actor's course of conduct, that increase the probability of detection or apprehension or that make more difficult the accomplishment of the criminal purpose. Renunciation is not complete if it is motivated by a decision to postpone the criminal conduct until a more advantageous time or to transfer the criminal effort to another but similar objective or victim.

(*Model Penal Code* §5.01(4))

So, the code identifies roughly four kinds of motives for abandonment that undermine mitigation. There is no mitigation if the defendant abandons because (a) there's a better chance he'll get caught than he expected, (b) completion is harder than he expected, (c) there will be a better time or place for the crime, or (d) there's a better victim for the crime.

Consider, first, defendants who abandon for the reasons described in (a). The bank robbery, for instance, is abandoned after the defendant walks into the bank, armed and ready to hold up the teller, but notices that a security camera has been installed since he cased the bank. In cases of this sort, *the abandonment is predicated upon completion being punished in a way that is typical*. The reason that the new security camera provides the defendant with a reason to walk away is that the defendant expects that completion would result in a certain punishment that he has a strong desire to avoid. For all we know, were he to anticipate a smaller than typical punishment, then the added risk of being caught, given the unanticipated camera, would not outweigh the possibility of filling his sack with money. Thus, by abandoning, he has not shown, as the argument for abandonment-based mitigation requires, that he would recognize sufficient reason not to complete the crime, even given a lower than typical sanction for completion. For all we know, a lower than typical sanction would not, given his motives for abandoning, provide him with sufficient reason to refrain, and so the argument for abandonment-based mitigation in his case loses its force.

Now consider cases in which the motive is of the sort described in (b). The bank robbery, for instance, is abandoned at the same point as in our previous example (after the defendant has walked into the bank, armed and intent on robbing it). But, in this case, the defendant abandons because he notices that the vault doors are closed, where they were open when he cased the bank, and so the robbery would require him to persuade a bank employee to open them for him. In this case, also, there is no reason to believe that the defendant would have recognized sufficient reason to refrain from completing the robbery had he anticipated a smaller than typical sanction. The reason is that any time anyone undertakes any complicated task, such a task is thought to be worth-while only if the rewards outweigh the costs that must be borne in order to earn them. For all we know, this defendant included the typical sanction (corrected for the probability that he would have to suffer it) in his calculations before he walked into the bank. The added work of having to open the vault doors tipped the scales against the robbery. But were a cost of the robbery lowered—were a lower than typical sanction for completion promised—then it is quite possible that the added work to open the vault doors would be worth undertaking. As in the previous hypothetical, in this kind of case, for all we know, a lower than typical sanction would persuade the defendant that he did not, after all, have sufficient reason to abandon. So, like before, the argument on offer in this section for abandonment-based mitigation fails when a defendant abandons for the reasons described in (b).

Similar considerations apply in cases in which the motives to abandon are like those in (c) and (d). Consider someone who abandons the bank robbery at the very same point when he realizes that a large daily deposit has been delayed, and so it will be worth a lot of money to him to rob the bank later. Such a person decides that the risk in this instance isn't worth the reward, but that the risk will be worth the reward at the later time. But if the completed crime promised a smaller than typical sanction, then, for all we know, the risk involved in robbing the bank now would be worth the reward to be expected from robbing it now; after all, less would be risked if the expected sanction were lower than typical, and so less would be gained by waiting to rob the bank later. Again, the promise of a lower than typical sanction, given the motive for abandonment, might actually prompt the defendant *not* to recognize sufficient reason to abandon. Similarly, the defendant who abandons his attempt to rob bank X because he decides he will be better off robbing bank Y instead (a case involving a motive of type (d)), sees attractions in robbing Y that outweigh the costs associated with the robbery, including the anticipated sanction (corrected for the probability of being apprehended). But if the robbery of X were to promise a lower than typical sanction, then there might not be sufficient reason to switch targets.

In all these hypothetical cases, the motive for abandonment shows a sensitivity on the defendant's part to the typical sanction. The defendant is weighing pros and cons and deciding to abandon *given an assumption on his part that there's a chance he'll suffer the typical sanction should he complete the crime*. Thus, when we have these motives for abandonment, it is also true that had the defendant known before he C'd that he would suffer a certain smaller than typical sanction for C-ing, then he might have seen there to be sufficient reason *not* to abandon his attempt. We thus have no reason to think that clause (2) in the Principle of Prospective Reasons is false: smaller sanctions might not have led the defendant to recognize sufficient reason not to commit the crime. Therefore, when the defendant has abandoned from the motives the *Model Penal Code* identifies, the reason for giving a particular sanction rather than a lower one supplied by the Principle of Prospective Reasons still applies. And so the argument for abandonment-based mitigation does not go through.

Notice that when a person abandons for the reasons that Arin Ahmed abandoned her attempted suicide bombing, there is every reason to think that clause (2) of the Principle of Prospective Reasons is false. Ahmed's reasons for abandoning are not of the sort that are sensitive to the expected sanction for the completed crime. That sanction—if it is even possible to imagine what kind of sanction there could be for such behavior, perhaps a penalty issued to one's surviving family members—plays no role in her reasoning; it is not something to be outweighed by other considerations, but is simply trumped by the reasons that she had for abandoning. Hence, even if the sanction were smaller, she still would have abandoned her attempt. What follows is that in her case, the argument for abandonment-based mitigation goes through, and so her abandonment is a legitimate mitigating factor.

Could there be other motives for abandonment that undermine the case for abandonment-based mitigation, motives that do not fall into any of the four categories the *Model Penal Code* identifies? Yes there can. Consider the case of *People v. Taylor* (598 N.E.2d 693 (N.Y. 1992)). George Taylor forced his way into the apartment of a stranger and, threatening her with a knife, he made aggressive sexual advances. The court describes what happened next:

Because of her fear of the knife, [the victim] sought to dissuade him—rather than fighting him or screaming—by "trying to make him believe he could be [her] boyfriend and he did not have to do it this way." Despite these efforts, he carried her into the bedroom where he continued to touch and rub himself against her and tried to pull down her pants. After [the victim] "told him he could come to [her] house anytime", he relented and they "went back to the living room and started talking". He took off the surgical gloves he had been wearing during the attack, saying that he was "not going to be needing these anymore".

A little later, the victim convinced Taylor to accompany her to a liquor store where they could get a bottle before returning to her apartment. On the way out, she ducked back into the apartment and locked the door behind her, leaving Taylor in the hall. Taylor knocked on the door and tried without success to get her to open it. She then called the police.

In *Taylor*, the court rejects the possibility of an abandonment defense under a statute derived from the *Model Penal Code*. The court does this on the grounds that the defendant's renunciation was not "voluntary and complete". However, it is far from clear why it was not, under the *Model Penal Code*'s official definitions of those terms. The best case for thinking that it was not comes from construing the defendant's motives as of type (c)—to construe him, that is, as having merely decided to postpone the rape until later, perhaps after the two returned from the liquor store. But it is hard to see why he would have stopped his attack if this were his motive. After all, if he was intent on rape, he could have completed it despite the victim's efforts to persuade him that he could later have consensual sex with her. Rather, it seems that Taylor forced his way into the apartment with a preference for consensual over non-consensual sex, but intent on having sex with the victim regardless. When he became convinced that consensual sex was a possibility, he pursued it, perhaps anticipating that, should it stop seeming possible, he would return to his pursuit of non-consensual sex. However, even construed in this way, it is not unreasonable to think of Taylor as having changed his mind. His intention to have non-consensual sex was predicated on an assumption: consensual sex was not possible. When he came to believe this assumption was false, he changed his mind and abandoned his plan to have non-consensual sex with the victim. This isn't to say that Taylor ought to enjoy abandonment-based mitigation. He ought not to. But why not? The *Model Penal Code* does not provide us with a tool for answering; only by distorting the facts are we able to construe Taylor's motive for abandonment as of one of the four sorts that undermine abandonment's mitigating force under the code.

The reason that Taylor's sentence for attempted rape should not be mitigated is because, for all we know, Taylor's preference for consensual over non-consensual sex was at least in part derived from the fact that non-consensual sex brings with it a certain punishment, the typical punishment for rape. So, if we ask whether someone who abandoned his rape for Taylor's reasons would have done so, even if the penalty for rape were lower than typical, we find that the answer might very well be "no". After all, were the penalty lower than typical, then Taylor may have thought that the prospect of consensual sex, bringing with it the risk that he would not have sex with the victim at all, was not worth pursuing. He abandons only if he thinks that consensual sex outweighs non-consensual, a calculation quite possibly made by considering, among other things, the typical penalty for non-consensual sex. Lower that penalty and the calculation might come out in favor of persevering with his plan to have non-consensual sex.

In short, the argument offered here helps us to identify the crucial question that must be answered in deciding whether to grant mitigation on the basis of abandonment: "Does the fact that the defendant abandoned his attempt show that the defendant would have been dissuaded from completing the crime even if a lower than typical sanction was given for completion?" The answer is "no" when the defendant abandoned for any of the four types of reasons identified by the *Model Penal Code*. But the anwer is "no", also, when the defendant abandoned for reasons like Taylor's, even though those reasons do not fall into any of the *Model Penal Code*'s four categories. Legitimate abandonment-based mitigation is hard to come by, even harder than under the *Model Penal Code*, since there are motives for abandonment that undermine its mitigating force but are not identified as such by the code.

## 3. What Other Crimes Deserve Abandonment-Based Mitigation?

It was noted in the introduction that a discussion of abandonment-based mitigation *of attempt* is not complete if its implications for mitigation of other sorts of crimes is not also considered. We might have reason to doubt an argument for abandonment-based mitigation of attempt, even if we cannot see which premise is false, or how the conclusion fails to follow from its premises, if a parallel argument would support mitigation in another domain where we are confident it should not be offered. On the other hand, it is also important that we follow our arguments where they lead. So, if an argument parallel to the one offered in section 2 supports mitigation in some other unexpected domain of criminal law, then that points to the correctness of that conclusion, unexpected as it is. There are two salient comparisons with abandoned attempt to be discussed in this section: completed crimes followed with remorse, and abandoned "substantive" inchoate crimes such as larceny and burglary, that have unfulfilled intentions as elements. Each will be considered in turn.

### 3.1 *Remorse*

Before the *Model Penal Code* elevated abandonment to an affirmative defense, it was common to find courts rejecting a defendant's appeal to abandonment as reason for acquittal or mitigation on the following grounds: abandonment of an attempt, like remorse for a completed crime, happens after the criminal conduct that forms the basis of the charge has occurred; hence, abandonment of attempt has no more relevance than remorse to criminal liability or to sentencing. If we agree that this is true, what are its implications for the relevance of abandonment? For sentencing purposes, judges have varying attitudes towards remorse—some reduce the sentence of a remorseful defendant, some do not; some do so only if the remorse was evidenced by more than just a verbal expression of it in court, such as an effort to make amends to a victim; some take such additional behavior to be either unnecessary for mitigation (a heartfelt verbal report will do), or insufficient for it (not even such behavior supports mitigation). So, if abandonment bears on sentencing for attempt, it would appear that the defendant who abandons his attempt is subject to the same vicissitudes in sentencing as the defendant who is remorseful following completion of his crime: maybe it will make a difference, maybe it will not, depending on which judge happens to be issuing sentence. However, as will be suggested in what follows, the argument for abandonment-based mitigation for attempt does not go through when what is at issue is not abandonment but remorse. If remorse mitigates, it is not for the same reasons that abandonment of attempt does. And hence a judge oughtn't to take the same attitude towards abandonment of an attempt as he does towards remorse following completion.

Remorse is importantly different from abandonment in two different ways. First, remorse typically takes place after completion. The reason for issuing a particular sanction, rather than a lower one, which is negated by the fact of abandonment, depends crucially on what reasons the defendant would have recognized and been guided by prior to completion. It is easiest to see why this is important by reflecting on the consequentialist rationale for the Principle of Prospective Reasons, although the same rationale can be accepted by the forms of retributivism which are consistent with the principle. Since one of the ways in which punishment achieves best consequences is by motivating agents to refrain from committing crimes, punishments must be large enough to give people sufficient reason to comply *at the time of the crime*. The fact that someone recognized *after completion* that he had sufficient reason not to commit the crime does not tell us anything about what reasons he would have recognized at the time that he committed the crime, if aware that he would suffer a particular sanction. Remorse is easier, in this respect, than abandonment. It is easier to see that you lacked sufficient reason to comply when you've already reaped the benefits of non-compliance.

Still, it is certainly possible to imagine remorse that takes place prior to completion. Imagine our bomber from earlier, who is remorseful after the fuse is lit but before the bomb explodes. However, even narrowing ourselves to cases in which remorse precedes completion, there is an important difference between abandonment and remorse. In particular, abandonment involves trying:

someone who abandons, *tries* to prevent the occurrence of a crime, namely the one that he was formerly trying to complete. By contrast, someone who feels remorse may not be trying to do anything. He might truthfully say, for instance, that he would take it back if he could; but because he cannot, he is not, in fact, trying to take it back. The argument for abandonment-based mitigation of attempt offered in the previous section goes through only when the defendant has genuinely tried to prevent the crime from being completed. The defendant must both recognize sufficient reason not to complete the crime, and be guided by that recognition. It is only because both things are true that we can be confident that he would have recognized sufficient reason to refrain, and been guided by that recognition, even if promised a lower sanction than some particular one. The remorseful defendant has at most met the first of these two requirements. He recognizes sufficient reason not to complete the crime, but if his attitude rests in remorse, and does not rise to the level of abandonment, then he is not guided by it. To see why this is important, consider again the consequentialist explanation of the Principle of Prospective Reasons, according to which a sanction must give people sufficient reason to comply if they are to dissuade people from committing crimes. Under that approach, a person who recognizes sufficient reasons for compliance, but is not moved by that recognition, is someone whom we might need to threaten with *greater* sanction, rather than less, if we are to induce compliance. For such a person, we need to overcome his irrational responses—he does what he recognizes as less well supported by reasons than an alternative—and that might require increasing sanction. In any event, it clearly does not speak in favor of a decrease.

## 3.2 Abandoned Substantive Inchoate Crimes

Dustin Buttrick, a 22-year-old man living in Maine, had a sexually explicit conversation with someone in a chat room claiming to be a 14-year-old girl. They arranged to meet in a particular parking lot in New Hampshire in order to have sex. Before the meeting, Buttrick told a friend that he was not sure whether the person he was chatting with was a 14-year-old girl, but that he was curious to find out. His friend advised him against going through with the meeting. In fact, Buttrick was chatting over the Internet with a detective. Buttrick arrived at the parking lot and drove past it twice before being pulled over and arrested. He was charged under a statute that reads as follows:

A person who travels in interstate commerce . . . for the purpose of engaging in any illicit sexual conduct with another person shall be fined under this title or imprisoned not more than 30 years, or both. (18 U.S.C. §2423(b))

At trial, Buttrick requested that the jury be instructed that abandonment of the intention to have illicit sex (for the purposes here, sex with a minor) is a defense to the charge. The trial judge refused to instruct the jury in this manner.

Buttrick had hoped to argue that although he had intended to have sex with a minor, somewhere along the line he decided to have sex with the person he was chatting with only if she turned out not to be a minor at all. After being convicted, Buttrick appealed in part on the grounds that the jury should have had the chance to hear this argument. His appeal was rejected.[10]

The statute under which Buttrick was charged defines a crime that, like burglary (requiring intent to commit a felony but not performance of the intended felony), or larceny (requiring intent to permanently deprive someone of his goods but not success in that endeavor), has as an element an intention that the defendant need not fulfill in order to be guilty of the crime. Assault with intent to kill, and possession of an illegal drug with intent to distribute are other examples of such crimes. (It differs from these crimes in an important way, too: it contains a "jurisdictional element", traveling in interstate commerce, the purpose of which is solely to bring the crime under federal jurisdiction. But let that pass.[11]) The relationship between crimes of this sort—what might be called "substantive inchoate crimes"—and attempts is far from clear. It was suggested in the introduction to this book that many substantive inchoate crimes—criminal liability for many of which, such as burglary, are much older than attempts—were initially created in order to criminalize certain attempts under some other name. This encourages the idea that substantive inchoate crimes are simply attempts in disguise. However, substantive inchoate crimes persist and continue to be created, even though we now have attempt liability. The legislature chose to criminalize "traveling in interstate commerce with intent to engage in illicit sexual conduct with another"; it might have, instead, criminalized "traveling in interstate commerce and intentionally having illicit sexual conduct with another", and thereby criminalized behavior such as Buttrick's on the grounds that it was an attempt of this crime. Are there ever good reasons for creating the substantive inchoate crime rather than creating the completed crime and allowing prosecution and punishment of attempts of it?

There is this important difference between substantive inchoate crimes and attempts: in substantive inchoate crimes, the prosecution bears no burden to show that the defendant's behavior meets the jurisdiction's standards for the act element of attempt; the prosecution bears, instead, a burden to show that the defendant engaged in behavior meeting the description of the acts involved

---

[10] *United States v. Buttrick* (432 F.3d 373).

[11] The crime with which Buttrick was charged is different from either burglary or larceny in another way, too. In burglary and larceny, the behavior that the intention is coupled with is an independent crime. It is a crime to enter a dwelling without permission, as in burglary, and it is a crime to take something of someone else's without permission, as in larceny. These behaviors are worse when accompanied by the objectionable intentions involved in burglary or larceny, but they are crimes even in the absence of those intentions. But it is not a crime to "travel in interstate commerce". That behavior becomes criminal only when accompanied by an intention to have illicit sex. It is not clear that this difference matters to the argument here.

in the substantive inchoate crime. In, to take an obvious example, jurisdictions employing the "last act" test for the act element of attempt—the test according to which, roughly, the defendant has not done enough for attempt unless he could complete the crime without any further action on his part—many who are guilty of substantive inchoate crimes have fallen short of attempt by the standards of that jurisdiction. Think, for instance, of possession with intent to distribute. Or, on the flip side, if in the jurisdiction one could attempt murder, for instance, with acts that fall short of assault, then in proving that the defendant committed assault with intent to kill, the prosecution bears a heavier burden than it would bear if trying to prove attempted murder. Assault, for instance, ordinarily requires harm to the victim, or the apprehension of imme-diate harm. If D pointed a gun at Victim's back, unbeknownst to Victim, intending to shoot him, and was stopped before he could pull the trigger, he would not have committed an assault—no harm and no apprehension of harm occurred—and so would not be guilty of assault with intent to kill. But if the jurisdiction's standards for the act element of attempt are low enough, D may have committed attempted murder in such a case. Whether or not someone who commits a particular substantive inchoate crime has also committed an attempt, or vice versa, depends on the conduct involved in the substantive inchoate crime, and on the jurisdiction's standards for the act element of attempt.

In fact, the relationship between attempts and substantive inchoate crimes is even more complicated than this, since substantive inchoate crimes often involve circumstantial elements that, under views in line with that defended in chapter 5, could be absent in attempt, provided the defendant believes them to be present. In such cases, it is possible to attempt a crime while falling short of commission of the correlated substantive inchoate crime, even if the juris-diction has very low standards for the act element of attempt. Imagine that D is at the airport and notices Victim put something of great value into a suitcase that happens to look just like D's. At their destination, D, aiming to steal Victim's valuable object, takes a suitcase that looks like his own, believing it to be Victim's, and he does so with intent never to return it. In fact, however, D took his own suitcase. D has attempted theft (he has even attempted larceny), but he hasn't committed larceny, since one of the elements of larceny is that the object taken not be the defendant's, and in this case the bag belongs to the defendant himself (although he does not know that).

In general, there is a very imperfect overlap between substantive inchoate crimes and attempts. True, it is common to find that the person who commits the substantive inchoate crime also commits the attempt: many burglars, on entering, have attempted the felony they intend. But there can be cases of defendants who commit the substantive inchoate crime but do not commit any attempt, and cases of defendants who commit an attempt, but not the corresponding substantive inchoate crime. What the possibility of divergence here shows is that substantive inchoate crimes are not criminalized under the

Transfer Principle—they are not criminalized merely on the grounds that the crime intended by those who commit them is justifiably criminalized. This is perhaps most obvious in a crime like Buttrick's. As noted earlier, the crime of traveling in interstate commerce with intent to have illicit sex is defined as it is in order to bring certain kinds of behaviors under federal jurisdiction. Further, the definition of the crime does not preclude the possibility that behaviors falling short of attempts to have illicit sex will be criminalized under it. What is criminalized under the relevant statute would not change with changes in the federal law regarding the act element of attempt. Were the federal law to change to the "last act" test, Buttrick would still have committed the crime, even though by that standard he would have fallen far short of guilt for an attempt. What this shows is that *if* it is legitimate to criminalize traveling in interstate commerce with intent to have illicit sex (and it might not be), the reasons for doing so do not derive from the reasons to criminalize the having of illicit sex in the way that is supported by the Transfer Principle.

The question, then, of whether it would be better to define the substantive inchoate crime, or, alternatively, to define the completed crime and criminalize attempts of it under the Transfer Principle, turns on whether there are good reasons to criminalize particular acts that fall under the definition of the substantive inchoate crime but are not attempts, and whether there are good reasons not to criminalize *as attempts* those instances of the substantive inchoate crime that are. Sometimes there might be. Consider burglary. Imagine someone who enters another's home intending to commit rape there, but who has not attempted rape since, for instance, in the jurisdiction in question such an attempt would require an act beyond the entrance of the home, such as some "direct movement towards" sex with another person. It is not hard to imagine a conception of the sanctity of the home, and the objectionable nature of invasions of it, under which this would appear to be much worse behavior than any charge of criminal trespass could accommodate. If such a view is coupled with a belief that attempted rape is worse yet than this imagined defendant's behavior, then we have found a view under which there are reasons to criminalize the substantive inchoate crime that do not require conceiving of it as an attempt. If so, then burglary is legitimately criminalized, but not because it falls under the Transfer Principle.

Thus, the question of whether abandonment ought to mitigate sentence for a substantive inchoate crime *for the reasons offered in* section 2 turns on whether or not any premise in the argument for abandonment-based mitigation for attempt is true only because attempts are criminalized under the Transfer Principle. If one of the premises of that argument is true only given that that is why attempts are criminalized, then it is not true of substantive inchoate crimes. What would follow is that abandonment ought not to mitigate sentence for substantive inchoate crimes for the reasons that it ought to mitigate sentence for attempts. And, in fact, this is so. Consider the rule that the attempt is not to be punished more severely than the completed crime, a rule that serves as a premise in the argument for abandonment-based mitigation of attempt. This rule does not, in general, apply to substantive inchoate crimes. Would it ever be appropriate, for instance, to punish someone who committed a robbery less severely than someone who broke into a house, at night, intending to commit a similar robbery inside? It seems perfectly possible that it could be appropriate. After all, the burglar, in this example, has taken a particular, objectionable means to committing robbery—namely a particularly intrusive and disturbing trespass. That trespass might be a more severe crime than the robbery intended. The sentence for the robbery does not set the ceiling for the sentence for the burglarly. The rationale for the crime of burglary—the reason for criminalizing it—does not derive from, and depend upon, the reasons for criminalizing the intended felony. Could it ever be appropriate to give a greater sanction to someone who travels in interstate commerce, intending to have illicit sex, than to someone who has illicit sex? The answer to this question will turn on what we think is objectionable about traveling in interstate commerce with this intention, as opposed to pursuing it in some other way. If, for instance, those who travel from one state to another for this purpose are much less likely to be caught than those who do not travel—they are able to escape notice of state authorities by returning to their home states after completion of the crime—then there might be reason to give a much greater disincentive to those who travel, in contrast to those who commit the crime in the states in which they live, and that might be sufficient reason to give a greater sanction to those who commit the substantive inchoate crime than to those who actually succeed in having illicit sex. The point is that attempts have a very special feature that distinguishes them from substantive inchoate crimes: all the reasons for criminalizing attempts derive from the reasons for criminalizing the crime attempted. There is no comparable relationship between the reasons for criminalizing the substantive inchoate crimes and the reasons for criminalizing the relevant completed crimes. But section 2's argument for abandonment-based mitigation of attempt relies crucially on this special relation between attempts and completions.

It therefore follows that abandonment does not mitigate substantive inchoate crimes *for the reasons that it mitigates attempts*. This is consistent with the possibility that abandonment does mitigate substantive inchoate crimes for distinct reasons. Ultimately, to answer the question of what it is appropriate to do with a defendant like Buttrick, who contends that he abandoned pursuit of the intention involved in his substantive inchoate crime, we will need to know more about the grounds, if there are adequate grounds, for the criminalization of substantive inchoate crimes. Armed with a conception of such grounds we may be in a position to say whether or not abandonment mitigates. After all, armed with a conception of the grounds of criminalization of attempts—the rationale for the Transfer Principle—we are able to see principled reasons for mitigation when the attempter abandons before completion.

## 4. Conclusion

Change of mind, as common as it is, is puzzling from a moral point of view. It is hard to know how to react to the person who acts in a way of which we disapprove, but changes his mind later. As the agent of a bad act, he seems worthy of censure; as the agent who prevented the bad act's occurrence, he seems worthy of praise. The puzzle arises from the fact that he is, indeed, both of these agents. This puzzle does not dissolve in the face of the argument for abandonment-based mitigation offered here. Rather, the logic of mitigation makes room for an expression of our ambivalence of attitude in an all-things-considered judgment about what sanction is appropriate. That judgment is the product of the mysterious process by which we weigh competing reasons in situations in which *some* outcome must be reached. There are reasons to blame and reasons to praise, and we need to do one or the other and to some particular degree. It is because the person who abandons his attempt attempted the crime—he engaged in behavior worthy of censure and sanction—that it makes sense to punish the attempter who abandons. But it is because he abandons, and so shows himself to be someone who recognizes sufficient reason to refrain, even in the face of a lower sanction, that it makes sense to give him a lower sanction than is typical for the attempt. The push and pull of moral intuition that we find when contemplating abandoned attempts to do wrong, that is, is accommodated by the view presented here, rather than shown to rest on a mistake.

What has also been shown here is that a comparable accommodation of our ambivalence of attitude cannot be made on the same grounds when it comes to crimes other than attempts. Attempts are special in this regard because they allow us to weigh competing claims to, on the one hand, sanction typically and, on the other, to sanction less than is typical, in just the way that we weigh such claims when it comes to consideration of those who abandon their attempts to do wrong, but do wrong nonetheless. The key to understanding the abandonment of attempt, that is, is to consider how to sentence those who abandon their attempts but complete their crimes nonetheless. Since there is a reason to issue a less than typical sanction to the person who abandons before completion, but completes the crime anyway, there is a parallel reason to issue a less than typical sanction to the person who abandons his attempt and falls short of completion. The reason transfers from the one case to the other only because justifiable criminalization transfers from completion to attempt.

# 12

# Is it Unfair to Punish Completed Crimes More than Attempts?

## 1. Introduction

Perhaps no question in criminal law theory has been more extensively explored in recent years than this one: "Is the causation of harm of relevance to punishment?" Should we treat differently defendants who differ only with respect to what they cause?[1] The question is made pointed through consideration of various real and hypothetical examples. However, every discussion of the issue uses one particular kind of example to illustrate the question's power, a kind of example of relevance to the topic of this book: the "last act" attempt that fails for fortuitous, unanticipated reasons. Consider D1, who shoots Victim1 in the chest, intending to kill, but fails only because Victim1 is, unbeknownst to D1, wearing a bulletproof vest; compare him to D2 who also shoots his victim in the chest, acting on the intention to kill, but, thanks to Victim2's failing to wear a bulletproof vest, kills him. Should we give different punishments to D1 and D2? Should the last act attempter be given a lesser punishment merely because the murderer's victim, in comparison to his, was insufficiently cautious when deciding that morning what to wear to his meeting with the defendant? After all, it wasn't up to either D1 or D2 what their respective victims would decide to wear.

There's a powerful intuition, brought out by this kind of example, to the effect that results ought to be irrelevant to punishment generally, and, particularly, when it comes to the punishment of last act attempts in comparison to the corresponding completed crimes. There's a powerful intuition, that is, that there's something wrong, somehow, with giving a greater punishment to a completed crime than would have been given to the last act attempt of it. But

---

[1] For a sampling of the large literature on the question see, Becker (1974), Schulhofer (1974), Parker (1984), Davis (1986), Lewis (1989), Kadish (1994), Moore (1994), Gardner (2004), Morse (2004), Alexander and Ferzan (2009a), and Alexander and Ferzan (2009b).

what, intuitively, is wrong with that? Broadly speaking, there are two kinds of answers to this question, one having to do with control, another having to do with fairness. We might think, that is, that at least some portion of the completer's sentence is being given for something over which he lacked sufficient control to warrant any punishment. Or, alternatively, we might think that when we sentence the completer and the last act attempter differently we treat unequally two agents who are the same in relevant respects, and thus treat one or both of them unfairly. As we will see, it is the second line of thought—the appeal to unfairness—which will be the target of our discussion here. This chapter argues, that is, that it is not unfair to give a lesser sentence to the last act attempt than would have been appropriate had that attempt been completed.

It is important to acknowledge two ways in which the discussion offered in this chapter fails to connect to recent discussions of this and closely related topics. Assessing many of the arguments concerned with control that one might offer in support of the claim that results don't matter requires grappling with the problem of freedom of will. The relevant questions are, first, what kind of control, and how much, a person must have over what he does in order to be rightly held responsible for his conduct, and, second, whether human beings ever have, or under what conditions they have, that kind of control and to that degree. These are fiendishly hard questions that will not be addressed here. Rather, here we will confine ourselves to consideration of arguments that appeal to fairness. According to such arguments, the problem with allowing results to matter to sentencing is not that we punish people for things over which they had insufficient control to justify such treatment; that might be true, but that's not the problem such arguments identify. Rather, the problem identified by such arguments is that by allowing results to matter we necessarily commit ourselves to treating differently defendants who are similar in all relevant respects.

The discussion here also does not bear on the disagreement between theorists of criminal law concerning the place to be given to widely shared *intuitions* to the effect that results make a difference to what punishment is deserved.[2] Most people take the reckless or negligent agent who causes harm to be deserving of greater punishment than the one who does not. It is possible to invoke similar intuitions in contrasting attempters and completers.[3] And there is little question that practices, such as that of aggravating the sentences of those who cause more harm, enjoy great public approval. There is a question of what to say about such intuitions. Should we take them seriously as pointing to something about our ordinary concept of desert in need of accommodation? Should we

---

[2] The issue is raised powerfully by Michael Moore's defense of retributivism. See Moore (1997), part 1.

[3] Empirical verification of this claim is offered in Robinson and Darley (1995).

take them, that is, to show that results are part of what Michael Moore has called "the desert basis" of the crime?[4] Should we take them to support the contention that the purpose of criminal law is served only by punishing more harshly on the basis of causation of harm? Should we take them, that is, as Peter Westen does, to show that the criminal law's function of expressing the community's condemnation requires that results be treated as relevant?[5] Or should we, in contrast, take them, as Larry Alexander and Kim Ferzan do, to be nothing but facts about our psyches that should influence our practices only if given independent, rational justification?[6] No progress on this debate will be made here.[7] The intuitions in question might, or might not, give us good reasons for having the sentencing policies we have, quite independently of the question of whether those policies are unfair. But unfairness is our topic here.

Recall that throughout this book various problems about attempts have been solved through reflection on one of three things: (a) what it is to commit an attempt, (b) what kind of evidence we must have of the commission of an attempt, given what attempts are, or (c) how attempts ought to be sentenced, given their intimate relation to completed crimes. The discussion in chapter 11 of attempts abandoned before completion fell into this last category. There it was suggested that it is because abandonment of an attempt shows that the defendant would have recognized sufficient reason to refrain and been guided by that recognition, even given the prospect of a lower sanction, that abandoned attempts should be mitigated, a conclusion that follows only because the reasons for punishing attempts are all reasons for punishing completions. Given this, any factor that silences a reason to issue a particular punishment for completion rather than a lower punishment—as abandonment does—silences a reason to issue that punishment for attempt (provided that the reason in question is both a reason to punish completion and attempt). The approach to the question of

---

[4] Moore (1994).

[5] Westen (2007).

[6] Alexander and Ferzan (2009a), Alexander and Ferzan (2009b).

[7] Still, it is worth observing that the question of what our intuitions about the relevance of harm to punishment show is not, in the first instance, a question that can be addressed independently of the problem of freedom of will. Our intuitions about what punishments people deserve are in part influenced by our beliefs about what kind of control they had over that for which they are being held responsible. Whether the person who recklessly backs over the child was sufficiently in control of that result to warrant responsibility for it is a hard question. And how one answers it will depend, in part, on how one answers the quite general question of what kind of control, and to what degree, one must have over what one does to warrant responsibility for it. This is, again, the problem of freedom of will. The comparison with the case of the agent who was just as reckless, but hurt no one, brings out vividly a fact about the agent who ran over the child, namely that crucial to the performance of his act was the occurrence of an event (namely, the child's crossing when he was) over which he had no control. But in so far as *that* is what gives us pause about imposing a harsh punishment on the person who backs over the child, it is our intuitions about how much control is required to warrant such treatment; such intuitions are rooted in judgments about how much, and what kind, of control is needed for responsibility.

whether last act attempters should be given the same or different punishments than those who complete crimes, the question to be addressed here, falls also into this third category. We find ourselves squarely in the theory of sentencing and not in the theory of attempt commission or its evidence. If there is a reason to give different, or similar, punishments to a last act attempter, to someone who completes the crime, or to a non-last act attempter, then that reason applies on the assumption that the attempters have committed the attempts and have been shown to have done so by the evidence.

Where the argument of chapter 11 for abandonment-based mitigation could be made in the absence of a theory of punishment—any defensible theory is compatible with it—the argument of this chapter cannot be. Section 2 explains the theory of punishment which informs the discussion that follows. Section 3 discusses an appealing argument for the claim that it is unfair to punish completion more harshly than last act attempt. The basic idea of the argument is that this is unfair since the completer and the last act attempter have done the same thing, namely perform the last act. It is shown that that argument fails. Section 4, then, considers a seemingly similar argument for the claim that it would be unfair to issue a harsher punishment to the last act attempter than to the *non-last act attempter* who fails to complete the last act. The basic idea of the argument is that it is unfair since the two agents have done the same thing, namely tried to commit the crime by trying to commit the last act. It is argued that this argument succeeds, and that it does so compatibly with the failure of the argument discussed in section 3. The result is that it is not unfair to give heavier sentences for completion than for attempt.

## 2. The Mixed Theory of Punishment

The view of punishment assumed here starts with the following observation: *the state typically censures by sanctioning.* The act of censuring a defendant found guilty of a crime is performed, that is, *by* subjecting the defendant to harsh treatment. Through such subjection, the state expresses its judgment of disapproval and condemnation of the defendant's act. Ultimately, that is, it is not only through disapproving remarks made by the judge at the time sentencing is issued, or through disapproving looks on the faces of the jury, that the state censures. Instead, the most important expression of the state's censorious disapproval is the act of sanctioning the defendant. There is a question as to whether this is justified. Perhaps the state should find another way to censure. But it is nonetheless a fact that the issuance of sanction is the most important form of censure, and it will be assumed here that the state is justified in expressing its censure that way.[8]

---

[8] Duff (2001) also places great emphasis on the way in which sanction expresses deserved censure. Over and above the expression of censure, however, Duff gives pride of place to the

The fact that censure is expressed through sanction places one very important constraint on the size of the sanction that is given to a defendant: *the sanction must not be either so small as to necessarily fall short of expressing the appropriate degree of censure of the act, but nor must be it be so large as to express greater censure than is appropriate.* The size of the sanction must be adjusted, that is, to its communicative purpose. A sanction that fails in either respect, either by being too small or too large to express a deserved degree of censure, is unjustified, precisely because it fails to accomplish a fundamental aim of sanction, which is to express censure.

Given this idea, there is a question as to the degree to which the appropriate level of sanction is fixed by the appropriate level of censure. To simplify matters, imagine that we could censure conduct on a scale of one to ten, with ten being the greatest censure, the strongest possible level of disapproval that can be expressed, and one being the least amount that can be expressed while still expressing disapproval. And imagine that sanction, too, can be ranked on such a scale, with ten being, for instance, the death penalty, and one being the smallest of prison terms, or the tiniest of fines. The question is whether the fact that a crime warrants censure of degree, say seven, determines what degree of sanction would serve to express that degree of censure. Could we express that degree of censure only through the issuance of a sanction of degree seven, or will a range of sanctions—say, six through eight—serve to express the appropriate level of censure?

It takes little reflection on the nature of communicative expression, whether linguistic or non-linguistic, to realize that a range of sanctions will serve to express any fixed degree of censure, if issued in the appropriate context. Imagine, for instance, that rolling through a stop sign rather than coming to a complete stop, and leaving a small pile of trash in the park are both given the same $100 fine: they are given the same sanction. Does this imply that they are censured equally by the state? No. The act of littering is censured to a somewhat lower degree. The reason is that it is publicly recognized that littering offenses must be given greater penalties than the expression of censure requires in order to prevent littering. In part this is *because* littering is not censured as heavily as minor reckless driving, and, hence, individuals who are considering littering are not deterred by the pangs of conscience to the same degree as those who are considering rolling through a stop sign. But it is also because it is publicly recognized that the harms that littering causes, unlike minor reckless driving, are produced only by widespread littering, and not by individual acts of littering. No single act of littering undermines the benefits of the park, although

---

role that sanction can play in improving the offender by encouraging repentance and reconciliation with victims. While I do not want to deny that these considerations are important, nor do I want to commit myself to the view that they are a more important part of sanction's purpose than are other additional purposes of sanction.

many such aggregated acts do, while single acts of even minor reckless driving can have catastrophic consequences and are criminalized in virtue of such possibilities. This difference between the harms involved in the act in virtue of which the act is criminalized—the harms of littering are aggregative, the harms of reckless driving are not—provides a context in which we express censure through sanction. That context is such as to make the same sanction expressive of different degrees of censure.

In this way, sanction expresses censure in something like the way in which the word "huge" expresses a judgment about an object's size. A pronouncement that a given mosquito is huge, and a pronouncement that a given elephant is, express different judgments, with the same word, of the size of the object described. Similarly, issuing a given sanction to a token of one type of act, and the same sanction to a token of another, can express different judgments of disapproval, given public recognition of relevant differences between the two types of act, particularly between the harms that attend such acts.

Just as it is not the case, in linguistic expression, that anything goes in the absence of context—some things just are not huge no matter what the context—it is not the case that any sanction can be used to express any given degree of censure in the absence of the kind of contextual factors that distinguish minor forms of reckless driving from littering. Some sanctions are simply too low to express the appropriate level of censure for, for instance, rape, quite independently of any contextual factors. And some sanctions are simply too high to express the appropriate level of censure for, for instance, spitting on the sidewalk, quite independently of any contextual factors. What we should say is that putting context aside, a given degree of censure can be expressed by a range of possible sanctions, with the understanding that any given level of sanction serves to express the targeted degree of censure only given appropriate contextual factors. The bottom of the range of sanctions appropriate when censure of degree c is appropriate is the lowest sanction that could express censure of degree c given appropriate contextual factors, while the top of the range is the highest. Given the impact of context on expression, generally, we should expect this range to be just that: we shouldn't expect there to be one and only one sanction that allows expression of a given degree of censure.

Add to this the following idea: the deserved sanction *just is* any sanction that would serve to express the deserved level of censure. In so far as the issuance of sanction is the expression of censure, sanction is deserved to the degree to which the censure thereby expressed is deserved. What follows, putting this idea together with the claim that a range of sanctions can express any given level of censure, is that *any member of a range of sanctions is deserved*, even when a fixed and given level of censure is deserved.

The framework sketched here—and I don't claim to have defended it—is an instance of what is sometimes called "a mixed theory" of punishment. Retributive considerations come in, in the first instance, to fix the appropriate level of censure: a defendant should be censured to precisely the degree to which he deserves censure, no more and no less. What level of censure is deserved is a moral question, and how it is answered is a difficult question in moral philosophy, not to be settled here. The deserved level of censure then fixes a range of possible sanctions: a defendant should be sanctioned in such a way as to express the level of censure he deserves, and thus should be sanctioned within a particular range. But what kind of factors can determine where in the range the defendant should be sanctioned? What kind of factors determine the "context" of the act of expressing censure through sanction? Here non-retributive considerations can come into play. In our example above, the fact that the harms associated with littering arise from repeated acts of littering, makes littering harder to deter: most people who want to avoid causing harm are not motivated to refrain from any given act of littering, since no token act causes the harm that multiple acts of littering cause. Every litterer can, in his mind, shift responsibility for the filth in the park to the other litterers who contributed, as a group, much more than he did, although individually no more and no less. This fact can warrant issuing a sanction at the top of the range within which the appropriate (low) level of censure is expressed, provided that the reasons for sanctioning are made appropriately public, and thus serve to influence the communicative force of the act of sanction. And, undoubtedly, deterability of conduct is not the only factor that can, when made public, lead to the expression of the appropriate level of censure by a given sanction within the deserved range. This theory of punishment will inform our treatment of the arguments regarding the unfairness of giving different punishment to attempters and completers in what follows.

## 3. The Same Act Argument

What is the argument being offered by those who hold that it is unfair to punish the last act attempter less harshly than the person who completes the crime? We can imagine such a person justifying his position by saying,

The reason we shouldn't punish differently people who differ only in what they cause is that two such people *do the same thing* for the same reasons: the last act attempter and the completer both perform the last act. Surely, the same actions should warrant the same punishments.

One of the interesting things about this line of thought is that it seems to cut, also, the other way. Compare D1, the last act attempter in the bulletproof vest example, to D3 who, acting on an intention to kill, loads his gun and points it at Victim3's chest, but never gets the chance to pull the trigger because he is stopped by the police. D3 has not yet committed the "last act" of pulling the trigger. Should D3 be given the same punishment as D1? We might offer the following in favor of this:

The reason we shouldn't punish differently the last act attempter and the non-last act attempter is that two such people *do the same thing*—they both try to commit the crime—for the same reasons. Surely, the same actions should warrant the same punishments.

The person concerned to argue that results are irrelevant points to one description under which the last act attempter and the completer did the same thing—they both "pulled the trigger"—while the advocate of similar punishment for last act and non-last act attempters points to a description under which *they* did the same thing—they both "tried to kill another". If "doing the same thing" is so important in the one case, it seems that it should be in the other, as well.

The advocate of results' irrelevance typically sees no problem with giving different punishments to last act attempters and non-last act attempters. He sees a crucial difference between the non-last act attempter and the completer: the completer (like the last act attempter) took that final step towards completion, and the non-last act attempter did not. However, there's a difference, also, between the last act attempter and the completer: the latter caused that objectionable result, while the former did not. Which similarity is crucial? Which difference? We need to know if the two lines of reasoning highlighted above—the one advising lumping last act attempters and completers together, the other lumping last act attempters and non-last act attempters together—are separable. Do the two lines of thought stand and fall together? The upshot of the discussion in this section and the next is that they are separable. Interestingly, however, it is the *second* that succeeds, while the first fails, contrary to the view of the advocate of results' irrelevance. While last act attempters and completers cannot be lumped together on the grounds that they did the same thing, last act attempters and non-last act attempters can and should be. At least, so it will be argued in this section and the next.

To appeal to a principle to the effect that the same acts should be given the same punishments is to appeal to *comparative* unfairness. The problem with punishing D1 and D2 differently, according to the advocate of results' irrelevance, is that to do so would be to treat people differently who are, in the relevant respect—namely, in what they *did*—the same. The same problem is noted by the person who advocates punishing the last act attempter and the non-last act attempter the same. Both are concerned with comparative fairness.

Comparative fairness, as the name suggests, is a relational concept. There are senses of the term "unfair" in which a person can be treated unfairly merely in virtue of facts about the way he is treated and facts about his properties, independently of any facts about the way other people with similar or different properties are treated. To say, for instance, that it is unfair to issue a life sentence to a person for a minor offense is not to appeal to *comparative* fairness: the unfairness (if that's the right word for it) derives entirely from a mismatch between what the person has done wrong and the length of the sentence imposed. We need know nothing about *other* agents, or the way they are treated, to recognize the unfairness in the treatment. By contrast, to say that someone is treated *comparatively unfairly* is to make explicit or implicit reference to someone else who is being treated in some way. Someone who criticizes a form of treatment of an agent on the grounds that it is comparatively unfair can remain agnostic about how the agent, or those to whom he is compared, are to be treated, given what they have done and what they are like. To say, for instance, that there is comparative unfairness in giving a lesser sentence to the last act attempt to possess crack cocaine than to completion of that offense is not to say that defendants who commit those crimes ought, or ought not, to be given sentences in excess of ten years in prison, as was common in the United States only a few years ago.[9] It is to say, instead, that whatever the right sentence is, the last act attempter ought not to be given a lesser sentence than the person who completes the crime.

The advocate of results' irrelevance who appeals, as in the quick remark in defense of his view offered above, to the comparative unfairness of letting results matter, is offering a particular argument for the claim he advocates. Let's call the argument "The Same Act Argument". It proceeds as follows:

(1) If two people did the same thing, for the same reasons, then they should not be given different punishments.
(2) If two people differ only in what they cause, then they do not differ in what they did, or the reasons for which they did it.
(3) ∴ If two people differ only in what they cause, then they should not be given different punishments.

The conclusion here is sweeping, and is intended to be. It speaks against any legal practice that entails a distinction in punishment between those who cause certain events and those who do not, even if that is the only difference between some members of each group. The conclusion, therefore, speaks against (i) defining crimes in such a way as to include result elements, (ii) defining the act elements of crimes in such a way that people could fall short of having performed them merely in virtue of what their acts failed to cause (for example, taking, killing, and deceiving would all be unacceptable act elements), and (iii) taking any facts about what a defendant's crime happened to cause as aggravating factors in sentencing. At the moment, we do all of these things. In fact, virtually every crime either has a result element or an act element that one can fall short of performing merely by failing to cause something through one's act. And, of course, taking the fact, for instance, that the defendant's act caused excruciating pain as an aggravating factor in sentencing is a

---

[9] For discussion, see United States Sentencing Commission (1995).

commonplace practice. So if this very simple argument works, our system is badly in need of reform. Although the argument's conclusion is sweeping, our concern here is with one of its somewhat less sweeping implications, namely, that last act attempts and corresponding completed crimes should not be given different sentences. If the argument's conclusion is true, then this follows, since the last act attempter and the completer differ only in what they cause.

Several commentators, including those who want to defend the *conclusion* of the Same Act Argument, have noted, however, that under one natural interpretation, premise (2) is false.[10] D2 (the agent who kills another in our bulletproof vest example), did do something different from what D1, the last act attempter, did: D2 *killed someone*, and D1 did not. The problem this fact poses for premise (2) is not that what one caused through one's act *sometimes* makes a difference to what one did: the problem is that it virtually *always* makes a difference. A person who shot another is rightly said to have performed that act in part because *he caused another to be shot*. (In chapter 3, the term "the agency involvement factor" was used to refer to that which needs to be added to causing another to be shot in order for it to count as shooting another.) Far more often than not, we identify what a person did by noting what he caused. So, if all that is meant in claiming that two people *did not do the same thing* is that there's a description of what one of them did that does not apply to what the other did, then it is very common to find that two people differ in what they did merely in virtue of a difference in what they caused. So much for premise (2).

There are, perhaps, exceptions to the general rule that acts are identified by appeal to what they cause; perhaps, that is, there are acts that are not so identified. Tryings are the most likely candidates to be in this category. But reflecting on this fact allows us to assert, instead of premise (2), only the following much weaker claim:

(2′) If two people differ only in what they cause, then they do not differ in what they tried to do, or the reasons for which they tried to do it.

(2′) is a more restricted version of (2). It limits the claim that differences in causation are insufficient for differences in action to the case of tryings. However, this adjustment merely shifts the problem with the argument. The problem is that in order to reach the conclusion, (3), from (2′), we need to assert the following instead of (1):

(1′) If two people tried to do the same thing, for the same reasons, then they should not be given different punishments.

Perhaps (1′) is true. But notice that we cannot assert (1′) as a premise in an argument intended to show that last act attempts should be given the same

---

[10] Cf. Thomson (1989).

punishment as corresponding completed crimes, which is one of the results that is sought by the advocate of the Same Act Argument. After all, (1') merely asserts that claim and so cannot be used to support it.[11]

There is, however, an alternative to premise (2), which differs from (2') and does not fall prey to this criticism. Perhaps what the person who asserts (2) is really getting at, really means to express, is the idea that two people who differ only in what they caused do not differ *in a normatively relevant way* in what they did. What such a person is trying to express, that is, is the idea that the description of what the two agents did under which they did the same thing is the relevant description for purposes of moral and legal assessment. Both D1 and D2, for instance, shot another person while intending to kill him. Both *tried* to kill another person. So, although there is a difference between them—D2 killed someone and D1 did not—that difference is not relevant when it comes to assessment. To see the point, consider the way we might express it under a "moral ledger" view, according to which the question of what punishment a person deserves is determined by what acts are on his moral ledger, where on his moral ledger is the list of acts that (i) he performed, and (ii) for which he owes an account. So, we might say, although the list of acts *performed* by D1 and D2 is different in an interesting way—D2's list includes "killed another" and D1's does not—the two agents' *moral ledgers* are the same; they each owe an account of their act of shooting another with intent to kill, and D2 does not owe an account of killing another despite the fact that he performed that act. Of course, the question is why. Why should we think that what is relevant when it comes to assessment is that both shot another intending to kill, and not that one actually killed someone and the other did not? Why should it be that only what one tries to do ends up on one's moral ledger, and not also what one did thanks to what one's trying caused?

At this point, the elusive notion of control re-enters the stage. What the advocate of the Same Act Argument is likely to say is that there is no unfairness in including an act on one person's moral ledger, despite its not appearing on the moral ledger of those who did not perform it, only if the act meets the following restriction: *the agent succeeded in performing it only because he exercised greater control over it than the agents who did not perform it*. To place "killed another" on D2's moral ledger is to hold him to account for something over which he had no more control than D1 had, in violation of this restriction. Call this the "Greater Control Restriction".

Unlike the various "control principles" that one finds in the literature on this topic—principles that say that such-and-such kind or degree of control over an

---

[11] In addition, many who advocate for the same punishment for completions as last act attempts also think it justified to give lesser punishments to non-last act attempts. See, for instance, Morse (2004). But (1') implies that all attempts should be punished the same regardless of whether they are last act attempts or non-last act attempts.

act is necessary for responsibility for the act—the Greater Control Restriction is comparative. What it says is that a person cannot be fairly held to account for something unless he exercised *more* control over it than the other agents who failed to perform it. This is not to say that he had "complete" or "total" control over it—whatever those kinds of control amount to—or even that he had sufficient control over it to hold him responsible for it. Say, for instance, that two agents, D4 and D5, play Russian roulette with their respective victims, Victim4 and Victim5. Both D4 and D5 spin the cylinder of a revolver containing one bullet, point it at the victim and pull the trigger. D4 fires no bullet—the chamber aligned with the barrel is empty—and Victim4 is unharmed, while D5's gun fires a bullet killing Victim5. Can we hold D5 to account for killing another, or would doing so necessarily treat him unfairly relative to D4? If there was just as good a chance that D5's gun would fire no bullet as that D4's would, then we cannot, under the Greater Control Restriction; we must hold them to account for the acts they both performed, acts like risking someone's death, but we cannot hold D5 to account for killing another. But if D5's gun had only six chambers—giving him a one in six chance of killing Victim5—while D4's had eight—giving him a one in eight chance of killing Victim4—then the situation is different. Now, under the Greater Control Restriction, we can place "killed another" on D5's moral ledger, despite its absence from D4's, without treating D5 unfairly in comparison to D4. Of course, we may find that there is some *other* agent, D6, who did not kill anyone, but had no less control over that than D5 had; in which case, *relative to D6*, it will be comparatively unfair to hold D5 to account for killing someone. But, still, even in that event it is not unfair to hold D5 to account for a killing *relative to D4*—D5 had greater control over that than D4 did—even though it is so *relative to D6*. To know whether or not a certain treatment is comparatively unfair we need to compare it to the treatment some particular other person is getting.

Two points illustrated by this example, and already made in the preceding paragraph, deserve emphasis. First, restricting acts on one's moral ledger to those that one exercised greater control over than otherwise identical agents does not restrict them to acts over which one had sufficient control for responsibility. Imagine, for instance, that the cylinder of the gun has one hundred million chambers and, still, only one bullet. The person who kills the victim in such a case surely had insufficient control over that result to warrant holding him responsible for it: he had a lower chance of killing another than any of us do whenever we drive to the grocery store; he had a lower chance of killing another than someone who gives "the finger" has of causing a lethal heart attack. Second, comparative unfairness, as it is being understood here, is a two-place relation. As such, it can hold between X and Y while failing to hold between X and Z. Hence an agent can be treated unfairly relative to one other person, but not relative to another. In one version of the example above, we imagine three agents: D4's cylinder has eight chambers and he does not kill anyone; D5's has six and he kills someone; D6's has six and he does not kill anyone. On the proposed restriction on what is placed on one's moral ledger, it is not comparatively unfair *relative to D4* to place killing another on D5's moral ledger, but it is relative to D6. Given what comparative fairness is, there is nothing puzzling or unexpected about such asymmetries.

Thus, we might take the idea sought to be expressed by the advocate of premise (2) in the Same Act Argument, not as the idea that where there is a difference in what two people cause there is no difference in their acts, but, instead, as the idea that in such a case there is no act that one performed *thanks to his exercising greater control over it than the other*. That is to say that differences in what two people cause can result in differences in their acts, but it can't result in differences in their acts *that are explicable by noting that one exercised greater control over the act he performed than the other*. Thus, it can't result in differences in what acts appear on two otherwise identical agents' moral ledgers, under the Greater Control Restriction.

So understood, the Same Act Argument proceeds as follows:

(1″) If someone performed an act over which he exercised no more control than someone otherwise identical who failed to perform it, then he should not be given a different punishment from that other person.

(2″) If two people differ only in what they caused, then one of them performed an act over which he exercised no more control than the other who failed to perform it.

(3) ∴ If two people differ only in what they cause, then they should not be given different punishments.

Under this version of the argument, the second premise, (2″), is true. But to use (2″) to reach (3), we needed to introduce a new premise, namely (1″). Where (1) said that where we find the same acts we ought to have no difference in punishment, and (1′) said that where we find the same tryings we ought to have no difference in punishment, (1″) says that where we find different acts, but the same exercise of control, we ought to have no difference in punishment. (1) is true, but can't help to reach the conclusion since (2) is false. (1′) begs the question since it amounts to asserting what is in need of proof, namely that last act attempts and completions should not be punished differently. What about (1″)? Like (1) and (1′), (1″) is a claim about comparative fairness. It should be understood as asserting that it is comparatively unfair to issue different punishments to two people who differ in what they did, and in nothing else, without any difference in control. Is (1″) true, and should it be recognized as such, independently of acceptance of the claims it is meant to support?

(1″) needs to be considered in relation to the distinction between censure and sanction. Punishment always involves both. Hence, assessment of premise (1″) requires disambiguating two claims that might be made by someone who asserts it:

*Same Control-Same Censure*: If someone performed an act over which he exercised no more control than someone otherwise identical who failed to perform it, then he should not be censured differently from that other person.

*Same Control-Same Sanction*: If someone performed an act over which he exercised no more control than someone otherwise identical who failed to perform it, then he should not be given a different sanction from that other person.

The fact that a person should not be given a pair of things does not imply that he should not be given each: it might be wrong to give a madman a gun and ammunition, but not wrong to give him a gun (provided he has no ammunition), and not wrong to give him ammunition (provided he has no gun). For this reason, (1″) logically entails neither Same Control-Same Censure, nor Same Control-Same Sanction. It is logically possible, that is, that it is wrong to censure to degree c the person who completes the crime and at the same time to sanction him to degree s, given that the otherwise identical last act attempter is given a different package of censure and sanction, while it is not wrong to censure him to degree c (provided he is not sanctioned to degree s), and not wrong to sanction him to degree s (provided he is not censured to degree c). Still, reflection on these two principles will help us to get a better idea of whether premise (1″) is true.

I believe that Same Control-Same Censure is true, and Same Control-Same Sanction is false. This result follows from the "mixed theory" of punishment sketched in section 2. Recall that, under that theory, a given level of censure can be expressed by quite different sanctions. The need to express only a deserved level of censure sets a range of admissible sanctions. However, where in that range a defendant is appropriately placed can be a function of much besides desert of censure. Considerations of general deterrence, of incapacitation, of mercy, of equality, of criminal history, and much more besides, can quite correctly inform the decision about where in the deserved range of sanction to place the defendant. By making those considerations parts of the context of the act of communication involved in sanction, the state thereby can sanction more or less heavily, while still expressing the same degree of censure.

Now, from within the mixed theory of punishment proposed, Same Control-Same Censure is quite plausible, or, at least, it is not impugned by anything said here. After all, it does seem that two people who try to do the same bad thing—who exercise control in precisely the same way—are worthy of the same kind and degree of disapproval: they are worthy of the same censure. After all, as suggested in chapter 1, the attempter and the completer recognize, weigh, and respond to reasons in the same way, and are both guided by their commitments in the same way. These commonalities between attempter and completer speak strongly to the idea that they are deserving of the same degree of censure. When one person is censured differently from another, despite no difference in desert of censure, one or the other has been treated comparatively unfairly. A principle of equal treatment for the equally deserving constrains us to express the same degree of censure to equally deserving defendants.

However, Same Control-Same Sanction is not nearly as plausible. The reason is that two defendants could have exercised the control they had in precisely the same way, and have come to do different things, while in different contexts. That difference in context can make a difference to what sanction needs to be issued in order to express the same level of censure. Hence, the fact that the differences in their actions is not explicable through a difference in the way they exercised control over their conduct does not imply that there is no difference between them that makes them deserving of different sanctions. The differences in the deserved sanctions derive, instead, from differences in context.

Putting the point this way obscures something important about the nature of these contextual factors. The relevant contextual factors often involve a variety of social goods that are achievable through issuing greater sanctions than would be needed to express the appropriate level of censure in their absence. If we recognize, for instance, that a $100 fine for littering keeps the parks clean, and we recognize publicly that it is with that end in mind that the litterer is given this sanction, that blunts the force of the expression of censure. It is as though we are saying, to the litterer, "I disapprove of what you did somewhat less than it might appear, but I sanction you this way in order to achieve goods that are of importance to us all." And, in general, to blunt the expressive force of a sanction—to express less censure than is sometimes expressed with that same amount of sanction—social goods must be at play in this way. We must express, to the defendant, that more is at stake for all of us in his sanction than the mere expression of censure, if we are to manage to express less censure than such sanction expresses in other contexts. The reason that the litterer cannot complain of the comparative unfairness of issuing him the same fine as the minor reckless driver, who deserves greater censure, is that different sorts of social goods are at stake in the censure of littering than are at stake in the censure of minor reckless driving, and thanks to this difference, different degrees of censure are expressed by the same fine. This is why it makes sense to say to the litterer who points to the minor reckless driver and says, "Why is he getting the same fine as me?" that the fine that he is being given keeps the parks clean. Such a response identifies the context thanks to which the fine the litterer is given expresses only the small degree of censure that he deserves.

But has it been shown, at this point, that (1″) is false? Not yet. After all, it is one thing to say that differences in "context" can result in the same degree of censure being expressed by different sanctions. It is quite another thing to say that a difference only in what is caused by the agent can make such a difference to the relevant context. But it is that claim that the argument really requires. The difference between the last act attempter and the otherwise identical person who completes the crime, that is, must be a difference *that makes the following difference*: it results in the same amount of censure being expressed by two different sanctions. If this is true, then the Same Act Argument fails.

And, in fact, it is true, as one can see by reflecting on the role that the issuance of sanction plays in public acknowledgement of victims of crime as people who have been wronged, and are entitled to recognition as such. To express, to the injured victim of a crime, the judgment that the perpetrator acted wrongly is part of what is called for. But it is not all that is called for. The reason is that to say that the perpetrator acted wrongly is not to express, directly, the judgment that the injuries of the victim are themselves to be mourned, quite independently of the perpetrator's wrongdoing. A person who both judges the perpetrator's act to be objectionable, and judges what the victim lost to be of value, must often find a way to express both judgments. This is not always true—we do not each of us owe this to every victim of wrongdoing—but there are certain conditions under which we do owe it. Of relevance here is the fact that the expression of these two judgments, both of them, is owed by the state to a particular citizen victim of a publicly recognized form of wrongdoing—a justifiably criminalized form—who has lost something that is, itself, a good of the sort that the state criminalizes conduct in order to protect. In these circumstances, which are the circumstances of moment to the criminal law, the state must show that it values what the victim lost; it is not enough to show that it condemns what the perpetrator did. Sanction can express both of these judgments, and often does.

This is not an unimportant form of expression. Sanction is expensive; and when the state issues a sanction it expresses the idea that the values that it affirms in issuing it are worth at least the costs that it incurs in order to do so. In this, the issuance of sanction is continuous with a variety of social practices, including those involved in mourning. Funerals are expensive. But they seem worth doing, even to those who believe that there is no life after death. A funeral expresses a shared judgment among its participants of the value of the life mourned. Similarly, the issuance of sanction can express a shared judgment of the value of the losses suffered by the victim. Although we can coolly say that the difference between the last act attempter and the person who completes the crime is sometimes only a difference in what is caused, we might just as well say that often there is only this difference: the latter has a *victim* and the former does not.

To point to the fact that the issuance of the sanction expresses acknowledgment of the injury to the victim is to point to something that *diminishes* the degree of censure that would have been expressed by the sanction in the absence of that fact. The sanction is acknowledging a judgment of the value of what was lost by injury, and such a judgment does not, in itself, express disapproval or condemnation for the person who is, through his act, the cause of the injury. So, in response to the person who completes the crime, and complains that he is being given a greater punishment than the last act attempter we can say, pointing to the victim, "He was injured." This explanation works not by increasing the censure expressed by the sanction, but by identifying the fact about the context that makes the sanction an expression of no greater censure than was expressed by the smaller sanction given to the last act attempter.

It is important to note that what was just said is not, despite appearances, an argument in favor of giving *greater* punishments to completed crimes than to last act attempts. After all, for all that has been said, it is *possible* to express both censure of the person who completes the crime and acknowledgment of the injury of the victim with a sanction that is just the same as the sanction issued to the last act attempter. If this is possible, then further arguments are needed to positively support giving a greater punishment to the person who completes the crime. Still, what has been argued is that it is also *possible* to give a greater punishment to the completer than to the last act attempter without thereby expressing any greater censure for the completer, as in the case in which the additional sanction serves merely to acknowledge the injury to the victim. But if this is possible, then nothing rules out the possibility of differences in punishment without comparative unfairness, contrary to what the advocate of the argument under discussion aims to establish.

(1″), therefore, is false. It is not necessarily the case that it is comparatively unfair to give different punishments to otherwise identical people who differ in their acts, despite no difference in the degree of control exercised by them. Such a difference in punishment can be fair, provided that the same degree of censure is expressed by different sanctions. And this is the case when the only difference between two people is that one, and not the other, injured a third. To acknowledge the injured is not to thereby express any greater disapproval of the injurer. Therefore, even in this developed form, the Same Act Argument for the irrelevancy of results fails. Or, rather, our conclusion should be conditional: the Same Act Argument fails *given* the mixed theory of punishment sketched in section 2.

## 4. The Same Attempt Argument

As noted in the last section, it is an interesting fact that advocates of results' irrelevance, while uncomfortable with punishing last act attempts less harshly than corresponding completed crimes, are entirely at ease with punishing attempts that are not last act attempts—attempts in which further action from the defendant would have been required for completion—less heavily than last act attempts. The obvious explanation for this is that there is a difference in the conduct of the last act attempter and the non-last act attempter: the last act attempter has done more to advance towards the fulfillment of the criminal intention than the non-last act attempter. But why should this matter? In one very important respect the last act and non-last act attempter have done precisely the same thing: they have both tried to commit the crime. There are differences, too, in what they have done: the last act attempter, for instance, has actually pulled the trigger, while the non-last act attempter merely aimed the gun, planning to pull the trigger, and was stopped before he could. So, "tried to kill another" appears on both agents' list of acts performed, but "pulled the trigger" appears only on the last act attempter's list. Is that difference enough to warrant a difference in punishment?

Some answer "yes" to this question on the grounds that the non-last act attempter might still change his mind, while the last act attempter has given up what is, for all he knows, his last chance to do so.[12] Is this response adequate? The first thing to note in response to this question is that performance of a last act does not, in itself, preclude change of mind prior to completion. D1 might wish he had never pulled that trigger as the bullet flies to its target, and he might do what useless things he can—yell, "Duck!", for instance—to prevent the bullet from reaching its mark after it is fired. Further, performance of what one believes to be a last act does not assure completion; D1, whose bullet is stopped by the bulletproof vest, does not complete the murder he intends, despite performing what he believes is the last act. What must be thought to be of significance, then, is not giving up one's last chance to change one's mind, nor taking steps that assure completion. Instead, what must be thought to be of significance is giving up what one believes will be one's last chance *to avoid completion through an exercise of one's agency.* However, performance of an act that one believes, at the time of action, to be such an act does not preclude having another opportunity to change one's mind, since one's belief might turn out to be false. When D1 discovers that Victim1 was wearing a bulletproof vest, and thus that his act of pulling the trigger was not the last after all, he might have the opportunity to finish the job, by firing a second shot at Victim1's head, say, or, instead, he might have the opportunity to abandon the attempt. So, under the effort to distinguish between the last act attempter and the non-last act attempter on offer, it is thought to be of great normative significance, great enough to warrant a harsher penalty, to act while believing, even falsely, that one will thereby achieve what one intends.

However, this is a very thin basis on which to hang a distinction in punishment. Notice that it is virtually always possible for an intending criminal to form a plan that involves no last act, and that will, if executed properly, lead to commission of the crime. To make a plan that involves a last act, a person must anticipate that he will, in the execution of his plan, perform an act that *he will believe at the time of action* to result, if nothing goes wrong, in completion. Someone who plans to kill another by shooting him in the chest typically makes such a plan. He plans to pull the trigger and expects that when he does so he will believe that no further action on his part will be necessary for commission of the murder. But it need not be this way. Even in this case, his

---

[12] Cf. Duff (1996), 40.

plan need not involve any last act. Perhaps he plans to shoot his victim in the chest and, if that does not kill him, to follow through with another shot to the head. If that is his plan then he does not plan for the pulling of the trigger to be the last act; he hopes it will be—it will save him time and ammunition if it is— but he does not expect that, when the time comes to pull the trigger, he will view himself as giving up his last chance to avoid completion through an exercise of his agency. For all he knows, he will have another chance to do so, a chance to choose not to give the shot to the head, when the victim fails to die from the shot to the chest. Other examples, even just restricting ourselves to murder, are more obvious. Someone who plans to kill another by slow poisoning does not anticipate that there will ever be an act that, when performed, he believes to be the last he will need to perform: his plan is to keep at it until his victim dies, and he anticipates that in each and every instance in which he administers a dose, he will not know if it is the last. Why should the fact that an agent acts on a plan involving no last acts—no acts that he will believe, at the time of action, to involve forsaking his last opportunity to prevent completion through an exercise of his agency—imply that his conduct is worthy of any less punishment than that of the person whose plan includes a last act which he actually performs?

Part of the issue here concerns the attitude of an agent towards contingency planning—planning about what to do should the aimed-at result of one's conduct fail to come to pass. Some agents engage in a great deal of contingency planning, and others do not. Those who do are much more likely to make plans that include no last acts. An agent who has made plans for what to do if the bullet he shoots fails to kill, does not expect to believe, when he fires that bullet, that his act is his last. If he has contingency plans regarding what to do if his *contingency plans* fail, then he does not anticipate that even those acts will be believed, at the time of action, to be his last. But, if anything, the contingency planner seems to be acting on a *worse* plan—it is, at the least, a plan more likely to result in completion of the crime—than the agent who makes no contingency plans, or few. Why should someone whose plans are worse in this respect be subject to lesser punishments?

Still, to say that a natural way of identifying the normatively crucial difference between the last act attempter and the non-last act attempter fails, despite its appeal, is not to say that there is comparative unfairness in punishing the last act attempter more harshly than the non-last act attempter. The argument for that claim requires independent discussion. Such an argument proceeds as follows, and unlike the Same Act Argument, this formulation will require no further refinement. but only defense against objections. Let's call this the "Same Attempt Argument":

(4) If two people committed the same crime, for the same reasons, and with the same results, they should not be given different punishments.

(5) The last act attempter and the otherwise identical non-last act attempter both committed an attempted crime, for the same reasons, and with the same results.

(6) ∴ The last act attempter and the otherwise identical non-last act attempter should not be given different punishments.

As in the Same Act Argument, the first premise of the Same Attempt Argument, premise (4), appeals (tacitly) to comparative fairness. The idea is, simply, that it is unfair to give different treatment to people who committed the same crime (assuming they did it for the same reasons and with the same results). According to the argument, the last act attempter, who is given a harsher punishment than some non-last act attempter who was acting on the very same intention but just didn't manage to complete the last act, has a point when he gestures towards that person and says, "Why is he being given a lesser punishment than I am? After all, we both tried to commit the crime, and we did it for the very same reasons and with the same results."

The remarks made in section 3 in discussion of the principles of Same Control-Same Censure and Same Control-Same Sanction would seem to apply in objection to premise (4). What we learned from that discussion is that it is comparatively unfair to censure two people differently when they did the same thing, but that it can be comparatively fair to sanction them differently, provided that differences in context allow for expression of equal degrees of censure through the issuance of different sanctions. Should we say here, then, that premise (4) is false since differences in context can allow for differences in sanction of people who committed the same crime for the same reasons and with the same results? No. The reason is that where two agents have committed the same crime for the same reasons and with the same results, *there is no difference in context*. And without a difference in context, different sanctions will express different degrees of censure.

Why is there no difference in context in this case? First, unlike the case of minor reckless driving sanctioned the same as littering, where the differences in the crime made a difference to the context, here we have the same crime, namely the attempt of a particular crime. Thus we do not have *that* difference in context. In addition, recall that in the case of the Same Act Argument it was observed that a difference in effects on victims is a difference in context that can make a difference to what degree of censure is expressed by particular sanctions. Where there is a difference in harm, there is a different need for the state to express its belief in the value of what the victim lost. It was suggested there that this need could be fulfilled through the issuance of different sanctions, without the state thereby expressing different degrees of censure. But, *by hypothesis*, the two agents we are imagining here—the last act attempter and the non-last act attempter of the same crime—do not have different effects on victims, and so this explanation cannot be used. Our objection to the Same

Act Argument, then, does not apply with equal force against the Same Attempt Argument.

Now why should the opponent agree that the last act attempter and the agent with whom he is being compared do not have different effects on victims? After all, compare D1, the last act attempter whose victim was wearing a bulletproof vest, to D3, the non-last act attempter who acted on the same intention to kill, but fell short of pulling the trigger. There is a very important difference in these two defendants' respective effects on their victims: D1 has actually shot someone, while D3 has not. Anyone who had a choice between standing in Victim1's shoes and standing in Victim3's would choose Victim3's; at least Victim3 didn't take a bullet. And this suggests that the state ought to find a way to express its judgment that Victim1 has suffered, has lost something of value that was not lost by Victim3. If such a difference in context was enough to defeat the Same Act Argument, it seems that it ought to be enough to defeat the Same Attempt Argument.

But it is not. The reason is that where the Same Act Argument required, by its nature, a comparison between agents, one of whom caused harm and the other of whom did not (or caused less), the Same Attempt Argument does not. Thus, the right response to the objection is to admit that to give a heavier punishment to D1 than to D3 does not, all by itself, show D1 to have been treated in a comparatively unfair way: these different punishments, thanks to differences in the effects on victims, might express the same degree of censure. But this shows only that D1's punishment is not unfair *relative to D3*. But the Same Attempt Argument does not require that the harsher penalty for the last act attempter is comparatively unfair relative to *all* non-last act attempters, but only that it is comparatively unfair relative to *some* such. So consider D7. Acting on an intention to kill, and knowing that Victim7 is wearing a bulletproof vest, D7 shoots Victim7 in the chest, expecting that the blow will knock him to the ground, giving D7 the chance to shoot him in the head. D7 shoots Victim7 in the chest and Victim7, like Victim1, falls to the ground, but before D7 can issue the kill-shot, he is wrestled to the ground by police. D1 and D7 have both attempted a murder, for the same reasons and with the same results, but only D1 has performed a last act. But here we have no difference in context that can cause it to be the case that different sanctions would express the same degree of censure. If D1 receives a harsher sanction than D7, then D1 is censured more harshly than D7, but since they deserve precisely the same degree of censure, D1 is being treated comparatively unfairly.

In general, for every last act attempter we can construct an example of a non-last act attempter who did the same thing, for the same reasons, and with the same results. To do so, simply take whatever result the last act attempter actually caused and imagine that (i) the non-last act attempter intended to cause that very same thing, and (ii) did so, but (iii) did so as a non-last step in a sequence of actions that would end with completion of the crime, but (iv) was prevented from performing any further acts in the envisioned sequence. Such an attempter differs from the last act attempter only in his head: he has a different plan for completing the crime, a plan involving a somewhat longer sequence of actions than the last act attempter's. Thus, for every last act attempter there is a non-last act attempter whom comparative fairness requires should be given the very same sanction. To give a different sanction to the last act attempter than to this non-last act attempter, then, is to treat the last act attempter comparatively unfairly relative to the non-last act attempter envisioned. Any sentencing policy, then, that gives greater sanction to last act attempters than to non-last act attempters is committed to engaging in comparatively unfair treatment of last act attempters.

Notice that I am not suggesting that all attempters should be given the same punishments. Different attempters have different effects on victims, and this difference, among other differences, can make a difference to what sanction is appropriate. Although all those who attempt the same crime are worthy of the same degree of censure, this degree of censure, when differences are present, can be expressed by different sanctions. The crucial point is that the right comparison class when we wonder whether an attempter is being treated fairly by being given a particular sanction *is the class of defendants who have attempted the same crime.* The right comparison class is not those who have *completed the crime.* Those who have completed the crime have, necessarily, had effects on others that the attempter has not, and such effects are relevant for the reasons offered here. In addition, and importantly, last act attempters are not a particularly important class of attempters when it comes to sentencing. There is no reason to think that it is comparatively unfair to give them lower punishments than those who complete the crime, and there are, necessarily, others who have not committed a last act but who ought to be given just the same punishment that they are to be given. Comparative fairness requires it.

## 5. Conclusion

It is important to emphasize both the sense in which the preceding discussion has, and the sense in which it has not advanced the long-standing debate among criminal law theorists about the relevance of results to sentencing. As indicated in the introduction to this chapter, many of the disputes that have arisen in that debate cannot be adjudicated independently of thought about the nature of freedom of will; this includes debates about the relevance of intuitions that both favor and oppose giving different treatment to those who differ only in what they have caused. No progress has been made here, then, in settling any such disputes. Where progress has been made is in adjudicating dispute over the comparative fairness of predicating differences in sanction on differences in effect. What has been argued is that, independently of objections to the mixed theory of punishment sketched in section 2, there is as yet no reason to believe that there is, generally, unfairness in doing so. Of course, sometimes there is comparative unfairness in such sentences, even given the mixed theory sketched, for sometimes different degrees of censure are expressed where the same degree of censure is deserved. But it need not be this way: it is possible to express the same degree of censure with different sanctions and so it is possible to predicate different treatments on differences in effect without comparative unfairness.

Further, and importantly, the Same Attempt Argument offered and defended in section 4 poses a powerful challenge to those who think it comparatively unfair to take results to be relevant to sentencing. What the argument indicates is that, just as we can often imagine a last act attempter who differs from a completer only in what he caused, we can *always* imagine a non-last act attempter who differs not at all from any given last act attempter, and whom it would be comparatively unfair to treat differently. What this implies is that anyone who accepts that *a completer* should be punished just the same as some last act attempter must also accept that a completer should be punished just the same *as some non-last act attempter.* It is thus incumbent on anyone who holds that results are irrelevant for reasons of fairness to avoid commitment to the claim that the difference between the last act attempter and the non-last act attempter is of a sort that he takes to be normatively relevant. In other words, one cannot say, in defense of the irrelevance of results, that it is "mere luck" that distinguishes the last act attempter and the completer, for it is not "mere luck" that separates the completer from the non-last act attempter, and yet there are principled reasons for thinking that if the last act attempter and the completer are to be lumped together, then the non-last act attempter is to be lumped together with them too. If they are all to be punished the same—if results really are irrelevant—it must be for some reason that obeys this constraint. If the completer and the last act attempter are similar in all "relevant" respects, then so must be the completer and the non-last act attempter; what is relevant in the one case must be treated as relevant in the other.

What is the right response to this conundrum? One response, motivated by a conviction in the unfairness of predicating differences in treatment on differences only in what is caused, involves searching for a way in which the completer, the last act attempter, *and* the non-last act attempter are all, at heart, the same. This, it seems to me, is a strategy that is likely to have diminishing returns. The better position it seems to me—although I cannot claim to have a fully satisfactory argument for it—involves accepting that results can make a difference to what sanction is deserved, even though they cannot make a difference to what degree of censure is deserved. There is moral sanction-luck, but no moral censure-luck. Such a position requires support from a theory of punishment, a theory that implies that this is possible. The mixed theory sketched here is such a theory, although, perhaps, there are other defensible theories of punishment that also provide the same support. In any event, from this we reach the conclusion that when it comes to attempts, our sentencing practices stand on firmer ground than one might have thought. One can, without unfairness, both punish an attempt less harshly than a completed crime, and punish some attempts more harshly than others.

# Bibliography

Alexander, L. and Ferzan, K. D. (2009a) *Crime and Culpability: A Theory of Criminal Law*, Cambridge: Cambridge University Press.

—— ——. (2009b) "Results Don't Matter" in *Criminal Law Conversations*, P. H. Robinson (ed.), Oxford: Oxford University Press, pp. 147–153.

——, and Kessler, Kimberly D. (1997) "Mens Rea and Inchoate Crimes" in *The Journal of Criminal Law and Criminology*, v. 87, pp. 1138–1193.

American Law Institute. (1985) *The Model Penal Code and Commentaries*, Philadelphia: The American Law Institute. [Cited by section and commentary page as *Model Penal Code*.]

Austin, J. L. (1979) "Ifs and Cans" in *Philosophical Papers*, New York: Oxford University Press, pp. 205–232.

Baier, A. (1997) "Doing Things with Others: The Mental Commons" in L. Alanen, S. Heinamaa, and T. Wallgren (eds.), *Commonality and Particularity in Ethics*, New York: St Martin's Press.

Becker, L. C. (1974) "Criminal Attempt and the Theory of the Law of Crimes" in *Philosophy & Public Affairs*, v. 3, pp. 262–294.

Bennett, J. (1981) "Morality and Cosequences" in S. M. McMurrin (ed.), *The Tanner Lectures on Human Values*, v. 2, Salt Lake City: University of Utah Press, pp. 46–116.

Bratman, M. (1987) *Intention, Plans and Practical Reason*, Cambridge: Harvard University Press.

——. (1999a) *Faces of Intention: Selected Essays on Intention and Agency*, Cambridge: Cambridge University Press.

——. (1999b) "I Intend That We J" in *Faces of Intention: Selected Essays on Intention and Agency*, Cambridge: Cambridge University Press, pp. 142–164.

——. (1999c) "Davidson's Theory of Intention" in *Faces of Intention: Selected Essays on Intention and Agency*, Cambridge: Cambridge University Press, pp. 209–224.

——. (2006) "What is the Accordion Effect?" in *Journal of Ethics*, v. 10, pp. 5–19.

——. (2007a) "Hierarchy, Circularity and Double Reduction" in *Structures of Agency*, Oxford: Oxford University Press, pp. 68–88.

——. (2007b) "Two Problems about Human Agency" in *Structures of Agency*, Oxford: Oxford University Press, pp. 89–105.

——. (2007c) "Valuing and the Will" in *Structures of Agency*, Oxford: Oxford University Press, pp. 47–67.

Chisholm, R. (1964) "The Descriptive Element in the Concept of Action" in *The Journal of Philosophy*, v. 61, pp. 613–624.

Danto, A. (1965) "Basic Actions" in *American Philosophical Quarterly*, v. 2, no. 2, pp. 141–148.

Darwall, S. (2006) *The Second-Person Standpoint: Morality, Respect, and Accountability*, Cambridge: Harvard University Press.

Davidson, D. (1980a) "Intending" in *Essays on Actions and Events*, Oxford: Oxford University Press, pp. 83–102.

——. (1980b) "Freedom to Act" in *Essays on Actions and Events*, Oxford: Oxford University Press, pp. 63–82.

——. (1980c) "Actions, Reasons and Causes" in *Essays on Actions and Events*, Oxford: Oxford University Press, pp. 3–19.

——. (1980d) "Agency" in *Essays on Actions and Events*, Oxford: Oxford University Press, pp. 43–61.

——. (2001a) "Radical Interpretation" in *Inquiries into Truth and Interpretation*, Oxford: Clarendon Press, pp. 125–140.

——. (2001b) "Three Varieties of Knowledge" in *Subjective, Intersubjective, Objective*, Oxford: Clarendon Press, pp. 205–220.

Davis, M. (1986) "Why Attempts Deserve Less Punishment than Complete Crimes" in *Law and Philosophy*, v. 5, pp. 1–32.

Davis, W. (1984) "A Causal Theory of Intending" in *American Philosophical Quarterly*, v. 21, pp. 43–54.

Donagan, A. (1987) *Choice: The Essential Element in Human Action*, London: Routledge & Kegan Paul.

Dressler, J. (2003) *Cases and Materials on Criminal Law* (4th edn), St Paul: Thomson-West.

——. (2009) *Understanding Criminal Law* (5th edn), Newark: LexisNexis.

Duff, R. A. (1991) "The Circumstances of an Attempt" in *Cambridge Law Journal*, v. 50, pp. 100–119.

——. (1996) *Criminal Attempts*, Oxford: Oxford University Press.

——. (2001) *Punishment, Communication and Community*, Oxford: Oxford University Press.

Dworkin, G. and Blumenfeld, D. (1966) "Punishment for Intentions" in *Mind*, v. 75, pp. 396–404.

Feinberg, J. (1970a) "Action and Responsibility" in *Doing and Deserving: Essays in the Theory of Responsibility*, Princeton: Princeton University Press, pp. 119–151.

——. (1970b) "Causing Voluntary Actions" in *Doing and Deserving: Essays in the Theory of Responsibility*, Princeton: Princeton University Press, pp. 152–186.

——. (2008) "The Classic Debate" in *Philosophy of Law* (8th edn), J. Feinberg and J. Coleman (eds), Belmont: Wadsworth-Thomson, pp. 624–629.

——. (2000) "When the Rule Swallows the Exception" in *Quinnipiac Law Review*, v. 19, pp. 505–533.

Fischer, J. and Ravizza, M. (1998) *Responsibility and Control: A Theory of Moral Responsibility*, Cambridge: Cambridge University Press.

——, ——, and Copp, D. (1993) "Quinn on Double Effect: The Problem of Closeness" in *Ethics*, v. 103, pp. 707–725.

Fletcher, G. (1986) "Constructing a Theory of Impossible Attempts" in *Criminal Justice Ethics*, v. 53, pp. 53–69.

——. (2000) *Rethinking Criminal Law* (2nd edn), Oxford: Oxford University Press.

Frege, G. (1948) "Sense and Reference" in *The Philosophical Review*, v. 57, pp. 209–230.

Gardner, J. (2004) "The Wrongdoing that Gets Results" in *Philosophical Perspectives*, v. 18, pp. 53–88.

Ginet, C. (1990) *On Action*, Cambridge: Cambridge University Press.

——. (2004) "Trying to Act" in *Freedom and Determinism*, J. K. Campbell, M. O'Rourke, and D. Shier (eds), Cambridge: MIT Press, pp. 89–102.

Grice, H. P. (1971) "Intention and Uncertainty" in *Proceedings of the British Academy*, v. 57, pp. 263–279.

Grimm, F. (1989) "Alleged Plot to Kill by Hex Puts Voodoo Man in Jail" in *Miami Herald*, Florida, March 31.

Hale, M. (1736) *Historia Placitorum Coronæ*: The History of the Pleas of the Crown, London.

Hall, J. (1960) *General Principles of Criminal Law* (2nd edn), Indiannapolis: Bobbs-Merrill.

Harman, G. (1976) "Practical Reasoning" in *Review of Metaphysics*, v. 29, pp. 431–463.

——. (1986) *Change in View*, Cambridge: MIT Press.

——. (2000) "Desired Desires" in *Explaining Value and Other Essays in Moral Philosophy*, Oxford: Oxford University Press, pp. 117–136.

Hart, H. L. A. (1981) "The House of Lords on Attempting the Impossible" in *Oxford Journal of Legal Studies*, v. 1, pp. 149–166.

——. and Honore, A. M. (1959) *Causation in the Law*, Oxford: Clarendon Press.

Hasnas, J. (2002) "Once More Unto The Breach: The Inherent Liberalism Of The Criminal Law And Liability For Attempting The Impossible" in *Hastings Law Journal*, v. 54, pp. 1–77.

Holmes, O. Wendell (1881) *The Common Law*, Cambridge: John Wilson & Son.

Hornsby, J. (1980) *Actions*, London: Routledge.

——. (1995) "Reasons for Trying" in *Journal of Philosophical Research*, v. 20, pp. 525–539.

Husak, D. (1996a) "Transferred Intent" in *Notre Dame Journal of Law, Ethics and Public Policy*, v. 10, pp. 65–97.

——. (1996b) "The 'But-Everyone-Does-That!' Defense" in *Public Affairs Quarterly*, v. 10, pp. 307–334.

——. (2007) "Rethinking the Act Requirement" in *Cardozo Law Review*, v. 28, pp. 2437–2460.

——. (2008) *Overcriminalization: The Limits of the Criminal Law*, Oxford: Oxford University Press.

Kadish, S. H. (1994) "The Criminal Law and the Luck of the Draw" in *Journal of Criminal Law and Criminology*, v. 84, pp. 679–702.

—— and Schulhofer, S. (2001) *Criminal Law and Its Processes: Cases and Materials* (7th edn), New York: Aspen.

Kavka, G. (1983) "The Toxin Puzzle" in *Analysis*, v. 43, pp. 33–36.

Keedy, E. (1954) "Criminal Attempts at Common Law" in *University of Pennsylvania Law Review*, v. 102, pp. 464–489.

Kolodny, N. (2005) "Why Be Rational?" in *Mind*, v. 114, n. 455, pp. 509–563.

LaFave, W. (2000) *Criminal Law*, St Paul: Westlaw.

Lee, E. T. (1997) "Cancelling Crime" in *Connecticut Law Review*, v. 30, pp. 117–156.

Levy-Barzilai, V. (2002) "Prisoner's Dilemmas" in *Harper's Magazine*, September, pp. 17–22.

Lewis, D. (1989) "The Punishment that Leaves Something to Chance", *Philosophy and Public Affairs*, v. 18, pp. 53–67.

McCann, H. (1974) "Volition and Basic Action" in *Philosophical Review*, v. 83, pp. 451–473.

——. (1998) "Trying, Paralysis and Volition" in *The Works of Agency: On Human Action, Will and Freedom*, Ithaca: Cornell University Press, pp. 94–109.

Mele, A. (1992) *Springs of Action*, New York: Oxford University Press.

——. (1999) "Is There a Place for Intention in an Analysis of Intentional Action?" in *Philosophia*, v. 27, pp. 419–432.

Michaels, A. C. "Acceptance: The Missing Mental State" in *Southern California Law Review*, v. 71, pp. 953–1035.

Moore, G. E. (1942) "A Reply to My Critics" in *The Philosophy of G. E. Moore*, P.A. Schilpp (ed.), Evanston: Northwestern University Press.

Moore, M. (1993) *Act and Crime*, Oxford: Clarendon Press.

——. (1994) "The Independent Moral Significance of Wrongdoing" in *Journal of Contemporary Legal Issues*, v. 5, pp. 237–281.

——. (1997) *Placing Blame*, Oxford: Clarendon Press.

——. (2009) *Causation and Responsibility*, Oxford: Oxford University Press.

Morris, H. (1965) "Punishment for Thoughts" in *Monist*, v. 49, pp. 342–376.

Morse, S. (2004) "Reasons, Results and Criminal Responsibility" in *University of Illinois Law Review*, pp. 364–435.

Nagel, T. (1979) "Moral Luck" in *Mortal Questions*, Cambridge: Cambridge University Press, pp. 24–38.

Parker, R. (1984) "Blame, Punishment and the Role of Result" in *American Philosophical Quarterly*, v. 21, pp. 269–276.

Pink, T. (1996) *The Psychology of Freedom*, Cambridge: Cambridge University Press.

Quinn, W. S. (1989) "Actions, Intentions, and Consequences: The Doctrine of Double Effect" in *Philosophy and Public Affairs*, v. 18, pp. 334–351.

Reid, T. (1969) *Essays on the Active Powers of Man*, Cambridge: MIT Press.

Robinson, P. H. (1984) "Imputed Criminal Liability" in *Yale Law Journal* 93, pp. 609–676.

—— and Darley, J. M. (1995) *Justice, Liability, and Blame: Community Views and the Criminal Law*, Boulder: Westview Press.

Rule, A. (2001) *Empty Promises*, New York: Pocket Books.

Sayre, F. B. (1928) "Criminal Attempts" in *Harvard Law Review* 41, pp. 821–859.

Scanlon, T. (2008) *Moral Dimensions*, Cambridge: Harvard University Press.

Schroeder, M. (2004) "The Scope of Instrumental Reason" in *Philosophical Perspectives (Ethics)* 18, pp. 337–364.

Schulhofer, S. (1974) "Harm and Punishment: A Critique of Emphasis on the Results of Conduct in the Criminal Law" in *University of Pennsylvania Law Review*, v. 122, pp. 1497–1607.

Searle, J. (1983) *Intentionality*, Cambridge: Cambridge University Press.

Skilton, R. H., (1937a) "The Mental Element in a Criminal Attempt" in *University of Pittsburgh Law Review*, v. 3, pp. 181–190.

——. (1937b) "The Requisite Act in Criminal Attempt" in *University of Pittsburgh Law Review*, v. 3, pp. 308–319.

Smith, J. C. (1957) "Two Problems in Criminal Attempts" in *Harvard Law Review*, v. 70, pp. 422–448.

——. (1962) "Two Problems in Criminal Attempts Re-Examined" in *Criminal Law Review*, pp. 135–144 and 212–222.

Spjut, R. J. (1987) "When is an Attempt to Commit an Impossible Crime a Criminal Act?" in *Arizona Law Review*, v. 29, pp. 247–279.

Stannard, J. E. (1987) "Making Up for the Missing Element—A Sideways Look at Attempts" in *Legal Studies*, v. 7, p. 199.

Stephen, J. F. (1883) *A Digest of Criminal Law*, London: Macmillan & Co.

Stoutland, F. (1997) "Why Are Philosophers of Action So Antisocial?" in L. Alanen, S. Heinamaa, and T. Wallgren (eds), *Commonality and Particularity in Ethics*, New York: St Martin's Press.

Strahorn, J. S. (1930) "The Effect of Impossibility on Criminal Attempts" in *University of Pennsylvania Law Review*, v. 78, pp. 962–998.

Thomson, J. J. (1989) "Morality and Bad Luck" in *Metaphilosophy*, v. 20, pp. 203–221.

Turner, J. W. Cecil (1935) "Attempts to Commit Crimes" in *Cambridge Law Journal*, v. 5, pp. 230–37.

United States Sentencing Commission. (1995) *Special Report to Congress: Cocaine and Federal Sentencing Policy*, Washington: GPO, February.

Velleman, J. D. (1989) *Practical Reflection*, Princeton: Princeton University Press.

——. (1997) "How To Share an Intention" in *Philosophy and Phenomenological Research*, v. 57, pp. 29–50.

Vermazen, B. (1993) "Objects of Intention" in *Philosophical Studies*, v. 71, pp. 223–265.

Westen, P. (2007) "Why Harm Matters: Plato's Abiding Insight in the Laws" in *Criminal Law & Philosophy*, v. 1, pp. 307–326.

——. (2008) "Impossible Attempts: A Speculative Thesis" in *Ohio State Criminal Law Journal*, v. 5, pp. 523–565.

Wharton, F. (1932) *Wharton's Criminal Law* (12th edn), Rochester: Lawyers Co-operative Publishing Co.

Williams, G. (1961) *Criminal Law: The General Part* (2nd edn), London: Stevens & Sons.

——. (1991) "Intents in the Alternative" in *Cambridge Law Journal*, v. 50, pp. 120–130.

Wilson, G. (1989) *The Intentionality of Human Action*, Stanford: Stanford University Press.

Yaffe, G. (2004) "Conditional Intent and Men Rea" in *Legal Theory*, v. 10, pp. 273–310.

——. (2005) "'The Government Beguiled Me': The Entrapment Defense and the Problem of Private Entrapment" in *The Journal of Ethics and Social Philosophy*, v. 1, pp. 1–50.

——. (2006) "Trying, Intending and Attempted Crimes" in *Philosophical Topics*, v. 32, pp. 505–532.

——. (2008a) "Trying, Acting and Attempted Crimes" in *Law and Philosophy*, v. 28, pp. 109–162.

——. (2008b) "Reasonableness in the Law and Second-Personal Address" in *Loyola Law Review*, v. 40, pp. 939–976.

# General Index